Lecture Notes in Computer Science 6550

Kurt Jensen   Susanna Donatelli
Maciej Koutny (Eds.)

Transactions on Petri Nets and Other Models of Concurrency IV

Springer

Editor-in-Chief

Kurt Jensen
Aarhus University
Faculty of Science
Department of Computer Science
IT-parken, Aabogade 34, 8200 Aarhus N, Denmark
E-mail: kjensen@cs.au.dk

Guest Editors

Susanna Donatelli
University of Turin
Computer Science Department
Corso Svizzera 185, 10149 Turin, Italy
E-mail: susi@di.unito.it

Maciej Koutny
Newcastle University
School of Computing Science
Newcastle upon Tyne, NE1 7RU, UK
E-mail: maciej.koutny@ncl.ac.uk

ISSN 0302-9743 (LNCS)
e-ISSN 1611-3349 (LNCS)
ISSN 1867-7193 (ToPNoC)
e-ISBN 978-3-642-18222-8
ISBN 978-3-642-18221-1
DOI 10.1007/978-3-642-18222-8
Springer Heidelberg Dordrecht London New York

Library of Congress Control Number: 2008942189

CR Subject Classification (1998): D.2.2-4, D.2, I.6, F.3-4, H.2.3, C.2, C.4

Typesetting: Camera-ready by author, data conversion by Scientific Publishing Services, Chennai, India

Printed on acid-free paper

Springer is part of Springer Science+Business Media (www.springer.com)

Preface by Editor-in-Chief

The fourth issue of LNCS Transactions on Petri Nets and Other Models of Concurrency (ToPNoC) contains revised and extended versions of a selection of the best papers from the workshops held at the 30th International Conference on Application and Theory of Petri Nets and Other Models of Concurrency, Paris, France, June 22–26, 2009, and from the 10th Workshop and Tutorial on Practical Use of Coloured Petri Nets and the CPN Tools, Aarhus, Denmark, October 19–22, 2009.

I would like to thank the two guest editors of this special issue: Susanna Donatelli and Maciej Koutny. Moreover, I would like to thank all authors, reviewers, and the organizers of the Petri net conference satellite workshops, without whom this issue of ToPNoC would not have been possible.

November 2010

Kurt Jensen
Editor-in-Chief
LNCS Transactions on Petri Nets and Other Models of Concurrency (ToPNoC)

LNCS Transactions on Petri Nets and Other Models of Concurrency: Aims and Scope

ToPNoC aims to publish papers from all areas of Petri nets and other models of concurrency ranging from theoretical work to tool support and industrial applications. The foundation of Petri nets was laid by the pioneering work of Carl Adam Petri and his colleagues in the early 1960s. Since then, an enormous amount of material has been developed and published in journals and books and presented at workshops and conferences.

The annual International Conference on Application and Theory of Petri Nets and Other Models of Concurrency started in 1980. The International Petri Net Bibliography maintained by the Petri Net Newsletter contains close to 10,000 different entries, and the International Petri Net Mailing List has 1,500 subscribers. For more information on the International Petri Net community, see: http://www.informatik.uni-hamburg.de/TGI/PetriNets/

All issues of ToPNoC are LNCS volumes. Hence they appear in all large libraries and are also accessible in LNCS Online (electronically). It is possible to subscribe to ToPNoC without subscribing to the rest of LNCS.

ToPNoC contains:

- revised versions of a selection of the best papers from workshops and tutorials concerned with Petri nets and concurrency;
- special issues related to particular subareas (similar to those published in the *Advances in Petri Nets* series);
- other papers invited for publication in ToPNoC; and
- papers submitted directly to ToPNoC by their authors.

Like all other journals, ToPNoC has an Editorial Board, which is responsible for the quality of the journal. The members of the board assist in the reviewing of papers submitted or invited for publication in ToPNoC. Moreover, they may make recommendations concerning collections of papers for special issues. The Editorial Board consists of prominent researchers within the Petri net community and in related fields.

Topics

System design and verification using nets; analysis and synthesis, structure and behavior of nets; relationships between net theory and other approaches; causality/partial order theory of concurrency; net-based semantical, logical and algebraic calculi; symbolic net representation (graphical or textual); computer tools for nets; experience with using nets, case studies; educational issues related to nets; higher level net models; timed and stochastic nets; and standardization of nets.

Applications of nets to: biological systems, defence systems, e-commerce and trading, embedded systems, environmental systems, flexible manufacturing systems, hardware structures, health and medical systems, office automation, operations research, performance evaluation, programming languages, protocols and networks, railway networks, real-time systems, supervisory control, telecommunications, and workflow.

For more information about ToPNoC, please see:
www.springer.com/lncs/topnoc

Submission of Manuscripts

Manuscripts should follow LNCS formatting guidelines, and should be submitted as PDF or zipped PostScript files to ToPNoC@cs.au.dk. All queries should be addressed to the same e-mail address.

LNCS Transactions on Petri Nets and Other Models of Concurrency: Editorial Board

Preface by Guest Editors

This issue of ToPNoC contains revised and extended versions of a selection of the best papers from the workshops held at the 30th International Conference on Application and Theory of Petri Nets and Other Models of Concurrency, Paris, France, June 22–26, 2009, and from the 10th Workshop and Tutorial on Practical Use of Coloured Petri Nets and the CPN Tools, Aarhus, Denmark, October 19–22, 2009.

We are indebted to the Program Committees (PCs) of the workshops and in particular their chairs. Without their enthusiastic work this volume would not have been possible. Many members of the PCs participated in reviewing the revised and extended papers considered for this issue. Papers from the following workshops were considered when selecting the best papers:

- APNOC 2009: International Workshop on Abstractions for Petri Nets and Other Models of Concurrency, organized by Natalia Sidorova and Alexander Serebrenik (The Netherlands);
- PNSE 2009: International Workshop on Petri Nets and Software Engineering, organized by Daniel Moldt (Germany);
- ORGMOD 2009: International Workshop on Organizational Modeling, organized by Michael Köhler-Bußmeier and Daniel Moldt (Germany);
- TiSto 2009: International Workshop on Timing and Stochasticity in Petri Nets and Other Models of Concurrency, organized by Andras Horvath (Italy) and Olivier H. Roux (France); and
- CPN 2009: The 10th Workshop and Tutorial on Practical Use of Coloured Petri Nets and the CPN Tools, organized by Kurt Jensen, Søren Christensen (Denmark), and Lars M. Kristensen (Norway).

The best papers of these workshops were selected in close cooperation with their chairs. The authors of these papers were invited to submit improved and extended versions. The papers needed to incorporate new results and to address comments made by the workshop's referees and those made during discussions at the workshop.

All invited papers were reviewed by three referees. We followed the principle of also asking for "fresh" reviews of the revised papers, i.e., from referees who had not been involved initially in reviewing the papers. After the first round of reviews, some papers were rejected while the authors of the others were asked to revise their papers in line with the reviewers' comments and to include a response to each comment to indicate how changes had been incorporated as a result of the comment. The revised paper and the responses were then forwarded to the reviewers for a final recommendation and comment. We would like to thank all authors and the reviewers for their excellent cooperation and for their outstanding work, which has led to a set of excellent papers in this issue.

After this rigorous review process, 9 papers were accepted out of the 15 initially considered as best papers. (Note that the workshops accepted about 60 papers in total and that the number of submissions to these workshops was considerably higher.)

This issue begins with a theoretical paper by Jörg Desel and Agathe Merceron, "Vicinity Respecting Homomorphisms for Abstracting System Requirements", which is concerned with structuring system requirements on an abstract conceptual level using the Channel/Agency Petri nets allowing one to represent functional and data aspects of the requirements in a graphical way. It is then shown that vicinity respecting homomorphisms can be applied to refine and abstract these nets as they preserve both dependencies between computational elements and important structural properties of nets.

The group of four papers that follows is concerned with formal verification of concurrent systems using model checking. The paper "Search-Order Independent State Caching" by Sami Evangelista and Lars Michael Kristensen revisits state caching which has been used to alleviate the state explosion problem in the context of depth-first search algorithms. The paper proposes and evaluates an extension of the state caching method for general state exploring algorithms that are independent of the search order. The second paper, "Bounded Parametric Model Checking for Elementary Net Systems" by Michał Knapik, Maciej Szreter, and Wojciech Penczek investigates formal verification of properties expressed in (timed) modal logics using bounded model checking (BMC). It shows that such a technique can be extended to the parametric extension of an existential fragment of CTL (PRTECTL).

The theme of BMC is continued in the third paper, "SAT-Based (Parametric) Reachability for Distributed Time Petri Nets", by Wojciech Penczek, Agata Półrola, and Andrzej Zbrzezny. The paper describes how to adapt the bounded model checking methods originally developed for timed automata to make them applicable to distributed time Petri nets and parametric reachability checking. The last two papers are complemented by the final (tool) paper of this group, "Parametric Model Checking with VerICS", by Michał Knapik et al. The paper presents the verification system VerICS extended features exploiting BMC for the verification of parametric reachability and properties expressed in PRTECTL.

The next two papers address various aspects of computer based support for business processes. Ronny Mans et al. present an approach that supports the seamless integration of unscheduled and scheduled tasks in workflow management systems in their paper "Schedule-Aware Workflow Management Systems". The proposed approach is illustrated using a real-life (hospital) case study. The second paper, "On-the-fly Auditing of Business Processes" by Kees van Hee et al., deals with the problem of ensuring that certain business rules are enforced in a business process. The proposed approach is based on a dedicated system, called a monitor, that collects the actual events of the business processes and then verifies business rules over finite system histories.

The last couple of papers discuss different aspects of the agent-based approach to software engineering. The paper "Modeling Organizational Units as

Modular Components of Systems of Systems" by Matthias Wester-Ebbinghaus, Daniel Moldt, and Michael Köhler-Bußmeier, is concerned with hierarchical and recursive system decomposition where classical agent orientation reaches its limits. The paper proposes the concept of an organizational unit that both embeds actors and is itself embedded as a collective actor in surrounding organizational units, and gives a precise notion of operational semantics. The following paper, "A Multi-Agent Organizational Framework for Coevolutionary Optimization" by Grégoire Danoy, Pascal Bouvry, and Olivier Boissier, introduces a distributed agent framework for optimization (DAFO) that helps in designing and applying coevolutionary genetic algorithms (CGAs). In particular, DAFO includes a complete organization and reorganization model, multi-agent system for evolutionary optimization, that permits the user to formalize CGAs structure, interactions, and adaptation.

The 9 papers of this issue provide a good mixture of theory, tools, and practical applications related to concurrency and provides a useful snapshot of current research. As guest editors we would like to thank Lars Madsen and Annemette Hammer of Aarhus University for providing administrative and technical support and the Springer/ToPNoC team for the final production of this issue.

November 2010

Susanna Donatelli
Maciej Koutny
Guest Editors, Fourth Issue of ToPNoC

Organization of This Issue

Guest Editors

Susanna Donatelli, Italy
Maciej Koutny, UK

Co-chairs of the Workshops

Andras Horvath (Italy)
Kurt Jensen (Denmark)
Michael Köhler-Bußmeier (Germany)
Daniel Moldt (Germany)
Natalia Sidorova (The Netherlands)
Olivier H. Roux (France)
Alexander Serebrenik (The Netherlands)

Referees

Wil van der Aalst
Guido Boella
Didier Buchs
Gianfranco Ciardo
José Manuel Colom
Jörg Desel
Ekkart Kindler
Berndt Farwer
Guy E. Gallasch
Serge Haddad
Kees van Hee
Thomas Hildebrandt
Gabriel Juhas
Victor Khomenko
Michael Köhler-Bußmeier
Fabrice Kordon
Johan Lilius
Robert Lorenz
Eric Matson
Daniel Moldt
Chun Ouyang
Lucia Pomello
Franck Pommereau
Matteo Risoldi
Heiko Roelke
Olivier H. Roux
Christophe Sibertin-Blanc
Jaime Sichman
Carla Simone
Martin Steffen
Mark-Oliver Stehr
Rüdiger Valk
Jan Martijn van der Werf
Karsten Wolf

Table of Contents

Vicinity Respecting Homomorphisms for Abstracting System Requirements 1
Jörg Desel and Agathe Merceron

Search-Order Independent State Caching 21
Sami Evangelista and Lars Michael Kristensen

Bounded Parametric Model Checking for Elementary Net Systems 42
Michał Knapik, Maciej Szreter, and Wojciech Penczek

SAT-Based (Parametric) Reachability for a Class of Distributed Time Petri Nets 72
Wojciech Penczek, Agata Półrola, and Andrzej Zbrzezny

Parametric Model Checking with VerICS 98
Michał Knapik, Artur Niewiadomski, Wojciech Penczek, Agata Półrola, Maciej Szreter, and Andrzej Zbrzezny

Schedule-Aware Workflow Management Systems 121
Ronny S. Mans, Nick C. Russell, Wil M.P. van der Aalst, Arnold J. Moleman, and Piet J.M. Bakker

On-the-Fly Auditing of Business Processes 144
Kees van Hee, Jan Hidders, Geert-Jan Houben, Jan Paredaens, and Philippe Thiran

Modeling Organizational Units as Modular Components of Systems of Systems 174
Matthias Wester-Ebbinghaus, Daniel Moldt, and Michael Köhler-Bußmeier

A Multi-Agent Organizational Framework for Coevolutionary Optimization 199
Grégoire Danoy, Pascal Bouvry, and Olivier Boissier

Author Index 225

Vicinity Respecting Homomorphisms for Abstracting System Requirements

Jörg Desel[1] and Agathe Merceron[2]

[1] FernUniversität in Hagen, Germany
joerg.desel@fernuni-hagen.de
[2] Beuth Hochschule für Technik Berlin, Germany
merceron@beuth-hochschule.de

Abstract. This paper is concerned with structuring system requirements on an abstract conceptual level. Channel/Agency Petri nets are taken as a formal model. They allow to represent functional aspects as well as data aspects of the requirements in a graphical way. Vicinity respecting homomorphisms are presented as a means to refine and abstract these nets. They preserve paths, i.e., dependencies between computational elements and they preserve important structural properties of nets, such as S- and T-components, siphons and traps and the free choice property. These properties have important interpretations for marked Petri nets and can therefore be used for the analysis of system models at more concrete levels.

Keywords: Channel/Agency Nets, Homomorphisms, Abstraction.

1 Introduction

A nontrivial task in the design of large and complex systems is to organize the requirements into a coherent structure. Usually, this organization is a gradual process which involves refinement and abstraction between different conceptual levels of the system. In this paper we take Channel/Agency Petri nets [22,24] to model systems and propose vicinity respecting homomorphisms as a means to refine and abstract these nets.

Channel/Agency Petri nets are a Petri net model where all elements of a net are labelled by informal descriptions. They have been proposed for the conceptual modelling of the architecture of information systems e.g. in [1,2,13]. As shown in [23,24] they can be used for different levels of abstraction, in particular in the early phases of system and software engineering. On a low level of abstraction containing all details nets can be equipped with markings and a notion of behavior which simulates the behavior of the modelled system. In this way Petri nets can be used as a means for prototyping.

We introduce vicinity respecting homomorphisms of Petri nets to formalize refinement and abstraction relations between nets. This encompasses modular techniques because each composition of subsystems may be viewed as an identification of the respective interface elements and thus as a particular abstraction. Vicinity respecting homomorphisms rely on the graph structure of a net. They

K. Jensen, S. Donatelli, and M. Koutny (Eds.): ToPNoC IV, LNCS 6550, pp. 1–20, 2010.

are special graph homomorphisms that are able to formalize abstractions including contractions of graphs not only in their breadth but also in their length.

The definition of vicinity respecting homomorphisms is based on the local vicinities of elements. This concept suffices to preserve important global structural properties like connectedness. If two elements of a net are connected by a path then the respective system components are in a causal dependency relation. Because they preserve paths, vicinity respecting homomorphisms not only respect dependency but also its complementary relation independency.

Petri nets not only allow to combine data- and function-oriented views of a system. They also allow to concentrate on either aspect. The data aspect including nondeterministic choice is reflected by S-components. T-components represent an activity-oriented view, where only transitions are branched. Petri nets that are covered by S- and T-components allow for a compositional interpretation of these two aspects. We show that vicinity respecting net homomorphisms preserve coverings by S- and T-components. As a consequence, they respect the notions of choice (a forward branching place) and of synchronization (a backward branching transition).

This paper gathers, generalizes and deepens results obtained in [4,16,6]. In the last years, research concentrated on abstraction techniques for Petri nets on a behavioral level, i.e. morphisms have been defined that preserve occurrence sequences or other behavioral notions. Structural relations between the respective nets appeared as a consequence of behavioral relations. For example, [14] concentrates on abstraction techniques for high-level Petri nets and explicitly distinguishes the advocated behavior-oriented approach from our structure-based work. Our work is different because we concentrate on local structural properties of the relation between nets, i.e., on properties of the homomorphism, and derive global structural properties which have consequences for behavior.

Another line of research considers abstraction and modularity techniques for Petri nets based on graph grammars, see e.g. [8]. Considering relations between Petri nets representing conceptual models, which do not necessarily have a formal behavior, was continued in [18,19]. It is important to notice that this work was not published in the Petri net community but in our intended application domain – hence it points out that there is a demand for structural abstraction techniques of process models.

Recently, there is a renewed interest in construction techniques for (unmarked) Petri nets, applied for requirement analysis [7] and in the context of modular Petri nets [25] that are composed via identification of common nodes.

Today, instead of Petri nets, diagram techniques of the UML play a more important role in practice. However, all these diagram languages are essentially graphs. At least for UML Activity Diagrams, a diagram type closely related to Petri nets, our approach can be applied as well.

Other diagram techniques have a different notion of abstraction; abstraction is a concept visible within a single diagram instead of a relation between diagrams. Examples for such abstractions are aggregation and generalization in data modelling. Also hierarchy notions in process modelling provide abstraction concepts within diagrams. Whereas a Petri net morphism relates two nets, particular morphisms representing abstractions can be depicted in single diagrams. In this paper we concentrate on so-called net quotients where the elements of the more abstract net can be viewed as equivalence sets of the net on the less abstract level. A net quotient is uniquely identified by the less abstract net together with the equivalence classes, which directly leads to a diagram technique comparable to the ones mentioned above.

In Section 2 we investigate homomorphisms of arbitrary graphs. Section 3 introduces Petri nets and transfers the notion of vicinity respecting homomorphisms to them. In Section 4 we show that vicinity respecting homomorphisms respect coverings by S- and T-components of Petri nets and draw consequences for Petri nets composition. Siphons and traps are concepts known from Petri net theory that allow for an analysis of the data contained in sets of places [3]. Section 5 proves that vicinity respecting homomorphisms preserve siphons, traps and the free choice property. Finally, Section 6 concludes this paper.

2 Graph Homomorphisms

Petri nets are special graphs. Vicinity respecting homomorphisms will be defined for arbitrary graphs in this section.

Figure 1 shows a model of a sender/receiver system on the left hand side and a coarser view of the same system on the right hand side. The left model can be viewed as a refinement of the right model. The interrelation between the graphs is given by a mapping which is a particular graph homomorphism. As we shall see, in this example dependencies between vertices of the source graph are strongly related to dependencies between vertices of the target graph. We start with a formal introduction of graphs and related concepts. We consider only finite directed graphs without multiple edges and without loops.

Definition 1. *A* graph *is a pair* (X, F) *where* X *is a finite set (*vertices*) and* $F \subseteq X \times X$ *(*edges*). A* loop *is an edge* (x, x)*. A graph is said to be* loop-free *if no edge is a loop.*

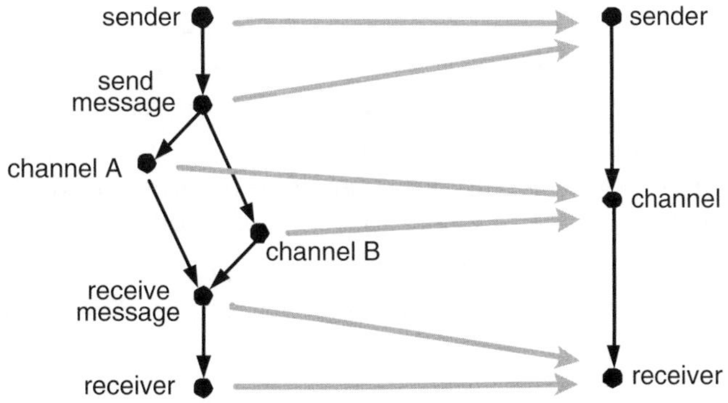

Fig. 1. A graph homomorphism as a mapping

The classical notion of graph homomorphism [20] respects edges in the sense that the images of connected vertices are again connected. Since we also consider contractions of loop-free graphs, where two connected vertices are mapped to one vertex without a loop, a slightly more liberal definition will be employed; we allow the images of connected vertices to be either connected or identical.

Definition 2. *Let (X, F) and (X', F') be graphs. A mapping $\varphi: X \to X'$ is a* graph homomorphism *(denoted by $\varphi: (X, F) \to (X', F')$) if, for every edge $(x, y) \in F$, either $(\varphi(x), \varphi(y)) \in F'$ or $\varphi(x) = \varphi(y)$.*

To describe the environment of an element we shall use the notions of pre- and post-sets and related notions of pre- and post-vicinities.

Definition 3. *Given a graph (X, F) and $x \in X$, we denote by ${}^\bullet x = \{y \in X \mid (y, x) \in F\}$ the pre-set of x and by $x^\bullet = \{y \in X \mid (x, y) \in F\}$ the post-set of x. The pre-vicinity of x is ${}^\odot x = \{x\} \cup {}^\bullet x$, the post-vicinity of x is $x^\odot = \{x\} \cup x^\bullet$.*

$\varphi({}^\bullet x) \subseteq {}^\bullet(\varphi(x))$ does not hold for arbitrary graph homomorphisms because in case of contractions elements of ${}^\bullet x$ can be mapped to $\varphi(x)$, and similarly for post-sets. However, we get:

Lemma 1. *Let (X, F) and (X', F') be graphs and $\varphi: X \to X'$ a mapping.*
The following three conditions are equivalent.

1. *φ is a graph homomorphism.*
2. *for each vertex x in X, $\varphi({}^\odot x) \subseteq {}^\odot(\varphi(x))$.*
3. *for each vertex x in X, $\varphi(x^\odot) \subseteq (\varphi(x))^\odot$.*

Proof: We only show $1 \iff 2$, $1 \iff 3$ being similar.

Assume that $\varphi: X \to X'$ is a graph homomorphism, let x be an element of X and let $y \in {}^\odot x$. If $x = y$ then $\varphi(y) = \varphi(x) \in {}^\odot(\varphi(x))$. If $(y, x) \in F$ then either $\varphi(y) = \varphi(x) \in {}^\odot(\varphi(x))$ or $(\varphi(y), \varphi(x)) \in F'$ since φ is a graph homomorphism and therefore $\varphi(y) \in {}^\odot(\varphi(x))$.

Conversely, assume for each x in X, $\varphi({}^\odot x) \subseteq {}^\odot(\varphi(x))$. Let $(y, x) \in F$. Then $y \in {}^\odot x$ and hence $\varphi(y) \in {}^\odot(\varphi(x))$. So either $\varphi(y) = \varphi(x)$ or $(\varphi(y), \varphi(x)) \in F'$.

□

Definition 4. *A sequence $x_1, x_2 \dots x_n$ $(n \geq 1)$ of vertices of a graph is a* path *if there exist edges $(x_1, x_2), \dots, (x_{n-1}, x_n)$ of the graph. A graph is* strongly connected *if for any two vertices x and y there exists a path $x \dots y$.*

We allow a single element to be a path. Since consecutive vertices of a graph can be mapped onto a single element without a loop, the sequence of images of path elements is not necessarily a path of the target graph. So we define, for loop-free graphs, the image of a path to ignore stuttering of vertices.

Definition 5. *Let (X, F), (X', F') be loop-free graphs and $\varphi: (X, F) \to (X', F')$ a graph homomorphism. The image of a path $x_1 \dots x_n$ of (X, F) is defined by*

$$\varphi(x_1 \dots x_n) = \begin{cases} \varphi(x_1) & \text{if } n = 1 \\ \varphi(x_1 \dots x_{n-1}) & \text{if } n > 1 \text{ and } \varphi(x_{n-1}) = \varphi(x_n) \\ \varphi(x_1 \dots x_{n-1})\, \varphi(x_n) & \text{if } n > 1 \text{ and } \varphi(x_{n-1}) \neq \varphi(x_n) \end{cases}$$

Using Definition 5, the image of the path *sender*, *send message*, *channel A* of the left hand graph in Figure 1 is the path *sender channel* of the target graph.

Graph homomorphisms do not preserve edges but they preserve paths:

Lemma 2. *Let (X, F), (X', F') be loop-free graphs and let $\varphi\colon (X, F) \to (X', F')$ be a graph homomorphism. If $x_1 \ldots x_n$ is a path of (X, F) then $\varphi(x_1 \ldots x_n)$ is a path of (X', F') leading from $\varphi(x_1)$ to $\varphi(x_n)$.*

Proof: We proceed by induction on n.

If $n = 1$ then $\varphi(x_1)$ is a path of (X', F').

Let $n > 1$ and assume that $\varphi(x_1 \ldots x_{n-1})$ is a path leading from $\varphi(x_1)$ to $\varphi(x_{n-1})$. We have $(x_{n-1}, x_n) \in F$ by the definition of a path. By the homomorphism property, we can distinguish two cases:

1. $(\varphi(x_{n-1}), \varphi(x_n)) \in F'$. Then $\varphi(x_1 \ldots x_n) = \varphi(x_1 \ldots x_{n-1})\varphi(x_n)$ is a path of (X', F') leading from $\varphi(x_1)$ to $\varphi(x_n)$.
2. $\varphi(x_{n-1}) = \varphi(x_n)$. Then $\varphi(x_1 \ldots x_n) = \varphi(x_1 \ldots x_{n-1})$. By assumption, this is a path leading from $\varphi(x_1)$ to $\varphi(x_{n-1})$. Since $\varphi(x_{n-1}) = \varphi(x_n)$ this path leads to $\varphi(x_n)$. □

Surjectivity is a first condition when graph homomorphisms are used for abstractions. Surjective graph homomorphisms preserve strong connectivity:

Corollary 1. *Let (X, F), (X', F') be loop-free graphs and $\varphi\colon (X, F) \to (X', F')$ a surjective graph homomorphism. If (X, F) is strongly connected then (X', F') is also strongly connected.*

Proof: Let $x', y' \in X'$. Since φ is surjective there are $x, y \in X$ such that $\varphi(x) = x'$ and $\varphi(y) = y'$. There is a path from x to y because (X, F) is strongly connected. Using Lemma 2, some path of (X', F') leads from x' to y'. □

Surjectivity concerns vertices only. An additional requirement is that every edge of a target graph reflects a connection between respective vertices of the source graph. We call such a graph homomorphism a quotient.

Definition 6. *Let (X, F), (X', F') be loop-free graphs. A surjective graph homomorphism $\varphi\colon (X, F) \to (X', F')$ is called* quotient *if, for every edge $(x', y') \in F'$, there exists an edge $(x, y) \in F$ such that $\varphi(x) = x'$ and $\varphi(y) = y'$.*

The graph homomorphism shown in Figure 1 is a quotient. The edges of the target graph are the equivalence classes of the edges of the source graph. There is a vertex connecting two edges of the target graph if and only if there is at least one edge connecting elements of the respective sets of vertices in the source graph.

The name "quotient" is justified because for quotients, target graphs are determined up to renaming by the equivalence classes of vertices that are mapped onto the same vertex (see [5]). Therefore, we can represent quotients graphically by solely depicting equivalence classes. Figure 2 represents the quotient shown in Figure 1 this way.

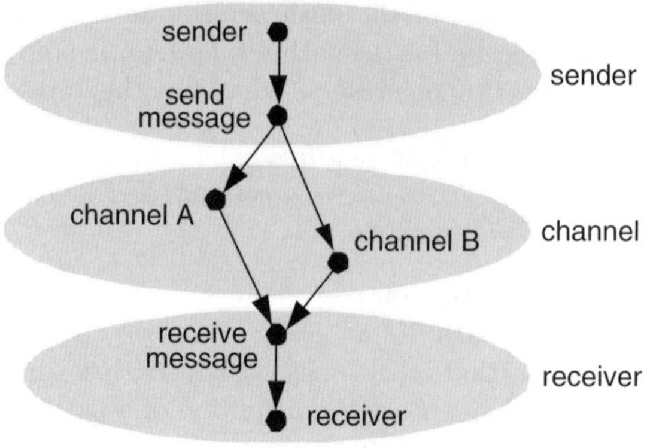

Fig. 2. Another representation of the graph homomorphism of Figure 1

When thinking of a graph (X', F') as of an abstraction of another graph (X, F), dependencies between nodes of X' that are represented through paths have to mirror dependencies already present in X. Therefore we look for a converse of Lemma 2. For quotients, this lemma has a weak converse by the definition of a quotient: every path of the target graph with at most two vertices is the image of a path of the source graph.

The same does not necessarily hold for longer paths, as shown in Figure 3. The target graph has a path $\varphi(a)\,\varphi(b)\,\varphi(f)$ which is not the image of a path of the source graph. What is wrong with this homomorphism? The post-vicinity of b is $\{b, d\}$. The post-vicinity of the image of b contains three vertices, namely $\varphi(b), \varphi(d)$ and $\varphi(f)$. So the image of the post-vicinity of b is properly included in the post-vicinity of the image. We say that the post-vicinity is not respected and define homomorphisms that respect vicinities of vertices:

Definition 7. *Let (X, F), (X', F') be loop-free graphs.*

A graph homomorphism $\varphi: (X, F) \to (X', F')$ is called pre-vicinity respecting *if, for every $x \in X$, either $\varphi({}^{\odot}x) = {}^{\odot}(\varphi(x))$ or $\varphi({}^{\odot}x) = \{\varphi(x)\}$.*

φ is called post-vicinity respecting *if, for every $x \in X$, either $\varphi(x^{\odot}) = (\varphi(x))^{\odot}$ or $\varphi(x^{\odot}) = \{\varphi(x)\}$.*

φ is called vicinity respecting *if it is pre-vicinity respecting and post-vicinity respecting.*

The following theorem states that for surjective post-vicinity respecting homomorphisms of strongly connected graphs there is a converse of Lemma 2. By symmetry, the same holds for pre-vicinity respecting graph homomorphisms.

Theorem 1. *Let (X, F), (X', F') be loop-free graphs such that (X, F) is strongly connected, and $\varphi: (X, F) \to (X', F')$ a surjective post-vicinity respecting graph homomorphism. For each path $x'_1 \dots x'_m$ of (X', F') there exists a path $x_1 \dots x_n$ of (X, F) such that $\varphi(x_1 \dots x_n) = x'_1 \dots x'_m$.*

Proof: We proceed by induction on m.

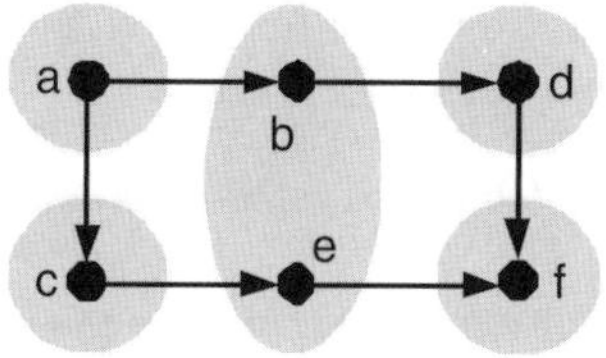

Fig. 3. A path of the target graph is not necessarily image of a source graph path

Let $m = 1$. Since φ is surjective, some $x_1 \in X$ satisfies $\varphi(x_1) = x'_1$. The path consisting of x_1 only satisfies the required property.

Let $m > 1$. Assume that $x_1 \dots x_k$ is a path of (X, F) such that $\varphi(x_1 \dots x_k) = x'_1 \dots x'_{m-1}$. Since φ is surjective, some $y \in X$ satisfies $\varphi(y) = x'_m$. Since the graph (X, F) is strongly connected, it contains a path leading from x_k to y. Consider the first vertex x_{i+1} in this path that is not mapped to x'_{m-1}. Such a vertex exists because the last vertex y in the path is mapped to x'_m and $x'_{m-1} \neq x'_m$ since (X', F') is loop-free. By definition, the predecessor x_i of x_{i+1} is mapped to x'_{m-1} and so are all vertices in the path $x_k \dots x_i$.

We have $x_{i+1} \in x_i^{\odot}$. Since $\varphi(x_{i+1}) \neq \varphi(x_i)$ we obtain $\varphi(x_i^{\odot}) \neq \{\varphi(x_i)\}$. Using the definition of a post-vicinity respecting homomorphism we conclude that $\varphi(x_i^{\odot}) = (\varphi(x_i))^{\odot}$. Therefore, since $x'_m \in {x'_{m-1}}^{\odot} = (\varphi(x_i))^{\odot}$, some vertex $z \in x_i^{\odot}$ is mapped to x'_m. This vertex z cannot be x_i itself, hence it is in $x_i^{\bullet}$.

Now the path $x_1 \dots x_k \dots x_i z$ is mapped to $x'_1 \dots x'_m$. □

The example in Figure 4 shows that in the previous theorem it is necessary that the source graph (X, F) is strongly connected. Moreover, neither requiring weak connectedness nor nonempty pre- or post-sets for all vertices constitute sufficient conditions. This graph homomorphism φ is a vicinity respecting quotient. The target graph has a path $\varphi(c)\,\varphi(d)\,\varphi(c)$ which is not the image of a path of the source graph.

Corollary 2. *Let (X, F), (X', F') be loop-free graphs such that (X, F) is strongly connected and let $\varphi\colon (X, F) \to (X', F')$ be a surjective post-vicinity respecting graph homomorphism. Then φ is a quotient.*

Proof: Let $(x', y') \in F'$. Then $x'\, y'$ is a path. By Theorem 1 there is a path $x_1 \dots x_n$ of X with $\varphi(x_1 \dots x_n) = x'\, y'$. Let x_i be the last element of the path with $\varphi(x_i) = x'$. Then $(x_i, x_{i+1}) \in F$ and $\varphi(x_{i+1}) = y'$, which was to prove. □

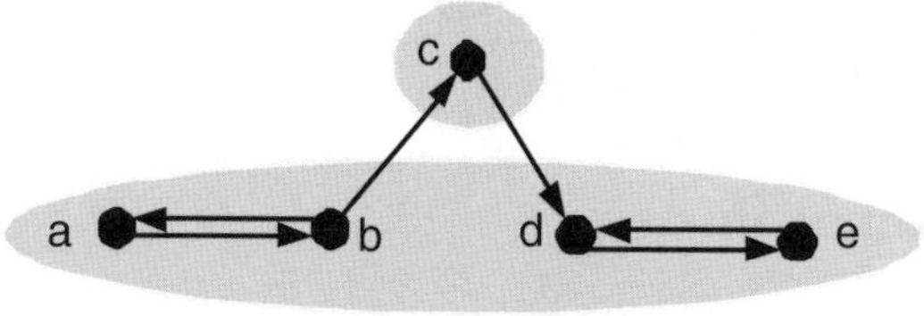

Fig. 4. For non-strongly connected graphs, a path of the target graph by a vicinity respecting quotient is not necessarily the image of a path

The following result, that will be used later, is weaker than Corollary 2 but holds for arbitrary surjective graph homomorphisms.

Lemma 3. *Let (X, F) be a strongly connected graph and let (X', F') be a graph satisfying $|X'| > 1$. If $\varphi: (X, F) \to (X', F')$ is a surjective graph homomorphism, then, for each $x' \in X'$, there are arcs $(y, x_1), (x_2, z) \in F$ with $\varphi(x_1) = x' = \varphi(x_2)$ and $\varphi(y) \neq x' \neq \varphi(z)$.*

Proof: We show only the first part, the second one being similar.
Let y' be an element of X' distinct from x' (which is possible because $|X'| > 1$). Since φ is surjective there are $c, d \in X$ with $\varphi(c) = x'$ and $\varphi(d) = y'$. Since (X, F) is strongly connected, there exists a path $x_1 \ldots x_n$ of (X, F) with $x_1 = c$ and $x_n = d$. Let i be the least index such that $\varphi(x_i) = x'$ and $\varphi(x_{i+1}) \neq x'$. With $(x, y) = (x_i, x_{i+1})$ we are finished. □

Concentrating on different elements which are mapped onto the same image instead of comparing source graph and target graph leads to another aspect of vicinity respecting homomorphisms in the case of quotients.

Lemma 4. *Let (X, F), (X', F') be loop-free graphs and $\varphi: (X, F) \to (X', F')$ a quotient. φ is vicinity respecting iff for all $x, y \in X$ satisfying $\varphi(x) = \varphi(y)$:*

1. $\varphi({}^{\odot}x) = \{\varphi(x)\}$ *or* $\varphi({}^{\odot}y) = \{\varphi(y)\}$ *or* $\varphi({}^{\odot}x) = \varphi({}^{\odot}y)$;
2. $\varphi(x^{\odot}) = \{\varphi(x)\}$ *or* $\varphi(y^{\odot}) = \{\varphi(y)\}$ *or* $\varphi(x^{\odot}) = \varphi(y^{\odot})$.

Proof: It is immediate that Definition 7 implies 1. and 2. We only show that 1. implies pre-vicinity respecting; showing that 2. implies post-vicinity respecting is similar.

Let $x \in X$ such that $\varphi({}^{\odot}x) \neq \{\varphi(x)\}$ and let $z' \in {}^{\bullet}\varphi(x)$. Then there exist $y, z \in X$ such that $z \in {}^{\bullet}y, \varphi(z) = z'$ and $\varphi(y) = \varphi(x)$ because φ is a quotient. By 1. we obtain that $\varphi({}^{\odot}x) = \varphi({}^{\odot}y)$. Since $z \in {}^{\odot}y$, some element in ${}^{\odot}x$ is mapped to z'. Since z' was chosen arbitrarily in ${}^{\bullet}\varphi(x)$ we finally obtain $\varphi({}^{\odot}x) = {}^{\odot}\varphi(x)$. □

In the proof of Lemma 4, we showed that for any element $z' \in {}^{\bullet}\varphi(x)$ there exists an element $z \in {}^{\bullet}x$ with $\varphi(z) = z'$. From this fact, we deduce immediately the following technical corollary that will be used later.

Corollary 3. *Let (X, F), (X', F') be loop-free graphs and $\varphi: (X, F) \to (X, F')$ a vicinity respecting quotient. Then, for every $x \in X$:*

1. *if* $\varphi({}^{\odot}x) \neq \{\varphi(x)\}$ *then* $|{}^{\bullet}\varphi(x)| \leq |{}^{\bullet}x|$;
2. *if* $\varphi(x^{\odot}) \neq \{\varphi(x)\}$ *then* $|\varphi(x)^{\bullet}| \leq |x^{\bullet}|$.

3 Net Homomorphisms

A (Petri) net can be seen as a loop-free graph (X, F) where the set X of vertices is partitioned into a set S of *places* and a set T of *transitions* such that the flow relation F must not relate two places or two transitions. Formally:

Definition 8. *A triple* $N = (S, T; F)$ *is called* net *if* S *and* T *are disjoint sets and* $F \subseteq (S \times T) \cup (T \times S)$*. The set* $X = S \cup T$ *is the set of* elements *of the net.*

This definition allows to consider nets with isolated elements, i.e. elements with empty pre- and post-sets. Graphically, places are represented by circles, transitions are represented by squares and the flow relation is represented by arrows between elements. We do not consider markings and behavioral notions but concentrate on the structure of net models. However, there are many relations between structure and behavior, whence our concepts have indirect consequences for the behavior of the considered nets as well.

We use the following convention: indices and primes used to denote a net N are carried over to all parts of N. For example, speaking of a net N_i', we implicitly understand $N_i' = (S_i', T_i'; F_i')$ and $X_i' = S_i' \cup T_i'$.

The $\bullet$-notation for pre- and post-sets and the $\odot$-notation for pre- and post-vicinities of vertices of graphs carries over to nets. A consequence of Definition 8 is that the pre-set and the post-set of a place are sets of transitions, and the pre-set and the post-set of a transition are sets of places. We will employ the $\bullet$-notation also for sets of elements as usual: The pre-set of a set of elements is the union of pre-sets of elements of the set, and similar for post-sets.

The transitions of a net model the active subsystems, i.e. functions, operators, transformers etc. They are only connected to places which model passive subsystems, i.e. data, messages, conditions etc. On a conceptual level, it is not always obvious to classify a subsystem active or passive. The decision to model it by a place or by a transition is based on the interaction of the subsystem with its vicinity. As an example, consider a channel that is connected to functional units that send and receive data through the channel. Then the channel has to be modelled by a place. In contrast, if the channel is connected to data to be sent on one side and to already received data on the other side then the channel is modelled by a transition. As we shall see, a transition may represent a subsystem that is modelled by a net containing places and transitions on a finer level of abstraction. The same holds respectively for places.

An arrow in a net either leads from a place to a transition or from a transition to a place. In the first case the place is interpreted as a pre-requisite (pre-condition, input) for the transition which can be consumed by the action modelled by the transition. In the second case the place is interpreted as a post-requisite (post-condition, output) for the transition which can be produced by the action modelled by the transition. In this sense, arrows are used to denote two different types of relations between the elements of a Petri net.

Homomorphisms of Petri nets are particular graph homomorphisms that additionally respect the type of relation between the elements given by arrows [21,11]. Since we again allow contractions, places can be mapped to transitions and transitions can be mapped to places. However, if two connected elements are not mapped to the same element of the target net, then the place of the two has to be mapped to a place and the transition has to be mapped to a transition. So Definition 2 becomes for Petri nets:

Definition 9. *Let N, N' be nets. A mapping $\varphi: X \to X'$ is called* net homomorphism, *denoted by $\varphi: N \to N'$, if for every edge $(x,y) \in F$ holds:*

1. *if $(x,y) \in F \cap (S \times T)$ then either $(\varphi(x), \varphi(y)) \in F' \cap (S' \times T')$ or $\varphi(x) = \varphi(y)$,*
2. *if $(x,y) \in F \cap (T \times S)$ then either $(\varphi(x), \varphi(y)) \in F' \cap (T' \times S')$ or $\varphi(x) = \varphi(y)$.*

This definition is equivalent to the one given in [10]. Notice that there are various different definitions of Petri net homomorphisms in the literature, for example [17].

A consequence of our definition is that a transition is only allowed to be mapped to a place if all places of its pre-set and its post-set are mapped to the same place, and similarly for places.

Lemma 5. *Let $\varphi: N \to N'$ be a net homomorphism. Then:*

1. *If a transition t is mapped to a place s' then $\varphi({}^{\odot}t \cup t^{\odot}) = \{s'\}$.*
2. *If a place s is mapped to a transition t' then $\varphi({}^{\odot}s \cup s^{\odot}) = \{t'\}$.*

Proof: We only show 1., 2. being similar.
Let $t \in T$, $s' \in S'$ such that $\varphi(t) = s'$. Then for each place $s \in {}^{\bullet}t$ we have $(s,t) \in F \cap S \times T$ and $(\varphi(s), \varphi(t)) \notin S' \times T'$ and therefore $\varphi(s) = \varphi(t)$. Likewise, each place $s \in t^{\bullet}$ satisfies $\varphi(s) = \varphi(t)$. Since $\varphi({}^{\odot}t \cup t^{\odot}) = \varphi({}^{\bullet}t) \cup \varphi(\{t\}) \cup \varphi(t^{\bullet})$ and $\varphi(t) = s$ we obtain the result. □

Corollary 4. *Let $\varphi: N \to N'$ be a net homomorphism and let $(x,y) \in F$ such that $\varphi(x) \neq \varphi(y)$. Then $\varphi(x) \in S'$ iff $x \in S$ and $\varphi(y) \in S'$ iff $y \in S$.*

For nets the vicinity respecting homomorphism definition can be split into two notions: homomorphisms that respect the vicinity of places and homomorphisms that respect the vicinity of transitions.

Definition 10. *Let $\varphi: N \to N'$ be a net homomorphism.*

1. *φ is* S-vicinity respecting *if, for every $x \in S$:*
   (a) *$\varphi({}^{\odot}x) = {}^{\odot}(\varphi(x))$ or $\varphi({}^{\odot}x) = \{\varphi(x)\}$ and*
   (b) *$\varphi(x^{\odot}) = (\varphi(x))^{\odot}$ or $\varphi(x^{\odot}) = \{\varphi(x)\}$.*
2. *φ is* T-vicinity respecting *if, for every $x \in T$:*
   (a) *$\varphi({}^{\odot}x) = {}^{\odot}(\varphi(x))$ or $\varphi({}^{\odot}x) = \{\varphi(x)\}$ and*
   (b) *$\varphi(x^{\odot}) = (\varphi(x))^{\odot}$ or $\varphi(x^{\odot}) = \{\varphi(x)\}$.*
3. *φ is* vicinity respecting *if it is both S- and T-vicinity respecting*

A subnet of a net is generated by its elements and preserves the flow relation between its elements. We will be interested in subnets that are connected to the remaining part only via places or only via transitions.

Definition 11. *Let N be a net and let X_1 be a subset of X, the set of places and transitions of N. The $\bullet$-notation refers to N in the sequel.*

1. *X_1 generates the* subnet *$N_1 = (S \cap X_1, T \cap X_1; F \cap (X_1 \times X_1))$.*
2. *N_1 is called* transition-bordered *if ${}^{\bullet}S_1 \cup S_1^{\bullet} \subseteq T_1$.*
3. *N_1 is called* place-bordered *if ${}^{\bullet}T_1 \cup T_1^{\bullet} \subseteq S_1$.*

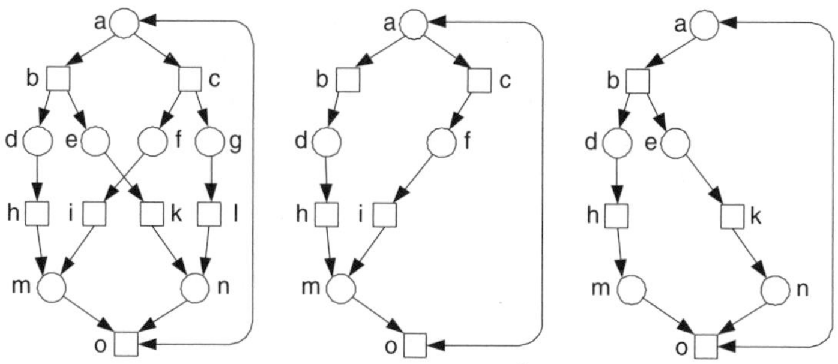

Fig. 5. A net with two subnets

A single transition of a net constitutes a transition-bordered subnet and a single place constitutes a place-bordered subnet. Figure 5 shows three nets. The net in the middle of the figure is a subnet of the net on the left hand side (notice that its set of places is a subset of the set of places of the left net and similar for transitions). This subnet is generated by its set of elements $\{a, b, c, d, f, h, i, m, o\}$. It is a transition-bordered subnet because, for its places a, d, f and m, it contains all transitions in the pre- and post-set of the places. Similarly, the subnet on the right hand side is place-bordered.

Net homomorphism allow to map places to transitions and vice versa. Nevertheless, the role of active and passive components of a net are preserved in the following sense. The refinement of a transition-bordered subnet is a transition-bordered subnet, i.e., the reverse image of the elements of a transition-bordered subnet generates a transition-bordered subnet of the source net. Similarly, the set of elements of the source net that are mapped to some place-bordered subnet of the target net constitute a place-bordered subnet of the source net. The following results were proven in [9] in a topological framework.

Lemma 6. *Let $\varphi: N \to N'$ be a net homomorphism.*

1. *If N'_1 is a transition-bordered subnet of N' then $\{x \in X \mid \varphi(x) \in X'_1\}$ generates a transition-bordered subnet of N.*
2. *If N'_1 is a place-bordered subnet of N' then $\{x \in X \mid \varphi(x) \in X'_1\}$ generates a place-bordered subnet of N.*

Proof: We show only 1, 2 being similar.
Let $(x, y) \in F$. Assume that $\varphi(x) \notin X'_1$ and $\varphi(y) \in X'_1$. Since N'_1 is a transition-bordered subnet of N', $\varphi(x)$ is a place and $\varphi(y)$ is a transition. By Corollary 4, x is a place and y is a transition. It is similarly shown that $\varphi(x) \in X'_1$ and $\varphi(y) \notin X'_1$ implies that x is a transition and y is a place. The result follows by the definition of a transition-bordered subnet. □

4 Transformation of S- and T-Components

An S-component of a net yields a data-oriented view of a part of the system. An S-component can contain nondeterministic choices that are modelled by branching places, i.e. by places with more than one output transitions. It does however not contain aspects of concurrency, whence its transitions are not branched [3]. Similarly, T-components concentrate on functional aspects. They do not contain branching places. Formally S-components and T-components are particular subnets. Figure 5 shows a net on the left hand side, one of its S-components in the middle and one of its T-components on the right hand side.

Definition 12. *Let N be a net. The $\bullet$-notation refers to N in the sequel.*

1. *A strongly connected transition-bordered subnet N_1 of N is called* S-component *of N if, for every $t \in T_1$, $|{}^\bullet t \cap S_1| \leq 1 \wedge |t^\bullet \cap S_1| \leq 1$. N is* covered by S-components *if there exists a family of S-components (N_i), $i \in I$, such that for every $x \in X$ there exists an $i \in I$ such that $x \in X_i$.*
2. *A strongly connected place-bordered subnet N_1 of N is called* T-component *of N if, for every $s \in S_1$, $|{}^\bullet s \cap T_1| \leq 1 \wedge |s^\bullet \cap T_1| \leq 1$. N is* covered by T-components *if there exists a family of T-components (N_i), $i \in I$, such that for every $x \in X$ there exists an $i \in I$ such that $x \in X_i$.*

When a net is mapped to another net, then so are its subnets. The following definition provides a notion for the induced mapping of a subnet.

Definition 13. *Let $\varphi: N \to N'$ be a net homomorphism and N_1 a subnet of N. The net $(\varphi(X_1) \cap S', \varphi(X_1) \cap T'; \{(\varphi(x), \varphi(y)) \mid (x, y) \in F_1 \wedge \varphi(x) \neq \varphi(y)\})$ is called the net image of N_1 by φ. It is denoted by $\varphi(N_1)$. By $\varphi_{N_1}: X_1 \to \varphi(X_1)$ we denote the restriction of φ to X_1, with the range of φ restricted to $\varphi(X_1)$.*

The induced graph homomorphism φ_{N_1} is surjective by definition. Note that $\varphi(N_1)$, the net image of N_1, is not necessarily a subnet of the target net N_1. Figure 6(a) gives an example. The image of the subnet generated by $\{a, b, c, d, e, f\}$ is not a subnet of the target net because the target net has an arrow from $\varphi(b)$ to $\varphi(e)$ whereas the net image of the subnet does not have this arrow.

Definition 13 immediately implies the following result:

Proposition 1. *If $\varphi: N \to N'$ is a net homomorphism and N_1 is a subnet of N then $\varphi_{N_1}: N_1 \to \varphi(N_1)$ is a quotient.*

Corollary 5. *A net homomorphism $\varphi: N \to N'$ is a quotient if and only if $N' = \varphi(N)$ and in this case $\varphi = \varphi_N$.*

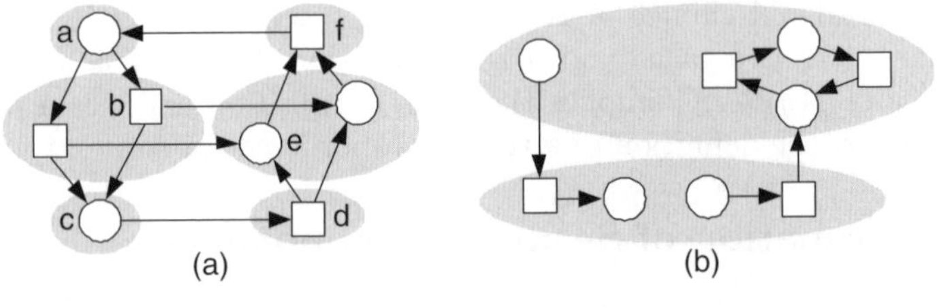

Fig. 6. Net images of subnets are not necessarily subnets

S-vicinity respecting net homomorphisms map a strongly connected transition-bordered subnet either onto a single element or onto a strongly connected transition-bordered subnet:

Theorem 2. *Let* $\varphi: N \to N'$ *be an S-vicinity respecting net homomorphism and let* N_1 *be a strongly connected transition-bordered subnet of* N. *Define* $N_1' = \varphi(N_1)$. *Then:*

1. N_1' *is a subnet of* N'.
2. *If* $|X_1'| > 1$ *then* N_1' *is a transition-bordered subnet of* N'.
3. $\varphi_{N_1}: N_1 \to N_1'$ *is S-vicinity respecting.*

Proof: Assume $|X_1'| > 1$ (otherwise the proposition trivially holds).

1. Obviously $S_1' \subseteq S', T_1' \subseteq T'$ and $F_1' \subseteq F' \cap ((S_1' \times T_1') \cup (T_1' \times S_1'))$.
Let $x', y' \in X_1'$ such that $(x', y') \in F'$. We show that $(x', y') \in F_1'$.
Assume that x' is a place. $\varphi_{N_1}: N_1 \to N_1'$ is a surjective net homomorphism. By Lemma 3 we can find an arc $(x, z) \in F_1$ such that $\varphi_{N_1}(x) = x'$ and $\varphi_{N_1}(z) \neq x'$. By Corollary 4, $x \in S_1$. Since φ is S-vicinity respecting and $\varphi(x^{\odot}) \neq \{\varphi(x)\}$ ($\odot$-notation w.r.t. F) there exists some $y \in T_1$ with $y \in x^{\bullet}$ and $\varphi(y) = y'$ since N_1 is a transition-bordered subnet. Hence $(x, y) \in F_1$ and $(\varphi(x), \varphi(y)) = (x', y') \in F_1'$.
The case $y' \in S'$ is analogous.
2. We only show $S_1'^{\bullet} \subseteq T_1'$, ${}^{\bullet}S_1' \subseteq T_1'$ being similar. Let $x' \in S_1'$, $y' \in T'$ such that $(x', y') \in F'$. Arguing like above, we can find an $x \in S_1$ with $\varphi_{N_1}(x) = x'$ and some $y \in x^{\bullet}$ with $\varphi(y) = y'$. We have $y \in T_1$ because ${}^{\bullet}S_1 \cup S_1^{\bullet} \subseteq T_1$. Hence $y' \in T_1'$, which was to prove.
3. Let $x \in S_1$. We show $\varphi_{N_1}({}^{\odot}x) = \{\varphi_{N_1}(x)\}$ or $\varphi_{N_1}({}^{\odot}x) = {}^{\odot}(\varphi_{N_1}(x))$.
If $\varphi({}^{\odot}x) = \{\varphi(x)\}$ then $\varphi_{N_1}(x) = \{\varphi(x)\} = \{\varphi_{N_1}(x)\}$ and we are done.
Otherwise, since ${}^{\odot}x \subseteq X_1$ we have $\varphi_{N_1}({}^{\odot}x) = \varphi({}^{\odot}x)$. Since φ is S-vicinity respecting, $\varphi({}^{\odot}x) = {}^{\odot}(\varphi(x))$. Since N_1' is a transition-bordered subnet by 2., ${}^{\odot}\varphi(x) \subseteq X_1'$. Therefore ${}^{\odot}(\varphi(x)) = {}^{\odot}(\varphi_{N_1}(x))$. □

The example in Figure 6(b) shows that being strongly connected is a necessary prerequisite for Theorem 2. The image of the left connected subnet by the S-vicinity respecting quotient is not a subnet because of the arc (a, b). In Figure 6(a) we gave an example of a strongly connected subnet which is not transition-bordered. Its image by the S-vicinity respecting quotient is also not a subnet of the target net.

An S-component is in particular a strongly connected transition-bordered subnet. For respecting coverings by S-components, stronger hypotheses have to be assumed. Let us continue considering the S-vicinity respecting quotient shown in Figure 7(a). This net is covered by S-components. The net homomorphism φ is an S-vicinity respecting quotient. However, the target net is not covered by S-components. Observe that the restriction of φ to any S-component is not T-vicinity respecting. Consider the S-component N_1 containing b. The image of N_1 is the entire target net. We have $\varphi_{N_1}(\{a, b\}) \neq \{\varphi_{N_1}(a)\} = \{u\}$ but

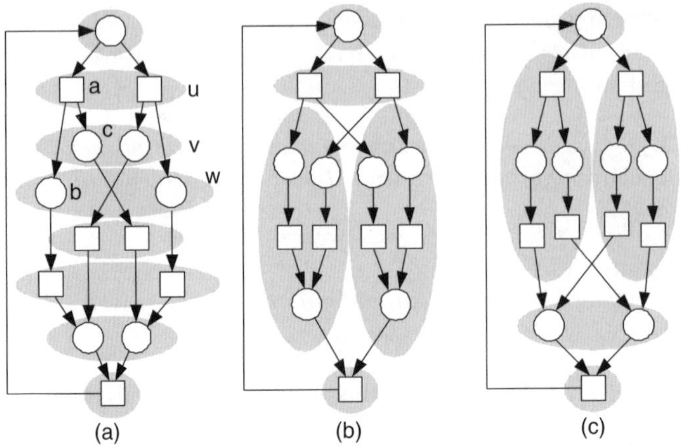

Fig. 7.

$\varphi_{N_1}(\{a,b\}) = \{u,w\} \neq (\varphi_{N_1}(a))^{\odot} = \{u,v,w\}$. The net image of N_1 is not an S-component of the target net.

In Figure 7(b) and 7(c), the quotients restricted to any S-component are T-vicinity respecting.

Proposition 2. *Let $\varphi: N \to N'$ be an S-vicinity respecting net homomorphism and let N_1 be an S-component of N. Define $N_1' = \varphi(N_1)$ and suppose $\varphi_{N_1}: N_1 \to N_1'$ is T-vicinity respecting. If $|X_1'| > 1$ then N_1' is an S-component of N'.*

Proof: Assume $|X_1'| > 1$. Since N_1 is an S-component, it is a transition-bordered subnet. Hence, by Theorem 2, N_1' is a transition-bordered subnet of N'.

It remains to prove: every $y' \in T_1'$ satisfies $|{}^\bullet y' \cap S_1'| \leq 1$ and $|y'^\bullet \cap S_1'| \leq 1$. Let $y' \in T_1'$. We show only: $|{}^\bullet y' \cap S_1'| \leq 1$ ($|y'^\bullet \cap S_1'| \leq 1$ is similar). Since φ_{N_1} is surjective we can find an arc $(x,y) \in F_1$ with $\varphi(x) \neq y'$ and $\varphi(y) = y'$ (Lemma 3). Since φ_{N_1} is a T-vicinity respecting quotient, Corollary 3 implies $|S_1' \cap {}^\bullet y'| \leq |S_1 \cap {}^\bullet y|$ and $|S_1 \cap {}^\bullet y| \leq 1$ because N_1 is an S-component. □

Theorem 3. *Let N be a net, covered by a family (N_i), $i \in I$ of S-components. Let $\varphi: N \to N'$ be an S-vicinity respecting quotient such that, for all $i \in I$, $\varphi_{N_i}: N_i \to \varphi(N_i)$ is T-vicinity respecting. Then N' is covered by S-components.*

Proof: In Proposition 2 we have shown that, given the assumptions above, every S-component of N is either mapped to an S-component of N' or to an element of N'.

Let $x' \in X'$. If x' is an isolated element then it is a trivial S-component. So assume that x' is not isolated. Then we can find a $y' \in X'$ such that $(x',y') \in F'$ or $(y',x') \in F'$.

Since φ is a quotient, there are $x \in S$, $y \in T$ with $\varphi(\{x,y\}) = \{x',y'\}$ and either $(x,y) \in F$ or $(y,x) \in F$. N is covered by S-components and hence we can

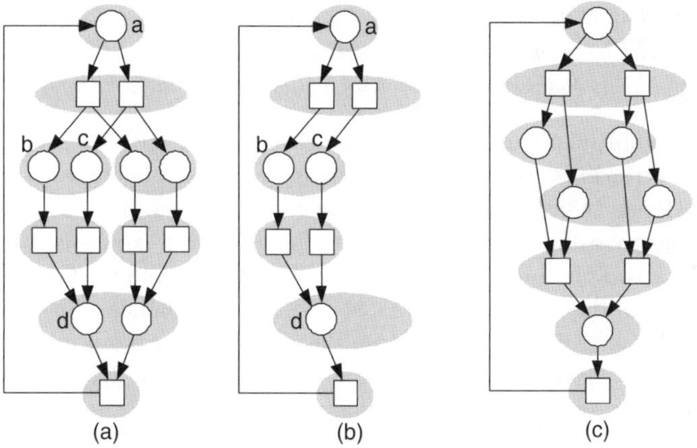

Fig. 8.

find an $i \in I$ such that $x \in S_i$ and $y \in T_i$. $|X'_i| > 1$ since x' and y' are distinct elements of $\varphi(N_i)$. Thus $\varphi(N_i)$ is an S-component of N'. □

By Theorem 2(3), 'φ is S-vicinity respecting' implies for all $i \in I$: 'φ_{N_i} is S-vicinity respecting'. So all the φ_{N_i} have to be both S- and T-vicinity respecting. However, this alone does not imply that φ is S-vicinity respecting and is not sufficient for N' to be covered by S-components as is shown in Figure 8(a). For the S-component N_1 of this net, shown in Figure 8(b), φ_{N_1} is S-and T-vicinity respecting. However, φ is not S-vicinity respecting and N' is not covered by S-components.

Theorem 3 implies that, given a family of S-components which cover the source net, a respective covering of the target net is obtained by the images of the S-components which are not mapped to single non-isolated places.

The choice of a covering family of S-components is decisive. In the example of Figure 8(c), the quotient is vicinity respecting. Its restriction to either the S-component N_1 which contains the respective left places or to the S-component N_2 which contains the respective right places is T-vicinity respecting. Taking the other two possible S-components as a cover of N, the restriction of φ to any of these S-components is not T-vicinity respecting. So the choice of an abstraction and the choice of an S-component covering are not independent.

By duality we get:

Corollary 6. *Let $\varphi: N \to N'$ be a T-vicinity respecting net homomorphism and N_1 a strongly connected place-bordered subnet of N. Define $N'_1 = \varphi(N_1)$. Then:*

1. *N'_1 is a subnet of N';*
2. *If $|X'_1| > 1$ then N'_1 is a place-bordered subnet of N';*
3. *$\varphi_{N_1}: N_1 \to N'_1$ is T-vicinity respecting.*

The dual version of Theorem 3 reads as follows:

Theorem 4. *Let N be a net, covered by a family $(N_i), i \in I$ of T-components. Let $\varphi: N \to N'$ be a T-vicinity respecting quotient such that, for all $i \in I$, $\varphi_{N_i}: N_i \to \varphi(N_i)$ is S-vicinity respecting. Then N' is covered by T-components.*

The net homomorphisms depicted in Figure 7(b) and 7(c) are vicinity respecting. Their restrictions to any S-component or T-component are also vicinity respecting. Hence their net images are covered by S- and T-components.

A particular case of Theorem 3 is the composition of S-components; the source net N is the disjoint union of a family of S-components and the mapping, restricted to each of these S-components, is injective (and hence a fortiori T-vicinity respecting). We can reformulate our result as a property of net homomorphisms as follows: For every place a of an S-component N_1 of a net N the entire vicinity belongs to the S-component as well by definition. Therefore the natural injection $\psi_1: N_1 \to N$ is S-vicinity respecting but not necessarily surjective. A covering by S-components $N_i (i \in I)$ can be expressed by a set of net homomorphisms $\psi_i (i \in I)$ such that each element of N is in $\psi_i(N_i)$ for at least one i. Using the disjoint union of the S-components ($\biguplus N_i$), the net homomorphisms ψ_i induce a quotient ψ from $\biguplus N_i$ to N. Now Theorem 3 reads as follows. Given

- a family (N_i), $i \in I$ of strongly connected nets with $|{}^\bullet t| \leq 1$, $|t^\bullet| \leq 1$ for all transitions t (S-components),
- S-vicinity respecting injective net homomorphisms $\psi_i: N_i \to N (i \in I)$ such that the induced mapping ψ is a quotient (i.e., N is covered by the N_i),
- an S-vicinity respecting quotient $\varphi: N \to N'$ such that φ_{N_i} is T-vicinity respecting for all $i \in I$,

we can find injective S-vicinity respecting mappings $\psi'_i: \varphi(N_i) \to N'$ such that the induced mapping $\psi': \bigcup \varphi(N_i) \to N'$ is surjective (N' covered by the $\varphi(N_i)$).

Again, by duality we can use the same formalism to capture the composition of T-components.

5 Siphons, Traps and Free Choice Property

Definition 14. *Let N be a net.*
A siphon of a net is a nonempty set of places A satisfying ${}^\bullet A \subseteq A^\bullet$.
A trap of a net is a nonempty set of places A satisfying $A^\bullet \subseteq {}^\bullet A$.
A siphon (trap) is minimal if it does not strictly include any other siphon (trap).

For marked Petri nets, siphons and traps are used to deduce behavioral properties of the system [3]. Also at the conceptual level of Channel/Agency nets, they can be used to analyze aspects of the data and information flow in the modelled system. Roughly speaking, if a set of places is a trap then information cannot get completely lost in the component modelled by these places. For the places of a siphon, it is not possible to add information without taking data from the siphon into account.

Minimal siphons and traps are particularly important for the analysis of marked Petri nets. We will show that vicinity respecting net homomorphisms map minimal siphons either onto singletons or onto siphons of the target net, and similarly for minimal traps. We begin with a preliminary result.

Proposition 3. *[3] Let A be a minimal siphon of a net N. Then the subnet generated by $^\bullet A \cup A$ is strongly connected.*

Proof: Let $N_A = (A, {}^\bullet A; F_A)$ be the subnet generated by A. First we observe that every transition t of N_A is an input transition of some place of A by the definition of N_A and also an output transition of some place of A because A is a siphon. Hence, for proving strong connectivity it suffices to show that for every two places $x, y \in A$ there is a path $x \dots y$ in N_A.

Let $y \in A$ and define the set $X = \{z \in A \mid \text{there is a path } z \dots y \text{ in } N_A\}$. We prove that $X = A$. This implies $x \in X$ and, by the definition of X, proves the result we are after.

Let $t \in {}^\bullet X$. Since $X \subseteq A$ and since A is a siphon we have $t \in A^\bullet$. By the definition of X there is a path $t \dots y$ in N_A. So every place in $^\bullet t \cap A$ belongs to X. Therefore $t \in X^\bullet$. So we have $^\bullet X \subseteq X^\bullet$. X is not the empty set because $y \in X$. So X is a siphon included in A. Since A was assumed to be a minimal siphon we conclude that $X = A$. □

Theorem 5. *Let $\varphi\colon N \to N'$ be a surjective S-vicinity respecting net homomorphism. If A is a minimal siphon of N then either $\varphi(A)$ is a single node (place or transition) or $\varphi(A) \cap S'$ is a siphon of N'.*

Proof: Since A is a minimal siphon, $\bullet A \cup A$ generates a strongly connected subnet N_1 by Proposition 3. Hence the subnet N_1' of N' generated by the set of elements $\varphi({}^\bullet A) \cup \varphi(A)$ is also strongly connected.

Assume that $\varphi(A)$ contains more than one node. Let x' be a place of N_1' and let $z' \in {}^\bullet x'$. We have to prove that z' has an input place of N_1'.

Since N_1' is strongly connected and since it contains more than one element, it contains a transition $y' \in {}^\bullet x'$. So there exist a place $x \in A$ and a transition $y \in {}^\bullet x$ such that $\varphi(x) = x'$ and $\varphi(y) = y'$. In particular $\varphi({}^\odot x) \neq \{\varphi(x)\}$. Since φ is S-vicinity respecting, we obtain $\varphi({}^\odot x) = {}^\odot \varphi(x)$. This implies that some $z \in {}^\bullet A$ is mapped to z'. Since A is a siphon, z has an input place of A. So z' has an input place of N_1' which completes the proof. □

By symmetrical arguments, an analogous result holds for traps:

Theorem 6. *Let $\varphi\colon N \to N'$ be a surjective S-vicinity respecting net homomorphism. If A is a minimal trap of N then either $\varphi(A)$ is a single node (place or transition) or $\varphi(A) \cap S'$ is a trap of N'.*

In Figure 9(a), $\{a, b\}$ is a minimal trap that is mapped to a single place which does not constitute a trap. The trap $\{a, b\}$ in Figure 9(b) is not minimal, and the single place of its image does not constitute a trap, too.

We close this section establishing that vicinity respecting quotients respect free choice Petri nets. Important behavioral properties are characterized in terms of traps, siphons for these nets and the class of free choice Petri nets which is

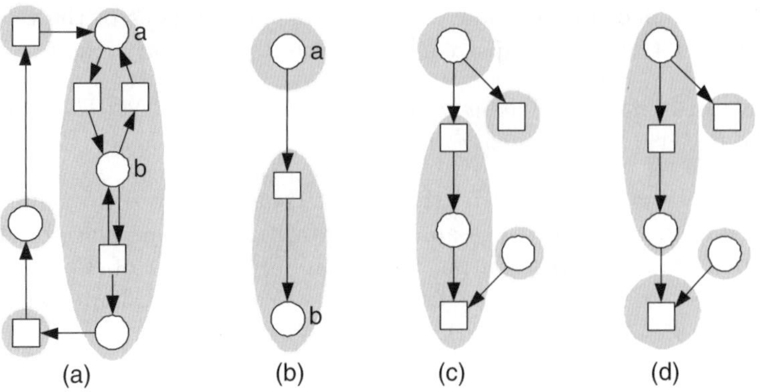

Fig. 9.

covered by S- and T-components is well established [3]. In a free choice net, if two transitions share some input places, then they share all their input places.

Definition 15. *A net N is called free choice if for any two places s_1 and s_2 either $s_1^\bullet \cap s_2^\bullet = \emptyset$ or $s_1^\bullet = s_2^\bullet$.*

Theorem 7. *Let N be a free choice net and $\varphi: N \to N'$ be a vicinity respecting quotient. Then N' is free choice as well.*

Proof: We show that for any two places s_1', s_2' of S' we have: ${s_1'}^\bullet \cap {s_2'}^\bullet = \emptyset$ or ${s_1'}^\bullet = {s_2'}^\bullet$.

We proceed indirectly. Let s_1' and s_2' be places of S' such that ${s_1'}^\bullet \cap {s_2'}^\bullet \neq \emptyset$ and ${s_1'}^\bullet \neq {s_2'}^\bullet$. Without loss of generality assume that there is a transition $t_2' \in {s_2'}^\bullet$ with $t_2' \notin {s_1'}^\bullet$. Let $t_1' \in {s_1'}^\bullet \cap {s_2'}^\bullet$. Since φ is a quotient we find $(s_2, t_1) \in F$ with $\varphi(s_2) = s_2'$ and $\varphi(t_1) = t_1'$. Since φ is S-vicinity respecting we have $\varphi(s_2^\odot) = (\varphi(s_2))^\odot$. Hence there is a transition $t_2 \in s_2^\bullet$ satisfying $\varphi(t_2) = t_2'$. Since φ is T-vicinity respecting, $\varphi({}^\odot t_1) = {}^\odot\varphi(t_1)$. Hence there is a place $s_1 \in {}^\bullet t_1$ with $\varphi(s_1) = s_1'$. Since φ is vicinity respecting and since $t_2' \notin {s_1'}^\bullet$ we get $t_2 \notin \varphi(s_1^\bullet)$ - a contradiction to the free-choice property of N. □

Figures 9(c) and 9(d) show that for the previous theorem, S-vicinity respecting and T-vicinity respecting alone are not sufficient.

6 Conclusion

Structuring system requirements is a gradual process which involves refinement/abstraction between different conceptual levels. Abstractions should bear formal relations with refinements because otherwise the analysis of some abstraction will be of no help for the induced refinement. We argued that vicinity respecting homomorphisms give a possible solution to these requirements for graph-based models of distributed systems. They provide a method to perform graphical abstraction/refinement such that every element is either glued together with its vicinity or its vicinity is the vicinity of its image.

The vicinity respecting concept is a local notion because its definition only uses local vicinities. However, it has global consequences since it preserves paths and, consequently, connectedness properties. For Petri nets, vicinity respecting homomorphisms preserve moreover important structural properties such as S- and T-components, siphons and traps and the free-choice property.

Other concepts for refinement and abstraction of Petri nets and of morphisms [26,17] have been proposed in the literature. However, all these approaches are concerned with marked Petri nets and aim results involving the behavior given by the token game. In contrast, we are concerned with the preliminary task of structuring software requirements down to a working system and aim at structure preservation. Generally, abstraction in our sense is more general than behavior preserving abstraction. However, structure influences behavior. The transition refinement considered in [12] turns out to induce a vicinity respecting homomorphism from the refined net to the coarser net.

As mentioned in the introduction and further in the paper, Petri net quotients can be graphically represented by the less abstract net together with equivalence classes of those elements that are identified by the abstracting morphism. Vicinity respecting quotients play a particular role because they preserve important structural properties. Concepts like aggregation and generalization can be adapted to process modelling and represented as particular vicinity respecting quotients, thus leading to a single diagram including such abstraction elements. Future work will concentrate on the identification of suitable abstraction notions for process models and their representation within single nets.

References

1. Bruno, G.: Model-Based Software Engineering. Chapman and Hall, Boca Raton (1995)
2. Deiters, W., Gruhn, V.: The FUNSOFT net approach to software process management. International Journal on Software Engineering and Knowledge Engineering 4(2) (1994)
3. Desel, J., Esparza, J.: Free Choice Petri Nets. Cambridge Tracts in Theoretical Computer Science, vol. 40. Cambridge University Press, Cambridge (1995)
4. Desel, J., Merceron, A.: Vicinity respecting net morphisms. In: Rozenberg, G. (ed.) APN 1990. LNCS, vol. 483, pp. 165–185. Springer, Heidelberg (1991)
5. Desel, J.: On abstractions of nets. In: Rozenberg, G. (ed.) APN 1991. LNCS, vol. 524, pp. 78–92. Springer, Heidelberg (1991)
6. Desel, J., Merceron, A.: Vicinity respecting homomorphisms for abstracting system requirements. Bericht No. 337 of Institut AIFB, Universität Karlsruhe (1996)
7. Desel, J., Petrucci, L.: Aggregating views for Petri net model construction. In: Petri Nets and Distributed Systems (PNDS 2008), Workshop at the 29th International Conference on Application and Theory of Petri Nets and Other Models of Councurrency, Xi'an, China (2008)
8. Ehrig, H., Hoffmann, K., Padberg, J.: Transformations of Petri nets. Electr. Notes Theor. Comput. Sci. 148(1), 151–172 (2006)

9. Fernández, C.: Net Topology I. Interner Bericht der GMD ISF-75-9 GMD St. Augustin, Germany (1975); Net Topology II. Interner Bericht der GMD ISF-76-2, GMD St. Augustin, Germany (1976)
10. Genrich, H.J., Lautenbach, K., Thiagarajan, P.S.: Elements of general net theory. In: Brauer, W. (ed.) Net Theory and Applications. LNCS, vol. 84, pp. 21–163. Springer, Heidelberg (1980)
11. Genrich, H.J., Stankiewicz-Wiechno, E.: A dictionary of some basic notions of net theory. In: Brauer, W. (ed.) Net Theory and Applications. LNCS, vol. 84, pp. 519–535. Springer, Heidelberg (1980)
12. van Glabbeek, R., Goltz, U.: Refinements of actions in causality based models. In: de Bakker, J.W., de Roever, W.-P., Rozenberg, G. (eds.) REX 1989. LNCS, vol. 430, pp. 267–300. Springer, Heidelberg (1990)
13. van Hee, K.M.: Information Systems Engineering - a Formal Approach. Cambridge University Press, Cambridge (1994)
14. Lakos, C.: Composing abstractions of coloured Petri nets. In: Nielsen, M., Simpson, D. (eds.) ICATPN 2000. LNCS, vol. 1825, pp. 323–345. Springer, Heidelberg (2000)
15. Luckham, D.C., Kenney, J.J., et al.: Specification and analysis of system architecture using Rapide. IEEE Transactions on Software Engineering, Special Issue on Software Architecture 21(4) (April 1995)
16. Merceron, A.: Morphisms to preserve structural properties of Petri nets. Computer Science – Research and Applications, pp. 439–454. Plenum Press, New York (1994)
17. Meseguer, J., Montanari, U.: Petri nets are monoids. In: Information and Computation, vol. 88, pp. 105–155 (1990)
18. Mikolajczak, B., Wang, Z.: Conceptual Modeling of Concurrent Systems through Stepwise Abstraction and Refinement Using Petri Net Morphisms. In: Song, I.-Y., Liddle, S.W., Ling, T.-W., Scheuermann, P. (eds.) ER 2003. LNCS, vol. 2813, pp. 433–445. Springer, Heidelberg (2003)
19. Mikolajczak, B.: Conceptual modeling of concurrent information systems with general morphisms of Petri nets. In: Intelligent Information Systems, Advances in Soft Computing, pp. 535–539. Springer, Heidelberg (2003)
20. Ore, O.: Theory of Graphs, vol. XXXVIII. American Mathematical Society, Colloquium Publications (1962)
21. Petri, C.A.: Concepts of net theory. In: Proceedings of Symposium and Summer School on Mathematical Foundations of Computer Science, High Tatras, September 3-8, 1973
22. Petri, C.A.: Introduction to General Net Theory. In: Brauer, W. (ed.) Net Theory and Applications. LNCS, vol. 84, pp. 1–20. Springer, Heidelberg (1980)
23. Reisig, W.: Petri nets in software engineering. In: Brauer, W., Reisig, W., Rozenberg, G. (eds.) APN 1986. LNCS, vol. 255, pp. 63–96. Springer, Heidelberg (1987)
24. Reisig, W.: A Primer in Petri Net Design. Springer, Heidelberg (1992)
25. Reisig, W.: Simple composition of nets. In: Franceschinis, G., Wolf, K. (eds.) PETRI NETS 2009. LNCS, vol. 5606, pp. 23–42. Springer, Heidelberg (2009)
26. Winskel, G.: Petri nets, algebras, morphisms and compositionality. In: Information and Computation, vol. 72, pp. 197–238 (1987)

Search-Order Independent State Caching*

Sami Evangelista[1,2] and Lars Michael Kristensen[3]

[1] Computer Science Department, Aarhus University, Denmark
[2] LIPN, Université Paris 13, France
sami.evangelista@lipn.univ-paris13.fr
[3] Department of Computer Engineering, Bergen University College, Norway
lmkr@hib.no

Abstract. State caching is a memory reduction technique used by model checkers to alleviate the state explosion problem. It has traditionally been coupled with a depth-first search to ensure termination. We propose and experimentally evaluate an extension of the state caching method for general state exploring algorithms that are independent of the search order (i.e., search algorithms that partition the state space into closed (visited) states, open (to visit) states and unmet states).

1 Introduction

Model checking is one of the techniques used to detect defects in system designs. Its principle is to perform an exhaustive exploration of all system states to track erroneous behaviors. Although it provides some advantages compared to other verification methods, its practical use is sometimes prohibited by the well-known state explosion problem: the state space of the system may be far too large to be explored with the available computing resources.

The literature is replete with examples of techniques designed to tackle, or at least postpone, the state explosion problem. While some techniques, like partial order reduction [12], reduce the part of the state space that must be explored while still guaranteeing soundness and completeness, more pragmatic approaches make a better use of available resources to extend the range of systems that can be analyzed. State compression [16], external memory algorithms [1], and distributed algorithms [24] are examples of such techniques. In this paper we focus on the *state caching* method first proposed by Holzmann in [14].

State caching is based on the idea that, in depth-first search (DFS), only the states on the current search path need to be in memory to detect cycles. All states that have been visited but have left the DFS stack can thus be deleted from memory without endangering the termination of the search. This comes at the cost of potentially revisiting states and for many state spaces, time becomes the main limiting factor.

The state caching method has been developed and mostly studied in the context of depth-first search since this search order makes it easy to guarantee

* Supported by the Danish Research Council for Technology and Production.

K. Jensen, S. Donatelli, and M. Koutny (Eds.): ToPNoC IV, LNCS 6550, pp. 21–41, 2010.

termination. In this paper we propose an extension of state space caching to General State Exploring Algorithms (GSEA). Following the definition of [5], we put in this family all algorithms that partition the state space into three sets: the set of *open* states that have been seen but not yet expanded (i.e., some of their successors may not have been generated); the set of *closed* states that have been seen and expanded; and the set of unseen states. DFS, BFS, and directed search algorithms [8] like Best-First Search and A* are examples of such general state exploring algorithms.

The principle of our extension is to detect cycles and guarantee termination by maintaining a tree rooted in the initial state and covering all open states. States that are part of that tree may not be removed from the cache, while others are candidates for replacement. Hence, any state that is not an ancestor in the search tree of an unprocessed state can be removed from memory. This tree is implicitly constructed by the state caching algorithm in DFS, since DFS always maintains a path from the initial state to the current state, while for GSEA it has to be explicitly built. However, our experimental results demonstrate that the overhead both in time and memory of this explicit construction is negligible.

The generalized state caching reduction is implemented in our model checker ASAP [26]. We report on the results of experiments made to assess the benefits of the reduction in combination with different search orders: BFS, DFS, and several variations and combinations of these two; and with the sweep-line method [20] which we show is compatible with our generalized state caching reduction. The general conclusions we draw from these experiments are that (1) the memory reduction is usually better with DFS than with BFS although we never really experienced a time explosion with BFS; (2) BFS is to be preferred for some classes of state spaces; (3) a combination of BFS and DFS often outperforms DFS with respect to both time and memory; (4) state caching can further enhance the memory reduction provided by the sweep-line method.

Structure of the Paper. Section 2 presents the principle of a general state exploring algorithm. Section 3 describes our state caching mechanism for the general algorithm. In Sect. 4 we put our generalized state caching method into context by discussing its compatibility with related reduction techniques. Section 5 reports on the results of experiments made with the implementation of the new algorithm. Finally, Sect. 6 concludes this paper.

Definitions and Notations. From now on we assume to be given a universe of system states $\mathcal{S}$, an initial state $s_0 \in \mathcal{S}$, a set of events $\mathcal{E}$, an enabling function $en : \mathcal{S} \rightarrow 2^{\mathcal{E}}$ and a successor function $succ : \mathcal{S} \times \mathcal{E} \rightarrow \mathcal{S}$; and that we want to explore the state space implied by these parameters, i.e., visit all its states. A state space is a triple (S, T, s_0) such that $S \subseteq \mathcal{S}$ is the set of reachable states and $T \subseteq S \times S$ is the set of transitions defined by:

$$\begin{aligned} S &= \{s_0\} \cup \{\, s \in \mathcal{S} \mid \exists s_1, \ldots, s_n \in \mathcal{S} \text{ with } s = s_n \ \wedge \ s_1 = s_0 \ \wedge \\ &\qquad \forall i \in \{1, \ldots, n-1\} : \exists e_i \in en(s_i) \text{ with } succ(s_i, e_i) = s_{i+1} \} \\ T &= \{(s, s') \in S \times S \mid \exists e \in en(s) \text{ with } succ(s, e) = s'\} \end{aligned}$$

Related Work. The principle of state caching dates back to an article of Holzmann [14] in 1985. He noted that, in DFS, cycles always eventually reach a state on the stack and, hence, keeping in memory the states on the current search path ensures termination. Forgetting other states comes at the cost of potentially re-exploring them. In the worst case, if any state leaving the stack is removed from memory, a state will be visited once for each path connecting it to the initial state leading to a potential explosion in run-time. Hence, depending on available memory, a set of states that have left the stack are cached in memory.

The question of the strategy to be used for replacing cached states has been addressed in several papers: [11,14,15,17,18,23]. States can be chosen according to various criteria (e.g., in- and out-degree, visit frequency, stack entry time) or in a purely random way. The experiments reported in [23] stress that no strategy works well on all models and that strategies are, to some extent, complementary.

The *sleep-set* reduction technique [12] is fully compatible with state caching [13]. This reduction eliminates most "useless" interleavings by exploiting the so-called *diamond property* of independent transitions: whatever their execution order they lead to the same state. This has the natural consequence to limit revisits of states removed from the cache. For some protocols (e.g., AT&T's Universal Receiver Protocol, MULOG's mutual exclusion protocol), the result of this combination is impressive: at a reasonable cost in time, the cache size can be reduced to less than 3% of the state space.

All the related work discussed above are coupled with depth-first search. To the best of our knowledge, the only work exploring the combination of state caching with BFS is [21] which is more closely related to our work. Termination in [21] is ensured by taking snapshots of the state space, i.e., memorizing full BFS levels. By increasing the period between two snapshots it is guaranteed that cycles will eventually reach a "pictured" state. This approach is in general incomparable with the present work. The algorithm of [21] has to keep full levels in memory while ours stores some states of each level. Besides this algorithm, [21] also introduces some hierarchical caching strategies and learning mechanisms.

Some other reduction techniques share the philosophy of state caching: only store a subset of the state space while still guaranteeing termination. Examples include the "to-store-or-not" method [3] and the sweep-line method [20]. The compatibility of our algorithm with these two works is discussed in Sect. 4.

2 General State Exploring Algorithm

A general state exploring algorithm is presented in Fig. 1. It operates on two data structures. The set of open states, $\mathcal{O}$, contains all states that have been reached so far, but for which some successor(s) have not yet been computed. Once all these successors have been computed, the state is moved from $\mathcal{O}$ to the set of closed states $\mathcal{C}$. Initially, the closed set is empty, and the open set only contains the initial state. A set of events *evts* is associated with each open state. It consists of its enabled events that have not been executed so far. In each iteration, the algorithm selects an open state s (l. 3), picks one of its executable events e (if any, since the state may be a terminal state) and removes it from the set of events to execute $s.evts$ (ll. 4–5). The successor state s' of s reached via the execution of e is computed, and if it is neither in the closed nor in the open set (ll. 7–9), it is put in $\mathcal{O}$ to be later visited and its enabled events are computed. Once the successor is computed, we check if all the enabled events of s have been executed (ll. 10–11), in which case we move s from $\mathcal{O}$ to the closed set $\mathcal{C}$.

1: $\mathcal{C} := \emptyset$; $\mathcal{O} := \{s_0\}$; $s_0.evts := en(s_0)$
2: **while** $\mathcal{O} \neq \emptyset$ **do**
3: $\quad s :=$ **choose from** $\mathcal{O}$
4: $\quad$ **if there exists** $e \in s.evts$ **then**
5: $\quad\quad s.evts := s.evts \setminus \{e\}$
6: $\quad\quad s' := succ(s, e)$
7: $\quad\quad$ **if** $s' \notin \mathcal{C} \cup \mathcal{O}$ **then**
8: $\quad\quad\quad \mathcal{O} := \mathcal{O} \cup \{s'\}$
9: $\quad\quad\quad s'.evts := en(s')$
10: $\quad$ **if** $s.evts = \emptyset$ **then**
11: $\quad\quad \mathcal{C} := \mathcal{C} \cup \{s\}$; $\mathcal{O} := \mathcal{O} \setminus \{s\}$

Fig. 1. A general state exploring algorithm

In the rest of this paper we shall use the following terminology. *Expanding* a state s consists of executing one of its enabled events and putting its successor in the open set if needed (ll. 6–9). A state s will be characterized as *expanded* if all its successor states have been computed, i.e., $s.evts = \emptyset$, and it has been moved to the closed set; and as *partially expanded* if some of its successors have been computed, but s is still in the open set. A state s *generates* state s' if $succ(s, e) = s'$ for some $e \in en(s)$ and $s' \notin \mathcal{C} \cup \mathcal{O}$ when expanding s. In this case, the transition (s, s') is said to be the *generating transition*.

The algorithm in Fig. 1 differs slightly from explicit state space search algorithms usually found in the literature, e.g., like the GSEA of [5]. In an iteration, the algorithm only executes one event rather than all executable events of a state. This variation is more flexible as it allows us to have open states that are partially expanded. Hence, it naturally caters for search order independence. Depending on the implementation of the open set, the search strategy can be, for instance, depth-first (with a stack), breadth-first (with a queue), or best-first (with a priority queue). Since each search order has its pros and cons, it is of interest to design reduction techniques that work directly on the generic search order independent template, e.g., like the partial order reduction proposed in [5], rather than on a specific instance.

3 State Caching for GSEA

The key principle of state caching for depth-first search is that cycles always eventually reach a state on the DFS stack. Hence, it is only necessary to keep this stack in memory to ensure termination of the algorithm. In breadth-first search, or more generally for a GSEA, we do not have such a structure to rely on in order to detect cycles. Hence, a BFS naively combined with state caching may never terminate.

To overcome this limitation, we propose to equip GSEA with a mechanism that allows it to avoid reentering cycles of states and thereby ensures termination. The principle of this modification is to maintain, as the search progresses, a so-called *termination detection tree* (`TD`-tree). The `TD`-tree is rooted in the initial state s_0 and keeps track of unprocessed states of the open set as explained below. To formulate the requirements of the TD-tree we shall use the term *search tree*. The search tree is the sub-graph of the state space which at any moment during the execution of GSEA covers all open and closed states, and contains only generating transitions. In other words, it consists of the state space explored so far from which we remove transitions of which the exploration led to an already seen state, i.e., in the set $\mathcal{C} \cup \mathcal{O}$.

The three following invariants related to the TD-tree must be maintained during the state space search:

I1 The TD-tree is a sub-tree of the search tree;
I2 All open states are covered by the TD-tree;
I3 All the leaves of the TD-tree are open states.

A sufficient condition for the modified GSEA to terminate is that we always keep in memory the states belonging to the TD-tree. Intuitively, when expanding a state s picked from the open set, we are sure (provided invariants I1 and I2 are valid) that any cycle covering s will at some point contain a state s' belonging to the TD-tree. States that can be deleted from memory are all closed states that are not part of the TD-tree: their presence is not required to detect cycles. Note that only the two first invariants are required for termination. Invariant I3 just specifies that the TD-tree is not unnecessarily large, i.e., it does not contain states we do not need to keep in the closed set to detect cycles. To sum up, all the states that may not be removed from the cache are (besides open states) all closed states that generated (directly or indirectly through a sequence of generating transitions) a state in the open set.

As an example, let us see see how a BFS extended with this mechanism will explore the state space of Fig. 2(top left). Each state is inscribed with a state number that coincides with the (standard) BFS search order. The TD-tree has been drawn in the right box for several steps of the algorithm. The legend for this box is shown in the bottom left box of the figure. Note that these graphical conventions are used throughout the paper. Some reference counters used to maintain the TD-tree appear next to the states. They will not be discussed now. Their use will become clear after the presentation of the algorithm.

After the expansion of the initial state 0, the queue contains its two successor states 1 and 2 and the TD-tree is equivalent to the search tree (see Step 1). At the next level, we expand open states 1 and 2. State 1 first generates states 3 and 4. As state 4 is already in the open set when state 2 is expanded, this one does not generate any new states, which means that at Step 2, state 2 does not have any successors in the search tree. It is deleted from the TD-tree, and we assume that the algorithm also removes it from the closed set. The expansion of open states 3 and 4 at the next level generates the three states 5, 6 and 7. At Step 3 all the states that were expanded at level 2 generated at least one (new) state. Hence, no state is deleted from the TD-tree. Level 3 is then processed. States 5 and 6 do not have any successors and state 7 has a single successor, state 2, which has been visited but deleted from memory. Hence, it is put in the

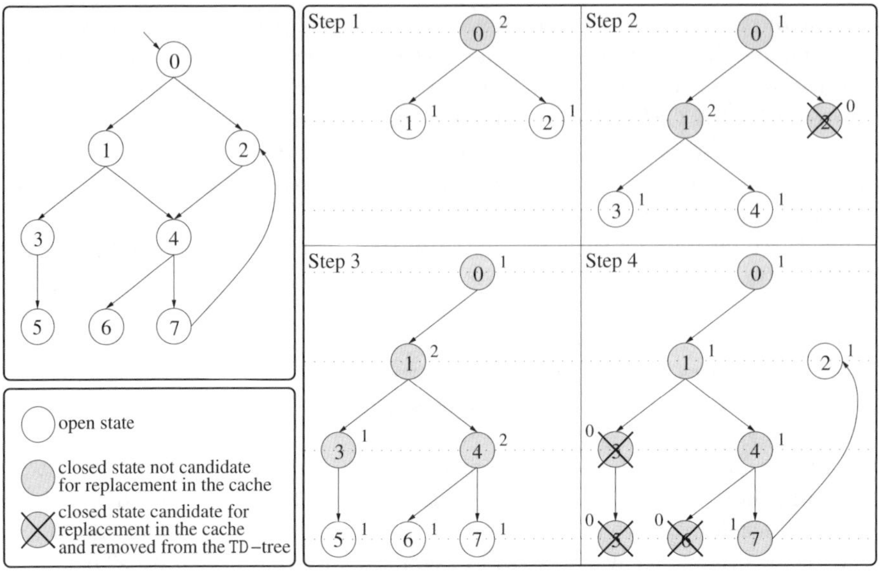

Fig. 2. A state space (top left), the TD-tree at three different stages of a BFS (right) and the legend for the right box (bottom left). Step 1: after the expansion of state 0. Step 2: after the expansion of states 1 and 2. Step 3: after the expansion of states 3 and 4. Step 4: after the expansion of states 5, 6 and 7.

open set. States 5 and 6 can be deleted from the TD-tree at Step 4 since they are terminal states and do not have any successors in the TD-tree. After the deletion of state 5, state 3 is in the same situation and becomes a leaf of the TD-tree. It is thus also deleted. The queue now only contains state 2 that had already been previously expanded. Its only successor, state 4, belongs to the TD-tree and, hence, is present in memory. The algorithm thus detects the cycle 2→4→7→2. After this last expansion, the queue is empty and algorithm terminates.

The operation of our algorithm is similar to the basic state caching reduction for DFS with the difference that the TD-tree is implicitly maintained by the DFS state caching algorithm: it consists of all the open states located on the DFS stack. Closed states have left the stack so they have not generated the states currently on the stack and do not need anymore to be part of the TD-tree.

We now introduce the algorithm of Fig. 3, a GSEA extended with the state caching mechanism we described above. The main procedure (on the left column) works basically as the algorithm of Fig. 1 except that we inserted the lines preceded by a ► to manage the state cache. Apart from the closed set $\mathcal{C}$ and open set $\mathcal{O}$, the algorithm also uses a set $\mathcal{D} \subseteq \mathcal{C}$ that contains all states candidate for deletion if memory becomes scarce, i.e., all the states that left the TD-tree. Hence, the TD-tree is composed of the states in $(\mathcal{C} \cup \mathcal{O}) \setminus \mathcal{D}$.

After each state expansion, the algorithm calls the *garbageCollection* procedure (l. 13) that checks if the number of states kept in memory exceeds some user-defined limit `MaxMemory`. In that case, one of the candidates for replacement

```
1:  C := ∅ ; O := {s0} ; s0.evts := en(s0)
2:  ► D := ∅ ; s0.refs := 1 ; s0.pred := nil
3:  while O ≠ ∅ do
4:     s := choose from O
5:     if there exists e ∈ s.evts then
6:        s.evts := s.evts \ {e}
7:        s' := succ(s, e)
8:        if s' ∉ C ∪ O then
9:           O := O ∪ {s'}
10:          s'.evts := en(s')
11:          ► s.refs := s.refs + 1
12:          ► s'.refs := 1 ; s'.pred := s
13:          ► garbageCollection()
14:    if s.evts = ∅ then
15:       C := C ∪ {s} ; O := O \ {s}
16:       ► unref(s)
17: procedure unref(s) is
18:    s.refs := s.refs − 1
19:    if s.refs = 0 then
20:       D := D ∪ {s}
21:       if s.pred ≠ nil then
22:          unref(s.pred)
23:
24: procedure garbageCollection() is
25:    if |O| + |C| > MaxMemory then
26:       if D = ∅ then
27:          report "out of memory"
28:       else
29:          s := choose from D
30:          C := C \ {s}
31:          D := D \ {s}
```

Fig. 3. A general state exploring algorithm combined with state caching

is selected from $\mathcal{D}$ according to a replacement strategy and deleted from both $\mathcal{C}$ and $\mathcal{D}$ (ll. 29–31) to make room for the state newly inserted in $\mathcal{O}$. If there is no candidate (ll. 26–27), the algorithm terminates with a failure: the TD-tree is too large to fit within user-defined available memory.

In order to maintain the TD-tree, two additional attributes are associated with states. The first one, *pred*, identifies the predecessor of the state that previously generated it, i.e., its predecessor in the search tree. It is set at l. 12 when a new state s' is generated from s. The second attribute, *refs*, is a reference counter used by the *garbageCollection* procedure to determine when a closed state leaves the TD-tree and can become a candidate for replacement. The following invariant is maintained by the algorithm for any $s \in \mathcal{C} \cup \mathcal{O}$:

$$\textbf{I4}\quad s.refs = |\{s' \in \mathcal{C} \cup \mathcal{O} \textbf{ with } s'.pred = s \wedge s'.refs > 0\}| + \begin{cases} 0 \textbf{ if } s \notin \mathcal{O} \\ 1 \textbf{ if } s \in \mathcal{O} \end{cases}$$

In other words, $s.refs$ records the number of successors of s in the TD-tree incremented by 1 if s is an open state. It directly follows from invariant I4 that any state s with $s.refs = 0$ must be moved to $\mathcal{D}$ and deleted from the TD-tree in order to satisfy invariant I3. This is the purpose of procedure *unref* called each time a state s leaves the open set (ll. 15–16). Its counter is decremented by 1, and if it reaches 0 (ll. 19–22), s is put in the candidate set and the procedure is recursively called on its predecessor in the TD-tree (if any).

Let us consider again the TD-trees depicted in Fig.2(right). Reference counters are given next to the states. At Step 4, after the expansion of states 5, 6, and 7 of level 3, the reference counter of 5 and 6 reaches 0: they have left the open set and have no successors in the search tree, i.e., they did not generate any new state. They can therefore be put in the candidate set and leave the TD-tree. *unref* is then also recursively called on states 3 and state 4 and their counters are decremented to 0 and 1, respectively. Hence, state 3 is also put in the candidate set. This finally causes *unref* to decrement the reference counter of state 1 to 1.

Lemma 1. *The algorithm of Fig.3 terminates after visiting all states.*

Proof. Let $\mathcal{T}$ be the (only) sub-tree of the search tree that satisfies invariants I1, I2 and I3 and assume that the states belonging to $\mathcal{T}$ always remain in set $\mathcal{C} \cup \mathcal{O}$. Let $s_1, \ldots, s_n \in \mathcal{S}$ be a cycle of states with $\forall i \in \{1, \ldots, n\} : succ(s_i, e_i) = s_{i \bmod n+1}$, and such that s_1 is its first state to enter $\mathcal{O}$. This cycle is necessarily detected, i.e, during the search we reach some $s_i \in \mathcal{C} \cup \mathcal{O}$. Let us suppose the contrary. Then, each state $s_i \in \{s_1, \ldots, s_{n-1}\}$ generates the state $s_j = s_{i+1}$, i.e., $s_j \notin \mathcal{C} \cup \mathcal{O}$ when event e_i is executed from s_i. Hence, after the execution of e_{n-1} by the algorithm it holds from invariants I1 and I2 that $\{s_1, \ldots, s_n\} \subseteq \mathcal{T}$ since $s_n \in \mathcal{O}$ and each $s_j \in \{s_2, \ldots, s_n\}$ was generated by s_{j-1}. Thus, $s_1 \in \mathcal{C} \cup \mathcal{O}$ when event e_n is executed from s_n, which contradicts our initial assumption.

It is straightforward to see from invariant I4 that $s.refs > 0 \Leftrightarrow s \in \mathcal{T}$. After an iteration of the algorithm (ll.3–16), invariant I4 is trivially ensured. This implies that any $s \in \mathcal{C}$ with $s.refs = 0$ ($\Leftrightarrow s \in \mathcal{D}$) can be deleted from $\mathcal{C}$.

The modified GSEA of Fig. 3 consumes slightly more memory per state to represent the *pred* and *refs* attributes. In our implementation *pred* is encoded with a 4 byte pointer and *refs* using a single byte. Nevertheless, these 5 bytes are usually negligible compared to the size of the bit vector used to encode states.

4 Compatibility with Other Reduction Techniques

We discuss in this section several aspects of our algorithm and its combination with some selected reduction techniques.

4.1 Single-Successor States Chain Reduction

Closely related to state caching, the idea of [3] is to use a boolean function that, given a state, determines if the state should be kept in the closed set or not. The paper proposes functions that guarantee the termination of the search. One is to only store states having several successors. The motivation is that the revisit of single-successor and deadlock states is cheap. It consists of reexecuting a sequence until reaching a branching state (which has several successors and which is therefore stored). To avoid entering cycles of single-successor states, the kth state of these sequences is systematically stored.

In order to combine this reduction of [3] with our state caching mechanism we have to carefully reduce chains that are part of the TD-tree. First we notice that we do not have to worry about cycles of single-successor states: they will eventually reach a state of the TD-tree and all their states will immediately leave the TD-tree becoming candidates for replacement. To reduce chains of single-successor states we associate with each open state s an attribute *ancestor* that points to the branching state that generated the first state of the chain to which s belongs, or is equal to **nil** if s is a branching state. The following piece of code specifies how this attribute is used to remove such chains from the TD-tree. It must be inserted after the generation of state s' from s at line 12.

$$s'.ancestor := \begin{cases} \textbf{if } |en(s')| = 1 \textbf{ and } s.ancestor = \textbf{ nil then } s \\ \textbf{if } |en(s')| = 1 \textbf{ and } s.ancestor \neq \textbf{ nil then } s.ancestor \\ \textbf{else nil} \end{cases}$$

if $s'.ancestor =$ **nil and** $s.ancestor \neq$ **nil then**
    $a := s.ancestor \; ; \; s'.pred := a \; ; \; a.refs := a.refs + 1 \; ; \; unref(s)$

ancestor is first set when a single-successor state is generated from a branching state and then propagated later along all the states of the chain. If s' is a branching state and $s.ancestor$ points to some state, this means that we just left a chain. The reduction is done by directly linking s' to $s.ancestor$ and removing all the states of the chain from the TD-tree, by unreferencing s.

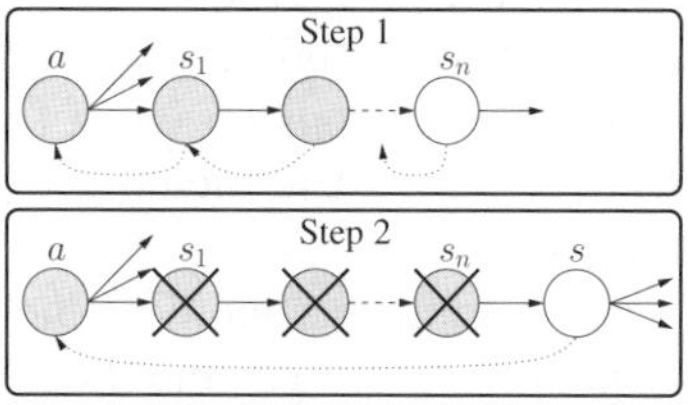

Fig. 4. Reduction of a single-successor state chain

Fig. 4 shows an example of this reduction. Dotted arcs graphically represent the *pred* pointer of each state in the TD-tree.At Step 1, $s_1, \ldots, s_n$ form a reducible chain of single-successor states. All their *ancestor* field points to a, the branching state that generated the first state of the chain. State s_n then generates s that has several successors (see Step 2). Hence $s.ancestor =$ **nil** $\neq s_n.ancestor$ and a reducible chain is detected. The consequence is to break the link from s to s_n and make $s.pred$ directly point to $s_n.ancestor = a$. The chain is then removed from the TD-tree by invoking $unref(s_n)$.

4.2 Distributed Memory Algorithms

Most works in the field of distributed verification follow the seminal work of Stern and Dill [24]. Their algorithm partitions the state space upon several processes using a partition function mapping states to processes. Each process involved in the verification is responsible of storing and exploring the states it is assigned by this function. Whenever a process p generates a state owned by process $q \neq p$ it has to pack it into a message and send it to q that, upon reception, will store it in its open state and expand it later.

Our reduction is compatible with this algorithm. The only issue is raised by the *unref* procedure, used to maintain the TD-tree. This one has to access the ancestors of the unreferenced state — ancestors that may be located on another process — hence generating communications. A possible way to overcome this problem is to only call that procedure when memory becomes scarce. Processes then enter a garbage collection phase where they clean the TD-tree and delete states from memory. Thus, if the aggregated memory is large enough to solve the problem without any reduction then there is no time overhead. This might also help to group states sent to the same owner and thereby reduce communication.

Another solution is to associate with each new state s received from another process a reference number of 2 (rather than 1) to ensure it will never leave the TD-tree (and that no communication will occur). It is then not necessary that the source state of the transition that generated the message keeps a reference to s. An example of a TD-tree (actually a forest) distributed over two processes can be seen in Fig 5. Dashed transitions are not part of the TD-tree. The reference counter of state s is set to 3 whereas it is closed and only has 2 successors. The reason is that it has been first discovered upon its reception by process 1. Hence, it will never leave the TD-tree, guaranteeing that the cycle $t_0.t_1.t_2$ will be detected regardless of the order in which states are visited. Another difference with a "sequential" TD-tree is that the counter of s_0 is set to 1 instead of 2 since it only has one successor in the TD-tree on the same process. Hence, although s will remain in the memory of process 1, s_0 will eventually be allowed to leave the cache.

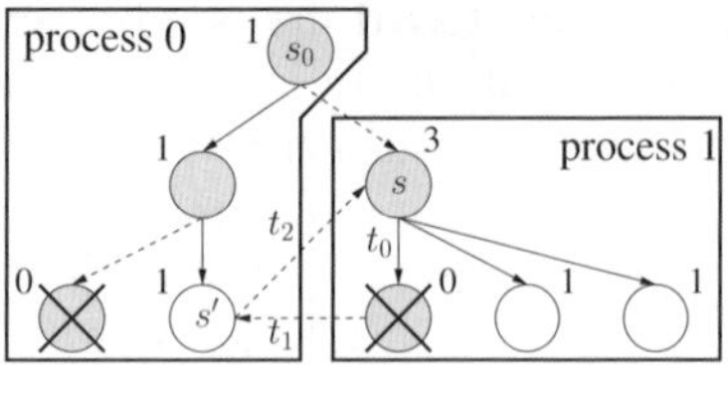

Fig. 5. A distributed TD-tree

Both solutions should benefit from a partitioning exhibiting few cross transitions linking states belonging to different processes. This will limit communications for the first solution and enhance the reduction in the second case.

4.3 Reductions Based on State Reconstruction

Our GSEA is also compatible with the reduction techniques proposed in [10] and [27]. Instead of keeping full state vectors in the closed and open sets, their principle is to represent a state s as a pair $(pred, e)$ where $pred$ is a pointer to the state s' that generated s during the search, and e is the event such that $succ(s', e) = s$. States can be reconstructed from this compressed representation by reexecuting the sequence of events that generated it. At a reasonable cost in time, it allows each state to be encoded by 12–16 bytes whatever the system being analyzed. This reduction fits nicely with the algorithm of this paper. The TD-tree can be compactly stored using this representation of states and, actually, both methods store with each state a pointer to its generating predecessor. The only states that have to be fully stored in memory are those who left the TD-tree since their generating predecessor may not be present anymore in memory.

4.4 The Sweep-Line Method

A sweep-line based algorithm alternates between exploration phases where states are visited and their successor(s) generated; with garbage collection phases where states are removed from memory. A key feature of the method is the progress measure ψ mapping states to (ordered) progress values. It is used to estimate "how far" states are from the initial states and guides the garbage collection procedure: if the minimal progress value found in the set of open states is $\alpha_{min} = \min_{s \in \mathcal{O}} \psi(s)$ then all closed states s with $\psi(s) < \alpha_{min}$ can be deleted from memory. The underlying idea is that if the progress mapping is monotonic, i.e., all transitions (s, s') are such that $\psi(s) \leq \psi(s')$, then a visited state s with a progress $\psi(s) < \alpha_{min}$ will not be visited again. In [20] the method is extended to support progress measures with regress transitions, i.e., transitions (s, s') with $\psi(s) > \psi(s')$, that with the basic method of [6] cause the algorithm to not terminate. The principle of this extension is to mark destination of regress transitions as persistent to prevent the garbage collector from deleting them.

The sweep-line method can also be used in conjunction with our reduction. This stems from the fact that the algorithm of [20] is also an instance of the GSEA of Fig. 1 that keeps open states in a priority queue (priority being given to states having the lowest progression). However, one has to proceed carefully when combining both methods: the *unref* procedure of our algorithm may not put in the set $\mathcal{D}$ of candidates for replacement an unreferenced state (i.e., with $s.refs = 0$) that has been marked as persistent by the sweep-line reduction. Note that the predecessor of a persistent state may however be unreferenced.

Running the sweep-line algorithm in combination with our state caching algorithm causes the deletion of non-persistent states stored in the `TD`-tree. This means that we only store the parts of the `TD`-tree corresponding to the states determined to be in memory by the sweep-line method. The role of the `TD`-tree (which now becomes a forest) is to ensure termination of each of the phases of the sweep-line method, while the overall termination of the combined search is guaranteed by the persistent states stored by the sweep-line method.

5 Experiments

The technique proposed in this paper has been implemented in the ASAP verification tool [26]. ASAP can load models written in DVE [7], the input language of the DiVinE verification tool [2]. This allowed us to perform numerous experiments with models from the BEEM (BEnchmarks for Explicit Model checkers) database [22] although "Puzzles" and "Planning and scheduling" problems were not considered. These are mostly toy examples having few characteristics in common with real-life models. We performed two experiments, studying the performance of our reduction in combination with basic search algorithms for the first one; and with the sweep-line method for the second one. Due to lack of space, some data has been left out in this section but may be found in [9].

5.1 Experiment 1: State Caching with Basic Search Strategies

State caching is a rather unpredictable technique in the sense that its performance depends on a large range of parameters, e.g., the size and replacement strategy for the cache, the characteristics of the state space. It is usually hard to guess which configuration should be used before running the model checker. State caching must therefore be experimented with in a wide range of settings and with many different state spaces in order to get a good insight into its behavior. In this experiment we performed more than 1,000,000 runs using different search algorithms, caching strategies, cache sizes, and state space reduction techniques.

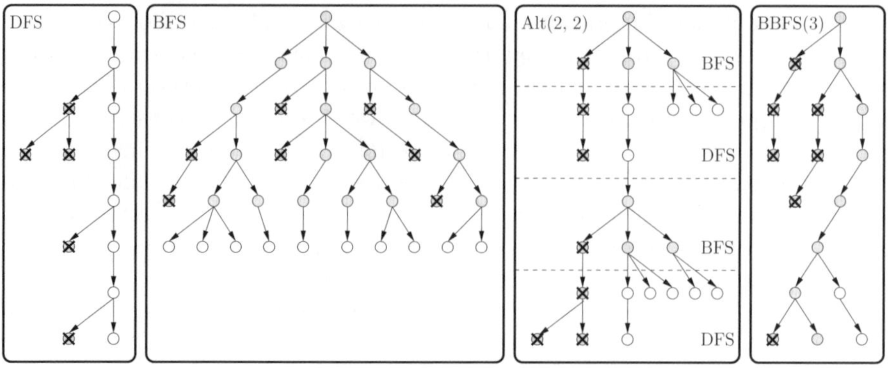

Fig. 6. Snapshot of the search trees with different search strategies

Experimentation Context

Search strategies. Several preliminary experiments revealed important variations of our state caching reduction when combined with DFS or BFS. Therefore, it seemed interesting to combine both algorithms to observe if such a combination could improve on pure breadth- or depth-first searches. Thus, in addition to DFS and BFS, we also experimented with the two following variations of these search strategies devised for the sake of our experimentation.

- *Alternation of breadth- and depth-first search.* This search strategy is parametrized by two integers b and d. It starts breadth-first on the b first levels. Then for the states at level b the search switches to a DFS until the depth $b+d$ is reached. At that point, the algorithm mutates back to a BFS and so on. This search will be denoted by Alt(b, d) in the following.
- *Bounded-width breadth-first search.* This search strategy, denoted BBFS(w), proceeds as a BFS except that the queue at each level may not contain more than w states (the width of the search). Open states of previous levels are kept in a stack to be expanded later when all next levels have been processed.

Note that DFS and BFS are special instances of these search strategies since it holds that DFS $\equiv$ BBFS(1) $\equiv$ Alt(0, ∞) and BFS $\equiv$ BBFS(∞) $\equiv$ Alt(∞, 0).

A snapshot of the search trees of different state spaces induced by these different strategies can be seen in Fig. 6. With DFS (left), all states outside the stack are candidates for replacement in the cache. With BFS (second left), any ancestor in the search tree of an open state must remain in the cache while others may be replaced. Open states, with algorithm Alt(2, 2) (second right) are those still present in the stacks and queues used to perform "local" DFSs and BFSs. At last, the tree of BBFS(3) (right) is a BFS tree where each level can contain at most 3 states. Unlike BFS, some previous levels may contain open states as is the case here with the penultimate level.

All these algorithms are implemented using the generic template of Fig. 3 and parametrized by the type of the $\mathcal{O}$ data structure. BFS is implemented with a queue, DFS with a stack, BBFS(w) with a stack of arrays of size w, and Alt(b, d) with a stack containing single states for DFS levels and queues for BFS levels.

Cache replacement strategies. We implemented various strategies from the literature. The garbage collector can select states according to their in- and out-degree, their distance from the initial state (i.e., the depth at which the state has been generated), or in a purely random fashion. Stratified caching [11] has also been implemented. Due to a lack of space, we will not compare these strategies here. For DFS, the reader may consult the large body of work on that subject, e.g., [11,23]. With BFS, distance seems to be the criterion with most impact.

State space reduction. Sleep-set reduction has been shown in [13] to drastically reduce state revisits when using state caching. Rather than sleep-sets, we implemented the reduction of [4] which proposes a sleep-set like technique for both DFS and BFS that has two advantages over it: it does not require any memory overhead whereas the algorithm of [13] associates a set of transitions (the sleep set) with each closed and open set; and it is easier to implement.

We also implemented and experimented with the single-successor state chain reduction of [3] which is compatible with our algorithm as explained in Sect. 4.1. This reduction will be denoted by CR in the following.

Table 1 summarizes the different parameters and instances we experimented with. Unlike the reduction of [4] which was always turned on, the reduction of [3] was a parameter of each run. A run ended in one of three situations:

success. The search could finish within allocated resources.
out of memory. The cache was two small to contain the TD-tree.
out of time. The algorithm visited more states than the specified threshold.

Experimental Results

Experimental data is reported in Table 2. Due to space constraints, the table only contains data for 25 selected instances although the average on all instances experimented with is reported on the last line. Under each instance name, we give its number of states |S| and its average degree d as the ratio of transitions over states. All tests performed for each instance were divided into 8 groups according to the search algorithm they used (columns DFS, BFS, BBFS, and Alt) and according to whether or not they used the chain compression reduction (column CR). We then ordered, within each group, all successful runs first by ascending cache size (i.e., memory) and then by ascending number of state visits (i.e., time). Each cell of the table contains data for the best run according to that order: the number of stored states, i.e., the cache size, (column S) and visited states (column V) both expressed as a percentage of the state space. Additionally, for algorithms Alt and BBFS, columns (b, d) and w specify the parameters of the search that the best run used.

Table 1. Instances and parameters used during Experiment 1

Selected instances	135 instances with { 1,000, ..., 1,000,000 } states
Maximal state visits	$5 \cdot \lvert S \rvert$ (where $\lvert S \rvert$ is the state space size)
Cache size	{ 5, 10, 15, 20, ...} (as a % of the state space size) until a successful run could be found
Cache replacement strategy	60 caching strategies selected after experimentation with a small sample of 10 instances
Search strategy	DFS, BFS, BBFS(w) for $w \in \{4, 16, 256\}$, Alt(b, d) for $b, d \in \{1, 4, 8\}$
Reductions used	Reduction of [4] for all runs and CR for some runs

State caching apparently provides a better memory reduction when coupled with DFS than with BFS. The size of the TD-tree, with BFS, is lower bounded by the width of the state space, i.e., the size of the largest level, which can be high for some models. The DFS stack can also contain a large proportion of the state space but the reduction of [4] not only reduces interleavings but also the stack size, whereas it is not helpful in BFS.

We still found some models for which BFS outperformed DFS with respect to both time and memory. This is the case for instances `extinction.3`, `firewire_tree.4` and `leader_election.4`. We will see later why BFS is to be preferred for these models.

Some instances like `cambridge.5` have typical characteristics that make state caching inadequate: many cycles and a high degree. This inevitably leads to a time explosion with DFS even using partial order reduction. BFS seems to be more resilient with respect to these instances. We found a couple of similar instances during our experiments.

Although state caching is generally more memory efficient when coupled with DFS, BFS still provides a notable advantage: it is less subject to a time explosion. Even in cases where the cache size was close to its lower bound, i.e., the maximal size of the TD-tree, the time brutally increased in very few cases. With BFS, the distribution of run failures is the following: 98% are "out of memory", and 2% are "out of time". With DFS, these percentages become respectively 61% and 39%. Even in cases where BFS "timed out", increasing the maximal number of state visits from $5 \cdot |S|$ to $20 \cdot |S|$ could turn all these runs into successes. This is, from the user point of view, an appreciable property. With DFS, when the user selects a small cache size, and the search takes a long time, he/she can not know if it is due to a high rate of state revisits or if it is because the state space is very large and state caching is efficient. This situation never occurred with BFS.

In general, we found out that BFS is far less sensitive to the caching strategy than DFS. For a specific cache size, it was not unusual, with DFS, that only one or two replacement strategies could make the run successful. Whereas, with BFS, once a successful run could be found with some strategy, it usually meant that many other runs using different strategies (and with the same cache size) could also terminate successfully. On an average made on all models we calculated

Table 2. Summary of data for Experiment 1

Model	CR	DFS		BFS		BBFS			Alt		
		S	V	S	V	S	V	w	S	V	(b,d)
at.2	no	35	228	40	130	30	369	4	30	219	(8,4)
|S|=49,443 d=2.9	yes	30	428	40	130	30	373	4	30	222	(8,4)
bakery.4	no	20	271	25	216	25	173	4	20	185	(8,4)
|S|=157,003 d=2.6	yes	20	271	25	149	25	168	4	20	185	(8,4)
bopdp.2	no	15	215	30	149	15	246	4	15	213	(1,8)
|S|=25,685 d=2.8	yes	10	437	25	162	10	398	4	10	406	(1,8)
brp.3	no	5	235	15	112	5	163	256	5	160	(8,8)
|S|=996,627 d=2.0	yes	5	152	10	116	5	168	256	5	153	(8,8)
brp2.5	no	5	141	30	112	5	130	4	5	135	(8,1)
|S|=298,111 d=1.4	yes	5	140	20	103	5	131	4	5	137	(8,1)
cambridge.5	no	45	285	35	121	45	203	4	45	232	(8,4)
|S|=698,912 d=4.5	yes	45	287	35	120	45	200	16	45	233	(8,8)
collision.3	no	10	484	30	119	10	487	16	10	239	(8,1)
|S|=434,530 d=2.3	yes	10	338	25	169	10	412	16	10	286	(8,1)
extinction.3	no	10	185	10	100	10	186	4	10	176	(4,4)
|S|=751,930 d=3.5	yes	10	184	10	100	10	187	4	10	176	(4,4)
firewire_link.7	no	5	327	25	101	5	278	256	5	214	(8,1)
|S|=399,598 d=2.7	yes	5	321	20	101	5	348	256	5	230	(8,1)
firewire_tree.4	no	10	337	10	100	15	190	4	10	313	(4,4)
|S|=169,992 d=3.7	yes	10	345	10	100	15	191	4	10	311	(4,4)
gear.2	no	15	109	10	100	10	100	256	10	102	(4,4)
|S|=16,689 d=1.3	yes	15	106	5	102	5	101	256	10	101	(4,4)
iprotocol.2	no	5	359	20	132	5	250	4	5	296	(8,1)
|S|=29,994 d=3.3	yes	5	364	20	132	5	245	16	5	294	(1,1)
lamport_nonatomic.3	no	45	398	50	120	45	257	4	45	237	(8,8)
|S|=36,983 d=3.3	yes	45	366	50	119	45	260	4	45	232	(8,1)
leader_election.4	no	15	450	10	100	15	456	16	15	273	(4,1)
|S|=746,240 d=5.0	yes	15	316	10	100	15	453	16	15	275	(4,1)
lifts.6	no	5	123	15	123	5	125	4	5	124	(1,1)
|S|=333,649 d=2.1	yes	5	124	15	112	5	132	4	5	124	(1,1)
lup.2	no	30	478	30	142	40	369	4	15	429	(8,8)
|S|=495,720 d=1.8	yes	30	294	30	142	35	324	4	15	428	(8,8)
needham.3	no	5	412	30	100	5	409	256	5	435	(1,1)
|S|=206,925 d=2.7	yes	5	415	30	100	5	417	256	5	435	(1,1)
peterson.3	no	25	345	35	142	25	374	4	25	329	(1,8)
|S|=170,156 d=3.1	yes	25	331	35	136	25	356	4	25	320	(8,8)
pgm_protocol.7	no	10	152	10	106	5	360	16	5	493	(8,1)
|S|=322,585 d=2.5	yes	10	152	5	112	5	392	4	10	145	(4,1)
plc.2	no	5	100	30	100	10	101	4	5	100	(1,8)
|S|=130,777 d=1.6	yes	5	100	10	100	5	113	4	5	101	(8,8)
production_cell.4	no	10	176	10	100	10	162	4	10	157	(8,1)
|S|=340,685 d=2.8	yes	10	175	10	100	10	162	4	10	158	(8,1)
rether.3	no	30	118	40	104	35	132	256	25	113	(8,1)
|S|=305,334 d=1.0	yes	25	152	15	111	15	117	256	15	128	(8,1)
synapse.6	no	5	148	30	111	5	133	16	5	129	(8,8)
|S|=625,175 d=1.9	yes	5	118	25	296	5	136	16	5	129	(8,8)
telephony.3	no	30	394	50	124	25	482	256	25	368	(8,1)
|S|=765,379 d=4.1	yes	25	491	50	123	25	470	16	25	388	(8,1)
train-gate.5	no	10	114	20	100	10	110	4	10	102	(4,1)
|S|=803,458 d=2.1	yes	10	114	20	100	10	105	256	10	102	(4,1)
Average on	no	18.5	259	30.1	131	19.4	236		16.4	239	
135 models	yes	17.7	251	26.3	143	17.4	241		15.5	249	

that, with DFS and for the smallest cache size for which at least a run turned out to be successful, only 25% of all runs were successful. With BFS, this same percentage goes up to 66%.

These observations are in line with a remark made in [21], p. 226: "*Compared to BFSWS* [BFS With Snapshots], *the success of DFS setups differs a lot from one case to another.*" One of our conclusions is indeed that BFS has the advantage of exhibiting more predictable performance.

The effect of reduction CR is more evident in the case of BFS. The cache size could be further reduced by an average of 4–5% for a marginal cost in time, whereas with DFS the reduction achieved is negligible. In some instances BFS could, with the help of this reduction, significantly outperform DFS with respect to memory consumption. This is for instance the case for `rether.3` which has a majority of single-successor states.

Lastly, we notice that Alt and BBFS sometimes cumulate the advantages of both BFS (w.r.t. time) and DFS (w.r.t. memory) and perform better than these, e.g., `at.2`, `bakery.4`, `firewire_link.7` and `lup.2`. Search Alt also seems to be more successful than BBFS. It could on average reduce the cache size from 17 to 15% of the state space, when compared to DFS.

Influence of the State Space Structure in BFS. We previously noticed that the width of the graph is a lower bound of the `TD`-tree in BFS. More generally, there is a clear link between the shape of the BFS level graph and the memory reduction in BFS. Figure 7 depicts this graph for several instances that are of particular interest to illustrate our purpose. For each BFS level, the value plotted specifies the number of states (as a percentage of the full state space) belonging to a specific level. For instances `telephony.3` and `synapse.6`, a large proportion of states is gathered on a few neighbor levels. The algorithm will thus have to store most states of these levels and it is not surprising to observe in Table 2 that state caching is not efficient in these cases. Instances `pgm_protocol.7` and `gear.2` have the opposite characteristic: the distribution of states upon BFS levels is rather homogeneous and there is no sequence of neighbor levels containing many states. This explains the good memory reduction observed with BFS on these examples.

With DFS, the time increase is closely related to the average degree of the state space. This factor has a lesser impact with BFS: the proportion of backward transitions[1] plays a more important role. Indeed, the search order of BFS implies the destination state of a forward transition to necessarily be in the open set. Hence, only backward transitions may be followed by state revisits. Instances `extinction.3` and `firewire_tree.4` have rather high (3–5) degrees but few or no backward transitions, which led to very few state revisits with BFS; whereas using DFS we often experienced a time explosion with these instances. The fact that state spaces of real-world problems often have few backward transitions [25] may explain the small state revisit factors usually observed with BFS.

[1] (s, s') is a backward transition if the BFS levels d and d' of s and s' are such that $d \geq d'$. The length of (s, s') is the difference $d - d'$.

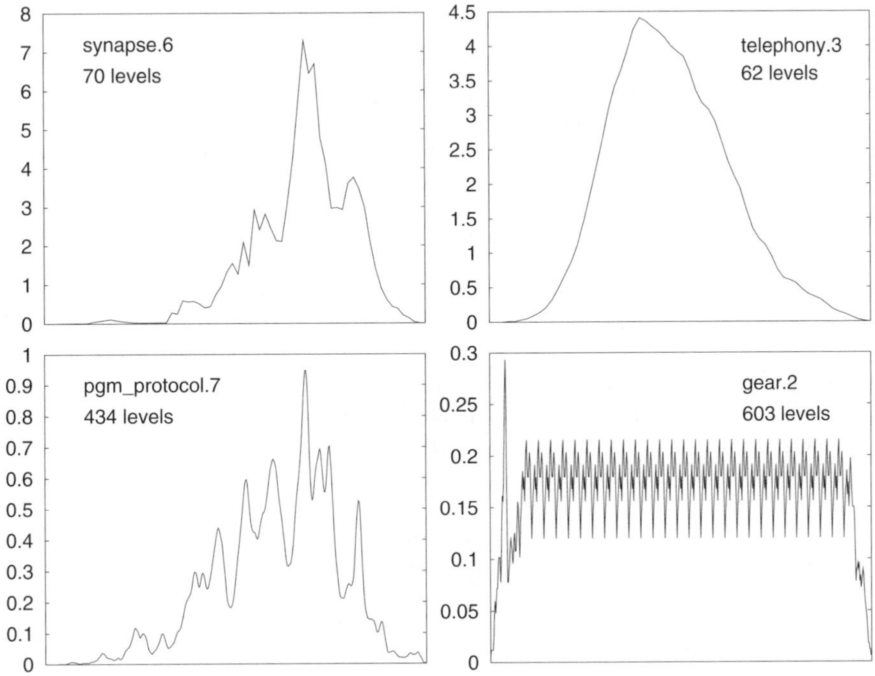

Fig. 7. BFS level graph of some instances

5.2 Experiment 2: State Caching with the Sweep-Line Method

In a second experiment we studied how our state caching algorithm combines in practice with the sweep-line method, as described in Section 4.4. We analyzed the same instances used in the first experiment. We automatically derived from their full state spaces several progress measures identified by a level ranging from 0 to 5. The higher the level, the more precise the progress mapping and the more aggressive the reduction. Our progress measures are abstractions in that they project states to some components of the underlying system. At level 0, the progress mapping is guaranteed to not generate any regress transition since we only consider components having a monotonic progression, e.g., an increasing sequence number; and as the level progresses, the mapping is refined by including in it more and more components in order to multiply the different progress values possible and increase the potential of the reduction (while also introducing more regress transitions). Progress values are then fixed-size vectors of (selected) components that can be compared via a lexical ordering. Each level corresponds to an estimation of the upper bound of the proportion of regress transitions: level 0 → no regress transition, level 1 → at most 1% of regress transitions, level 2 → 2%, level 3 → 5%, level 4 → 10% and level 5 →20%.

Table 3 summarizes the data collected during this experiment for some selected instances and progress measures. For each instance (column Model) and progress measure (of which the level appears in column PM) we performed a first

Table 3. Summary of data for Experiment 2

Model	|S|	PM	SL				SL + SC	
			S	V	P	L	S	V
bopdp.2	25,685	3	52.4	231	0.5	51.9	20.4	498
		4	26.8	242	0.8	26.0	14.9	480
		5	13.7	259	1.9	8.3	12.7	482
brp.3	996,627	2	13.3	145	0.1	8.3	4.9	203
		3	10.6	126	0.5	2.9	9.7	154
		4	10.0	122	2.4	0.3	9.9	120
		5	8.1	124	3.8	0.1	8.2	119
collision.3	434,530	4	24.1	100	0.0	24.1	13.5	482
		5	21.1	232	9.0	12.2	16.0	337
iprotocol.1	6,814	5	50.4	100	0.0	47.3	21.0	416
lifts.4	112,792	5	33.3	100	0.0	33.3	8.5	489
needham.3	206,925	5	20.9	100	0.0	0.1	21.0	101
pgm_protocol.3	195,015	3	2.4	144	1.1	0.0	2.1	129
		4	3.2	110	3.1	0.0	3.1	110
		5	9.0	110	8.9	0.0	9.0	108
plc.2	130,777	3	1.8	100	0.0	1.7	0.6	102
		4	1.2	105	1.2	0.0	1.3	105
		5	1.2	105	1.2	0.0	1.3	105
production_cell.4	340,685	4	27.7	100	0.0	22.7	14.1	485
		5	11.1	100	2.0	6.9	5.5	438
rether.3	305,334	4	25.3	161	3.9	21.8	5.0	200
		5	6.3	152	6.0	0.6	6.1	144
synapse.6	625,175	3	26.6	100	0.0	26.6	7.4	477
		4	27.4	316	2.7	16.4	17.2	477
		5	18.1	150	10.8	2.9	17.4	136

run with the sweep-line algorithm of [20] (column SL) and then several runs with the same algorithm extended with our state caching reduction (column SL + SC) using different cache sizes. We used a variation of the stratified caching strategy [11] that revealed to be the most efficient one during the first experiment. As in the first experiment we only kept, for algorithm SL + SC, the "best" run, that is, the one that used the smallest amount of memory with a state visit factor less than 5. For these two runs columns S and V provide the number of stored and visited states. Additionally, for algorithm SL the table gives in column P the number of persistent states at the end of the search ; and in column L the size of the largest class of states sharing the same progress value and present in memory at the same time (before being garbage collected). All these values are expressed as a percentage of the state space size given in column |S|. The data of the run that provided the best memory reduction for a model has been highlighted using a gray background.

To have a better understanding of these results it seems necessary to briefly recall the principle of algorithm SL. At each step the algorithm explores a class of states sharing a common progress value ψ. All their successors are put in the priority queue implementing the open set, and once this expansion step is finished, i.e., no state with progress value ψ is in the queue, the algorithm deletes from memory all expanded states. It then reiterates this process with the next progress value found in the queue until it is empty. The size of the largest class of states with the same progress value given in column L is thus a lower bound on the memory consumption of the algorithm. By implementing state caching on top of this algorithm we can hope to reduce only the class of states the algorithm is currently working on. Indeed if we denote by ψ the progress value of this class then all the states with a progress value $\psi' < \psi$ have been garbage collected by the sweep-line reduction and states with a progress value $\psi' > \psi$ present in memory are necessarily in the open set and hence can not be removed from the cache. The potential of the state caching reduction is thus given by the ratio $\frac{\mathsf{L}}{\mathsf{S}}$ (in column SL). It is therefore not surprising that the gain of using state caching depends on the size L of this largest class. Instances `brp.3`, `plc.2` and `pgm_protocol.3` are the typical examples of models for which the sweep-line method is well suited: they have long state spaces with a clear progression which enables progress mappings to be defined that divide the state space into many small classes. Hence, the sweep-line method used solely can provide a very good reduction that can not be significantly enhanced by state caching.

Increasing the PM level has three noteworthy consequences. First, for most models, the peak number of states stored by SL decreases although this is not always the case: by refining the progress mapping we usually increase the proportion of regress transitions generating persistent states that will never be garbage collected. Instance `pgm_protocol.3` is a good illustration. Second, by multiplying progress values we naturally decrease the effect of state caching since, as we previously saw, state caching is helpful to reduce classes of states sharing the same progress value. We indeed observe that the values in column L decrease as we increase the PM level, with the consequence that numbers converge to the same values with both algorithms. A last observation is that, regarding the number of states stored, SL and SL + SC often follow opposite behaviors. For instances `brp.3`, `collision.3`, `plc.2`, `rether.3` and `synapse.6`, SL consumes less memory when we refine the progress measure whereas SL + SC needs a larger cache. More generally, we observed that the average ratio of the number of states stored by SL over the number of states stored by SL + SC is maximal at level 3 (2.93) and then decreases to 1.97 at level 5. This is an interesting property from a user perspective. This indeed means that he/she does not necessarily have to provide a very fine tuned progress mapping to the model checker. In many cases, a basic mapping that extracts some monotonic component(s) from the model will be sufficient: the state caching reduction will then fully complement the sweep-line reduction flaws and provide an even better reduction compared to a very precise progress mapping that will cancel the benefits of state caching.

6 Conclusion

In this paper we have proposed an extension of state caching to general state exploring algorithms. Termination is guaranteed by maintaining, as the search progresses, a tree rooted in the initial state that covers all open states. This ensures that any cycle will eventually reach a state of the tree. Closed states that have left the tree can therefore be deleted from memory without endangering the termination of the algorithm. Extensive experimentation with models from the BEEM database has revealed that state caching can reduce the memory requirements of a BFS by a factor of approximately 4. Although this is usually not as good as the reduction observed with DFS, BFS offers an advantage in that the reduction comes almost for free: the average increase in run-time that we observed with BFS was usually around 30–40%, and we observed very few cases of time explosion, whereas this is quite common with DFS even when using partial order reduction. Combining both search strategies can also bring advantages: in some cases, we found that state caching coupled with a combination of BFS and DFS could bring the same (or an even better) reduction as with DFS while limiting the run-time explosion that could occur with this one. Last but not least, our experiments revealed that our reduction can also enhance the sweep-line method as the algorithm it relies on is also an instance of the GSEA.

The algorithm we proposed is fully language-independent in that it only relies on a successor function to explore the state space. Nevertheless, it should be worth experimenting it with other formalisms than DVE and especially Colored Petri Nets (CPN) [19]. It is possible that the high level constructs provided by CPN to express the successor function may impact the structural characteristics of state spaces that, as previous works on state caching and our own experiments revealed, are tightly linked to the performance of state caching. Such an experimentation is therefore the next research direction we will focus on.

References

1. Bao, T., Jones, M.: Time-Efficient Model Checking with Magnetic Disk. In: Halbwachs, N., Zuck, L.D. (eds.) TACAS 2005. LNCS, vol. 3440, pp. 526–540. Springer, Heidelberg (2005)
2. Barnat, J., Brim, L., Černá, I., Moravec, P., Ročkai, P., Šimeček, P.: DiVinE – A Tool for Distributed Verification. In: Ball, T., Jones, R.B. (eds.) CAV 2006. LNCS, vol. 4144, pp. 278–281. Springer, Heidelberg (2006)
3. Behrmann, G., Larsen, K.G., Pelánek, R.: To Store or Not to Store. In: Hunt Jr., W.A., Somenzi, F. (eds.) CAV 2003. LNCS, vol. 2725, pp. 433–445. Springer, Heidelberg (2003)
4. Bošnački, D., Elkind, E., Genest, B., Peled, D.: On Commutativity Based Edge Lean Search. In: Arge, L., Cachin, C., Jurdziński, T., Tarlecki, A. (eds.) ICALP 2007. LNCS, vol. 4596, pp. 158–170. Springer, Heidelberg (2007)
5. Bošnački, D., Leue, S., Lafuente, A.L.: Partial-Order Reduction for General State Exploring Algorithms. In: Valmari, A. (ed.) SPIN 2006. LNCS, vol. 3925, pp. 271–287. Springer, Heidelberg (2006)
6. Christensen, S., Kristensen, L.M., Mailund, T.: A Sweep-Line Method for State Space Exploration. In: Margaria, T., Yi, W. (eds.) TACAS 2001. LNCS, vol. 2031, pp. 450–464. Springer, Heidelberg (2001)
7. DVE Language, `http://divine.fi.muni.cz/page.php?page=language`

8. Edelkamp, S., Leue, S., Lluch-Lafuente, A.: Directed Explicit-State Model Checking in the Validation of Communication Protocols. STTT 5, 247–267 (2004)
9. Evangelista, S., Kristensen, L.M.: Search-Order Independent State Caching. Technical report (2009), http://daimi.au.dk/~evangeli/doc/caching.pdf
10. Evangelista, S., Pradat-Peyre, J.-F.: Memory Efficient State Space Storage in Explicit Software Model Checking. In: Godefroid, P. (ed.) SPIN 2005. LNCS, vol. 3639, pp. 43–57. Springer, Heidelberg (2005)
11. Geldenhuys, J.: State Caching Reconsidered. In: Graf, S., Mounier, L. (eds.) SPIN 2004. LNCS, vol. 2989, pp. 23–38. Springer, Heidelberg (2004)
12. Godefroid, P.: Partial-Order Methods for the Verification of Concurrent Systems. LNCS, vol. 1032. Springer, Heidelberg (1996)
13. Godefroid, P., Holzmann, G.J., Pirottin, D.: State-Space Caching Revisited. In: Probst, D.K., von Bochmann, G. (eds.) CAV 1992. LNCS, vol. 663, pp. 178–191. Springer, Heidelberg (1993)
14. Holzmann, G.J.: Tracing Protocols. AT&T Technical J. 64(10), 2413–2434 (1985)
15. Holzmann, G.J.: Automated Protocol Validation in Argos: Assertion Proving and Scatter Searching. IEEE Trans. Software Eng. 13(6), 683–696 (1987)
16. Holzmann, G.J.: State Compression in Spin: Recursive Indexing and Compression Training Runs. In: SPIN 1997 (1997)
17. Jard, C., Jéron, T.: On-Line Model Checking for Finite Linear Temporal Logic Specifications. In: Sifakis, J. (ed.) CAV 1989. LNCS, vol. 407, pp. 189–196. Springer, Heidelberg (1990)
18. Jard, C., Jéron, T.: Bounded-memory Algorithms for Verification On-the-fly. In: Larsen, K.G., Skou, A. (eds.) CAV 1991. LNCS, vol. 575, pp. 192–202. Springer, Heidelberg (1992)
19. Jensen, K., Kristensen, L.M.: Coloured Petri Nets — Modeling and Validation of Concurrent Systems. Springer, Heidelberg (2009)
20. Kristensen, L.M., Mailund, T.: A Generalised Sweep-Line Method for Safety Properties. In: Eriksson, L.-H., Lindsay, P.A. (eds.) FME 2002. LNCS, vol. 2391, pp. 549–567. Springer, Heidelberg (2002)
21. Mateescu, R., Wijs, A.: Hierarchical Adaptive State Space Caching Based on Level Sampling. In: Kowalewski, S., Philippou, A. (eds.) TACAS 2009. LNCS, vol. 5505, pp. 215–229. Springer, Heidelberg (2009)
22. Pelánek, R.: BEEM: Benchmarks for Explicit Model Checkers. In: Bošnački, D., Edelkamp, S. (eds.) SPIN 2007. LNCS, vol. 4595, pp. 263–267. Springer, Heidelberg (2007)
23. Pelánek, R., Rosecký, V., Sedenka, J.: Evaluation of State Caching and State Compression Techniques. Technical report, Masaryk University, Brno (2008)
24. Stern, U., Dill, D.L.: Parallelizing the Murphi Verifier. In: Grumberg, O. (ed.) CAV 1997. LNCS, vol. 1254, pp. 256–278. Springer, Heidelberg (1997)
25. Tronci, E., Della Penna, G., Intrigila, B., Venturini Zilli, M.: Exploiting Transition Locality in Automatic Verification. In: Margaria, T., Melham, T.F. (eds.) CHARME 2001. LNCS, vol. 2144, pp. 259–274. Springer, Heidelberg (2001)
26. Westergaard, M., Evangelista, S., Kristensen, L.M.: ASAP: An Extensible Platform for State Space Analysis. In: Franceschinis, G., Wolf, K. (eds.) PETRI NETS 2009. LNCS, vol. 5606, pp. 303–312. Springer, Heidelberg (2009)
27. Westergaard, M., Kristensen, L.M., Brodal, G.S., Arge, L.: The ComBack Method – Extending Hash Compaction with Backtracking. In: Kleijn, J., Yakovlev, A. (eds.) ICATPN 2007. LNCS, vol. 4546, pp. 445–464. Springer, Heidelberg (2007)

Bounded Parametric Model Checking for Elementary Net Systems*

Michał Knapik[1], Maciej Szreter[1], and Wojciech Penczek[1,2]

[1] Institute of Computer Science, PAS, J.K. Ordona 21, 01-237 Warszawa, Poland
{Michal.Knapik,mszreter}@ipipan.waw.pl
[2] Institute of Informatics, Podlasie Academy, Sienkiewicza 51, 08-110 Siedlce, Poland
penczek@ipipan.waw.pl

Abstract. Bounded Model Checking (BMC) is an efficient verification method for reactive systems. BMC has been applied so far to verification of properties expressed in (timed) modal logics, but never to their parametric extensions. In this paper we show, for the first time that BMC can be extended to PRTECTL – a parametric extension of the existential version of CTL. To this aim we define a bounded semantics and a translation from PRTECTL to SAT. The implementation of the algorithm for Elementary Net Systems is presented, together with some experimental results.

1 Introduction

Bounded Model Checking (BMC) [4] is a method of performing verification by stepwise unwinding a verified model and translating the resulting fragment, as well as the property in question, to a propositional formula. The resulting formula is then checked by means of efficient external tools, i.e., SAT-solvers. This method is usually incomplete from the practical point of view, but can find counterexamples in systems that appear too large for other approaches.

BMC was invented in late 1990s, and since then has become an established method among verification approaches. BMC is applied to verification of properties specified in temporal, dynamic, epistemic, and timed logics [3], [2], [7], [11], [13]. In fact, for many system specifications and property languages devised for explicit-state model checking, the BMC counterparts have been developed. In this paper we show how parametric model checking can be performed by means of BMC.

The rest of the paper is organized as follows. In Section 2 we shortly explore the motivations for the choice of the parameterized temporal logics vRTCTL and PRTCTL to which the BMC method is applied. Referenced and cited works are mentioned along with an outline of the contents. Section 3 recalls from [6] the syntax and semantics of the logics used in this work. In Section 3 we define existential fragments of the considered logics – vRTECTL and PRTECTL,

* Partly supported by the Polish Ministry of Science and Higher Education under the grant No. N N206 258035.

K. Jensen, S. Donatelli, and M. Koutny (Eds.): ToPNoC IV, LNCS 6550, pp. 42–71, 2010.

respectively. Section 4 introduces k-models together with bounded semantics for vRTECTL and PRTECTL. In Section 5 a translation of a model and a property under investigation is presented together with an algorithm for BMC. Section 6 contains an application of the above method to Elementary Net Systems. We choose three standard problems: the Mutual Exclusion, the Dining Philosophers, and the Generic Pipelining Paradigm. Some associated parameterized properties are verified in Section 7. The concluding remarks and an outline of some future work are in Section 8.

2 Related Work

The work presented in this paper falls into a broad area of Parametric Model Checking – an ambiguous term which may mean that we deal with the parameters in models (as in [1] and [8]), in logics (as in [6] and [5]) or in both (as in [12]). There are two reasons limiting the practical applications of Parametric Model Checking. The first – computational complexity of the problem – is the result of the presence of satisfiability in the Presburger Arithmetic (PA) as a subproblem. In case of the translation of the existential fragment of TCTL to PA formulae proposed in [5], the joint complexity of the solution is 3EXPTIME. The second – undecidability of the problem for Parametric Timed Automata in general [1] – results in a fact that some of the proposed algorithms do not need to stop [8].

In this paper we consider the parametric extension of Computation Tree Logic (CTL), introduced in [6] – namely PRTCTL (Parametric CTL). The logic is interpreted in Kripke structures, and we assume that traversing a transition takes one unit of time. As motivated in [6], such models, while less sophisticated than many other approaches, are often sufficient in systems modelling and analysis. The PRTCTL model checking problem is decidable, and does not contain PA-satisfiability as a subproblem. The Kripke models (marking graphs) induced by elementary Petri nets tend to be very large, which motivates our decision to apply bounded model checking ([4]) methods to the problem. The application of BMC to the existential fragment of the CTL originates from [11] with a further optimization in [14].

To the best knowledge of the authors, this paper presents the first extension of BMC to parameterized temporal logics.

3 Parameterized Temporal Logics

In this section we recall the temporal logics vRTCTL and PRTCTL, first defined in [6], both being extensions of CTL. The logic vRTCTL allows superscripts of form $^{\leq\eta}$, where η is a linear expression over path quantifiers of CTL. An example of a formula of this logic is $EF^{\leq\Theta_1+\Theta_2}(w_1 \wedge EG\neg c_1)$. The formulae of PRTCTL are built from formulae of vRTCTL by adding additional existential or universal quantifiers which may be restricted or unrestricted. As an example of a PRTCTL formula consider $\exists_{\Theta_1\leq 1}\forall_{\Theta_2\leq 2}EF^{\leq\Theta_1+\Theta_2}(w_1 \wedge EG\neg c_1)$. Following

E. A. Emerson's approach [6], the formulae are interpreted in standard Kripke structures, which seem to be appropriate for application in many computer science fields. The logics mentioned above essentially extend CTL, as they allow to formulate properties involving lengths of paths in a model. We interpret superscripts as time bounds, assuming that a transition in a model takes one unit of time. Throughout this paper by $\mathbb{N}$ we denote the set of all natural numbers (including 0). By a *sentence* of a logic we mean a formula without free variables, and by $\alpha(\Theta_1, \ldots, \Theta_n)$ we point out that the formula α contains free parameters $\Theta_1, \ldots, \Theta_n$.

3.1 Syntax

Let $\Theta_1, \ldots, \Theta_n$ be natural variables, called here *parameters*. An expression of the form $\eta = \sum_{i=1}^{n} c_i \cdot \Theta_i + c_0$, where $c_0, \ldots, c_n \in \mathbb{N}$, is called a *linear expression*. A function $\upsilon : \{\Theta_1, \Theta_2, \ldots, \Theta_n\} \longrightarrow \mathbb{N}$ is called a *parameter valuation*. Let Υ be the set of all the parameter valuations.

Definition 1. *Let $\mathcal{PV}$ be a set of propositional variables (propositions). Define inductively the formulae of* vRTCTL :

1. *every member of $\mathcal{PV}$ is a formula,*
2. *if α and β are formulae, then so are $\neg\alpha$, $\alpha \wedge \beta$ and $\alpha \vee \beta$,*
3. *if α and β are formulae, then so are $EX\alpha$, $EG\alpha$, and $E\alpha U\beta$,*
4. *if η is a linear expression, α and β, then so are $EG^{\leq\eta}\alpha$, $E\alpha U^{\leq\eta}\beta$.*

The conditions 1, 2, and 3 alone define CTL. Notice that η is allowed to be a constant. The logic defined by a modification of the above definition, where $\eta = a$ for $a \in \mathbb{N}$, is called RTCTL in [6]. For example $EF^{\leq 3}(w_1 \wedge EG\neg c_1)$ is an RTCTL formula.

Next, we extend vRTCTL with quantifiers.

Definition 2. *The formulae of* PRTCTL *are defined as follows:*

1. *if $\alpha \in$ vRTCTL, then $\alpha \in$ PRTCTL,*
2. *if $\alpha(\Theta) \in$ PRTCTL, where Θ is a free parameter,*
   then $\forall_\Theta \alpha(\Theta), \exists_\Theta \alpha(\Theta), \forall_{\Theta \leq a} \alpha(\Theta), \exists_{\Theta \leq a} \alpha(\Theta) \in$ PRTCTL for $a \in \mathbb{N}$.

Notice that the following inclusions hold: CTL $\subseteq$ RTCTL $\subseteq$ vRTCTL $\subseteq$ PRTCTL. In this paper we consider only sentences of PRTCTL.

By *true* we mean the formula $p \vee \neg p$, for some proposition p. Additionally we use the derived modalities: $EF\alpha \stackrel{def}{=} E(trueU\alpha)$, $AF\alpha \stackrel{def}{=} \neg EG\neg\alpha$, $AX\alpha \stackrel{def}{=} \neg EX\neg\alpha$, $AG\alpha \stackrel{def}{=} \neg EF\neg\alpha$ (CTL modalities) and $EF^{\leq\eta}\alpha \stackrel{def}{=} E(trueU^{\leq\eta}\alpha)$, $AF^{\leq\eta}\alpha \stackrel{def}{=} \neg EG^{\leq\eta}\neg\alpha$, $AG^{\leq\eta}\alpha \stackrel{def}{=} \neg EF^{\leq\eta}\neg\alpha$. Each modality of CTL has an intuitive meaning. The path quantifier A stands for "on every path" and E means "there exists a path". The modality X means "in the next state", G stands for "in the all states", F means "in some state", and U has a meaning of "until".

The introduced superscripts will become clear when the semantics of vRTCTL is presented. As to give an example of the intuitive meaning of an RTCTL formula, $EG^{\leq 3}p$ may be perceived as the statement "there exists a path such that in the first four states of this path p holds". The logic vRTCTL adds a possibility of expressing similar properties under parameter valuations, while PRTCTL allows for stating that some property holds in a model under some class of parameter valuations.

Definition 3. *The logics* vRTECTL, RTECTL, *and* PRTECTL *are defined as the restrictions of, respectively,* vRTCTL, RTCTL, *and the set of sentences of* PRTCTL *such that the negation can be applied to the propositions only.*

The main idea of bounded model checking is to unwind the computation tree of a model up to some finite depth, therefore in general with this approach it is not possible to verify the properties which deal with all the possible paths. This motivates our choice of the logics in Definition 3 (see [11]) – the formulae of the above restrictions contain the non-negated existential path quantifiers only.

3.2 Semantics

We evaluate the truth of the sentences and the formulae accompanied with parameter valuations in Kripke structures.

Definition 4. *Let $\mathcal{PV}$ be a set of propositional variables. A Kripke structure (a* model*) is defined as a tuple $M = (S, \rightarrow, \mathcal{L})$, where:*

1. *S is a finite set of* states*,*
2. *$\rightarrow \subseteq S \times S$ is a transition relation such that for every $s \in S$ there exists $s' \in S$ with $s \rightarrow s'$ (i.e., the relation is total),*
3. *$\mathcal{L} : S \longrightarrow 2^{\mathcal{PV} \cup \{true\}}$ is a labelling function satisfying $true \in \mathcal{L}(s)$ for $s \in S$.*

Notice that totality of the transition relation guarantees that there are no deadlocks (we need this assumption as the considered logics are interpreted over infinite runs). The labelling function assigns to an each state s a set of propositions which are assumed to be true at s. An infinite sequence $\pi = (s_0, s_1, \ldots)$ of states of a model such that $s_i \rightarrow s_{i+1}$ for $i \in \mathbb{N}$ is called a *path.* By $\pi(i)$ we denote the i–th position on a path π. The number of the states of model M is called the size of M and denoted by $|M|$. For a parameter valuation υ and a linear expression η, by $\upsilon(\eta)$ we mean the evaluation of η under υ.

Definition 5 (Semantics of vRTCTL**).** *Let* M *be a model, s – a state, α, β – formulae of* vRTCTL. *$M, s \models_\upsilon \alpha$ denotes that α is true at the state s in the model M under the parameter valuation υ. We omit M where it is implicitly understood. The relation $\models_\upsilon$ is defined inductively as follows:*

1. $s \models_\upsilon p \iff p \in \mathcal{L}(s)$
2. $s \models_\upsilon \neg p \iff p \notin \mathcal{L}(s)$,
3. $s \models_\upsilon \alpha \wedge \beta \iff s \models_\upsilon \alpha$ *and* $s \models_\upsilon \beta$,
4. $s \models_\upsilon \alpha \vee \beta \iff s \models_\upsilon \alpha$ *or* $s \models_\upsilon \beta$,
5. $s \models_\upsilon EX\alpha \iff \exists_\pi \big(\pi(0) = s \wedge \pi(1) \models_\upsilon \alpha\big)$,

6. $s \models_\upsilon EG\alpha \iff \exists_\pi\big(\pi(0) = s \wedge \forall_{i\geq 0}\pi(i) \models_\upsilon \alpha\big)$,
7. $s \models_\upsilon E\alpha U\beta \iff \exists_\pi\big(\pi(0) = s \wedge \exists_{i\geq 0}\big[\pi(i) \models_\upsilon \beta \wedge \forall_{j<i}\pi(j) \models_\upsilon \alpha\big]\big)$,
8. $s \models_\upsilon EG^{\leq\eta}\alpha \iff \exists_\pi\big(\pi(0) = s \wedge \forall_{0\leq i\leq\upsilon(\eta)}\pi(i) \models_\upsilon \alpha\big)$,
9. $s \models_\upsilon E\alpha U^{\leq\eta}\beta \iff \exists_\pi\big(\pi(0) = s \wedge \exists_{0\leq i\leq\upsilon(\eta)}\big[\pi(i) \models_\upsilon \beta \wedge \forall_{j<i}\pi(j) \models_\upsilon \alpha\big]\big)$.

If α is a formula of RTCTL, then the validity of $s \models_\upsilon \alpha$ does not depend on the parameter valuation υ, as there are no parameters in the formula. In this case we write $M, s \models \alpha$ omitting the parameter valuation subscript.

Observe that for every formula α of RTCTL there exists a formula β of vRTCTL and a parameter valuation υ such that $\alpha = \upsilon(\beta)$, where $\upsilon(\beta)$ denotes the formula obtained by substituting all the linear expressions with their evaluations under υ. For example the formula $EF^{\leq 5}(w_1 \wedge EG\neg c_1)$ can be obtained from $EF^{\leq\Theta_1}(w_1 \wedge EG\neg c_1)$ by a valuation υ such that $\upsilon(\Theta_1) = 5$ or from $EF^{\leq\Theta_1+\Theta_2}(w_1 \wedge EG\neg c_1)$ by a valuation υ' such that $\upsilon'(\Theta_1) = 3$ and $\upsilon'(\Theta_2) = 2$.

The semantics of PRTCTL is defined in such a way that by eliminating the quantifiers we eventually arrive at a sequence of conjunctions and/or disjunctions of RTCTL formulae. By a *fresh (integer) variable* we mean a new variable which is not a parameter and is not present in the considered formula.

Definition 6 (Semantics of PRTCTL**).** *Let* M *be a model, s – a state, and α – a formula of* PRTCTL. *$M, s \models \alpha$ denotes that α holds at the state s in the model M. The relation $\models$ is defined inductively as follows:*

1. $s \models \forall_\Theta\alpha(\Theta)$ *iff* $\bigwedge_{i_\Theta\geq 0} s \models \alpha(i_\Theta)$,
2. $s \models \forall_{\Theta\leq a}\alpha(\Theta)$ *iff* $\bigwedge_{0\leq i_\Theta\leq a} s \models \alpha(i_\Theta)$,
3. $s \models \exists_\Theta\alpha(\Theta)$ *iff* $\bigvee_{i_\Theta\geq 0} s \models \alpha(i_\Theta)$,
4. $s \models \exists_{\Theta\leq a}\alpha(\Theta)$ *iff* $\bigvee_{0\leq i_\Theta\leq a} s \models \alpha(i_\Theta)$,

where i_Θ is a fresh integer variable.

For example:

$$M, s \models \forall_{\Theta_1\leq 1}\exists_{\Theta_2\leq 2} EF^{\leq\Theta_1+\Theta_2}(w_1 \wedge EG\neg c_1)$$

$$\iff \bigwedge_{0\leq i_{\Theta_1}\leq 1}\ \bigvee_{0\leq i_{\Theta_2}\leq 2} M, s \models EF^{\leq i_{\Theta_1}+i_{\Theta_2}}(w_1 \wedge EG\neg c_1).$$

It is straightforward to check that for a model M and a state s, $M, s \models_\upsilon EG\alpha$ iff $M, s \models_\upsilon EG^{\leq|M|}\alpha$ and $M, s \models_\upsilon E\alpha U\beta$ iff $M, s \models_\upsilon E\alpha U^{\leq|M|}\beta$. The proof of this fact is based on the observation that in every path prefix of length greater or equal than $|M|$ there is a state that occurs (at least) two times, i.e., the path contains a loop.

Let's recall Theorem 1 from [6]:

Theorem 1. *Let M be a model and $Q_{1\Theta_1} \ldots Q_{n\Theta_n}\alpha(\Theta_1, \ldots, \Theta_n)$, where $Q_i \in \{\forall, \exists\}$ and $\alpha(\Theta_1, \ldots, \Theta_n) \in$ vRTCTL, be a* PRTCTL *sentence. Then, $M, s \models Q_{1\Theta_1} \ldots Q_{n\Theta_n}\alpha(\Theta_1, \ldots, \Theta_n)$ iff $M, s \models Q_{1\Theta_1\leq|M|} \ldots Q_{n\Theta_n\leq|M|}\alpha(\Theta_1, \ldots, \Theta_n)$.*

Next, we enhance the above theorem by the following lemma.

Lemma 1. *Let M be a model and $Q_{1\Theta_1 \leq c_1} \cdots Q_{n\Theta_n \leq c_n}\alpha(\Theta_1, \ldots, \Theta_n)$ where $Q_i \in \{\forall, \exists\}$, $c_i \in \mathbb{N}$, and $\alpha(\Theta_1, \ldots, \Theta_n) \in$ vRTCTL be a sentence of* PRTCTL. *Then $M, s \models Q_{1\Theta_1 \leq c_1} \cdots Q_{n\Theta_n \leq c_n}\alpha(\Theta_1, \ldots, \Theta_n)$ iff*
$M, s \models Q_{1\Theta_1 \leq min(c_1, |M|)} \cdots Q_{n\Theta_n \leq min(c_n, |M|)}\alpha(\Theta_1, \ldots, \Theta_n)$.

Proof. See the Appendix 1.

Basically, Theorem 1 allows for replacing the unrestricted quantifiers with their versions bounded with the size of the model, and Lemma 1 states that it suffices to consider the bounds not greater that $|M|$. Therefore, in the rest of this paper we restrict our research to the vRTCTL and PRTCTL formulae with superscripted modalities and restricted quantifiers. Such an approach is typical for model checking, which aims at verifying a given property in a fixed model. Notice, however, that PRTCTL allows for unbounded quantifiers – hence it is possible to express general quantitative properties abstracting from the underlying system. Let us recall an exemplary formula from [6]:

$$\forall_\Theta\big(AG(request \Rightarrow AF^{\leq \Theta} receive) \Rightarrow AG(request \Rightarrow AF^{\leq 2\cdot\Theta} grant)\big).$$

In a scenario where a system consists of a communicating client and a server, the meaning of the above property is that for each time value Θ if it takes at most Θ time steps for a request from the client to reach the server, then it takes at most $2 \cdot \Theta$ time steps to obtain the grant (e.g. to some resources). Notice that when we deal with a fixed model, we can easily create a CTL equivalent of the above formula. However, it is not possible to present its general non-parameterized counterpart due to the presence of an unbounded quantifier.

3.3 Example

In Figure 1 the states of the model M are drawn as circles, whereas the values of the labelling function (a set of propositions assumed to be true) are rendered inside. The transitions are drawn as arrows connecting states. The presented Kripke structure is induced by the Petri net modelling the classical problem of Mutual Exclusion for 2 processes (see Subsection 7.1). It is straightforward to check that:

$$M, start \models \forall_{\Theta_1 \leq 1}\exists_{\Theta_2 \leq 2} EF^{\leq \Theta_1 + \Theta_2}(w_1 \wedge EG\neg c_1),$$

$$M, start \models \exists_{\Theta_1 \leq 3}\forall_{\Theta_2} E\big(w_1 U^{\leq \Theta_1} EG^{\leq \Theta_2} r_2\big).$$

Notice that in the first formula there is no superscript over EG, nevertheless, as we have shown it can be rewritten in the following equivalent form:

$$M, start \models \forall_{\Theta_1 \leq 1}\exists_{\Theta_2 \leq 2} EF^{\leq \Theta_1 + \Theta_2}(w_1 \wedge EG^{\leq 8}\neg c_1).$$

Similarly, the second formula can be rewritten in an equivalent form, with the parameter Θ_2 bounded by $|M|$ as follows:

$$M, start \models \exists_{\Theta_1 \leq 3}\forall_{\Theta_2 \leq 8} E\big(w_1 U^{\leq \Theta_1} EG^{\leq \Theta_2} r_2\big).$$

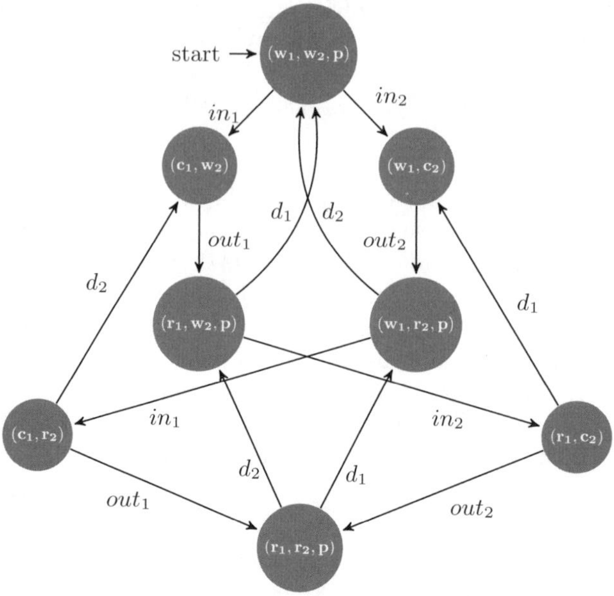

Fig. 1.

4 Bounded Semantics

The idea of bounded model checking is based on a concept of unfolding the computation tree of a given model only to a limited depth. In order to make things more clear we need the following definitions.

Definition 7. *Let M be a model and $k \in \mathbb{N}$. Let $Path_k$ be the set of all sequences $(s_0, \ldots, s_k)$ of states of M, where $s_i \rightarrow s_{i+1}$ for each $0 \leq i < k$. The pair $(Path_k, \mathcal{L})$ is called the k-*model *of M and is denoted by M_k.*

An element of $Path_k$ is called a *k-path* and denoted by π_k.

Definition 8. *Let M_k be the k-model of M and $\pi_k \in Path_k$. Define a function $loop : Path_k \longrightarrow 2^{\mathbb{N}}$ as:*

$$loop(\pi_k) = \{l \mid l \leq k \text{ and } \pi_k(k) \rightarrow \pi_k(l)\}.$$

A k-path π_k is called a *loop* if $loop(\pi_k) \neq \emptyset$. Observe that loops are essentially a way of representing some infinite paths in a finite way.

Definition 9 (Bounded semantics for vRTECTL**).** *Let M_k be the k-model, s – a state, $\alpha, \beta \in$ vRTECTL, p – a propositional variable, η – a linear expression, and υ – a parameter valuation. By $M_k, s \models_\upsilon \alpha$ let us denote that α is true (valid) at the state s of M_k. Again, M_k is omitted if it is implicitly understood. Define the relation $\models_\upsilon$ as follows:*

1. $s \models_\upsilon p$ *iff* $p \in \mathcal{L}(s)$
2. $s \models_\upsilon \neg p$ *iff* $p \notin \mathcal{L}(s)$,
3. $s \models_\upsilon \alpha \wedge \beta$ *iff* $s \models_\upsilon \alpha$ *and* $s \models_\upsilon \beta$,
4. $s \models_\upsilon \alpha \vee \beta$ *iff* $s \models_\upsilon \alpha$ *or* $s \models_\upsilon \beta$,
5. $s \models_\upsilon EX\alpha$ *iff* $\exists_{\pi_k \in Path_k}(\pi_k(0) = s \wedge \pi_k(1) \models_\upsilon \alpha)$,
6. $s \models_\upsilon EG^{\leq\eta}\alpha$ *iff* $\exists_{\pi_k \in Path_k}\big(\pi_k(0) = s \wedge \big[((\upsilon(\eta) \leq k) \wedge \bigwedge_{0\leq i\leq \upsilon(\eta)} \pi_k(i) \models_\upsilon \alpha) \vee ((\upsilon(\eta) > k) \wedge \bigwedge_{0\leq i\leq k} \pi_k(i) \models_\upsilon \alpha \wedge loop(\pi_k) \neq \emptyset)\big]\big)$,
7. $s \models_\upsilon E(\alpha U^{\leq\eta}\beta)$ *iff* $\exists_{\pi_k \in Path_k}\big(\pi_k(0) = s \wedge \exists_{0\leq i\leq min(k,\upsilon(\eta))}\big[\pi_k(i) \models_\upsilon \beta \wedge \bigwedge_{0\leq j<i} \pi_k(i) \models_\upsilon \alpha\big]\big)$.

The above definition differs from its counterpart for ECTL ([11]) in the points 6 and 7. In case of the point 6, we need to consider two subcases. The first subcase deals with the situation when α is checked along a finite path of length $\upsilon(\eta)$ smaller or equal than the depth k of the unfolding of the model. Each such a finite path is then a prefix of some k-path. In the second subcase we deal with the situation when α should be checked along a finite path of length strictly greater than k. Therefore, we have to check α along the loop – hence we have the *loop* condition. Both the subcases are combined in a disjunction. In case of the point 7, we check the existence of such a k-path π_k that the subformula β is valid on its position $\pi_k(i)$ where $i \leq min(k, \upsilon(\eta))$, and for all the positions $\pi_k(j)$ where $j < i$ we have $\pi_k(j) \models_\upsilon \alpha$.

Definition 10 (Bounded semantics for PRTECTL**).** *Let M_k be the k-model of M, s – a state, α – a sentence of* PRTECTL *and $a \in \mathbb{N}$. Define the relation $\models$ as follows:*

1. $M_k, s \models \forall_\Theta\alpha(\Theta)$ *iff* $\bigwedge_{i_\Theta\geq 0} M_k, s \models \alpha(i_\Theta)$,
2. $M_k, s \models \forall_{\Theta\leq a}\alpha(\Theta)$ *iff* $\bigwedge_{0\leq i_\Theta\leq a} M_k, s \models \alpha(i_\Theta)$,
3. $M_k, s \models \exists_\Theta\alpha(\Theta)$ *iff* $\bigvee_{i_\Theta\geq 0} M_k, s \models \alpha(i_\Theta)$,
4. $M_k, s \models \exists_{\Theta\leq a}\alpha(\Theta)$ *iff* $\bigvee_{0\leq i_\Theta\leq min(a,k)} M_k, s \models \alpha(i_\Theta)$,

where i_Θ is a fresh integer variable.

The next two lemmas bring forward the essential properties of bounded semantics. Basically they state that the truth of a formula in some k-model is maintained also in a larger l-model and in the whole model M. Therefore if we prove that a formula holds in the k-model (hopefully k is much smaller than $|M|$), then we obtain also the validity of the formula in the model M. These lemmas form a base for the idea of Bounded Model Checking. Namely, we start the search for a proof in the k-model with $k = 0$, then the length k of the paths is incremented until the proof is found or k reaches $|M|$. Then, the conditions 2 of Lemmas 2 and 3 guard that the property holds also in the model M. On the other hand, the conditions 3 of Lemmas 2 and 3 show that if $k = |M|$ is reached and no proof was found, the considered property is not valid in M.

Lemma 2. *Let M_k be the k-model of M, s – a state, υ – a parameter valuation, and α – a formula of* vRTECTL*. Then, the following conditions hold:*

1. $\forall_{l \geq k} \big(M_k, s \models_\upsilon \alpha$ *implies* $M_l, s \models_\upsilon \alpha\big)$,
2. $M_k, s \models_\upsilon \alpha$ *implies* $M, s \models_\upsilon \alpha$,
3. $M, s \models_\upsilon \alpha$ *implies* $M_{|M|}, s \models_\upsilon \alpha$.

Notice that Lemma 2 has its counterpart concerning PRTECTL as stated below.

Lemma 3. *Let M be a model, s – a state and α – a* PRTECTL *sentence. Then, the following conditions hold:*

1. $\forall_{l \geq k} \big(M_k, s \models \alpha$ *implies* $M_l, s \models \alpha\big)$,
2. $M_k, s \models \alpha$ *implies* $M, s \models \alpha$,
3. $M, s \models \alpha$ *implies* $M_{|M|}, s \models \alpha$.

Proofs of both the above lemmas can be found in the Appendix 1.

Both the above lemmas also hold when $|M|$ is substituted with the diameter of the model. However, while the BMC method is complete for PRTECL (see clause 3 in Lemma 3), in practice for complex models (e.g., induced by Petri nets) unwinding of the computation tree up to the size (or diameter) of the model is not possible. The main appeal of Bounded Model Checking is the ability to verify properties in a partial unfolding of a model which is especially valuable when looking for counterexamples, e.g., errors in system design.

4.1 Example

Recall the formulae and the model M from Example 3.3. One can check that

$$M_2, start \models \forall_{\Theta_1 \leq 1} \exists_{\Theta_2 \leq 2} EF^{\leq \Theta_1 + \Theta_2}(w_1 \wedge EG\neg c_1),$$

while this property does not hold in the bounded semantics for the k–models with k strictly smaller than 2. Similarly, we have

$$M_2, start \models \exists_{\Theta_1 \leq 3} \forall_{\Theta_2} E\big(w_1 U^{\leq \Theta_1} EG^{\leq \Theta_2} r_2\big),$$

while this does not hold for the k–models with k strictly smaller than 2.

5 Bounded Model Checking

The BMC algorithm is based on the idea of a translation of a part of the given model together with a temporal formula to a propositional formula. Satisfiability of the result means that the formula is true in the model. The first part of this section gives definitions and theorems concerning submodels, the second part presents the rules for the translation, whereas the last part includes the description of the BMC algorithm.

5.1 Submodels

We aim at giving a method of checking the validity of temporal formulae in k-models. In order to obtain an acceptable efficiency, the algorithm works on submodels of the k-model.

Definition 11. *Let $M_k = (Path_k, \mathcal{L})$ be the k-model of a model M. A substructure $M'_k = (Path'_k, \mathcal{L}')$, where $Path'_k \subseteq Path_k$ and $\mathcal{L}'$ is the restriction of $\mathcal{L}$ to the states present in the paths of $Path'_k$ is called a* submodel *of M_k.*

The bounded semantics of vRTECTL formulae and PRTECTL sentences over submodels is defined as for k-models. If $M'_k = (Path'_k, \mathcal{L}')$ and $M''_k = (Path''_k, \mathcal{L}'')$ are submodels of some k-model M_k, such that $Path''_k \subseteq Path'_k$, we write $M''_k \subseteq M'_k$.

Lemma 4. *Let M_k be the k-model of a model M, M'_k and M''_k – its submodels, such that $M''_k \subseteq M'_k$ and s a state present in some path of M''_k. Then, we have:*

1. $M''_k, s \models_\upsilon \alpha \Rightarrow M'_k, s \models_\upsilon \alpha$ *for* $\alpha \in$ vRTECTL *and any parameter valuation* υ,
2. $M''_k, s \models \alpha \Rightarrow M'_k, s \models \alpha$, *for* $\alpha \in$ PRTECTL.

Proof. The first part of the lemma is easily proven by the structural induction. In order to prove the second part, notice that in the bounded semantics the non-modal quantifiers are rewritten as, respectively, conjunctions or disjunctions, and use the result of the first part.

It was proven in [11] that in order to determine the truth of an ECTL formula in M_k it is sufficient to consider only submodels of a size (that is – the value of $|Path'_k|$) given by a special function on the checked formula. We extend these results to vRTECTL and PRTECTL.

Definition 12. *Let $\alpha, \beta \in$ vRTECTL, p – a propositional variable, η – a linear expression, and υ – a parameter valuation. Recall that Υ is the set of all parameter valuations. We define recursively the special function g_k : vRTECTL $\times \Upsilon \longrightarrow \mathbb{N}$ as follows:*

1. $g_k(p, \upsilon) = g_k(\neg p, \upsilon) = 0$,
2. $g_k(\alpha \vee \beta, \upsilon) = max(g_k(\alpha, \upsilon), g_k(\beta, \upsilon))$,
3. $g_k(\alpha \wedge \beta, \upsilon) = g_k(\alpha, \upsilon) + g_k(\beta, \upsilon)$,
4. $g_k(EX\alpha, \upsilon) = g_k(\alpha, \upsilon) + 1$,
5. $g_k(EG^{\leq\eta}\alpha, \upsilon) = (min(\upsilon(\eta), k) + 1) \cdot g_k(\alpha, \upsilon) + 1$,
6. $g_k(E\alpha U^{\leq\eta}\beta, \upsilon) = min(\upsilon(\eta), k) \cdot g_k(\alpha, \upsilon) + g_k(\beta, \upsilon) + 1$.

Let us build some intuitions on the above function. For a given k, let M_k be the k–model, s – a fixed state present in some path of M_k, α – a vRTECTL formula, and υ – a parameter valuation. The function $g_k(\alpha, \upsilon)$ returns the size of some submodel M'_k of M_k, such that $M_k, s \models_\upsilon \alpha$ iff $M'_k, s \models_\upsilon \alpha$. Let us focus on the fifth clause of the above definition. If $EG^{\leq\eta}\alpha$ holds in M_k under valuation υ, then there exists a k–path containing $min(\upsilon(\eta), k) + 1$ states along which α is satisfied. This path, together with $(min(\upsilon(\eta), k) + 1) \cdot g_k(\alpha, \upsilon)$ others, form the $Path'_k$ set of such a model M'_k that $M'_k, s \models_\upsilon EG^{\leq\eta}\alpha$. For all the remaining cases, consult the proof of Lemma 5.

Definition 13. *Let* $\alpha \in$ PRTECTL. *We define recursively the special function* f_k : PRTECTL $\longrightarrow \mathbb{N}$ *as follows:*

1. *if* $\alpha \in$ RTCTL *then* $f_k(\alpha) = g_k(\alpha, \upsilon)$ *for any* υ,
2. *if* $\alpha = \forall_{\Theta \leq c} \beta(\Theta)$ *then* $f_k(\alpha) = \sum_{i_\Theta \leq c} f_k(\beta(i_\Theta))$,
3. *if* $\alpha = \exists_{\Theta \leq c} \beta(\Theta)$ *then* $f_k(\alpha) = max_{i_\Theta \leq min(c,k)} \{f_k(\beta(i_\Theta))\}$,

where i_Θ *is a fresh integer variable.*

As the RTCTL formulae considered in the condition 1 of Definition 13 contain no free parameters, the above definition is unambiguous. The following lemmas state that we can determine the truth of the vRTECTL and PRTECTL formulae in the k-model using submodels of size bounded by the value of the appropriate function f_k or g_k.

Lemma 5. *Let* $\alpha \in$ vRTECTL, M_k *be the* k*-model of a model* M, *and* υ *– a parameter valuation. For any state* s *present in some path of* M_k, $M_k, s \models_\upsilon \alpha$ *if and only if there exists a submodel* M'_k *of* M_k *such that* $M'_k, s \models_\upsilon \alpha$ *and* $|Path'_k| \leq g_k(\alpha, \upsilon)$.

Proof. See the Appendix 1.

Lemma 6. *Let* β *be a* PRTECTL *sentence and* M_k *be the* k*-model of a model* M. *For any state* s *present in some path of* M_k, $M_k, s \models \beta$ *if and only if there exists a submodel* M'_k *of* M_k *such that* $M'_k, s \models \beta$ *and* $|Path'_k| \leq f_k(\beta)$.

Proof. See the Appendix 1.

From Lemmas 5,6, Lemma 4 (notice that the k-model is also a submodel) and Lemmas 2 and 3 we obtain that the truth of a formula in some submodel of size bounded by the appropriate g_k or f_k function implies the truth in a model. On the other hand, Lemmas 2 and 3 state that if a formula is true in a model, then it is also true in some k-model, or equivalently, by Lemmas 2 and 3 in its submodel of size bounded by the value of appropriately g_k or f_k.

5.2 Translation to SAT

In order to translate the problem of validity of a sentence $\alpha \in$ PRTECTL in the submodel M'_k to the problem of satisfiability of a propositional formula $[\alpha]_k$ we have to encode M'_k and α, and then combine the results together. We present an adapted version of the efficient translation introduced in [14].

Consider a model M. As the number of the states of M is finite, they can be perceived as bit vectors of the length $r = \lceil log|M| \rceil$. Therefore, we can represent the states as the valuations of the vector $w = (w_1, \ldots, w_r)$. This vector is called a *global state variable* while each its member w_i is called a *state variable*. Denote by $\mathcal{SV}$ the set of state variables, then a valuation $V : \mathcal{SV} \longrightarrow \{0,1\}$ naturally extends to the valuation of the global state variables $\hat{V} : \mathcal{SV}^r \longrightarrow \{0,1\}^r$ in such a way that $\hat{V}(w_1, \ldots, w_r) = (V(w_1), \ldots, V(w_r))$. With a slight notational abuse, we denote by $\hat{V}(w)$ a state encoded by bit vector. The *symbolic k-path* is a vector of global state variables. As we need a number of symbolic k-paths to represent the k-paths in a translated submodel, by $(w_{0,i}, w_{1,i}, \ldots, w_{r,i})$ we denote the i-th symbolic k-path, where $w_{j,i}$ is a global state variable.

Let w, w' be global state variables, s a state and p a proposition. In the rules of the translation the following propositional formulae are used:

1. $p(w)$ denotes a formula such that $V \models p(w)$ iff $p \in \mathcal{L}(\hat{V}(w))$,
2. $T(w, w')$ denotes a formula such that $V \models T(w, w')$ iff $\hat{V}(w) \to \hat{V}(w')$ (i.e., there exists a transition between $\hat{V}(w)$ and $\hat{V}(w')$ in the model M),
3. $H(w, w')$ is a formula such that $V \models H(w, w')$ iff $\hat{V}(w) = \hat{V}(w')$ (encoding the equality of states),
4. $L_k(j) = \bigvee_{i=0}^{k} T(w_{k,j}, w_{i,j})$ encodes a loop, that is $V \models L_k(j)$ iff $loop((V(w_{0,j}), \ldots, V(w_{k,j}))) \neq \emptyset$,
5. $I_s(w)$ is a formula such that $V \models I_s(w)$ iff $\hat{V}(w) = s$ (encoding the initial state).

Let M be a model and let A be a finite subset of $\mathbb{N}$. Then, the *unfolding of the transition relation* is defined as

$$[M]_k^A := \bigwedge_{j \in A} \bigwedge_{i=0}^{k-1} T(w_{i,j}, w_{i+1,j}).$$

It is easy to see that $V \models [M]_k^A$ iff for each $j \in A$, $(V(w_{0,j}), \ldots, V(w_{k,j}))$ is a k-path in M. As the translation introduced in [14] was an essential improvement over the original one of [11], we follow A. Zbrzezny's approach in our work. We recall the following definitions from [14].

Let A and B be finite subsets of $\mathbb{N}$. By $A \prec B$ we denote that $x < y$ for all $x \in A$ and $y \in B$. Let $k, m, p \in \mathbb{N}$ and $m \leq |A|$, then:

1. $\hat{g}_L(A, m)$ is the subset B of A such that $|B| = m$ and $B \prec A \backslash B$,
2. $\hat{g}_R(A, m)$ denotes the subset B of A such that $|B| = m$ and $A \backslash B \prec B$,
3. $h_X(A)$ is the set $A \backslash \{min(A)\}$,
4. if $k+1$ divides $|A| - 1$ then $h_G(A, k)$ is the sequence of sets $(B_0, \ldots, B_k)$ such that $\bigcup_{i=0}^{k} B_i = A \backslash \{min(A)\}$, $|B_i| = |B_j|$ and $B_i \prec B_j$ for every $0 \leq i < j \leq k$,
5. if k divides $|A| - 1 - p$, then $h_U(A, k, p)$ denotes the sequence of sets $(B_0, \ldots, B_k)$ such that $\bigcup_{i=0}^{k} B_i = A \backslash \{min(A)\}$, $B_i \prec B_j$ for every $0 \leq i < j \leq k$, $|B_0| = \ldots = |B_{k-1}|$ and $|B_k| = p$.

We also need a sequence element selector, that is if $h_G(A, k) = (B_0, \ldots, B_k)$ then define $h_G(A, k)(i) = B_i$ for $0 \leq i \leq k$ and if $h_U(A, k, p) = (B_0, \ldots, B_k)$, define $h_U(A, k, p)(i) = B_i$ for $0 \leq i \leq k$.

The functions $\hat{g}_L$ and $\hat{g}_R$ are used to divide the set of path indices into the two parts of the sizes sufficient to perform the independent translation of subformulae α and β of formula $\alpha \wedge \beta$. Similarly, the functions h_G and h_U are used to divide the set of path indices into the sequences (hence the use of the selector) of subsets which are of the sizes sufficient to perform the translation of subformulae α and α together with β of, respectively, formulae $EG^{\leq\eta}\alpha$ and $E\alpha U^{\eta}\beta$. These functions were not present in [11], where all the proper subformulae of a given formula α of ECTL were translated using the full set $\{i \in \mathbb{N} \mid 1 \leq i \leq g_k(\alpha)\}$ of indices. For a more in depth description we refer the reader to [14].

Definition 14 (Translation of vRTECTL**).** *Let $\alpha, \beta \in$ vRTECTL, p – a propositional variable, υ – a parameter valuation, η – a linear expression, $(m,n) \in \mathbb{N} \times \mathbb{N}$, and $A \subseteq \mathbb{N}$.*

$$\left[p\right]_k^{[m,n,A,\upsilon]} := p(w_{m,n}) \text{ and } \left[\neg p\right]_k^{[m,n,A,\upsilon]} := \neg p(w_{m,n}),$$

$$\left[\alpha \wedge \beta\right]^{[m,n,A,\upsilon]} := \left[\alpha\right]^{[m,n,\hat{g}_L(A,g_k(\alpha,\upsilon)),\upsilon]} \wedge \left[\beta\right]^{[m,n,\hat{g}_R(A,g_k(\beta,\upsilon)),\upsilon]},$$

$$\left[\alpha \vee \beta\right]^{[m,n,A,\upsilon]} := \left[\alpha\right]^{[m,n,\hat{g}_L(A,g_k(\alpha,\upsilon)),\upsilon]} \wedge \left[\beta\right]^{[m,n,\hat{g}_L(A,g_k(\beta,\upsilon)),\upsilon]},$$

$$\left[EX\alpha\right]^{[m,n,A,\upsilon]} := H(w_{m,n}, w_{0,min(A)}) \wedge \left[\alpha\right]_k^{[1,min(A),h_X(A),\upsilon]}.$$

The translation of the formula $EG^{\leq\eta}\alpha$ depends on the value of $\upsilon(\eta)$. If $\upsilon(\eta) > k$, then:

$$\left[EG^{\leq\eta}\alpha\right]^{[m,n,A,\upsilon]} := H(w_{m,n}, w_{0,min(A)}) \wedge L_k(min(A)) \wedge \bigwedge_{j=0}^{k} \left[\alpha\right]_k^{[j,min(A),h_G(A,k)(j),\upsilon]}$$

and if $\upsilon(\eta) \leq k$, then

$$\left[EG^{\leq\eta}\alpha\right]^{[m,n,A,\upsilon]} := H(w_{m,n}, w_{0,min(A)}) \wedge \bigwedge_{j=0}^{\upsilon(\eta)} \left[\alpha\right]_k^{[j,min(A),h_G(A,\upsilon(\eta))(j),\upsilon]}.$$

The translation of $E\alpha U^{\leq\eta}\beta$ is defined as follows:

$$\left[E\alpha U^{\leq\eta}\beta\right]^{[m,n,A,\upsilon]} := H(w_{m,n}, w_{0,min(A)})$$
$$\wedge \bigvee_{i=0}^{min(\upsilon(\eta),k)} \Big(\left[\beta\right]_k^{[i,min(A),h_U(A,min(\upsilon(\eta),k),g_k(\beta,\upsilon))(min(\upsilon(\eta),k)),\upsilon]}$$
$$\wedge \bigwedge_{j=0}^{i-1} \left[\alpha\right]_k^{[j,min(A),h_U(A,min(\upsilon(\eta),k),g_k(\beta,\upsilon))(j),\upsilon]}\Big).$$

The above encoding is based on the definition of the bounded semantics for vRTECTL – see Definition 9 together with the associated comment.

Definition 15 (Translation of PRTECTL**).** *Let $\alpha \in$ PRTECTL, $A \subseteq \mathbb{N}$, $(m,n) \in \mathbb{N} \times \mathbb{N}$, and $c \in \mathbb{N}$. If α contains no quantifiers and no free parameters, then:*

$$\left[\alpha\right]_k^{[m,n,A]} := \left[\alpha\right]_k^{[m,n,A,\upsilon]}, \text{ where } \upsilon \text{ is any parameter valuation.}$$

As in the above case $\alpha \in$ vRTECTL and it contains no free parameters, the choice of υ is irrelevant.

$$\left[\forall_{\Theta\leq c}\alpha(\Theta)\right]_k^{[m,n,A]} := \left[\alpha(c)\right]_k^{[m,n,\hat{g}_L(A,f_k(\alpha(c)))]} \wedge \left[\forall_{\Theta\leq c-1}\alpha(\Theta)\right]_k^{[m,n,\hat{g}_R(A,f_k(\forall_{\Theta\leq c-1}\alpha(\Theta)))]},$$

Let $d = min(c, k)$, then:

$$\big[\exists_{\Theta \leq c}\alpha(\Theta)\big]_k^{[m,n,A]} := \big[\alpha(d)\big]_k^{[m,n,\hat{g}_L(A,f_k(\alpha(d)))]} \vee \big[\exists_{\Theta \leq d-1}\alpha(\Theta)\big]_k^{[m,n,\hat{g}_L(A,f_k(\exists_{\Theta \leq d-1}\alpha(\Theta)))]}.$$

Let M_k be the k-model of a model M. If $\alpha \in$ vRTECTL and υ is a parameter valuation, then define $G_k(\alpha, \upsilon) := \{i \in \mathbb{N} \mid 1 \leq i \leq g_k(\alpha, \upsilon)\}$. Similarly, if $\beta \in$ PRTECTL, then define $F_k(\beta) := \{i \in \mathbb{N} \mid 1 \leq i \leq f_k(\beta)\}$. The sets G_k and F_k contain the indices of symbolic k-paths used to perform the translation. The formulae $\big[M\big]_k^{G_k(\alpha,\upsilon)}$ and $\big[M\big]_k^{F_k(\beta)}$ encode all the M_k submodels of the size not greater than needed to validate the truth of formulae α, β as indicated in Lemmas 5, 6.

Now, we are in the position to complete the translation of the problem of validity in vRTECTL and PRTECTL to the problem of satisfiability of propositional formulae. Let M_k be the k-model of a model M, $\alpha \in$ vRTECTL and υ be a parameter valuation. Denote

$$\big[M\big]_k^{\alpha,\upsilon} := \big[M\big]_k^{G_k(\alpha,\upsilon)} \wedge I_s(w_{0,0}) \wedge \big[\alpha\big]_k^{[0,0,G_k(\alpha,\upsilon),\upsilon]}.$$

Similarly, let $\beta \in$ PRTECTL, then denote

$$\big[M\big]_k^{\beta} := \big[M\big]_k^{F_k(\beta)} \wedge I_s(w_{0,0}) \wedge \big[\beta\big]_k^{[0,0,F_k(\beta)]}.$$

The following theorems ensure completeness and correctness of the translation.

Theorem 2. *Let M_k be the k-model of M, υ – a parameter valuation, α – a formula of* vRTECTL *containing at least one modality, and s a state. Then, the following equivalence holds: $M_k, s \models_\upsilon \alpha$ iff $\big[M\big]_k^{\alpha,\upsilon}$ is satisfiable.*

Proof. See the Appendix 2.

Theorem 3. *Let M_k be the k-model of M, β – a sentence of* PRTECTL *containing at least one modality, and s – a state. Then, the following equivalence holds: $M_k, s \models \beta$ iff $\big[M\big]_k^{\beta}$ is satisfiable.*

Proof. Replace the non-modal quantifiers in a formula of PRETCTL with, appropriately, conjunctions or disjunctions. To conclude use Theorem 2.

5.3 Example

Consider the model M from Example 3.3 and the formula:

$$\alpha = \forall_{\Theta_1 \leq 1}\exists_{\Theta_2 \leq 2} EF^{\leq \Theta_1 + \Theta_2}(w_1 \wedge EG\neg c_1).$$

The number of the paths needed to encode α in the 2–model is computed as follows:

$$f_k(\alpha) = \sum_{i_{\Theta_1} \leq 1} max_{i_{\Theta_2} \leq 2}\{f_k(EF^{\leq i_{\Theta_1} + i_{\Theta_2}}(w_1 \wedge EG\neg c_1))\}.$$

Let $\beta = EF^{\leq i_{\Theta_1}+i_{\Theta_2}}(w_1 \wedge EG\neg c_1))$, and observe that if $i_{\Theta_1} \leq 1$ and $i_{\Theta_2} \leq 2$ are fixed, then $f_k(\beta) = g_k(\beta, \upsilon)$ where $\upsilon(\Theta_1) = i_{\Theta_1}$ and $\upsilon(\Theta_2) = i_{\Theta_2}$. As $g_k(true, \upsilon) = 0$, we have $g_k(\beta, \upsilon) = g_k(w_1 \wedge EG\neg c_1, \upsilon) + 1 = 2$, therefore $f_k(\alpha) = 4$. Thus, the encoding in the 2–model of M is as follows:

$$\left[\forall_{\Theta_1 \leq 1} \exists_{\Theta_2 \leq 2} EF^{\leq \Theta_1 + \Theta_2}(w_1 \wedge EG\neg c_1)\right]_2^{[0,0,\{1,2,3,4\}]}$$

$$= \left[\exists_{\Theta_2 \leq 2} EF^{\leq \Theta_2}(w_1 \wedge EG\neg c_1)\right]_2^{[0,0,\{1,2\}]} \wedge \left[\exists_{\Theta_2 \leq 2} EF^{\leq 1+\Theta_2}(w_1 \wedge EG\neg c_1)\right]_2^{[0,0,\{3,4\}]}$$

$$= \bigvee_{i=0}^{2} \left[EF^{\leq i}(w_1 \wedge EG\neg c_1)\right]_2^{[0,0,\{1,2\}]} \wedge \bigvee_{j=1}^{2} \left[EF^{\leq j}(w_1 \wedge EG\neg c_1)\right]_2^{[0,0,\{3,4\}]}.$$

As the illustration of the further steps of the translation, consider:

$$\left[EF^{\leq 2}(w_1 \wedge EG\neg c_1)\right]_2^{[0,0,\{3,4\}]} = H(w_{0,0}, w_{0,3}) \wedge \bigvee_{i=0}^{2} \left[w_1 \wedge EG\neg c_1\right]_2^{[i,3,\{3,4\}]}$$

$$= H(w_{0,0}, w_{0,3}) \wedge \bigvee_{i=0}^{2} \left(\left[w_1\right]^{[i,3,\emptyset]} \wedge \left[EG\neg c_1\right]_2^{[i,3,\{4\}]}\right)$$

$$= H(w_{0,0}, w_{0,3}) \wedge \bigvee_{i=0}^{2} \left(p_{w_1}(w_{i,3}) \wedge H(w_{i,3}, w_{0,4}) \wedge L_2(4) \wedge \bigwedge_{j=0}^{2} \neg p_{c_1}(w_{j,4})\right).$$

5.4 The BMC Algorithm

Let M be a model and $\alpha \in$ PRTECTL.

```
BMCverifyPRTECTL(α)
    for k := 1 to |M|
        compute the translation [M]_k^{α,υ}
        if [M]_k^{α,υ} is satisfiable return true
    end for
    return false
```

Checking satisfiability of a propositional formula is delegated to an efficient SAT-solver. Obviously the algorithm terminates in a finite number of iterations. By Theorem 2 and Lemma 3 the result is positive (that is – the translation of the formula α is satisfiable) if and only if α is valid in the state s of a model M.

It is easy to present a similar algorithm for checking the validity of vRTECTL formulae under a parameter valuation υ – the only difference is the choice of the appropriate translation.

6 Implementation of Parametric BMC for Elementary Net Systems

In this section we recall some basic definitions concerning Elementary Net Systems (called also Elementary Petri Nets) and present the implementation of BMC for a model generated by a net. The formulations of this section originate from [11]. We consider only the *safe* Petri Nets, i.e., Petri Nets, where each place can be marked with at the most one token.

6.1 Elementary Net Systems

Definition 16. *A* net *is a triple* $N = (B, E, F)$, *where* B *(the* places*) and* E *(the* transitions*) are finite sets satisfying* $B \cap E = \emptyset$, *the relation (called a* flow relation*)* $F \subseteq (B \times E) \cup (E \times B)$ *has the property that for every* $t \in E$ *there exists* $p, q \in B$ *such that* $(p, t), (t, q) \in F$.

Let N be a net and $t \in E$, then $\bullet t = \{p \in B \mid (p, t) \in F\}$ is called the *pre-set* of t and $t\bullet = \{p \in B \mid (t, p) \in F\}$ is called the *post-set* of t. A *configuration* of a net $N = (B, E, F)$ is a subset C of B. An usual method of visualisation of nets is where the places are rendered as circles, the transitions as boxes, the elements of flow relation as arrows, and the configuration C is represented by placing a token in every circle corresponding to a place in C. A place not marked by a token is called *free*.

Definition 17. *A quadruple* $EN = (B, E, F, C_{in})$, *where* (B, E, F) *is a net and* $C_{in} \subseteq B$ *is the initial configuration, is called an* elementary net system.

Definition 18. *Let* $EN = (B, E, F, C_{in})$ *be an elementary net system and* $t \in E$.

1. *Let* $C \subseteq B$ *be a configuration. If* t *is a transition,* $\bullet t \subseteq C$, *and* $(t\bullet \setminus \bullet t) \cap C = \emptyset$, *then the transition* t *is* enabled *in* C *(denoted by* $C[t\rangle$*).*
2. *Let* $C, D \subseteq B$ *be configurations. A transition* t fires *from* C *to* D *(denoted by* $C[t\rangle D$*) if* $C[t\rangle$ *and* $D = (C \setminus \bullet t) \cup t\bullet$.
3. *A configuration* $C \subseteq B$ *is* reachable *if there are configurations* $C_0, C_1, \ldots, C_n \subseteq B$ *with* $C_0 = C_{in}, C_n = C$ *and transitions* $t_1, \ldots, t_n \in E$ *such that* $C_{i-1}[t_i\rangle C_i$ *for all* $1 \leq i \leq n$. *We denote the set of all the reachable configuration by* C_{EN}.

Informally, the arrows of the flow relation can be thought of as the directed paths of movement of tokens. If there is an arrow directed from a place b to a transition t, then we say that b *enters* t. If there exists an arrow directed from a transition t to a place b, then we say that t *fills* b. The transition t is enabled if all the places entering t are marked with tokens and all the places filled by t and not entering the transition t are free. If a transition t fires, then the tokens from all the places entering t disappear and appear in all the places filled by t.

6.2 Implementation

Our goal is to construct a Kripke model reflecting the states (markings) and actions (firings) in an elementary net system. Consider an elementary net system $EN = (B, E, F, C_{in})$ and number the places of the net with integers smaller or equal than $n = |B|$. We use a set $\{p_1, \ldots, p_n\}$ of propositions, where p_i is interpreted as the presence of a token in the place number i. If w is a state, then by $p_i \in w$ we mean that the i-th place is marked in the corresponding configuration.

We define the model $M = (S, \rightarrow, \mathcal{L})$ for EN by placing $S = C_{EN}$ (the reachable configurations are the states), $w \rightarrow v$ iff there exists $t \in E$ such that $w[t\rangle v$ (the transitions model the firings) for $w, v \in S$, and $p_i \in \mathcal{L}(w)$ iff $p_i \in w$ (the labelling models the markings).

It is easy to see that we can encode the states of S by valuations of a vector of the state variables $w = (w[1], \ldots, w[n])$, where $w[i] = p_i$ for $0 \leq i \leq n$. Moreover, let $P = \{1, \ldots, n\}$ and let $pre(t), post(t) \subseteq P$ be finite sets of the indices of the places of, respectively, $pre\text{−}set(t)$ and $post\text{−}set(t)$. Let $\xi(C_{in}) \subseteq P$ be the set of indices of the places in C_{in}.

Now, we are in the position to present the definitions:

1. $I_{C_{in}}(w) := \bigwedge_{i \in \xi(C_{in})} w[i] \wedge \bigwedge_{i \in P \setminus \xi(C_{in})} \neg w[i]$,
2. $T(w,v) := \bigvee_{t \in E} \big(\bigwedge_{i \in pre(t)} w[i] \wedge \bigwedge_{i \in (post(t) \setminus pre(t))} \neg w[i] \wedge \bigwedge_{i \in (pre(t) \setminus post(t))} \neg v[i]$ $\wedge \bigwedge_{i \in post(t)} v[i] \wedge \bigwedge_{i \in (P \setminus (pre(t) \cup post(t))) \cup (pre(t) \cap post(t))} w[i] \iff v[i] \big)$,
3. $p_i(w) := w[i]$,
4. $H(w,v) := \bigwedge_{1 \leq i \leq n} w[i] \iff v[i]$.

7 Experimental Results

We have implemented the presented algorithm on top of the BMC module of Verics. Elementary Net Systems are used as an input specification formalism, whereas PRTECTL is used as an input logic.

In order to show the performance and present some case studies we use standard scalable benchmarks. The detailed descriptions of these examples can be found in [11] and [10]. We have implemented our methods exactly as they are presented in this paper, the only optimization consists in using an efficient translation originating from [14].

The tables with results show the following data in the columns from left to right: the formula verified, the number of processes (denoted by NoP), the depth k of the unfolding of the model, the size of the corresponding propositional formula (numbers of variables and clauses) together with the description of how much resources (time and memory) does the translation take, the time it took for MiniSat SAT solver to check the satisfiability, and finally the SAT? column indicating whether the tested formula is satisfiable (√) or not satisfiable (×).

The experiments have been performed on a Linux machine with dual core 1.6 GHz processor. We tested satisfiability using the MiniSAT solver [9].

The presented models are relatively simple, yet classical, and the considered formulae have been chosen as to show the difference between the expressive power of CTL and PRECTL. As our work is still in its preliminary stage, we do not include any real-world example, however it should be mentioned that many of problems lead to models similar to presented in Examples 7.1 and 7.2. Tables 1 and 2 show some quantitative details of the experiments.

7.1 Mutual Exclusion

The elementary net system of Figure 2 models the well-known mutual exclusion problem. The system consists of $n+1$ processes (where $n \geq 2$) of which n compete for the access to the shared resource and one, called the permission process, guards so that no two processes use the resource simultaneously. The presence of a token in the place labelled by w_i means that the i-th process is waiting for the access to the critical section while the token in c_i means that the i-th process has acquired the permission and entered the critical section. The place r_i models the unguarded part of the process and the presence of token in place p indicates that the resource is available.

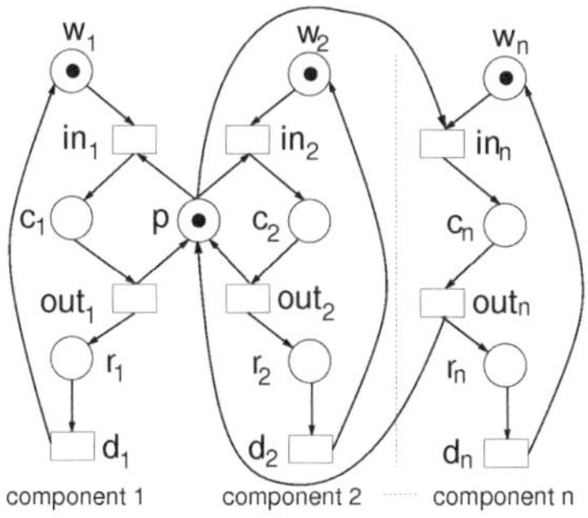

Fig. 2. Mutual exclusion

The Kripke structure constructed for 3 processes along the lines of Subsection 6.2 is presented in Figure 1. Let us consider the formula $\varphi_1^b = \forall_{\Theta \leq b} EF(\neg p \wedge EG^{\leq \Theta} c_1)$. We explore the validity of this formula with respect to the value of b. We can see that in order for the restricted EG operator to hold we need to have a path on which the first process enters its critical section and then other processes execute their local transitions d_i.

Let us explain how the verification works for this formula. For example, for 3 processes and $b = 2$, first the processes 2 and 3 enter their places r_2 and r_3 resp., then the process 1 enters its place c_1 and then 2 and 3 execute d_2 and d_3 respectively along the path of the length 2 on which c_1 holds. Notice that for $b = 3$ this formula does not hold in this model. Note that the non-parameterized counterpart of the formula φ_1, i.e., $EF(\neg p \wedge EGc_1)$ does not hold in our model as there is no cycle in which c_1 is true starting in a state where p is false.

Table 1. Mutual exclusion, testing the formula φ_1^b

formula	NoP	k	PBMC				MiniSAT	SAT?
			vars	clauses	sec	MB	sec	√/×
φ_1^1	3	2	1063	2920	0.01	1.3	0.003	×
φ_1^1	3	3	1505	4164	0.01	1.5	0.008	√
φ_1^2	3	4	2930	8144	0.01	1.5	0.01	×
φ_1^2	3	5	3593	10010	0.01	1.6	0.03	√
φ_1^2	30	4	37825	108371	0.3	7.4	0.2	×
φ_1^2	30	5	46688	133955	0.4	8.9	0.52	√
φ_1^3	4	6	8001	22378	0.06	2.5	0.04	×
φ_1^3	4	7	9244	25886	0.05	2.8	0.05	√

7.2 Dining Philosophers

Another benchmark we consider is the Dining Philosophers Problem. Consider n ($n \geq 2$) philosophers sitting around a round table. Each philosopher has a plate in front of him, and between the two neighbouring plates there lies a fork. Whenever a philosopher eats, he uses both the forks from both the sides of his plate. When a philosopher has finished eating, he lays back both of his forks on the table and starts thinking. The elementary net system modelling the system described above is shown in Fig. 3. The conditions r_i, w_i, s_i denote that i-th philosopher is thinking, waiting for both the forks and eating, respectively; c_i represents that the i-th fork is not taken.

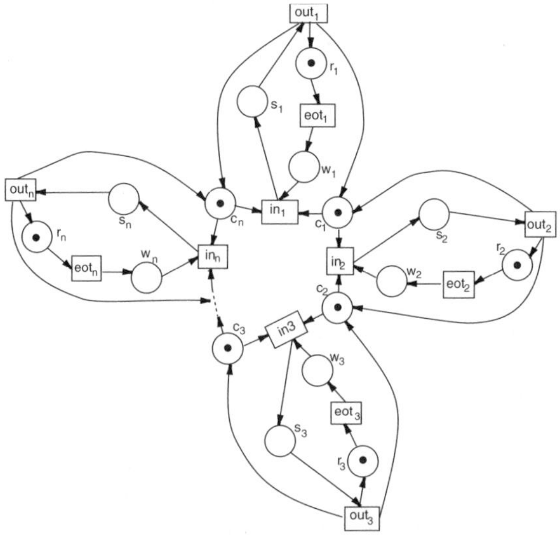

Fig. 3. Dining Philosophers

Let us consider the following properties: $\varphi_2^b = \forall_{\Theta \leq b} EF(s_1 \wedge EG^{\leq \Theta}(\neg c_1 \wedge \neg c_n \wedge \bigwedge_{1<i<n} c_i))$ and $\varphi_3^b = \forall_{\Theta \leq b} EF(s_1 \wedge EG^{\leq \Theta} \bigwedge_{1 \leq i \leq n} \neg c_i)$. The formula φ_2^b expresses that it is possible that in the future there exists a state where for b time units the first philosopher has eaten (therefore his forks are taken) while all the remaining forks are laid on the table. The formula φ_2^b states a similar property, namely that there exists a future state in which for b time units the first philosopher has eaten while all the remaining forks are taken.

Note that φ_3^3 does not hold in the model because there is no path of length 3 along which the first process can stay in the s_1 state.

Table 2. Dining philosophers, testing the formulae φ_2^b and φ_3^b

formula	NoP	k	PBMC				MiniSAT	SAT?
			vars	clauses	sec	MB	sec	√/×
φ_2^1	4	1	1240	3347	0.01	1.5	0.008	×
φ_2^1	4	2	2124	5839	0.02	1.64	0.004	√
φ_2^3	4	1	2518	6821	0.01	1.8	0.004	×
φ_2^3	4	2	4298	11837	0.01	2.01	0.01	√
φ_3^1	4	3	3014	8343	0.02	1.8	0.1	×
φ_3^1	4	4	3898	10385	0.03	1.9	0.2	√
φ_3^2	4	3	4549	12600	0.04	2.07	0.008	×
φ_3^2	4	4	5875	16338	0.06	2.32	0.04	√
φ_3^2	10	9	37981	107724	0.25	7.3	3.78	×
φ_3^2	10	10	42043	119310	0.28	8	8.97	√

7.3 Generic Pipeline Paradigm

The final benchmark we consider is the Generic Pipeline Paradigm model [10]. It consists of three parts, namely: Producer which is able to produce data ($ProdReady$), Consumer being able to receive data ($ConsReady$) and a chain of n intermediate Nodes – having data receiving ($Node_i Ready$), processing ($Node_i Proc_j$), and sending ($Node_i Send$) capabilities. Notice that the example can be scaled in order to see how the size of the system influences performance, and whether the truth of the verified formulae is affected. In particular, we extend the "processing" states with subsequent transitions, which model time needed to process data.

Let us consider the following property:

$$\varphi_4^{n,m} = \forall_{\Theta \leq nm-1} EFEG^{\leq \Theta}(\neg ProdReady \wedge \neg ConsReady \wedge \bigvee_{i=1}^{n} \neg Node_i Ready).$$

The intuitive meaning is that it is possible that for some state of the system, during some time (bounded by $nm - 1$) neither Producer is able to produce, nor Consumer is able to receive, while the intermediate Node chain is processing or transferring data. Note that the CTL nonsuperscripted counterpart does not hold in the model, as the data always eventually will reach Consumer.

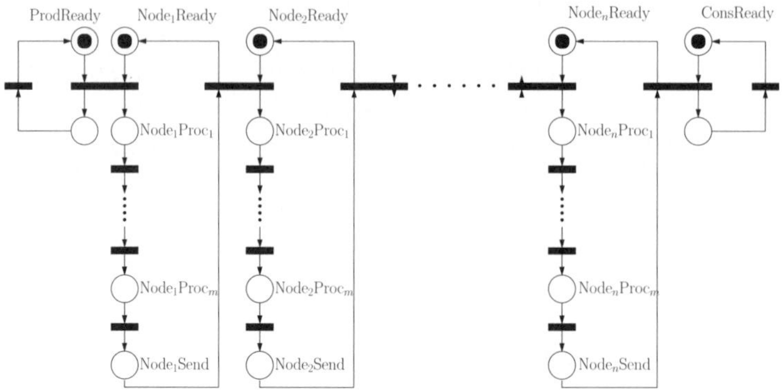

Fig. 4. Generic Pipeline Paradigm

Table 3. Generic Pipeline Paradigm, testing the formula $\varphi_4^{n,m}$

formula	n	m	k	PBMC				MiniSAT	SAT?
				vars	clauses	sec	MB	sec	√/×
$\varphi_4^{2,1}$	2	1	6	4086	11315	0.03	2.07	0.008	×
$\varphi_4^{2,1}$	2	1	7	4696	13079	0.036	2.7	0.02	√
$\varphi_4^{2,2}$	2	2	8	5980	16811	0.06	2.6	0.01	×
$\varphi_4^{2,2}$	2	2	9	13484	37927	0.08	2.7	0.06	√
$\varphi_4^{2,3}$	2	3	10	8844	24873	0.07	2.9	0.02	×
$\varphi_4^{2,3}$	2	3	11	9776	27509	0.08	3.1	0.2	√
$\varphi_4^{3,1}$	3	1	8	7416	20739	0.04	2.6	0.01	×
$\varphi_4^{3,1}$	3	1	9	8292	23207	0.03	2.7	0.07	√
$\varphi_4^{3,2}$	3	2	11	20025	56568	0.12	4.6	0.04	×
$\varphi_4^{3,2}$	3	2	12	21768	61517	0.14	4.7	0.43	√
$\varphi_4^{10,1}$	10	1	24	74488	212315	0.4	13.2	0.43	×
$\varphi_4^{10,1}$	10	1	25	77548	221055	0.52	13.6	19.2	√
$\varphi_4^{10,2}$	10	2	32	111844	320863	1.6	37.3	0.98	×
$\varphi_4^{10,2}$	10	2	33	230812	662175	1.64	38.4	23.1	√

8 Conclusions

In this paper we showed how parametric model checking can be performed by means of Bounded Model Checking. We presented an implementation and tested it against some benchmarks. Our work is still in its preliminary phase and can be extended in several directions. One of them is to investigate the remaining parametric logics presented in [6], of which General Parametric CTL (GPCTL) seems to be the most interesting. The formulae of GPCTL allow for referring to the number of occurrences of some event. In case of GPCTL, the computational complexity of the model checking problem is at least NP-complete, which is likely to make the BMC approach especially fruitful. Another possibility is to include parameters to the model. Introducing the real time can also be considered, given it has been done for non-parametric BMC.

References

1. Alur, R., Henzinger, T., Vardi, M.: Parametric real-time reasoning. In: Proc. of the 25th Ann. Symp. on Theory of Computing (STOC 1993), pp. 592–601. ACM, New York (1993)
2. Benedetti, M., Cimatti, A.: Bounded model checking for past LTL. In: Garavel, H., Hatcliff, J. (eds.) TACAS 2003. LNCS, vol. 2619, pp. 18–33. Springer, Heidelberg (2003)
3. Biere, A., Cimatti, A., Clarke, E., Fujita, M., Zhu, Y.: Symbolic model checking using SAT procedures instead of BDDs. In: Proc. of the ACM/IEEE Design Automation Conference (DAC 1999), pp. 317–320 (1999)
4. Biere, A., Cimatti, A., Clarke, E., Zhu, Y.: Symbolic model checking without bDDs. In: Cleaveland, W.R. (ed.) TACAS 1999. LNCS, vol. 1579, pp. 193–207. Springer, Heidelberg (1999)
5. Bruyére, V., Dall'Olio, E., Raskin, J.-F.: Durations and parametric model-checking in timed automata. ACM Transactions on Computational Logic 9(2), 1–21 (2008)
6. Emerson, E.A., Trefler, R.: Parametric quantitative temporal reasoning. In: Proc. of the 14th Symp. on Logic in Computer Science (LICS 1999), pp. 336–343. IEEE Computer Society Press, Los Alamitos (July 1999)
7. Heljanko, K.: Bounded reachability checking with process semantics. In: Larsen, K.G., Nielsen, M. (eds.) CONCUR 2001. LNCS, vol. 2154, pp. 218–232. Springer, Heidelberg (2001)
8. Hune, T., Romijn, J., Stoelinga, M., Vaandrager, F.: Linear parametric model checking of timed automata. In: Margaria, T., Yi, W. (eds.) TACAS 2001. LNCS, vol. 2031, pp. 189–203. Springer, Heidelberg (2001)
9. MiniSat (2006), `http://www.cs.chalmers.se/Cs/Research/FormalMethods/MiniSat`
10. Peled, D.: All from one, one for all: on model checking using representatives. In: Courcoubetis, C. (ed.) CAV 1993. LNCS, vol. 697, pp. 9409–9423. Springer, Heidelberg (1993)
11. Penczek, W., Woźna, B., Zbrzezny, A.: Bounded model checking for the universal fragment of CTL. Fundamenta Informaticae 51(1-2), 135–156 (2002)
12. Bruyère, V., Raskin, J.-F.: Real-time model-checking: Parameters everywhere. In: Pandya, P.K., Radhakrishnan, J. (eds.) FSTTCS 2003. LNCS, vol. 2914, pp. 100–111. Springer, Heidelberg (2003)
13. Woźna, B.: ACTL* properties and bounded model checking. In: Czaja, L. (ed.) Proc. of the Int. Workshop on Concurrency, Specification and Programming (CS&P 2003), vol. 2, pp. 591–605. Warsaw University (2003)
14. Zbrzezny, A.: Improving the translation from ECTL to SAT. Fundamenta Informaticae 85(1-4), 513–531 (2008)

Appendix 1

Let η be a linear expression. In what follows, by $Parameters(\eta)$ we denote the set of all the parameter variables present in η. If $i \in \mathbb{N}$ and Θ is a parameter variable, then by v^i_Θ we denote a valuation satisfying $v^i_\Theta(\Theta) = i$. A formula $\alpha(\Theta)$ containing exactly one free variable Θ is called a *one–parameter* formula.

Lemma 1. *Let M be a model and $Q_{1\Theta_1 \leq c_1} \cdots Q_{n\Theta_n \leq c_n} \alpha(\Theta_1, \ldots, \Theta_n)$ be a sentence of* PRTCTL, *where $Q_i \in \{\forall, \exists\}$, $c_i \in \mathbb{N}$, and $\alpha(\Theta_1, \ldots, \Theta_n) \in$* vRTCTL. *Then $M, s \models Q_{1\Theta_1 \leq c_1} \cdots Q_{n\Theta_n \leq c_n} \alpha(\Theta_1, \ldots, \Theta_n)$ iff $M, s \models Q_{1\Theta_1 \leq min(c_1, |M|)} \cdots Q_{n\Theta_n \leq min(c_n, |M|)} \alpha(\Theta_1, \ldots, \Theta_n)$.*

Proof. Throughout this proof we assume $k = |M|$. Let ψ be a formula of vRTCTL. Let v be a parameter valuation such that $v(\Theta') > k$ for some parameter Θ'. Define another parameter valuation v' such that:

$$v'(\Theta) = \begin{cases} v(\Theta), & \text{for } \Theta \neq \Theta' \\ k, & \text{for } \Theta = \Theta'. \end{cases} \tag{1}$$

We prove that $M, s \models_v \psi \iff M, s \models_{v'} \psi$ for each state $s \in S$. The proof goes by structural induction. The cases of $\psi = p$, $\psi = \neg\alpha$, $\psi = \alpha \vee \gamma$, $\psi = \alpha \wedge \gamma$ and $\psi = EX\alpha$ are easy to prove.

Let us focus on proving $M, s \models_v EG^{\leq\eta}\alpha \iff M, s \models_{v'} EG^{\leq\eta}\alpha$. If $\Theta' \notin Parameters(\eta)$, then the equivalence is valid by $v(\eta) = v'(\eta)$ and the inductive assumption. Assume that $\Theta' \in Parameters(\eta)$, and π is a path such that $\pi(0) = s$ and $M, \pi(i) \models_v \alpha$ for all $i \leq v(\eta)$. As $v'(\eta) \geq k$, there exists an $l \leq v'(\eta)$ such that $\pi(l) = \pi(n)$ for some $n < l$. Therefore we define the path π' as follows:

$$\pi'(i) = \begin{cases} \pi(i), & \text{for } i < l \\ \pi(n + (i - l) mod (l - n)), & \text{for } i \geq l. \end{cases} \tag{2}$$

As $\pi'(0) = \pi(0) = s$ and $M, \pi'(i) \models_{v'} \alpha$ for all $i \in \mathbb{N}$, by the inductive assumption we obtain $M, s \models_{v'} EG^{\leq\eta}\alpha$.

Now, let us move to the case of $\psi = E\alpha U^{\leq\eta}\beta$. We deal with the case of $\Theta' \in Parameters(\eta)$ only. If $M, s \models_v E\alpha U^{\leq\eta}\beta$, then there exists a path π with $\pi(0) = s$, such that for some $i \leq v(\eta)$ we have that $M, \pi(i) \models_v \beta$ and $M, \pi(j) \models_v \alpha$ for all $j < i$. If $i \leq v'(\eta)$, then $M, s \models_{v'} E\alpha U^{\leq\eta}\beta$ follows immediately from the inductive assumption. If $i > v'(\eta)$, then notice that from $v'(\eta) \geq k$ we get $i > k$. Therefore, there exist $n, m \in \mathbb{N}$ such that $n < m \leq i$ and $\pi(n) = \pi(m)$. By removing the subsequence $\pi(n+1), \ldots, \pi(m)$ from π we obtain a new path consisting of the states $\pi(0), \pi(1), \ldots, \pi(n), \pi(m+1), \pi(m+2), \ldots$. By consecutive elimination of such subsequences we eventually arrive at the path π' such that $\pi'(0) = s$, $\pi'(j) \models_v \beta$ for some $j < k$ and $\pi'(l) \models_v \alpha$ for all $l < j$. Therefore, by the inductive assumption we obtain $M, s \models_{v'} E\alpha U^{\leq\eta}\beta$.

By induction on the number of parameters we get that for formulae $\psi \in$ vRTCTL, the parameter valuation v and valuation v' defined as $v'(\Theta) = min(v(\Theta), k)$ for all the parameters Θ, we have $M, s \models_v \psi \iff M, s \models_{v'} \psi$.

In order to prove the general case, consider a one–parameter vRTCTL formula $g(\Theta)$. We have

$$M, s \models \forall_{\Theta \leq c} g(\Theta) \iff \bigwedge_{0 \leq i \leq c} M, s \models_{v^i_\Theta} g(\Theta).$$

Based on what we have already proven concerning vRTCTL formulae, we can substitute v^i_Θ by $v^i_\Theta[\Theta \leftarrow min(i,k)]$ in the right-hand side of the above formula, obtaining:

$$\bigwedge_{0 \leq i \leq c} M, s \models_{v^i_\Theta[\Theta \leftarrow min(i,k)]} g(\Theta) \iff \bigwedge_{0 \leq i \leq min(c,k)} M, s \models_{v^i_\Theta} g(\Theta).$$

Therefore, we have $M, s \models \forall_{\Theta \leq c} g(\Theta) \iff M, s \models \forall_{\Theta \leq min(c,k)} g(\Theta)$. The equivalence $M, s \models \exists_{\Theta \leq c} g(\Theta) \iff M, s \models \exists_{\Theta \leq min(c,k)} g(\Theta)$ is proven in the similar way. To conclude, notice that for formula of PRTCTL

$$h = Q_{1\Theta_1 \leq min(c_1,k)} \cdots Q_{t\Theta_t \leq min(c_t,k)} f(\Theta_1, \ldots, \Theta_t),$$

where $Q_i \in \{\exists, \forall\}$ and $f \in$ vRTCTL, we can define an one–parameter subformula $\mu(\Theta_1) = Q_{2\Theta_2 \leq min(c_2,k)} \cdots Q_{t\Theta_t \leq min(c_t,k)} f(\Theta_1)$. The thesis of the lemma follows by induction on the number of parameters.

Lemma 2. *Let M_k be the k-model of M, s – a state, v – a parameter valuation, and α – a formula of* vRTECTL. *Then, the following conditions hold:*

1. $\forall_{l \geq k} \big(M_k, s \models_v \alpha$ *implies* $M_l, s \models_v \alpha\big)$,
2. $M_k, s \models_v \alpha$ *implies* $M, s \models_v \alpha$,
3. $M, s \models_v \alpha$ *implies* $M_{|M|}, s \models_v \alpha$.

Proof. We start with the first implication. We omit the basic case of propositional variables and their negations as trivial. Let α, β be formulae satisfying the considered property, then $M_k, s \models_v \alpha \wedge \beta$ iff $M_k, s \models_v \alpha$ and $M_k, s \models_v \beta$, from which by the inductive assumption follows that $M_l, s \models_v \alpha$ and $M_l, s \models_v \beta$ which is equivalent to $M_l, s \models_v \alpha \wedge \beta$. The case of disjunction follows similarly. For the case of $M_k, s \models_v EX\alpha$ let us notice that a finite path π_k in M_k such that $\pi_k(0) = s$ and $M_k, \pi_k(1) \models_v \alpha$ is a prefix of some finite path in M_l, therefore $M_l, s \models_v EX\alpha$. Now, the case of $M_k, s \models_v EG^{\leq \eta}\alpha$ can be divided into two subcases. If $v(\eta) < k$, then define π_l as any finite path in M_l containing π_k as a prefix. If $v(\eta) \geq k$, then there exists an infinite path π along which α holds (see the proof of Lemma 1). Define π_l as a prefix of length l of π. In both the cases α holds along π_l, therefore $M_l, s \models_v EG^{\leq \eta}\alpha$. In the final case of $M_k, s \models_v E\alpha U^{\leq \eta}\beta$ let us notice that if for some path π_k in M_k we have $\pi_k(0) = s$, $M_k, \pi_k(i) \models_v \beta$, $M_k, \pi_k(j) \models_v \alpha$ for all $0 \leq j < i$ and $i \leq v(\eta)$, then the same path is a prefix of some path in M_l satisfying $M_l, s \models_v E\alpha U^{\leq \eta}\beta$.

The second implication is proven by the structural induction, similarly to the above reasoning. The only nontrivial case is when we consider $M_k, s \models_v EG^{\leq \eta}\alpha$. Notice that if $v(\eta) < k$, then a finite path along which α is satisfied up to $v(\eta)$

steps can be extended to an infinite path (due to the fact that the transition relation is total). On the other hand, if $\upsilon(\eta) \geq k$, then the finite path along which α is satisfied contains a loop, and can be transformed into an infinite path by traversing the loop, as in the proof of Lemma 1.

In the proof of the last implication we focus on two modalities, starting from the case of $M, s \models_\upsilon EG^{\leq\eta}\alpha$. If this formula is valid, then there exists an infinite path π in M such that $\pi(0) = s$ and $M, \pi(i) \models_\upsilon \alpha$ for all $0 \leq i \leq \upsilon(\eta)$. There are two possible subcases. We omit the easier subcase when $\upsilon(\eta) \leq |M|$. If $\upsilon(\eta) > |M|$, then the path π contains a loop with a return from position $l \leq |M|$. Therefore, by unwinding a loop in π we can create an infinite path such that α is satisfied in each of its position – also along a prefix of length $|M|$. Considering $M, s \models_\upsilon E\alpha U^{\leq\eta}\beta$, notice that there exists an infinite path π in M such that $\pi(0) = s$ and for some $l \leq \upsilon(\eta)$ we have $M, \pi(l) \models_\upsilon \beta$ and $M, \pi(i) \models_\upsilon \alpha$ for all $0 \leq i < l$. Again, there are two subcases. We omit the easier case of $l \leq |M|$. If $l > |M|$, then there exist $n, m \in \mathbb{N}$ such that $n < m \leq l$ and $\pi(n) = \pi(m)$. By consecutive elimination of blocks of type $\pi(n+1), \ldots, \pi(m)$, as in the proof of Lemma 1, we eventually obtain the path π' such that $\pi'(0) = s$, $\pi'(j) \models_\upsilon \beta$ for some $j \leq |M|$, and $\pi'(i) \models_\upsilon \alpha$ for all $i < j$.

Lemma 3. *Let M be a model, s – a state and α – a* PRTECTL *sentence. Then, the following conditions hold:*

1. $\forall_{l \geq k} \big(M_k, s \models \alpha$ *implies* $M_l, s \models \alpha\big)$,
2. $M_k, s \models \alpha$ *implies* $M, s \models \alpha$,
3. $M, s \models \alpha$ *implies* $M_{|M|}, s \models \alpha$.

Proof. Notice that due to the results of Lemma 1 and Theorem 1 we can assume that all the quantifiers are bounded in α.

Let us focus on the first implication. If α is a closed formula without existential or universal quantifiers, then α can be obtained from some vRTECTL formula ϕ through substitution of parameters by means of some parameter valuation υ. Therefore, as $M_k, s \models \alpha$ iff $M_k, s \models_\upsilon \phi$, then using Lemma 2 we obtain $M_l, s \models_\upsilon \phi$, from which $M_l, s \models \alpha$ follows. Now, assume that $\alpha(\Theta)$ is a one–parameter vRTECTL formula satisfying the property considered. Then

$$M_k, s \models \forall_{\Theta \leq c}\alpha(\Theta) \iff \bigwedge_{0 \leq i \leq c} M_k, s \models_{\upsilon^i_\Theta} \alpha(\Theta) \Rightarrow$$

$$\bigwedge_{0 \leq i \leq c} (M_l, s \models_{\upsilon^i_\Theta} \alpha(\Theta)) \iff M_l, s \models \forall_{\Theta \leq c}\alpha(\Theta).$$

We deal with the existential quantifier in a similar way, noticing that $\min(c, k) \leq \min(c, l)$. The proof follows by induction on the number of quantifiers in a formula. The remaining two implications are proven in the similar manner.

Lemma 5. *Let $\alpha \in$ vRTECTL, M_k be the k-model of M, and υ – a parameter valuation. For any state s present in some path of M_k, $M_k, s \models_\upsilon \alpha$ if and only if there exists a submodel M'_k of M_k such that $M'_k, s \models_\upsilon \alpha$ and $|Path'_k| \leq g_k(\alpha, \upsilon)$.*

Proof. The "if" part follows directly from Lemma 4. For the "only if" part, we use structural induction. The base cases of $M_k, s \models_\upsilon p$ and $M_k, s \models_\upsilon \neg p$ are trivial. Notice that $M_k, s \models_\upsilon \alpha \vee \beta$ iff $M_k, s \models_\upsilon \alpha$ or $M_k, s \models_\upsilon \beta$. From the inductive assumption there is M'_k such that $M'_k, s \models_\upsilon \alpha$ and $|Path'_k| \leq g_k(\alpha, \upsilon)$, or $M'_k, s \models_\upsilon \beta$ and $|Path'_k| \leq g_k(\beta, \upsilon)$. Thus $M'_k, s \models_\upsilon \alpha \vee \beta$ and $|Path'_k| \leq max(g_k(\alpha, \upsilon), g_k(\beta, \upsilon)) = g_k(\alpha \vee \beta, \upsilon)$.

Recall that $M_k, s \models_\upsilon \alpha \wedge \beta$ iff $M_k, s \models_\upsilon \alpha$ and $M_k, s \models_\upsilon \beta$. By the inductive assumption there exist submodels M''_k and M'''_k of M_k such that $M''_k, s \models_\upsilon \alpha, |Path''_k| \leq g_k(\alpha, \upsilon)$ and $M'''_k, s \models_\upsilon \beta, |Path'''_k| \leq g_k(\beta, \upsilon)$. Consider the submodel M'_k such that $Path'_k = Path''_k \cup Path'''_k$, then from Lemma 4 and the inclusions $M''_k \subseteq M'_k, M'''_k \subseteq M'_k$ we obtain $M'_k, s \models_\upsilon \alpha \wedge \beta$. Moreover, $|Path'_k| \leq |Path''_k| + |Path'''_k| \leq g_k(\alpha, \upsilon) + g_k(\beta, \upsilon) = g_k(\alpha \wedge \beta, \upsilon)$.

Now consider the case of $M_k, s \models_\upsilon EX\alpha$. From the definition of bounded semantics we obtain that there is some k–path $\pi_k \in Path_k$, such that $\pi_k(0) = s$ and $M_k, \pi_k(1) \models_\upsilon \alpha$. From the inductive assumption there exists a submodel M''_k such that $M''_k, \pi_k(1) \models_\upsilon \alpha$ and $|Path''_k| \leq g_k(\alpha, \upsilon)$. Define the submodel M'_k having $Path'_k = Path''_k \cup \{\pi_k\}$. Then from $\pi_k \in Path'_k$ and Lemma 4 we obtain $M'_k, \pi_k(1) \models_\upsilon \alpha$, therefore $M'_k, s \models_\upsilon EX\alpha$. Moreover, $|Path'_k| \leq |Path''_k| + 1 \leq g_k(\alpha, \upsilon) + 1 = g_k(EX\alpha, \upsilon)$.

Let us move to the case of $M_k, s \models_\upsilon EG^{\leq \eta}\alpha$. We have to consider two subcases. In the first case of $\upsilon(\eta) \leq k$, there exists a path $\pi_k \in Path_k$ such that $\pi_k(0) = s$ and $M_k, \pi_k(i) \models_\upsilon \alpha$ for all $0 \leq i \leq \upsilon(\eta)$. Let M^i_k denote submodel of M_k such that $M^i_k, \pi_k(i) \models_\upsilon \alpha$ and $|Path^i_k| \leq g_k(\alpha, \upsilon)$ for $0 \leq i \leq \upsilon(\eta)$. Define the submodel M'_k such that $Path'_k = \bigcup_{0 \leq i \leq \upsilon(\eta)} Path^i_k \cup \{\pi_k\}$. Then by Lemma 4 we have $M'_k, \pi_k(i) \models_\upsilon \alpha$ for all $0 \leq i \leq \upsilon(\eta)$, thus $M'_k, s \models_\upsilon EG^{\leq \eta}\alpha$. From the inductive assumption we obtain

$$|Path'_k| \leq \sum_{0 \leq i \leq \upsilon(\eta)} |Path^i_k| + 1 \leq (\upsilon(\eta) + 1) g_k(\alpha, \upsilon) + 1 = g_k(EG^{\leq \eta}\alpha, \upsilon).$$

We deal with the subcase of $\upsilon(\eta) > k$ in a similar way.

In the final case of $M_k, s \models_\upsilon E\alpha U^{\leq \eta}\beta$ there exists a path $\pi_k \in Path_k$ and $0 \leq j < min(\upsilon(\eta), k)$ such that $M_k, \pi_k(j) \models_\upsilon \beta$ and $M_k, \pi_k(i) \models_\upsilon \alpha$ for all $0 \leq i \leq j$. From the inductive assumption there exists a submodel M^j_k satisfying $M^j_k, \pi_k(j) \models_\upsilon \beta$ and $|Path^j_k| \leq g_k(\beta, \upsilon)$ and the submodels M^i_k such that $M^i_k, \pi_k(i) \models_\upsilon \alpha$ for all $0 \leq i < j$ and $|Path^i_k| \leq g_k(\alpha, \upsilon)$. Define M'_k such that $Path'_k = \bigcup_{0 \leq l \leq j} Path^l_k \cup \{\pi_k\}$. Then, by Lemma 4 we have $M'_k, \pi_k(i) \models_\upsilon \alpha$ for all $0 \leq i < j$, and $M'_k, \pi_k(j) \models_\upsilon \beta$. As from the latter follows $M'_k, s \models_\upsilon E\alpha U^{\leq \eta}\beta$ and

$$|Path'_k| \leq \sum_{0 \leq i < j} |Path'_k| + |Path^j_k| + 1 \leq j \cdot g_k(\alpha, \upsilon) + g_k(\beta, \upsilon) + 1$$

$$\leq min(\upsilon(\eta), k) g_k(\alpha, \upsilon) + g_k(\beta, \upsilon) + 1 = g_k(E\alpha U^{\leq \eta}\beta, \upsilon),$$

we conclude the proof of this case and of the lemma.

Lemma 6. *Let β be a* PRTECTL *sentence and M_k be the k-model of M. For any state s present in some path of M_k, $M_k, s \models \beta$ if and only if there exists a submodel M'_k of M_k such that $M'_k, s \models \beta$ and $|Path'_k| \leq f_k(\beta)$.*

Proof. Consider a one–parameter formula $\alpha(\Theta) \in$ vRTECTL, and let $i \in \mathbb{N}$. It follows from Lemma 5 that if $M_k, s \models_{\upsilon^i_\Theta} \alpha(\Theta)$, then there exists a submodel M^i_k such that $M^i_k, s \models_{\upsilon^i_\Theta} \alpha(\Theta)$ and $|Path^i_k| \leq g_k(\alpha, \upsilon^i_\Theta)$. Recall that $M_k, s \models \forall_{\Theta \leq c}\alpha(\Theta)$ iff $M_k, s \models_{\upsilon^i_\Theta} \alpha(\Theta)$ for all $0 \leq i \leq c$. Using the above observation we obtain that $M^i_k, s \models_{\upsilon^i_\Theta} \alpha(\Theta)$ for all $0 \leq i \leq c$, and $|Path^i_k| \leq g_k(\alpha, \upsilon^i_\Theta)$. Define M'_k as a submodel such that $Path'_k = \bigcup_{0 \leq i \leq c} Path^i_k$, then by Lemma 4 we have $M'_k, s \models_{\upsilon^i_\Theta} \alpha(\Theta)$ for all $0 \leq i \leq c$, therefore $M_k, s \models \forall_{\Theta \leq c}\alpha(\Theta)$. Moreover

$$|Path'_k| \leq \sum_{0 \leq i \leq c} |Path^i_k| \leq \sum_{0 \leq i \leq c} g_k(\alpha, \upsilon^i_\Theta) = \sum_{0 \leq i \leq c} f_k(\alpha[\Theta \leftarrow i])$$

$$= f_k(\forall_{\Theta \leq c}\alpha(\Theta)).$$

Similarly, notice that $M_k, s \models \exists_{\Theta \leq c}\alpha(\Theta)$ iff $\bigvee_{0 \leq i \leq min(c,k)} M_k, s \models_{\upsilon^i_\Theta} \alpha(\Theta)$. Therefore if the right side of the above equivalence holds true, then based on Lemma 5 we obtain that for some $0 \leq j \leq min(c, k)$ there exists a submodel M'_k such that $M'_k, s \models_{\upsilon^i_\Theta} \alpha(\Theta)$ and $|Path'_k| \leq g_k(\alpha, \upsilon^i_\Theta)$, from which $M'_k, s \models \exists_{\Theta \leq c}\alpha(\Theta)$ and

$$|Path'_k| \leq max_{i \leq min(c,k)}(g_k(\alpha, \upsilon^i_\Theta) = f_k(\exists_{\Theta \leq c}\alpha(\Theta)).$$

In order to prove the general case, notice that the PRTECTL sentence $h = Q_{1\Theta_1 \leq c_1} \cdots Q_{t\Theta_t \leq c_t} f(\Theta_1, \ldots, \Theta_t)$, where f is a formula of vRTECTL and $Q \in \{\forall, \exists\}$ can be rewritten in a form of a one–parameter formula and use the induction on the number of parameters, similarly as in the proof of Lemma 1.

Appendix 2

Throughout this section by $\mathbb{N}_+$ we denote the set of positive naturals. Let M be a model, α a formula of vRTECTL, and β a subformula of α. By $[\beta]_k^{[\alpha,m,n,A,\upsilon]}$ we denote the propositional formula $[M]_k^{G_k(\alpha,\upsilon)} \wedge [\beta]_k^{[m,n,A,\upsilon]}$.

Theorem 2. *Let M_k be the k-model of M, υ – a parameter valuation, α – a formula of* vRTECTL *containing at least one modality, and s a state. Then, the following equivalence holds: $M_k, s \models_\upsilon \alpha$ iff $[M]_k^{\alpha,\upsilon}$ is satisfiable.*

In order to prove the above theorem, we need the following two lemmas. The first one is a counterpart of Lemma 3.1 from [14], and deals with the correctness of a translation.

Lemma A. *Let M be a model, α – a formula of* vRTECTL, *υ – a parameter valuation, and $k \in \mathbb{N}$. For every subformula β of the formula α, every $A \subseteq G_k(\alpha, \upsilon)$ such that $|A| = g_k(\beta, \upsilon)$, every $(m, n) \in \{(0, 0)\} \cup \{0, \ldots, k\} \times \mathbb{N}_+$, and every state variables valuation V such that $\hat{V}(w_{m,n})$ is a state of M, the following condition holds: if $V \models [\beta]_k^{[\alpha,m,n,A,\upsilon]}$, then $M_k, \hat{V}(w_{m,n}) \models_\upsilon \beta$.*

Proof. The proof is by induction on the complexity of β. Let A, (m,n), and V be as in the thesis of the theorem.

For the base case of $\beta = p$, where p is an atomic proposition, notice that from $V \models [p]_k^{[\alpha,m,n,A,\upsilon]}$ it follows that $V \models p(w_{m,n})$, i.e., $p \in \mathcal{L}(\hat{V}(w_{m,n}))$, therefore $M_k, \hat{V}(w_{m,n}) \models_\upsilon p$. The case of $\beta = \neg p$ is proven in a similar way.

Now let $\beta = \gamma \wedge \phi$, and let $B = \hat{g}_L(A, g_k(\gamma,\upsilon))$, and $C = \hat{g}_R(A, g_k(\phi,\upsilon))$. Then from $V \models [\gamma \wedge \phi]_k^{[\alpha,m,n,A,\upsilon]}$ it follows that $V \models [\gamma]_k^{[\alpha,m,n,B,\upsilon]}$ and $V \models [\phi]_k^{[\alpha,m,n,C,\upsilon]}$. By the inductive argument we obtain that $M_k, \hat{V}(w_{m,n}) \models_\upsilon \gamma$, and $M_k, \hat{V}(w_{m,n}) \models_\upsilon \phi$, thus $M_k, \hat{V}(w_{m,n}) \models_\upsilon \gamma \wedge \phi$. The case of $\beta = \gamma \vee \phi$ follows similarly.

Notice that the sequence $(\hat{V}(w_{0,j}), \ldots, \hat{V}(w_{k,j}))$, where $j \in G_k(\alpha,\upsilon)$, is a k–path, as it satisfies the propositional formula $[M]_k^{G_k(\alpha,\upsilon)}$. In what follows we denote this k–path by π_j. In the case of $\beta = EX\gamma$, we have $V \models [EX\gamma]_k^{[\alpha,m,n,A,\upsilon]}$ iff $V \models [M]_k^{G_k(\alpha,\upsilon)} \wedge H(w_{m,n}, w_{0,min(A)}) \wedge [\gamma]_k^{[1,min(A),h_X(A),\upsilon]}$. The latter means that $\pi_{min(A)}(0) = \hat{V}(w_{m,n})$, and by the inductive argument $M_k, \pi_{min(A)}(1) \models_\upsilon \gamma$, therefore $M_k, \hat{V}(w_{m,n}) \models_\upsilon EX\gamma$.

In the case of $\beta = EG^{\leq \eta}\gamma$ we have to consider two subcases. In the first subcase, when $\upsilon(\eta) > k$, we have $V \models [EG^{\leq \eta}\gamma]_k^{[\alpha,m,n,A,\upsilon]}$ iff:

$$V \models [M]_k^{G_k(\alpha,\upsilon)} \wedge H(w_{m,n}, w_{0,min(A)}) \wedge L_k(min(A)) \wedge \bigwedge_{j=0}^{k} [\gamma]_k^{[\alpha,j,min(A),h_G(A,k)(j),\upsilon]}.$$

Now the k–path $\pi_{min(A)}$ satisfies $\pi_{min(A)}(0) = \hat{V}(w_{m,n})$, by the inductive argument $M_k, \pi_{min(A)}(j) \models_\upsilon \gamma$ for all $0 \leq j \leq k$, and for some $0 \leq i < k$ we have $\pi_{min(A)}(k) \to \pi_{min(A)}(i)$ (the k–path is a loop). Therefore, $M_k, \hat{V}(w_{m,n}) \models_\upsilon EG^{\leq \eta}\gamma$. The second subcase, when $\upsilon(\eta) \leq k$, is proven in a similar way, namely in this subcase $V \models [EG^{\leq \eta}\gamma]_k^{[\alpha,m,n,A,\upsilon]}$ means that:

$$V \models [M]_k^{G_k(\alpha,\upsilon)} \wedge H(w_{m,n}, w_{0,min(A)}) \wedge \bigwedge_{j=0}^{\upsilon(\eta)} [\gamma]_k^{[j,min(A),h_G(A,\upsilon(\eta))(j),\upsilon]}.$$

As previously we have $\pi_{min(A)}(0) = \hat{V}(w_{m,n})$, and $M_k, \pi_{min(A)}(j) \models_\upsilon \gamma$ for all $0 \leq j \leq \upsilon(\eta)$, therefore $M_k, \hat{V}(w_{m,n}) \models_\upsilon EG^{\leq \eta}\gamma$.

The final case is when $\beta = E\gamma U^{\leq \eta}\phi$. If $V \models [E\gamma U^{\leq \eta}\phi]_k^{[\alpha,m,n,A,\upsilon]}$, then:

$$V \models [M]_k^{G_k(\alpha,\upsilon)} \wedge \bigvee_{i=0}^{min(\upsilon(\eta),k)} \Big([\phi]_k^{[i,min(A),h_U(A,min(\upsilon(\eta),k),g_k(\phi,\upsilon))(min(\upsilon(\eta),k)),\upsilon]}$$

$$\wedge \bigwedge_{j=0}^{i-1} [\gamma]_k^{[j,min(A),h_U(A,min(\upsilon(\eta),k),g_k(\phi,\upsilon))(j),\upsilon]}\Big) \wedge H(w_{m,n}, w_{0,min(A)}).$$

Now it suffices to notice that $\pi_{min(A)}$ is such a k–path that $\pi_{min(A)}(0) = \hat{V}(w_{m,n})$, and by the inductive argument there exists $0 \leq j \leq min(\upsilon(\eta),k)$

such that $M_k, \pi_{min(A)}(j) \models_\upsilon \phi$, and $M_k, \pi_{min(A)}(i) \models_\upsilon \gamma$ for all $0 \le i < j$. Therefore $M_k, \hat{V}(w_{m,n}) \models_\upsilon E\gamma U^{\le\eta}\phi$.

The following lemma is a counterpart of Lemma 3.2 [14], and deals with completeness of the translation. By $Var(\psi)$ we denote the set of variables present in a propositional formula ψ.

Lemma B. *Let M be a model, α – a formula of* vRTECTL, *υ – a parameter valuation, and $k \in \mathbb{N}$. For every subformula β of the formula α, every $A \subseteq G_k(\alpha, \upsilon)$ such that $|A| = g_k(\beta, \upsilon)$, every $(m, n) \in \{(0,0)\} \cup \{0, \ldots, k\} \times (\mathbb{N}_+ \setminus A)$, and every state s of M, the following condition holds: if $M_k, s \models_\upsilon \beta$, then there exists a valuation V such that $\hat{V}(w_{m,n}) = s$ and $V \models [\beta]_k^{[\alpha,m,n,A,\upsilon]}$.*

Proof. The proof proceeds by induction on the complexity of β. Let A, (m, n), and V be as in the thesis of the theorem, and s be any state of M.

In the base case of $\beta = p$, where p is an atomic proposition, it suffices to take any valuation V, such that $\hat{V}(w_{m,n}) = s$. As $M_k, s \models_\upsilon p$ means that $p \in \mathcal{L}(\hat{V}(w_{m,n}))$, we have $V \models p(w_{m,n})$, therefore $V \models [p]_k^{[\alpha,m,n,A,\upsilon]}$. The case of $\beta = \neg p$ is proven in a similar way.

Now let us consider the case of $\beta = \gamma \wedge \phi$, and let $B = \hat{g}_L(A, g_k(\gamma, \upsilon))$, and $C = \hat{g}_R(A, g_k(\phi, \upsilon))$. By the inductive argument there exist valuations V_1 and V_2 such that $V_1 \models [\gamma]_k^{[\alpha,m,n,B,\upsilon]}$, $V_2 \models [\phi]_k^{[\alpha,m,n,C,\upsilon]}$, and $V_1(w_{m,n}) = V_2(w_{m,n}) = s$. Now it suffices to notice that $Var([\gamma]_k^{[m,n,B,\upsilon]}) \cap Var([\phi]_k^{[m,n,C,\upsilon]}) = w_{m,n}$, therefore there exists a valuation V such that $V \models [\gamma]_k^{[\alpha,m,n,B,\upsilon]} \wedge [\phi]_k^{[\alpha,m,n,C,\upsilon]}$ which means that $V \models [\gamma \wedge \phi]_k^{[\alpha,m,n,A,\upsilon]}$. The case of $\beta = \gamma \vee \phi$ is proven similarly.

Let us move to the case of $\beta = EX\gamma$. If $M_k, s \models_\upsilon EX\gamma$, then there exists a k–path π_k such that $\pi_k(0) = s$, and $M_k, \pi_k(1) \models_\upsilon \gamma$. By the inductive argument there exists a valuation V_1 such that $\hat{V}_1(w_{1,min(A)}) = \pi_k(1)$, and $V_1 \models [\gamma]_k^{[\alpha,1,min(A),h_X(A)]}$. Notice that $Var([\gamma]_k^{[1,min(A),h_X(A)]})$ contains at most one state variable of form $w_{i,min(A)}$ – namely $w_{1,min(A)}$. Therefore it is possible to find such a valuation V that $\pi_k = (\hat{V}(w_{0,min(A)}), \ldots, \hat{V}(w_{k,min(A)}))$, $\hat{V}(w_{m,n}) = \pi_k(0) = s$, $\hat{V}(w_{1,min(A)}) = \pi_k(1)$ and $V(w_{r,t}) = V_1(w_{r,t})$ for all $w_{r,t} \in Var([\gamma]_k^{[1,min(A),h_X(A)]})$. As this means that $V \models [EX]_k^{[\alpha,m,n,A,\upsilon]}$, we conclude the case.

Now let us consider the case of $\beta = EG^{\le\eta}\gamma$. For all $0 \le j \le min(\upsilon(\eta))$ let us denote $B_j = h_G(A, min(\upsilon(\eta), k))(j)$. If $M_k, s \models_\upsilon EG^{\le\eta}\gamma$, then there exists a k–path π_k such that $\pi_k(0) = s$, and $M_k, \pi(j) \models_\upsilon \gamma$ for all $0 \le j \le min(\upsilon(\eta), k)$. Notice that for all $0 \le j \le min(\upsilon(\eta), k)$ we have $|B_j| = g_k(\gamma, \upsilon)$, and $(j, min(A)) \notin B_j$, thus by the inductive argument there exist such valuations V_j that $V_j \models [\gamma]_k^{[\alpha,j,min(A),B_j,\upsilon]}$ for all $0 \le j \le min(\upsilon(\eta), k)$. Notice that $Var([\gamma]_k^{[r,min(A),B_r,\upsilon]}) \cap Var([\gamma]_k^{[t,min(A),B_t,\upsilon]}) = \emptyset$ for all $0 \le r, t \le min(\upsilon(\eta), k)$ such that $r \neq t$. It means that there exists such a valuation V that $(\hat{V}(w_{0,min(A)}), \ldots, \hat{V}(w_{k,min(A)}))$ is a k–path where for all $0 \le j \le min(\upsilon(\eta), k)$ it holds that $\hat{V}(w_{j,min(A)}) = \pi_k(j)$, and $V(w_{r,t}) = V_j(w_{r,t})$ given that $w_{r,t} \in$

$Var([\gamma]_k^{[j,min(A),B_j,\upsilon]})$. As it is easy to see that $V \models L_k(min(A))$ iff π_k is a loop, the case is proven.

The final case of $\beta = E\gamma U^{\leq\eta}\phi$ is proven similarly to the previous one. From $M_k, s \models_\upsilon E\gamma U^{\leq\eta}\phi$ we obtain the existence of such a k–path π_k that $\pi_k(0) = s$, $M_k, \pi_k(j) \models_\upsilon \phi$ for some $0 \leq j \leq min(\upsilon(\eta), k)$, and $M_k, \pi_k(i) \models_\upsilon \gamma$ for all $0 \leq i < j$. Let us denote $B_j = h_U(A, min(\upsilon(\eta), k), g_k(\phi, \upsilon))(j)$ for all $0 \leq j \leq min(\upsilon(\eta), k)$. As previously, notice that $|B_{min(\upsilon(\eta),k)}| = g_k(\phi, \upsilon)$, $(min(\upsilon(\eta), k), min(A)) \notin B_{min(\upsilon(\eta),k)}$, and $|B_i| = g_k(\gamma, \upsilon)$, $(i, min(A)) \notin B_i$ for all $0 \leq i < min(\upsilon(\eta), k)$. To conclude, use the inductive assumption, and the similar reasoning as in the case of $\beta = EG^{\leq\eta}\gamma$.

Now, in order to obtain the proof of Theorem 2 it suffices to apply both the above lemmas with $(m, n) = (0, 0)$, and $\hat{V}(w_{0,0}) = s$.

SAT-Based (Parametric) Reachability for a Class of Distributed Time Petri Nets*

Wojciech Penczek[1,2], Agata Półrola[3], and Andrzej Zbrzezny[4]

[1] Polish Academy of Sciences, ICS, Ordona 21, 01-237 Warsaw, Poland
[2] University of Podlasie, ICS, Sienkiewicza 51, 08-110 Siedlce, Poland
penczek@ipipan.waw.pl
[3] University of Łódź, FMCS, Banacha 22, 90-238 Łódź, Poland
polrola@math.uni.lodz.pl
[4] Jan Długosz University, IMCS, Armii Krajowej 13/15, 42-200 Częstochowa, Poland
a.zbrzezny@ajd.czest.pl

Abstract. Formal methods - among them the model checking techniques - play an important role in the design and production of both systems and software. In this paper we deal with an adaptation of the bounded model checking methods for timed systems, developed for timed automata, to the case of time Petri nets. We consider distributed time Petri nets and parametric reachability checking, but the approach can be easily adapted to verification of other kinds of properties for which the bounded model checking methods exist. A theoretical description is supported by some experimental results, generated using an extension of the model checker VerICS.

1 Introduction

The process of design and production of both systems and software – among others, the concurrent ones – involves testing whether the product conforms its specification. To this aim, various kinds of formal methods can be applied. One of the possible approaches, widely used and intensively developed, are *model checking techniques*.

In order to perform a formal verification, the system to be tested is usually modelled using a theoretical formalism, e.g., a version of automata, Petri nets, state diagrams etc. Obviously, the kind of the formalism depends on the features of the system to be described. One of the approaches, used to represent concurrent systems with timing dependencies [10,11,20], are *time Petri nets* (TPNs) by Merlin and Farber [21]. After modelling the system in the above way, a suitable verification method is applied.

The main problem to cope with while verifying timed systems is the so-called *state explosion*: in order to check whether the system satisfies a property we usually need to search through its state space, which in most cases is very large due to infinity of the dense time domain. Furthermore, in the case of concurrent systems the size of the state space is likely to grow exponentially when the number of the components increases. So, searching for verification methods which are able to overcome the above problem is an important subject of research.

* Partly supported by the Polish Ministry of Science and Higher Education under the grant No. N N206 258035.

K. Jensen, S. Donatelli, and M. Koutny (Eds.): ToPNoC IV, LNCS 6550, pp. 72–97, 2010.

Bounded model checking (BMC) is an efficient verification method whose main idea consists in considering a model truncated up to a specific depth. In turn, SAT-based BMC verification consists in translating a model checking problem solvable on a fraction of a model into a test of propositional satisfiability, which is then made using a SAT-checker. The method has been successfully applied to verification of both timed and untimed systems [3,4,7,12,16,27,32,36]. In this paper we show how to adapt the SAT-based BMC methods, presented in [27,35,36,38] and developed for timed automata, to the case of time Petri nets. The adaptation exploits, in some sense, a method of translating a time Petri net to a timed automaton, described in [28]. However, we perform no structural translation between these two formalisms, but use directly the transition relation defined by the translation. In order to benefit from the concurrent structure of the system, we focus on *distributed* nets (i.e., sets of communicating processes), and exploit a non-standard approach to their concrete semantics, which consists in associating a clock with each of the processes [28]. In this work we deal with testing whether the system (net) can ever be in a state satisfying certain properties (i.e., with *reachability* checking), but the presented solutions can be also easily adapted to verification of other classes of properties for which SAT-based BMC methods exist (see [23] for a survey). The algorithm has been implemented as an extension of the model checker VerICS [13]. The next topic we dealt with was searching for bounds on which the property tested can be reached (searching for a value of the parameter c in formulas $\mathrm{EF}^{\sim c}p$, corresponding to these considered in [14]). In the final part of the paper we provide some preliminary experimental results.

To our knowledge, no BMC method for time Petri nets has been defined so far, although some solutions for untimed Petri nets exist [16,25]. Therefore, the main contribution of this work consists in showing how to apply and implement for TPNs the above technique of verification (a general idea of the approach has been already sketched in [23], but no details are given there). As a result, we obtain an efficient method of checking reachability, as well as searching for counterexamples for the properties expressible by formulas of the logics ACTL^* and TACTL. Although the adaptation of the BMC methods is almost straightforward, the practical consequences seem to be quite useful.

The rest of the paper is organised as follows: in Sect. 3 we introduce time Petri nets, and the abstraction of their state spaces, i.e., an *extended detailed region graph*. In the further part we sketch the idea of reachability checking using BMC and SAT (Sect. 4), and show its implementation for time Petri nets (Sect. 5). Searching for bounds on time at which a state satisfying a property can be reached (parametric reachability) is considered in Sect. 6. Sections 7 and 8 contain experimental results and concluding remarks.

2 Related Work

The methods of reachability checking for time Petri nets, mostly consisting in building an *abstract model* of the system, are widely studied in the literature [6,5,8,9,15,19]. Detailed region graphs for time Petri nets, based on their standard semantics (i.e., the one associating a clock with each transition of the net) were presented in [22,34]. Some BMC methods for (untimed) Petri nets were described in [16,26]. Parametric verification for time Petri nets was considered in [33].

The current work is a modification and extension of the paper [24] (published in proceedings of a local workshop with the status of a technical report).

3 Time Petri Nets

Let $\mathbb{R}_+$ denote the set of non-negative reals, $\mathbb{Q}$ the set of rationals, and $\mathbb{N}$ ($\mathbb{N}_+$) - the set of (positive) natural numbers. We start with a definition of time Petri nets:

Definition 1. *A time Petri net (TPN, for short) is a six-element tuple* $\mathcal{N}=(P,T,F,m^0,Eft,Lft)$, *where* $P=\{p_1,\ldots,p_{n_P}\}$ *is a finite set of* places, $T=\{t_1,\ldots,t_{n_T}\}$ *is a finite set of* transitions, $F\subseteq(P\times T)\cup(T\times P)$ *is the* flow relation, $m^0\subseteq P$ *is the* initial marking *of* $\mathcal{N}$, *and* $Eft:T\to\mathbb{N}$, $Lft:T\to\mathbb{N}\cup\{\infty\}$ *are functions describing the* earliest *and the* latest firing time *of the transition; where for each* $t\in T$ *we have* $Eft(t)\le Lft(t)$.

For a transition $t\in T$ we define its *preset* $\bullet t=\{p\in P\mid (p,t)\in F\}$ and *postset* $t\bullet=\{p\in P\mid (t,p)\in F\}$, and consider only the nets such that for each transition the preset and the postset are non-empty. We need also the following notations and definitions:

- a *marking* of $\mathcal{N}$ is any subset $m\subseteq P$;
- a transition $t\in T$ is *enabled* at m ($m[t\rangle$ for short) if $\bullet t\subseteq m$ and $t\bullet\cap(m\setminus\bullet t)=\emptyset$; and *leads from* m *to* m', if it is enabled at m, and $m'=(m\setminus\bullet t)\cup t\bullet$. The marking m' is denoted by $m[t\rangle$ as well, if this does not lead to misunderstanding;
- $en(m)=\{t\in T\mid m[t\rangle\}$ is the set of all the transitions enabled at the marking m of $\mathcal{N}$;
- a marking $m\subseteq P$ is *reachable* if there exists a sequence of transitions $t_1,\ldots,t_l\in T$ and a sequence of markings $m_0,\ldots,m_l$ such that $m_0=m^0$, $m_l=m$, and for each $i\in\{1,\ldots,l\}$ $t_i\in en(m_{i-1})$ and $m_i=m_{i-1}[t_i\rangle$;
- a marking m *concurrently enables* two transitions $t,t'\in T$ if $t\in en(m)$ and $t'\in en(m\setminus\bullet t)$;
- a net is *sequential* if no reachable marking of $\mathcal{N}$ concurrently enables two transitions.

It should be mentioned that the time Petri nets defined as above are often called *1-safe* in the literature.

Next, we introduce the notion of a *distributed time Petri net*. The definition is an adaptation of the one from [17]:

Definition 2. *Let* $\mathfrak{I}=\{\mathfrak{i}_1,\ldots,\mathfrak{i}_n\}$ *be a finite ordered set of indices, and let* $\mathfrak{N}=\{N_\mathfrak{i}=(P_\mathfrak{i},T_\mathfrak{i},F_\mathfrak{i},m^0_\mathfrak{i},Eft_\mathfrak{i},Lft_\mathfrak{i})\mid \mathfrak{i}\in\mathfrak{I}\}$ *be a family of 1-safe, sequential time Petri nets (called* processes*), indexed with* $\mathfrak{I}$, *with the pairwise disjoint sets* $P_\mathfrak{i}$ *of places, and satisfying the condition* $(\forall \mathfrak{i}_1,\mathfrak{i}_2\in\mathfrak{I})(\forall t\in T_{\mathfrak{i}_1}\cap T_{\mathfrak{i}_2})$ $(Eft_{\mathfrak{i}_1}(t)=Eft_{\mathfrak{i}_2}(t)\wedge Lft_{\mathfrak{i}_1}(t)=Lft_{\mathfrak{i}_2}(t))$. *A* distributed time Petri net $\mathcal{N}=(P,T,F,m^0,Eft,Lft)$ *is the union of the processes* $N_\mathfrak{i}$, *i.e.,* $P=\bigcup_{\mathfrak{i}\in\mathfrak{I}}P_\mathfrak{i}$, $T=\bigcup_{\mathfrak{i}\in\mathfrak{I}}T_\mathfrak{i}$, $F=\bigcup_{\mathfrak{i}\in\mathfrak{I}}F_\mathfrak{i}$, $m^0=\bigcup_{\mathfrak{i}\in\mathfrak{I}}m^0_\mathfrak{i}$, $Eft=\bigcup_{\mathfrak{i}\in\mathfrak{I}}Eft_\mathfrak{i}$, *and* $Lft=\bigcup_{\mathfrak{i}\in\mathfrak{I}}Lft_\mathfrak{i}$.

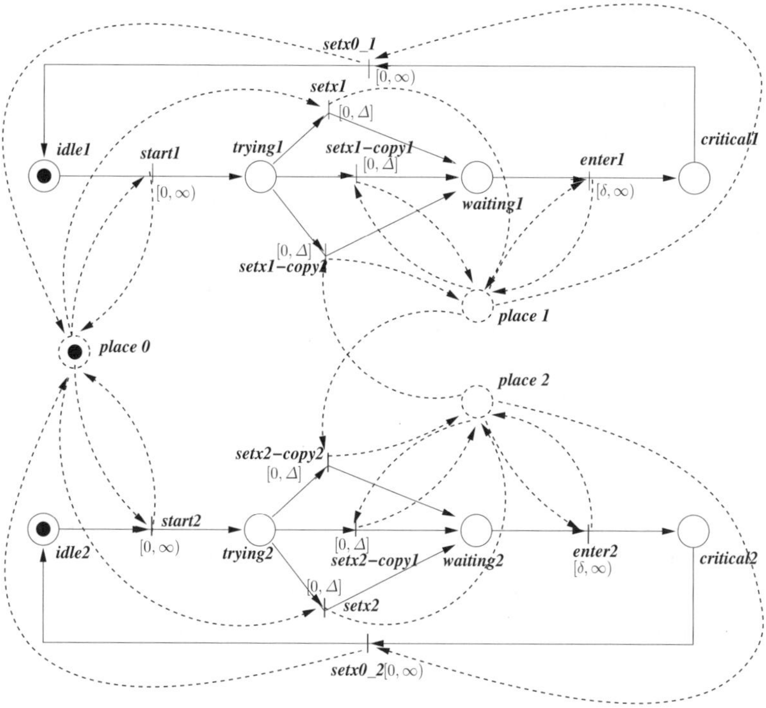

Fig. 1. A net for Fischer's mutual exclusion protocol for $n = 2$

Notice that the function $Eft_{\mathfrak{i}_1}$ ($Lft_{\mathfrak{i}_1}$) coincides with $Eft_{\mathfrak{i}_2}$ ($Lft_{\mathfrak{i}_2}$, resp.) for the joint transitions of each two processes $\mathfrak{i}_1$ and $\mathfrak{i}_2$. The interpretation of such a system is a collection of sequential, non-deterministic processes with communication capabilities (via joint transitions).

An example of a distributed TPN (Fischer's mutual exclusion protocol[1]) is shown in Fig. 1. The net consists of three communicating processes with the sets of places $P_i = \{idle_i, trying_i, enter_i, critical_i\}$ for $i = 1, 2$, and $P_3 = \{place0, place1, place2\}$. All the transitions of the process N_1 and all the transitions of the process N_2 are joint with the process N_3.

In what follows, we consider distributed nets only, and assume that their initial markings contain exactly one place of each of the processes of the net, and that all their processes are *state machines* (i.e., for each $\mathfrak{i} \in \mathfrak{I}$ and each $t \in T_\mathfrak{i}$, $| \bullet t| = |t \bullet | = 1$). This implies that in any marking of $\mathcal{N}$ there is exactly one place of each process. It is important to mention that a large class of distributed nets can be decomposed to satisfy the above requirement [18]. Moreover, for $t \in T$ we define $\mathcal{IV}(t) = \{\mathfrak{i} \in \mathfrak{I} \mid \bullet t \cap P_\mathfrak{i} \neq \emptyset\}$, and say that a process $N_\mathfrak{i}$ is *involved in a transition* t iff $\mathfrak{i} \in \mathcal{IV}(t)$.

[1] The system consists of some (here two) processes trying to enter their critical sections, and a process used to coordinate their access. It is parameterised by the time-delay constants δ and Δ, whose relation influences preservation of the mutual exclusion property (see Sec. 7).

3.1 Concrete State Spaces and Models

The current state of the net is given by its marking and the time passed since each of the enabled transitions became enabled (which influences the future behaviour of the net). Thus, a *concrete state* σ of a distributed TPN $\mathcal{N}$ can be defined as an ordered pair $(m, clock)$, where m is a marking, and $clock : \mathfrak{I} \rightarrow \mathbb{R}_+$ is a function which for each index $\mathfrak{i}$ of a process of $\mathcal{N}$ gives the time elapsed since the marked place of this process became marked most recently [28]. The set of all the concrete states is denoted by Σ. The initial state of $\mathcal{N}$ is $\sigma^0 = (m^0, clock^0)$, where m^0 is the initial marking, and $clock^0(\mathfrak{i}) = 0$ for each $\mathfrak{i} \in \mathfrak{I}$.

For $\delta \in \mathbb{R}_+$, let $clock + \delta$ denote the function given by $(clock + \delta)(\mathfrak{i}) = clock(\mathfrak{i}) + \delta$, and let $(m, clock) + \delta$ denote $(m, clock + \delta)$. The states of $\mathcal{N}$ can change when the time passes or a transition fires. In consequence, we introduce a labelled timed consecution relation $\rightarrow_c \subseteq \Sigma \times (T \cup \mathbb{R}_+) \times \Sigma$ given as follows:

- In a state $\sigma = (m, clock)$ a time $\delta \in \mathbb{R}_+$ can pass leading to a new state $\sigma' = (m, clock + \delta)$ (denoted $\sigma \xrightarrow{\delta}_c \sigma'$) iff for each $t \in en(m)$ there exists $\mathfrak{i} \in \mathcal{IV}(t)$ such that $clock(\mathfrak{i}) + \delta \leq Lft(t)$ (*time-successor relation*);
- In a state $\sigma = (m, clock)$ a transition $t \in T$ can fire leading to a new state $\sigma' = (m', clock')$ (denoted $\sigma \xrightarrow{t}_c \sigma'$) if $t \in en(m)$, for each $\mathfrak{i} \in \mathcal{IV}(t)$ we have $clock(\mathfrak{i}) \geq Eft(t)$, and there is $\mathfrak{i} \in \mathcal{IV}(t)$ such that $clock(\mathfrak{i}) \leq Lft(t)$. Then, $m' = m[t\rangle$, and for all $\mathfrak{i} \in \mathfrak{I}$ we have $clock'(\mathfrak{i}) = 0$ if $\mathfrak{i} \in \mathcal{IV}(t)$, and $clock'(\mathfrak{i}) = clock(\mathfrak{i})$ otherwise (*action-successor relation*).

Intuitively, the time-successor relation does not change the marking of the net, but increases the clocks of all the processes, provided that no enabled transition becomes disabled by passage of time (i.e., for each $t \in en(m)$ the clock of at least one process involved in the transition does not exceed $Lft(t)$). Firing of a transition t takes no time - the action-successor relation does not increase the clocks, but only sets to zero the clocks of the involved processes (note that each of these processes contains exactly one input and one output place of t, as the processes are state machines); and is allowed provided that t is enabled, the clocks of all the involved processes are greater than $Eft(t)$, and there is at least one such process whose clock does not exceed $Lft(t)$.

Then, we define a *timed run* of $\mathcal{N}$ starting at a state $\sigma_0 \in \Sigma$ (σ_0-*run*) as a maximal sequence of concrete states, transitions and time passings $\rho = \sigma_0 \xrightarrow{\delta_0}_c \sigma_0 + \delta_0 \xrightarrow{t_0}_c \sigma_1 \xrightarrow{\delta_1}_c \sigma_1 + \delta_1 \xrightarrow{t_1}_c \sigma_2 \xrightarrow{\delta_2}_c \ldots$, where $\sigma_i \in \Sigma$, $t_i \in T$ and $\delta_i \in \mathbb{R}_+$ for all $i \in \mathbb{N}$. A state $\sigma_* \in \Sigma$ is *reachable* if there exists a σ^0-run ρ and $i \in \mathbb{N}$ such that $\sigma_* = \sigma_i + \delta_i$, where $\sigma_i + \delta_i$ is an element of ρ. The set of all the reachable states of $\mathcal{N}$ is denoted by $Reach_{\mathcal{N}}$.

Given a set of propositional variables PV, we introduce a *valuation function* $V_c : \Sigma \rightarrow 2^{PV}$ which assigns the same propositions to the states with the same markings. We assume the set PV to be such that each $q \in PV$ corresponds to exactly one place $p \in P$, and use the same names for the propositions and the places. The function V_c is defined by $p \in V_c(\sigma) \Leftrightarrow p \in m$ for each $\sigma = (m, \cdot)$. The structure $M_c(\mathcal{N}) =$

$((T \cup \mathbb{R}_+, \Sigma, \sigma^0, \to_c), V_c)$ is called a *concrete (dense) model of* $\mathcal{N}$. It is easy to see that concrete models are usually infinite[2].

The concrete model $M_c(\mathcal{N})$ defined above involves timed steps of arbitrary length. However, it can be proven that without loss of generality one can consider a model with a restricted set of timed labels, i.e. $\widetilde{M}_c(\mathcal{N}) = ((T \cup [0, c_{max}(\mathcal{N}) + 1], \Sigma, \sigma^0, \to_r), V_c)$, where by $c_{max}(\mathcal{N})$ we mean the greatest finite value of Eft and Lft of the net $\mathcal{N}$. In order to show that $\widetilde{M}_c(\mathcal{N})$ preserves the behaviours of the net, we shall prove that it is *bisimulation equivalent* with $M_c(\mathcal{N})$, where the bisimulation equivalence is defined in the following way:

Definition 3. *Let* $M = ((L, S, s_0, \to), V)$ *and* $M' = ((L', S', s'_0, \to'), V')$ *be two models of a time Petri net* $\mathcal{N}$. *A relation* $\rightsquigarrow_s \subseteq S' \times S$ *is a* simulation *from* M' *to* M *if the following conditions hold:*

- $s'_0 \rightsquigarrow_s s_0$,
- *for each* $s \in S$ *and* $s' \in S'$, *if* $s' \rightsquigarrow_s s$, *then* $V(s) = V'(s')$, *and for every* $s_1 \in S$ *such that* $s \xrightarrow{l} s_1$ *for some* $l \in L$, *there is* $s'_1 \in S'$ *such that* $s' \xrightarrow{l'}{}' s'_1$ *for some* $l' \in L'$ *and* $s'_1 \rightsquigarrow_s s_1$.

The model M' simulates M *(*$M' \rightsquigarrow_s M$*) if there is a simulation from* M' *to* M. *Two models* M *and* M' *are called* bisimulation equivalent *if* $M' \rightsquigarrow_s M$ *and* $M (\rightsquigarrow_s)^{-1} M'$, *where* $(\rightsquigarrow_s)^{-1}$ *is the inverse of* $\rightsquigarrow_s$.

Let $c_{\mathbf{m1}}$ denote the value $c_{max}(\mathcal{N}) + 1$. Then, we can prove the following lemma:

Lemma 1. *For a given distributed time Petri net* $\mathcal{N}$ *the models* $M_c(\mathcal{N}) = ((T \cup \mathbb{R}_+, \Sigma, \sigma^0, \to_c), V_c$ *and* $\widetilde{M}_c(\mathcal{N}) = (T \cup [0, c_{\mathbf{m1}}], \Sigma, \sigma^0, \to_r), V_c)$ *are bisimulation equivalent.*

A proof can be found in the appendix.

3.2 Extended Detailed Region Graph

In order to deal with countable structures instead of uncountable ones, we introduce *extended detailed region graphs* for distributed TPNs. They correspond to the well-known graphs defined for timed automata in [1] and adapted for time Petri nets [22,34], but involve disjunctions of constraints, the reflexive transitive closure of the time successor of [1], and make no use of the maximal constant appearing in the invariants and enabling conditions. To do this, we assign a clock to each of the processes of a net.

Given a distributed time Petri net $\mathcal{N}$ whose processes are indexed with a set of indices $\mathfrak{I}$ with $|\mathfrak{I}| = n$ for some $n \in \mathbb{N}_+$. Let $\mathcal{X} = \{x_1, \ldots, x_n\}$ be a finite set of real-valued variables, called *clocks*. A *clock valuation* on $\mathcal{X}$ is a n-tuple $v \in \mathbb{R}^n_+$. The value of a clock $x_\mathfrak{i}$ in v is denoted by $v(x_\mathfrak{i})$. For a valuation v and a subset of clocks $X \subseteq \mathcal{X}$, by $v[X := 0]$ we denote the valuation v' such that $v'(x) = 0$ for all $x \in X$, and $v'(x) = v(x)$ for all $x \in \mathcal{X} \setminus X$. Moreover, for some $\delta \in \mathbb{R}_+$, by $v + \delta$ we denote the

[2] Finite concrete models are e.g. these for nets in which for each transition t it holds $Eft(t) = Lft(t) = 0$.

valuation v' such that $v'(x) = v(x) + \delta$ for all $x \in \mathcal{X}$. The set $\mathcal{C}_\mathcal{X}$ of *clock constraints* over $\mathcal{X}$ is defined by the following grammar:

$$\mathfrak{cc} := \mathit{true} \mid x_\mathfrak{i} \sim c \mid \mathfrak{cc} \wedge \mathfrak{cc} \mid \mathfrak{cc} \vee \mathfrak{cc},$$

where $x_\mathfrak{i} \in \mathcal{X}$, $\sim \in \{\leq, <, =, >, \geq\}$ and $c \in \mathbb{N}$. A valuation v *satisfies* a constraint $\mathfrak{cc} \in \mathcal{C}_\mathcal{X}$ (denoted $v \models \mathfrak{cc}$) iff

- $\mathfrak{cc}$ is of the form true,
- $v(x_\mathfrak{i}) \sim c$, and $\mathfrak{cc}$ is of the form $x_\mathfrak{i} \sim c$,
- $v \models \mathfrak{cc}_1 \ \wedge \ v \models \mathfrak{cc}_2$, and $\mathfrak{cc}$ is of the form $\mathfrak{cc}_1 \wedge \mathfrak{cc}_2$,
- $v \models \mathfrak{cc}_1 \ \vee \ v \models \mathfrak{cc}_2$, and $\mathfrak{cc}$ is of the form $\mathfrak{cc}_1 \vee \mathfrak{cc}_2$.

The set of clock valuations satisfying a given constraint $\mathfrak{cc}$ is denoted by $[\![\mathfrak{cc}]\!]$ ($[\![\mathfrak{cc}]\!] \subseteq \mathbb{R}^n_+$).

We assume the clock valuations to be such that for any concrete state $\sigma = (m, \mathit{clock})$, for each $\mathfrak{i} \in \mathfrak{I}$ we have $v(x_\mathfrak{i}) = \mathit{clock}(\mathfrak{i})$. Thus, the clock constraint expressing the conditions under which the net can be in a marking m (the *marking invariant*) can be written as

$$\mathit{inv}(m) = \bigwedge_{t \in en(m) \text{ s.t. } Lft(t) < \infty} \ \bigvee_{\mathfrak{i} \in \mathcal{IV}(t)} x_\mathfrak{i} \leq Lft(t),$$

if $\{t \in T \mid t \in en(m) \wedge Lft(t) < \infty\} \neq \emptyset$, and as $\mathit{inv}(m) = \mathit{true}$ otherwise, which intuitively means that staying in m is allowed as long as for each enabled transition t with finite latest firing time there is a process $N_\mathfrak{i}$, involved in this transition, whose clock is not greater than $Lft(t)$ (and therefore t has not been disabled by passage of time). Moreover, for a marking m and a transition $t \in en(m)$ we define the constraint

$$\mathit{fire}_t(m) = \bigwedge_{\mathfrak{i} \in \mathcal{IV}(t)} x_\mathfrak{i} \geq Eft(t)$$

which expresses the condition under which t can be fired at m (note that the marking invariant, which obviously holds if $\mathcal{N}$ is in the marking m, implies that at least one process involved in t has the value of its clock not greater than $Lft(t)$). Given a marking m and $t \in en(m)$, firing t at m results in assigning the value 0 to the clocks belonging to the set

$$\mathit{reset}(m,t) = \{x_\mathfrak{i} \in \mathcal{X} \mid \mathfrak{i} \in \mathcal{IV}(t)\}.$$

Having all the above components, we can introduce the extended detailed region graph for $\mathcal{N}$. Let $\mathcal{C}_\mathcal{N} \subseteq \mathcal{C}_\mathcal{X}$ be a non-empty set of constraints defined by

$$\mathfrak{cc} := x_\mathfrak{i} \geq Eft(t) \mid x_\mathfrak{i} \leq Lft(t') \mid \mathfrak{cc} \wedge \mathfrak{cc},$$

where $x_\mathfrak{i} \in \mathcal{X}$, and, for a given $i \in \mathfrak{I}$, $t \in T_\mathfrak{i}$ and $t' \in T_\mathfrak{i} \cap \{t \in T \mid Lft(t) < \infty\}$. Moreover, let $\mathit{frac}(a)$ denote the fractional part of a number $a \in \mathbb{R}_+$, and $\lfloor a \rfloor$ denote its integral part. Then, we define equivalence classes of clock valuations [39]:

Definition 4. *For two clock valuations $v, v' \in \mathbb{R}^n_+$, $v \simeq_\mathcal{N} v'$ iff for all $x, x' \in \mathcal{X}$ the following conditions are met:*

1. $\lfloor v(x) \rfloor = \lfloor v'(x) \rfloor$,
2. $frac(v(x)) = 0$ *iff* $frac(v'(x)) = 0$,
3. $frac(v(x)) < frac(v(x'))$ *iff* $frac(v'(x)) < frac(v'(x'))$.

The last condition implies that $frac(v(x)) = frac(v(x'))$ iff $frac(v'(x)) = frac(v'(x'))$.

We call the equivalence classes of the relation $\simeq_{\mathcal{N}}$ *(extended) detailed zones* for $\mathcal{X}$, and denote the set of all of them by $DZ(n)$. It is easy to see from the definition of $\simeq_{\mathcal{N}}$ that the number of extended detailed zones is countable, and that for each $\mathfrak{cc} \in \mathcal{C}_{\mathcal{N}}$ and each $Z \in DZ(n)$ either $v \models \mathfrak{cc}$ for all $v \in Z$, or $v \not\models \mathfrak{cc}$ for all $v \in Z$. We say that $Z \in DZ(n)$ *satisfies a clock constraint* $\mathfrak{cc} \in \mathcal{C}_{\mathcal{X}}$ (denoted by $Z \models \mathfrak{cc}$) iff we have $v \models \mathfrak{cc}$ for each $v \in Z$. Given an extended detailed zone $Z \in DZ(n)$, we introduce the operation $Z[X := 0] = \{v[X := 0] \mid v \in Z\}$. Moreover, let $Z^0 = \{v \in \mathbb{R}^n_+ \mid (\forall x \in \mathcal{X})\ v(x) = 0\}$.

By an *(extended detailed) region* we mean a pair (m, Z), where $m \subseteq P$ and $Z \in DZ(n)$. Notice that the set of all the extended detailed regions is countable. Given a concrete state $\sigma = (m', clock')$ we define $\sigma \in (m, Z)$ if $m = m'$ and $v \in Z$, where v is the clock valuation satisfying $v(x_{\mathfrak{i}}) = clock'(\mathfrak{i})$ for all $\mathfrak{i} \in \mathfrak{I}$. Next, we define a countable abstraction of the concrete state space of $\mathcal{N}$ - an *extended detailed region graph*.

Definition 5. *The* extended detailed region graph *for a net $\mathcal{N}$ is a structure $\Gamma(\mathcal{N}) = (T \cup \{\tau\}, W, w^0, \to)$, where $W = 2^P \times DZ(n)$, $w^0 = (m^0, Z^0)$, and the successor relation $\to \subseteq W \times (T \cup \{\tau\}) \times W$, where $\tau \notin T$, is defined in the following way:*

- $(m, Z) \xrightarrow{\tau} (m, Z')$ *iff* $Z, Z' \models inv(m)$ *and for each* $v \in Z$ *there exists* $\delta \in [0, c_{\mathbf{m1}}]$ *such that* $v + \delta \in Z'$ *(*time successor*);*
- *for* $t \in T$, $(m, Z) \xrightarrow{t} (m', Z)$ *iff* $t \in en(m)$, $m' = m[t\rangle$, $Z \models fire_t(m) \wedge inv(m)$, $Z' = Z[reset(m, t) := 0]$, *and* $Z' \models inv(m')$ *(*action successor*).*

By an abstract model *based on $\Gamma(\mathcal{N})$ we mean a structure $M_\Gamma(\mathcal{N}) = (\Gamma(\mathcal{N}), V)$, where for each $w \in W$ and each $\sigma \in w$ we have $V(w) = V_c(\sigma)$.*

Notice that the definition of $\xrightarrow{\tau}$ is correct: in spite of a possibly non-convex form of $[\![inv(m)]\!]$, its definition ensures that if $Z, Z' \in DZ(n)$, $Z, Z' \models inv(m)$ and $(m, Z) \xrightarrow{\tau} (m, Z')$, then for any other $Z'' \in DZ(n)$ s.t. $(m, Z) \xrightarrow{\tau} (m, Z'')$ and $(m, Z'') \xrightarrow{\tau} (m, Z')$ (i.e., for a region (m, Z'') "traversed" when the time passes between (m, Z) and (m, Z')) the condition $Z'' \models inv(m)$ is satisfied as well. This follows from the fact that if in the zone Z some $x_{\mathfrak{i}} \in \mathcal{X}$ satisfies the condition $v(x_{\mathfrak{i}}) > Lft(t)$, then the same holds also for all the time successors of (m, Z), and, on the other hand, if it satisfies $v(x_{\mathfrak{i}}) \leq Lft(t)$ and this condition is violated for some Z'' s.t. $(m, Z) \xrightarrow{\tau} (m, Z'')$, then there is no Z' s.t. $(m, Z'') \xrightarrow{\tau} (m, Z')$ for which it holds again.

In order to show that the model $M_\Gamma(\mathcal{N})$ preserves the behaviours of the net, we shall prove the following lemma:

Lemma 2. *For a given distributed time Petri net $\mathcal{N}$ the models $\widetilde{M}_c(\mathcal{N}) = ((T \cup [0, c_{\mathbf{m1}}], \Sigma, \sigma^0, \to_r), V_c)$ and $M_\Gamma(\mathcal{N}) = ((T \cup \{\tau\}, W, w^0, \to), V)$ are bisimulation equivalent.*

A proof can be found in the appendix.

4 Testing Reachability via BMC and SAT

The reachability problem for a system S consists in checking, given a property p, whether S can ever be in a state where p holds (which can be described by the CTL formula EFp - "there exists a path s.t. at that path the property p finally holds"). The property is expressed in terms of propositional variables. In the case the system S is represented by a time Petri net $\mathcal{N}$, the propositions correspond to the set of its places P. Therefore, the reachability verification can be translated to testing whether the set $Reach_{\mathcal{N}}$ contains a state whose marking includes a given subset of P. Checking this can be performed by an explicit exploration of the concrete state space (model), but due to its infinite size such an approach is usually very inefficient in practice.

If a reachable state satisfying the property p exists, this can be usually proven exploiting a part of the model only. This enables us to apply the bounded model checking approach. The basic idea of testing reachability using BMC consists in searching for a *reachability witness* of a bounded length k (i.e., for a path of a length $k \in \mathbb{N}_+$, called a k*-path*, which leads from the initial state to a state satisfying p). Searching for a reachability witness is performed by generating a propositional formula that is satisfiable iff such a witness exists. Satisfiability of this formula is checked using a SAT-solver.

To apply the above procedure, we represent the states of a model $M(\mathcal{N})$ for a given time Petri net $\mathcal{N}$ as vectors of boolean variables, and express the transition relation of the model in terms of propositional formulas. Then, we *encode* all the k-paths of $M(\mathcal{N})$ starting at its initial state as a propositional formula α_k, and check satisfiability of a formula γ_k which is the conjunction of α_k and a propositional formula expressing that the property p holds at some state of a k-path. The above process is started from $k = 1$, and repeated iteratively up to $k = |M|$. It, however, can be stopped, since if for some k the formula γ_k is satisfiable, then reachability of a state is proven, and no further tests are necessary.

The above method can be inefficient if no state satisfying p exists, since the length of the k-path strongly influences the size of its propositional encoding. Therefore, in order to prove unreachability of a state satisfying p, another solution, shown in [38], is applied. A sketch of the idea is as follows: using the BMC procedures, we search for a longest k-path starting from an arbitrary state of M (a *free path*) such that p holds only in the last state of this path. If such a path π is found, then this means that in order to learn whether a state satisfying p is reachable we need to explore the model only to the depth equal to the length of π.

5 Implementation for Time Petri Nets

In order to apply the above approach to verification of a particular distributed time Petri net $\mathcal{N}$, we deal with a model obtained by a *discretisation* of its extended detailed region graph. The model is of an infinite but countable structure, which, however, is sufficient for BMC (which deals with finite sequences of states only). Below, we show this discretisation, and then encode the transition relation of the model.

5.1 Discretisation of Extended Detailed Region Graphs

Let $\Gamma(\mathcal{N}) = (T \cup \{\tau\}, W, w^0, \rightarrow)$ be the extended detailed region graph for a distributed time Petri net $\mathcal{N}$, and $\mathcal{X}$ be the set of clocks corresponding to its processes. Instead of dealing with the whole extended detailed region graph $\Gamma(\mathcal{N})$, we *discretise* this structure, choosing for each region one or more appropriate representatives. The discretisation scheme is based on the one for timed automata [39], and preserves the qualitative behaviour of the underlying system.

Let n be the number of clocks, and $c_{max}(\mathcal{N})$ be the largest constant appearing in $\mathcal{C}_{\mathcal{N}}$ (i.e., the greatest finite value of Eft and Lft), and let $c_{\mathbf{m1}} = c_{max}(\mathcal{N}) + 1$. For each $m \in \mathbb{N}$, we define

$$\mathbb{D}_m = \{d \in \mathbb{Q} \mid (\exists k \in \mathbb{N})\ d \cdot 2^m = k\},$$

and

$$\mathbb{E}_m = \{e \in \mathbb{Q} \mid (\exists k \in \mathbb{N})\ e \cdot 2^m = k \wedge e \leq c_{\mathbf{m1}}\}.$$

The *discretised clock space* is defined as $\mathbb{D}^n$, where $\mathbb{D} = \bigcup_{m=1}^{\infty} \mathbb{D}_m$. Similarly, the set of possible values of time passings is defined as $\mathbb{E} = \bigcup_{m=1}^{\infty} \mathbb{E}_m$. Such a clock space and the set of lengths of timed steps ensure that for any representative of an extended detailed region there is another representative of this region which can be reached by a time step of a length $e \in \mathbb{E}$. It should be mentioned that such a solution (different than in [24]) allows us to compute precisely the time passed along a k-path, what is important for the algorithms for parametric verification (and was difficult while using the so-called "adjust transitions" of [24]).

The discretised region graphs and models are defined as follows:

Definition 6. *The* extended discretised region graph *based on the extended detailed region graph $\Gamma(\mathcal{N})$, is a structure $\widetilde{\Gamma}(\mathcal{N}) = (T \cup \mathbb{E}, \widetilde{W}, w^0, \rightarrow_d)$, where $\widetilde{W} = 2^P \times \mathbb{D}^n$, $w^0 = (m^0, Z^0)$, and the labelled transition relation $\rightarrow_d \subseteq \widetilde{W} \times (T \cup \mathbb{E}) \times \widetilde{W}$ is defined as*

1. *for $t \in T$, $(m, v) \xrightarrow{t}_d (m', v')$ iff $t \in en(m)$, $m' = m[t\rangle$, $v \models fire_t(m) \wedge inv(m)$, $v' = v[reset(m,t) := 0]$, and $v' \models inv(m')$ (*action transition*);*
2. *for $\delta \in \mathbb{E}$, $(m, v) \xrightarrow{\delta}_d (m, v')$ iff $v' = v + \delta$ and $v, v' \models inv(m)$ (*time transition*).*

Given an abstract model $M_\Gamma(\mathcal{N}) = (\Gamma(\mathcal{N}), V)$ based on $\Gamma(\mathcal{N}) = (T \cup \{\tau\}, W, w^0, \rightarrow)$ and the discretised model $\widetilde{\Gamma}(\mathcal{N})$, we can define a *discretised model* based on $\widetilde{\Gamma}(\mathcal{N})$, which is a structure $\widetilde{M_\Gamma}(\mathcal{N}) = (\widetilde{\Gamma}(\mathcal{N}), \widetilde{V})$, where $\widetilde{V} : \widetilde{W} \rightarrow 2^{PV}$ is a valuation function such that for each $\widetilde{w} \in \widetilde{W}$ being a representative of $w \in W$ we have $\widetilde{V}(\widetilde{w}) = V(w)$. The model has the following property:

Lemma 3. *For a given time Petri net $\mathcal{N}$ the models $M_\Gamma(\mathcal{N}) = (\Gamma(\mathcal{N}), V)$ and $\widetilde{M_\Gamma}(\mathcal{N}) = (\widetilde{\Gamma}(\mathcal{N}), \widetilde{V})$ are bisimulation equivalent.*

A proof can be found in the appendix. From Lemmas 1, 2 and 3 the discretised model is bisimulation equivalent with the concrete one. So, it preserves the behaviours of the net, and can be used for reachability verification.

5.2 Encoding of the Transition Relation of the Discretised Model

In order to apply SAT-based verification methods described in Sec. 4, we need to represent (encode) the discretised model $\widetilde{M}_{\Gamma}(\mathcal{N})$ as a boolean formula. To do that, we assume that each state $w \in \widetilde{W}$ is given in a unique binary form, i.e., $\widetilde{w} \in \{0,1\}^r$, where $r(m)$ is a function of the greatest exponent appearing in the denominators of clock values in $\widetilde{w}$ (see the appendix or [39] for details). The digits in the binary form of w are denoted by $w(1), \ldots, w(r(m))$. Therefore, the elements of $\widetilde{W}$ can be "generically" represented by a vector $\mathbf{w} = (\mathrm{w}[1], \ldots, \mathrm{w}[r(m)])$ of propositional variables (called a *symbolic state*), whose valuation (i.e., assignment of values to the variables) represents w iff for each $j \in \{1, \ldots, r(m)\}$ we have $\mathrm{w}[j] = true$ iff $w(j) = 1$, and $\mathrm{w}[j] = false$ otherwise. Moreover, each k-path in $\widetilde{\Gamma}(\mathcal{N})$ can be represented by a finite sequence $\mathbf{w}_0, \ldots, \mathbf{w}_k$ of symbolic states, and again, such a representation is called a *symbolic k-path.*

In what follows, by *state variables* we mean propositional variables used to encode the states of $\widetilde{\Gamma}(\mathcal{N})$. The set of all the state variables, containing the symbols $true$ and $false$, will be denoted by SV, and the set of all the propositional formulas built over SV - by SF. The elements of SF are called *state formulas.*

In order to encode the transition relation of $\widetilde{M}_{\Gamma}(\mathcal{N})$, we introduce the following functions and propositional formulas:

- $lit : \{0,1\} \times SV \to SF$, which is defined by $lit(0,p) = \neg p$ and $lit(1,p) = p$;
- $I_w(\mathbf{w}) := \bigwedge_{j=1}^{r} lit(w(j), \mathrm{w}[j])$ which is true iff the vector $\mathbf{w}$ represents the state w;
- $\mathbf{T}(\mathbf{w}, \mathbf{w}')$ which is true iff for the states $w, w' \in \widetilde{W}$, represented by vectors $\mathbf{w}$ and $\mathbf{w}'$, respectively, it holds $w \xrightarrow{e}_d w'$ for some $e \in T \cup \mathbb{E}$.

The formula which encodes all the k-paths in $\widetilde{\Gamma}(\mathcal{N})$ starting at the initial state is of the form

$$\alpha_k := I_{w^0}(\mathbf{w}_0) \wedge \bigwedge_{j=0}^{k-1} \mathbf{T}(\mathbf{w}_j, \mathbf{w}_{j+1}),$$

where $\mathbf{w}_0, \ldots, \mathbf{w}_k$ is a symbolic k-path. In practice, we consider k-paths with some restrictions on repetition of the action and time transitions, and on lengths of the time steps (see the appendix for details). Encoding the fact that a state satisfies a given property is straightforward.

6 Parametric Reachability Checking

Besides testing whether a state satisfying a property p is reachable, one can be interested in finding a minimal time in which a state satisfying p can be reached, or finding a minimal time after which p does not hold. To this aim, *parametric reachability checking* can be used.

In order to be able to perform the above verification, we introduce an additional restriction on the nets under consideration, i.e., require they contain no cycle C of transitions such that for each $t \in C$ we have $Eft(t) = 0$ (which guarantees that the

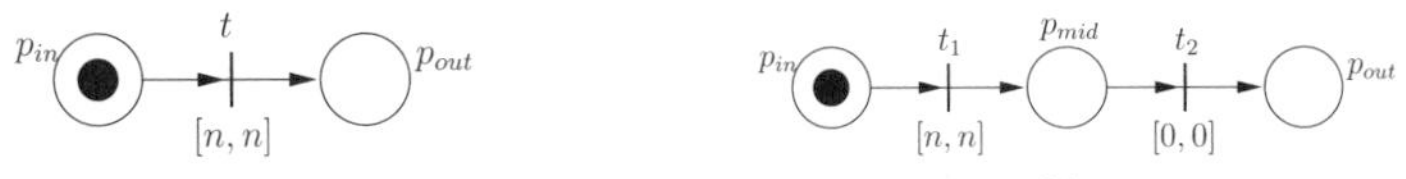

Fig. 2. The processes added to the nets to test parametric reachability

time increases when the net progresses, and is a typical assumption when analysing timed systems). Moreover, we introduce the notations $\mathrm{EF}^{\sim c}p$, with $\sim \in \{\leq, <, >, \geq\}$ and $c \in \mathbb{N}$, which express that a state satisfying p is reached in a time satisfying the constraint in the superscript[3]. The problems intuitively presented at the beginning of the section can be expressed respectively as finding a minimal c such that $\mathrm{EF}^{<c}p$ (or $\mathrm{EF}^{\leq c}p$) holds, and finding a maximal c such that $\mathrm{EF}^{>c}p$ (or $\mathrm{EF}^{\geq c}p$) holds.

An algorithm for finding a minimal c such that $EF^{\leq c}p$ holds looks as follows:

1. Using the standard BMC approach, find a reachability witness of minimal length[4];
2. read from the witness the time required to reach p (denoted x). Now, we know that $c \leq \lceil x \rceil$ (where $\lceil \cdot \rceil$ is the *ceiling* function);
3. extend the verified TPN with a new process N, which is composed of one transition t s.t. $Eft(t) = Lft(t) = n$, and two places p_{in}, p_{out} with $\bullet t = \{p_{in}\}$ and $t\bullet = \{p_{out}\}$ (see Fig. 2(a)),
4. set n to $\lceil x \rceil - 1$,
5. Run BMC to test reachability of a state satisfying $p \wedge p_{in}$ in the extended TPN,
6. if such a state is reachable, set $n := n - 1$ and go to 5,
7. if such a state is unreachable, then $c := n + 1$, STOP.

Some comments on the above algorithm are in place. First of all, it should be explained that the BMC method described in Sec. 4 finds a reachability witness of a shortest length (i.e., involving the shortest possible k-path). However, the shortest path is not necessarily that of minimal time. An example can be seen in Fig. 3, where the shortest path leading to the place satisfying the property p_{fin} consists of two time steps and two action steps (i.e., passing one unit of time, then firing t_2, passing 10 time units and then firing t_4), whereas minimal time of reaching such a state is 3, which corresponds to firing t_1, t_3 and t_5, each of them preceded by passing one unit of time. Due to this, after finding a reachability witness for p in Step 1 of the algorithm, we test whether p can be reached in a shorter time. Extending the net with a new process allows us to express the requirement that the time at which p is reached is not greater than n ($n \in \mathbb{N}$), since at time n the transition t has to fire, which unmarks the place p_{in}.

The second comment to the algorithm concerns the possible optimisations. Firstly, the algorithm can be optimised by applying one of the well-known searching algorithms instead of decreasing n by one in each step. Secondly, it is easy to see that if BMC finds a reachability witness for p of length k, then a witness for reaching p in a smaller time cannot be shorter than k (if such a witness existed, it would have been found previously).

[3] The full version of the logic, for a discrete semantics and with $\sim$ restricted to $\leq$ only, can be found in [14].

[4] If we cannot find such a witness, then we try to prove unreachability of p.

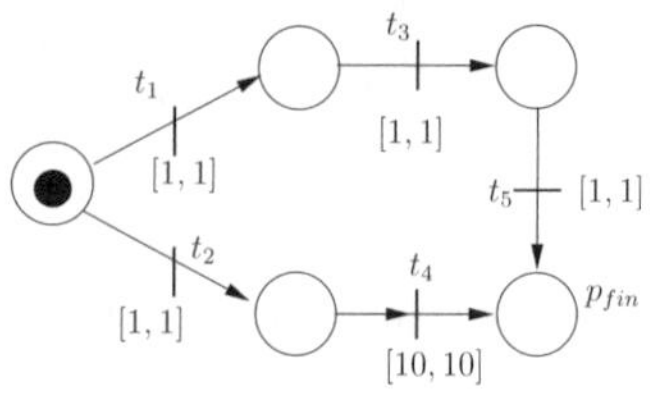

Fig. 3. An example net

Thus, in Step 5 of the algorithm the BMC method can start with k equal to the length of the witness found in the previous run, instead of with $k = 1$.

Finally, Step 7 of the algorithm should be explained. In order to decide that no state satisfying $p \wedge p_{in}$ is reachable, we should either prove unreachability of that state using the method of [38], or to find an upper bound on the length of the k-paths such that unreachability of $p \wedge p_{in}$ on the paths up to this length allows us to decide that no state of interest is reachable. We can do the latter in some cases only, i.e., when some restrictions on the nets considered are assumed. This is specified by the following two lemmas:

Lemma 4. *If a net $\mathcal{N}$ contains no transition t with $Eft(t) = 0$, then the length of a reachability witness for $\mathrm{EF}^{\leq c}p$, in which time- and action steps alternate, is bounded by $2 \cdot c$.*

Proof. We make use of the result of [29], which states that each reachable marking of a TPN can be reached on a path whose time steps are of integer values only. Since from the structure of the net and from the structure of the path we have that zero-time steps are not allowed, the shortest time steps are of length one. The bound $2c$ is then straightforward.

Lemma 5. *Let $\mathcal{N}$ be a distributed net consisting of n processes $N_\mathfrak{i} = (P_\mathfrak{i}, T_\mathfrak{i}, F_\mathfrak{i}, m_\mathfrak{i}^0, Eft_\mathfrak{i}, Lft_\mathfrak{i})$ ($\mathfrak{i} \in \mathfrak{I} = \{1, \ldots, n\}$), each of which contains no cycle besides (possibly) being a cycle itself and satisfies the condition $\forall t_1, t_2 \in T_\mathfrak{i}\ (\bullet t_1 \cap P_\mathfrak{i} = \bullet t_2 \cap P_\mathfrak{i} \iff t_1 \bullet \cap P_\mathfrak{i} = t_2 \bullet \cap P_\mathfrak{i})$. The length of a reachability witness for $\mathrm{EF}^{\leq c}p$, in which time- and action steps alternate, is bounded by $K = 2 \cdot \Sigma_{\mathfrak{i}=1}^{n} z_\mathfrak{i}$, where each $z_\mathfrak{i}$, for $\mathfrak{i} \in \mathfrak{I}$, is computed according to the following algorithm:*

1. *set $g := 0$, $time := 0$, and $nextTrans$ to such $t \in T_\mathfrak{i}$ that $\bullet t = m_\mathfrak{i}^0$ and $Eft(t) = min(Eft(t') \mid t' \in T_\mathfrak{i} \wedge \bullet t' = m_\mathfrak{i}^0)$,*
2. *do*
   - $*$ *$time := time + Eft(nextTrans)$;*
   - $*$ *if $time \leq c$ then set $g := g + 1$ and $s_g := nextTrans$;*
   - $*$ *set $nextTrans$ to such $t \in T_\mathfrak{i}$ that $\bullet t = s_{g-1}\bullet$ and $Eft(t) = min(Eft(t') \mid t' \in T_\mathfrak{i} \wedge \bullet t' = s_{g-1}\bullet)$,*

   while $time <= c$ and $s_g \bullet \cap P_\mathfrak{i} \neq \emptyset$,

3. *while* $Eft(s_g) = 0$ *and* $(\bullet s_g \cap P_i) \notin Prop(p)$, *where* $Prop(p)$ *is the set of propositions occurring in the property* p, *do* $g := g - 1$;
4. *set* $z_i := g$.

Proof. From the structure of a process of $\mathcal{N}$, we have that the algorithm for z_i computes first the number of transitions which can be executed in time c provided that $\mathcal{N}_i$ proceeds as fast as possible, and then optimises the value obtained by removing a number of final steps which influence neither the time nor reaching the property tested. The length of the path in which time- and action steps alternate is therefore equal to $2z_i$. Taking the sum of these values for all the processes corresponds to considering the worst case, in which all the processes proceed independently, performing as many steps as possible.

An algorithm for finding a minimal c such that $\text{EF}^{<c}p$ holds is similar to the previous one:

1. Using the standard BMC approach, find a reachability witness of minimal length[5];
2. read from the witness the time required to reach p (denoted x). Now, we know that $c \leq \lceil x \rceil$;
3. extend the verified TPN with a new process N, which is composed of two transitions t_1, t_2 s.t. $Eft(t_1) = Lft(t_1) = n$, $Eft(t_2) = Lft(t_2) = 0$, $\bullet t_1 = \{p_{in}\}$, $t_1\bullet = \bullet t_2 = \{p_{mid}\}$ and $t_2\bullet = \{p_{out}\}$ (see Fig. 2(b)),
4. set n to $\lceil x \rceil - 1$,
5. run BMC to test reachability of a state satisfying $p \wedge p_{in}$ in the extended TPN,
6. if such a state is reachable, set $n := n - 1$ and go to 5,
7. if such a state is unreachable, set $n := n + 1$ and run BMC to test reachability of a state satisfying $p \wedge p_{mid}$ in the extended TPN,
8. if such a state is reachable, then $c := n + 1$, STOP,
9. if such a state is unreachable, then $c := n$, STOP.

In this case, the additional process contains the place which can be marked only if the time passed since the net started is equal to n. The algorithm proceeds in the following way: the Steps 1 - 6 (analogous as in the previous algorithm) are aimed at finding a minimal n such that $\text{EF}^{\leq n}p$ holds. Then, it is tested whether p can be reached exactly at time n. Depending on the result of this test, the bound returned is either n or $n+1$ (which follows from the result of [30] stating that the minimal time duration of a transition sequence is an integer value). The improvements to the algorithms, as well as methods of deciding unreachability in Steps 7 and 9, are the same as in the previous case.

The next pair of the algorithms is aimed at finding a minimal time after which no state satisfying p is reachable. This can be done by searching for a maximal c for which $\text{EF}^{\geq c}p$ (or $\text{EF}^{>c}p$) holds. The algorithm for $\text{EF}^{\geq c}p$ is as follows:

1. using a standard BMC approach, test whether there is a k-path π such that p is reachable from its arbitrary state (which is done by testing the condition W specified below),
2. if such a k-path can be found, then no maximal c exists, STOP.

[5] If we cannot find such a witness, then we try to prove unreachability of p.

3. if such a k-path cannot be found then, using the standard BMC approach, find a reachability witness for p of a minimal length[6].
4. read from the witness the time x required to reach p,
5. extend the verified TPN with a new process which is composed of one transition t s.t. $Eft(t) = Lft(t) = n$, and two places p_{in}, p_{out} with $t\bullet = \{p_{out}\}$ and $\bullet t = \{p_{in}\}$,
6. set n to $\lceil x \rceil$, and set an upper bound b ($b \geq n$) on c to be searched for[7],
7. run BMC to test reachability of a state satisfying $p \wedge p_{out}$ in the extended TPN,
8. if such a state is reachable and $n + 1 < b$, then set $n := n + 1$ and go to 7,
9. if such a state cannot be found or $n + 1 \geq b$, then set $c := n - 1$, STOP.

Testing whether there is a k-path s.t. p is reachable from its arbitrary state (testing the condition W) is done by checking whether there is a path which has a loop, and there is a state of this loop at which p holds. In order to ensure that there is no maximal c, we need also the path to be progressive, i.e., such that its loop contains at least one non-zero time step[8].

Again, some optimisations to the algorithm can be introduced. The first one can consist in applying a well-known searching technique instead of increasing n by one in each step. The second is based on an observation that each reachability witness for $\mathrm{EF}^{\geq n}p$ is also a reachability witness for $\mathrm{EF}^{\geq n-1}p$. Thus, no witness for $\mathrm{EF}^{\geq n}p$ can be shorter than the shortest one found for $\mathrm{EF}^{\geq n-1}p$ (if a shorter witness existed, it would have been found while searching for a witness for $\mathrm{EF}^{\geq n-1}p$). Thus, while running Step 7 of the algorithm, we can start with k equal to the length of the witness found in the previous run, instead of with $k = 1$.

It should be noted that, contrary to the former cases, we cannot set any upper bound on the length of k-paths to be tested in Step 9, besides the one which follows from the value b assumed in the algorithm. In this case, computing the bound is done analogously as we shown in the description of the algorithm for $\mathrm{EF}^{\leq c}p$.

An algorithm for checking $EF^{>c}p$ (and searching for a maximal c) is as follows:

1. using a standard BMC approach, test whether there is a k-path π such that p is reachable from its arbitrary state (which is done by testing the condition W),
2. if such a k-path can be found, then no maximal c exists, STOP.
3. if such a k-path cannot be found then, using the standard BMC approach, find a reachability witness for p of a minimal length[9].
4. read from the witness the time x required to reach p,
5. extend the verified TPN with a new process N, which is composed of two transitions t_1, t_2 s.t. $Eft(t_1) = Lft(t_1) = n$, $Eft(t_2) = Lft(t_2) = 0$, $\bullet t_1 = \{p_{in}\}$, $t_1\bullet = \bullet t_2 = \{p_{mid}\}$ and $t_2\bullet = \{p_{out}\}$,

[6] If we cannot find such a k, then we try to prove unreachability of p.

[7] The value b can be also a parameter of the algorithm.

[8] Formally, let π be a k-path, $\pi(i)$ be the i-th state of the path, $\delta_\pi(i, i+1)$ be the time passed while moving from $\pi(i)$ to $\pi(i+1)$, $loop(\pi) = \{h \mid 0 \leq h \leq k \wedge \pi(k) \rightarrow \pi(h)\}$, and $\Pi_k(s)$ be the set of all the k-paths starting at s. The bounded semantics for W is as follows: $s \models W \iff (\exists \pi \in \Pi_k(s))(loop(\pi) \neq \emptyset \wedge (\exists l \in loop(\pi)(\exists l \leq j \leq k)(\pi(j) \models \alpha \wedge \Sigma_{l \leq j < k}\delta_p i(j, j+1) > 0))$.

[9] If we cannot find such a k, then we try to prove unreachability of p.

6. set n to $\lceil x \rceil$, and set an upper bound b ($b \geq n$) on c to be searched for[10],
7. run BMC to test reachability of a state satisfying $p \wedge p_{out}$ in the extended TPN,
8. if such a state is reachable and $n+1 < b$, then set $n := n+1$ and go to 7,
9. if such a state is unreachable or $n+1 > b$, set $n := n-1$ and run BMC to test reachability of $p \wedge p_{mid}$) in the extended TPN,
10. if such a state is reachable, then $c := n-1$, STOP;
11. if such a state is unreachable, then $c := n$, STOP.

The idea behind the algorithm is similar to the previous approaches: first a maximal n for which $\mathrm{EF}^{\geq n}p$ is found, then the algorithm tests whether reaching p at time n is possible. The final result depends on the answer to the latter question.

It should be mentioned that in practice all the above methods are not complete (as the BMC itself is not). It can happen that we are not able to prove unreachability of a state, compute an upper bound on the length of a k-path to be tested, or, in spite of finding such an upper bound, are not able to test the paths up to this length using the resources given. However, the preliminary experiments show that the methods can give quite good results.

7 Experimental Results

The experimental results presented below are preliminary, since some methods mentioned in the previous sections are not represented. We have performed our experiments on the computer equipped with Intel Pentium Dual CPU (2.00 GHz), 2 GB main memory and the operating system Linux 2.6.28. We have tested some distributed time Petri nets for the standard *Fischer's mutual exclusion protocol* (mutex) [2]. The system consists of n time Petri nets, each one modelling a process, plus one additional net used to coordinate their access to the critical sections. A distributed TPN modelling the system is shown in Figure 1, for the case of $n = 2$. *Mutual exclusion* means that no two processes are in their critical sections at the same time. The preservation of this property depends on the relative values of the time-delay constants δ and Δ. In particular, the following holds: "*Fischer's protocol ensures mutual exclusion iff* $\Delta < \delta$".

Our first aim was to check that if $\Delta \geq \delta$, then the mutual exclusion is violated. We considered the case with $\Delta = 2$ and $\delta = 1$. It turned out that the conjunction of the propositional formula encoding the k-path and the negation of the mutual exclusion property (denoted p) is unsatisfiable for every $k < 12$. The witness was found for $k = 12$. We were able to test 40 processes. The results are shown in Fig. 4 (left).

Our second aim was to search for a minimal c such that $\mathrm{EF}^{\leq c}p$ holds. The results are presented in Fig. 4 (right). In the case of this net, we are not able to compute an upper bound on the length of the k-path. Unfortunately, we also could not test unreachability, since the method is not implemented yet. Again, we considered the case with $\Delta = 2$ and $\delta = 1$, and the net of 25 processes. The witness was found for $k = 12$, and the time of the path found was between 8 and 9. The column n shows the values of the parameter in the additional component. For $n = 1$ and $k = 12$ unsatisfiability was returned, and testing the property on a longer path could not be completed in a reasonable time.

[10] The value b can be also a parameter of the algorithm.

		tpnBMC				RSat		
k	n	variables	clauses	sec	MB	sec	MB	sat
0	-	1937	5302	0.2	3.5	0.0	1.7	NO
2	-	36448	107684	1.4	7.9	0.4	9.5	NO
4	-	74338	220335	2.9	12.8	3.3	21.5	NO
6	-	112227	332884	4.2	17.6	14.3	37.3	NO
8	-	156051	463062	6.1	23.3	257.9	218.6	NO
10	-	197566	586144	7.8	28.5	2603.8	1153.2	NO
12	-	240317	712744	9.7	34.0	87.4	140.8	YES
				32.4	34.0	2967.1	1153.2	

		tpnBMC				RSat		
k	n	variables	clauses	sec	MB	sec	MB	sat
0	-	840	2194	0.0	3.2	0.0	1.4	NO
2	-	16263	47707	0.5	5.2	0.1	4.9	NO
4	-	33835	99739	1.0	7.3	0.6	9.1	NO
6	-	51406	151699	1.6	9.6	1.8	13.8	NO
8	-	72752	214853	2.4	12.3	20.6	27.7	NO
10	-	92629	273491	3.0	14.8	321.4	200.8	NO
12	-	113292	334357	3.7	17.5	14.3	39.0	YES
12	7	120042	354571	4.1	18.3	45.7	59.3	YES
12	6	120054	354613	4.0	18.3	312.7	206.8	YES
12	5	120102	354763	4.0	18.3	64.0	77.7	YES
12	4	120054	354601	4.1	18.3	8.8	35.0	YES
12	3	115475	340834	3.9	17.7	24.2	45.0	YES
12	2	115481	340852	3.9	17.8	138.7	100.8	YES
12	1	115529	341008	3.9	17.7	2355.4	433.4	NO
				40.1	18.3	3308.3	433.4	

Fig. 4. Results for mutex, $\Delta = 2$, $\delta = 1$, mutual exclusion violated. Left: proving reachability for 40 processes, right: parametric verification for 25 processes. The tpnBMC column shows the results for the part of the tool used to represent the problem as a propositional formula (a set of clauses); the column RSat displays the results of running the RSat solver for the set of clauses obtained from tpnBMC.

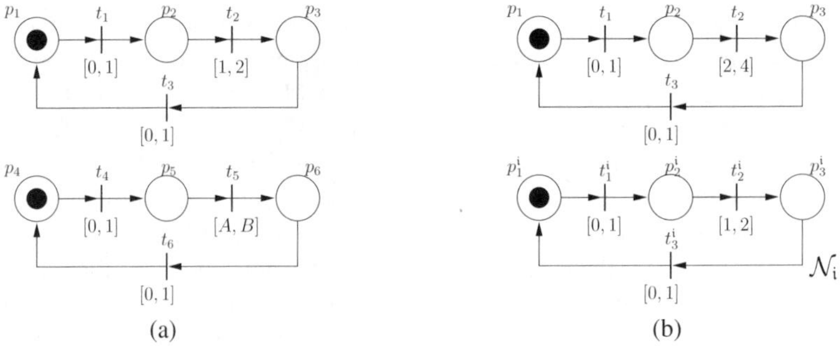

Fig. 5. Time Petri nets tested in experiments

The next two (scalable) examples were the nets shown in Fig. 5. The net (a) shown in the left-hand side of the figure was scaled by increasing $Eft(t_2)$ and $Lft(t_2)$, according to the schema $A = 2u$, $B = 4u$, for $u = 1, 2, \ldots$. The property tested was $\mathrm{EF}(p_3 \wedge p_6)$. The net (b) shown on the right was scaled by increasing the number of components $\mathcal{N}_{\mathrm{i}}$ ($\mathrm{i} = 1, 2, \ldots$). In this case, reachability of a state satisfying $p_3 \wedge \bigwedge_{\mathrm{i}=1}^{j} p_3^{\mathrm{i}}$ was checked (where j is a number of identical processes). For both the nets we searched for a minimal time c at which a given property can be reached, and for both of them we were able to compute an upper bound on the length of the k-path to be tested while checking reachability in a time not exceeding n. For the net (a) the bound is $K = 2(z_1 + z_2 + z_3)$, where $z_1 = 3n - 1$, $z_2 = 3\lceil n/(2u) \rceil - 1$ and $z_3 = 1$ (where the third process is that added to test reachability in time n); whereas for the net (b) containing j identical components it is given by $K = z_0 + \Sigma_{i=1}^{j} z_i + z_{j+1}$, where the bound for the first

		tpnBMC				RSat		
k	n	variables	clauses	sec	MB	sec	MB	sat
0	-	21	34	0.0	3.0	0.0	1.3	NO
2	-	603	1653	0.0	3.0	0.0	1.4	NO
4	-	1396	3909	0.0	3.1	0.0	1.6	NO
6	-	2174	6097	0.0	3.2	0.0	1.7	NO
8	-	3347	9429	0.1	3.3	0.0	2.0	NO
10	-	4345	12213	0.1	3.5	0.0	2.2	NO
12	-	5413	15175	0.1	3.6	0.0	2.5	NO
14	-	6551	18315	0.1	3.7	0.1	2.8	YES
14	7	8812	24886	0.1	4.0	0.1	3.3	NO
16	7	11299	31987	0.2	4.2	0.1	3.8	NO
18	7	13151	37159	0.2	4.5	0.2	4.2	NO
20	7	15103	42595	0.2	4.8	118.9	17.1	NO
22	7	17155	48295	0.3	5.0	15.6	8.3	NO
24	7	19307	54259	0.3	5.2	18.9	9.7	NO
26	7	21559	60487	0.3	5.5	133.5	19.0	NO
28	7	23911	66979	0.4	5.8	167.1	26.5	NO
30	7	27930	78424	0.4	6.2	96.4	18.5	NO
32	7	30586	85756	0.5	6.5	224.9	32.6	NO
34	7	33342	93352	0.5	6.8	339.8	36.4	NO
36	7	36198	101212	0.5	7.2	549.8	50.2	NO
38	7	39154	109336	0.6	7.5	339.8	50.7	NO
40	7	42210	117724	0.6	7.9	266.5	45.6	NO
42	7	45366	126376	0.7	8.2	1026.9	85.0	NO
44	7	48622	135292	0.7	8.6	558.6	83.3	NO
46	7	51978	144472	0.8	9.0	574.7	75.6	NO
				7.6	9.0	4431.9	85.0	

		tpnBMC				RSat		
k	n	variables	clauses	sec	MB	sec	MB	sat
0	-	21	34	0.0	3.0	0.0	1.3	NO
2	-	619	1707	0.0	3.0	0.0	1.4	NO
4	-	1428	4017	0.0	3.1	0.0	1.6	NO
6	-	2467	6985	0.0	3.2	0.0	1.8	NO
8	-	3411	9645	0.0	3.3	0.0	2.0	NO
10	-	4425	12483	0.1	3.5	0.0	2.2	NO
12	-	5994	16945	0.1	3.6	0.0	2.6	NO
14	-	7228	20379	0.1	3.7	0.1	2.9	NO
16	-	8532	23991	0.1	3.9	0.1	3.2	NO
18	-	9906	27781	0.1	4.1	0.1	3.5	NO
20	-	11350	31749	0.2	4.2	0.1	3.8	YES
20	10	15223	42995	0.2	4.8	0.2	4.8	YES
20	9	15303	43255	0.2	4.8	5.1	6.0	NO
22	9	17375	49021	0.3	5.0	58.9	10.9	NO
24	9	20802	58804	0.3	5.4	9.1	9.7	NO
26	9	23178	65410	0.3	5.7	73.4	16.4	NO
28	9	25654	72280	0.4	5.9	139.2	21.1	NO
30	9	28230	79414	0.4	6.3	185.2	22.6	NO
32	9	30906	86812	0.5	6.6	1974.1	115.3	NO
34	9	33682	94474	0.5	6.9	566.0	64.9	NO
36	9	36558	102400	0.5	7.2	955.7	67.8	NO
38	9	39534	110590	0.6	7.6	2931.3	160.6	NO
40	9	42610	119044	0.7	8.0	4771.1	187.6	NO
				5.7	8.0	11669.7	187.6	

Fig. 6. Results for net (a). Left: $u = 4$, $K = 46$ (unreachability proven). Right: $u = 5$, $K = 58$ (unreachability not proven).

process is $z_1 = 3\lceil n/2 \rceil - 1$, the bound for each of the identical processes is $z_i = 3n - 1$ ($i = 1, \ldots, j$), and the bound for the additional process is $z_{j+1} = 1$. The results for the net (a), with the values of the coefficient u given, are presented in Fig. 6. In the case of

		tpnBMC				RSat		
k	n	variables	clauses	sec	MB	sec	MB	sat
0	-	71	124	0.0	3.0	0.0	1.3	NO
2	-	1567	4394	0.0	3.1	0.0	1.6	NO
4	-	3754	10753	0.1	3.3	0.0	2.1	NO
6	-	6661	19240	0.1	3.7	0.0	2.8	NO
8	-	9273	26794	0.2	4.0	0.0	3.4	NO
10	-	12105	34956	0.2	4.4	0.1	4.0	NO
12	-	16672	48307	0.3	4.9	0.2	5.1	NO
14	-	20194	58445	0.4	5.4	0.5	5.9	NO
16	-	23936	69191	0.4	5.8	1.4	6.8	NO
18	-	27898	80545	0.5	6.3	2.9	8.0	NO
20	-	32080	92507	0.6	6.8	10.1	10.2	NO
22	-	39247	113458	0.7	7.7	88.9	19.0	NO
24	-	44119	127396	0.8	8.3	341.1	26.9	NO
26	-	49211	141942	0.8	8.9	489.3	42.4	NO
28	-	54523	157096	0.9	9.6	6.2	14.5	YES
28	2	60704	175021	1.0	10.3	40.6	24.0	YES
28	1	60816	175385	1.1	10.4	3027.4	243.0	NO
30	1	67021	193096	1.1	11.1	393.9	75.2	NO
				9.4	11.1	4402.6	243.0	

Fig. 7. Results for net (b) containing 6 identical processes; the bound $K = 30$

$u = 4$ we were able to test the k-paths up to the upper bound $K = 46$, and to show that the parameter searched for is $c = 8$; for $u = 5$ we can only assume that the value of c is 10, since we were not able to test all the k-paths of the lengths up to $K = 58$. Concerning the net (b), we were able to test the net containing 6 identical processes and to show that $c = 2$; the results are given in Fig. 7.

We have compared the efficiency of parametric part of our implementation with the tool Romeo [31], using the benchmark of Fischer's mutual exclusion protocol to this aim. The results are shown in Fig 8.

	Romeo		**VerICS**	
N	**sec**	**MB**	**sec**	**MB**
2	0.1	1	0.65	3
3	0.14	6	2.65	4
4	0.61	9	1.92	5
5	4.99	38	2.93	6
6	44.76	364	6.02	7
7	>360	>2000	8.63	9
8	-	-	12.67	12
9	-	-	20.74	15
10	-	-	30.28	23
12	-	-	43.72	32
15	-	-	136.78	92
20	-	-	551.64	299
25	-	-	1304.2	538

Fig. 8. Results for mutex, $\Delta = 2$, $\delta = 1$ - a comparison with the tool Romeo. N denotes the number of processes.

8 Final Remarks

We have shown that the BMC method for checking reachability properties of TPNs is feasible. Our preliminary experimental results prove the efficiency of the method. However, it would be interesting to check practical applicability of BMC for other examples of time Petri nets. On the other hand, it would be also interesting to check efficiency of the above solutions for other (non-distributed) nets (which could be done by applying the translations from [28]).

References

1. Alur, R., Courcoubetis, C., Dill, D.: Model checking for real-time systems. In: Proc. of the 5th Symp. on Logic in Computer Science (LICS 1990), pp. 414–425. IEEE Computer Society Press, Los Alamitos (1990)
2. Alur, R., Courcoubetis, C., Dill, D., Halbwachs, N., Wong-Toi, H.: An implementation of three algorithms for timing verification based on automata emptiness. In: Proc. of the 13th IEEE Real-Time Systems Symposium (RTSS 1992), pp. 157–166. IEEE Computer Society Press, Los Alamitos (1992)
3. Audemard, G., Cimatti, A., Kornilowicz, A., Sebastiani, R.: Bounded model checking for timed systems. In: Peled, D.A., Vardi, M.Y. (eds.) FORTE 2002. LNCS, vol. 2529, pp. 243–259. Springer, Heidelberg (2002)

4. Benedetti, M., Cimatti, A.: Bounded model checking for past LTL. In: Garavel, H., Hatcliff, J. (eds.) TACAS 2003. LNCS, vol. 2619, pp. 18–33. Springer, Heidelberg (2003)
5. Berthomieu, B., Diaz, M.: Modeling and verification of time dependent systems using time Petri nets. IEEE Trans. on Software Eng. 17(3), 259–273 (1991)
6. Berthomieu, B., Menasche, M.: An enumerative approach for analyzing time Petri nets. In: Proc. of the 9th IFIP World Computer Congress. Information Processing, vol. 9, pp. 41–46. North Holland/IFIP (September 1983)
7. Biere, A., Cimatti, A., Clarke, E., Fujita, M., Zhu, Y.: Symbolic model checking using SAT procedures instead of BDDs. In: Proc. of the ACM/IEEE Design Automation Conference (DAC 1999), pp. 317–320 (1999)
8. Boucheneb, H., Barkaoui, K.: Relevant timed schedules / clock valuations for constructing time petri net reachability graphs. In: Cassez, F., Jard, C. (eds.) FORMATS 2008. LNCS, vol. 5215, pp. 265–279. Springer, Heidelberg (2008)
9. Boucheneb, H., Berthelot, G.: Towards a simplified building of time Petri nets reachability graph. In: Proc. of the 5th Int. Workshop on Petri Nets and Performance Models, pp. 46–55 (October 1993)
10. Bucci, G., Fedeli, A., Sassoli, L., Vicaro, E.: Modeling flexible real time systems with preemptive time Petri nets. In: Proc. of the 15th Euromicro Conference on Real-Time Systems (ECRTS 2003), pp. 279–286. IEEE Computer Society Press, Los Alamitos (2003)
11. Bucci, G., Vicaro, E.: Compositional validation of time-critical systems using communicating time Petri nets. IEEE Trans. on Software Eng. 21(12), 969–992 (1995)
12. Clarke, E., Biere, A., Raimi, R., Zhu, Y.: Bounded model checking using satisfiability solving. Formal Methods in System Design 19(1), 7–34 (2001)
13. Dembinski, P., Janowska, A., Janowski, P., Penczek, W., Półrola, A., Szreter, M., Woźna, B.z., Zbrzezny, A.: VerICS: A tool for verifying timed automata and Estelle specifications. In: Garavel, H., Hatcliff, J. (eds.) TACAS 2003. LNCS, vol. 2619, pp. 278–283. Springer, Heidelberg (2003)
14. Emerson, E.A., Trefler, R.: Parametric quantitative temporal reasoning. In: Proc. of the 14th Symp. on Logic in Computer Science (LICS 1999), pp. 336–343. IEEE Computer Society Press, Los Alamitos (July 1999)
15. Gardey, G., Roux, O.H., Roux, O.F.: Using zone graph method for computing the state space of a time Petri net. In: Larsen, K.G., Niebert, P. (eds.) FORMATS 2003. LNCS, vol. 2791, pp. 246–259. Springer, Heidelberg (2004)
16. Heljanko, K.: Bounded reachability checking with process semantics. In: Larsen, K.G., Nielsen, M. (eds.) CONCUR 2001. LNCS, vol. 2154, pp. 218–232. Springer, Heidelberg (2001)
17. Huhn, M., Niebert, P., Wallner, F.: Verification based on local states. In: Steffen, B. (ed.) TACAS 1998. LNCS, vol. 1384, pp. 36–51. Springer, Heidelberg (1998)
18. Janicki, R.: Nets, sequential components and concurrency relations. Theoretical Computer Science 29, 87–121 (1984)
19. Lilius, J.: Efficient state space search for time Petri nets. In: Proc. of MFCS Workshop on Concurrency, Brno 1998. ENTCS, vol. 18. Elsevier, Amsterdam (1999)
20. Mascarenhas, R., Karumuri, D., Buy, U., Kenyon, R.: Modeling and analysis of a virtual reality system with time Petri nets. In: Proc. of the 20th Int. Conf. on Software Engineering (ICSE 1998), pp. 33–42. IEEE Computer Society Press, Los Alamitos (1998)
21. Merlin, P., Farber, D.J.: Recoverability of communication protocols – implication of a theoretical study. IEEE Trans. on Communications 24(9), 1036–1043 (1976)
22. Okawa, Y., Yoneda, T.: Symbolic CTL model checking of time Petri nets. Electronics and Communications in Japan, Scripta Technica 80(4), 11–20 (1997)

23. Penczek, W., Półrola, A.: Specification and Model Checking of Temporal Properties in Time Petri Nets and Timed Automata. In: Cortadella, J., Reisig, W. (eds.) ICATPN 2004. LNCS, vol. 3099, pp. 37–76. Springer, Heidelberg (2004)
24. Penczek, W., Półrola, A., Woźna, B., Zbrzezny, A.: Bounded model checking for reachability testing in time Petri nets. In: Proc. of the Int. Workshop on Concurrency, Specification and Programming (CS&P 2004). Informatik-Berichte, vol. 170(1), pp. 124–135. Humboldt University (2004)
25. Penczek, W., Woźna, B., Zbrzezny, A.: Bounded model checking for the universal fragment of CTL. Fundamenta Informaticae 51(1-2), 135–156 (2002)
26. Penczek, W., Woźna, B., Zbrzezny, A.: Branching time bounded model checking for elementary net systems. Technical Report 940, ICS PAS, Ordona 21, 01-237 Warsaw (January 2002)
27. Penczek, W., Woźna, B., Zbrzezny, A.: Towards bounded model checking for the universal fragment of TCTL. In: Damm, W., Olderog, E.-R. (eds.) FTRTFT 2002. LNCS, vol. 2469, pp. 265–288. Springer, Heidelberg (2002)
28. Półrola, A., Penczek, W.: Minimization algorithms for time Petri nets. Fundamenta Informaticae 60(1-4), 307–331 (2004)
29. Popova, L.: On time Petri nets. Elektronische Informationsverarbeitung und Kybernetik 27(4), 227–244 (1991)
30. Popova-Zeugmann, L., Schlatter, D.: Analyzing paths in time Petri nets. Fundamenta Informaticae 37(3), 311–327 (1999)
31. Romeo: A tool for time Petri net analysis (2000), `http://www.irccyn.ecnantes.fr/irccyn/d/en/equipes/TempsReel/logs`
32. Strichman, O.: Tuning SAT checkers for bounded model checking. In: Emerson, E.A., Sistla, A.P. (eds.) CAV 2000. LNCS, vol. 1855, pp. 480–494. Springer, Heidelberg (2000)
33. Traonouez, L.-M., Lime, D., Roux, O.H.: Parametric model-checking of time petri nets with stopwatches using the state-class graph. In: Cassez, F., Jard, C. (eds.) FORMATS 2008. LNCS, vol. 5215, pp. 280–294. Springer, Heidelberg (2008)
34. Virbitskaite, I.B., Pokozy, E.A.: A partial order method for the verification of time petri nets. In: Ciobanu, G., Păun, G. (eds.) FCT 1999. LNCS, vol. 1684, pp. 547–558. Springer, Heidelberg (1999)
35. Woźna, B.: ACTL* properties and bounded model checking. Fundamenta Informaticae 63(1), 65–87 (2004)
36. Woźna, B., Zbrzezny, A., Penczek, W.: Checking reachability properties for timed automata via SAT. Fundamenta Informaticae 55(2), 223–241 (2003)
37. Yovine, S.: Model checking timed automata. In: Rozenberg, G. (ed.) EEF School 1996. LNCS, vol. 1494, pp. 114–152. Springer, Heidelberg (1998)
38. Zbrzezny, A.: Improvements in SAT-based reachability analysis for timed automata. Fundamenta Informaticae 60(1-4), 417–434 (2004)
39. Zbrzezny, A.: SAT-based reachability checking for timed automata with diagonal constraints. Fundamenta Informaticae 67(1-3), 303–322 (2005)

Appendix

Concrete Models – Proofs

Below we provide a proof of Lemma 1:

Proof. We shall show that the relation $\mathcal{R} = \{((m, clock), (m', clock')) \mid m = m' \wedge \forall(\mathrm{i} \in \mathfrak{I} \text{ s.t. } clock(\mathrm{i}) \leq c_{max}(\mathcal{N}))\ clock(\mathrm{i}) = clock'(\mathrm{i}) \ \wedge\ \forall(\mathrm{i} \in \mathfrak{I} \text{ s.t. } clock(\mathrm{i}) > c_{max}(\mathcal{N}))\ clock'(\mathrm{i}) > c_{max}(\mathcal{N})\}$ is a bisimulation. It is easy to see that $\sigma^0 \mathcal{R} \sigma^0$, and the valuations of the related states are equal (due to equality of their markings). Consider $\sigma = (m, clock) \in \Sigma$ and $\sigma' = (m, clock') \in \Sigma$ such that $\sigma \mathcal{R} \sigma'$.

- if $\sigma \xrightarrow{\delta}_c \sigma_1$, where $\delta \in \mathrm{IR}_+$, then for each $t \in en(m)$ there exists $\mathrm{i} \in I\mathcal{V}(t)$ s.t. $clock(\mathrm{i}) + \delta \leq Lft(t)$. Consider the following cases:
  - if $en(m)$ contains at least one transition t with $Lft(t) < \infty$, then this implies that $\delta \leq c_{max}(\mathcal{N})$. In this case consider $\delta' = \delta$; it is easy to see from the definition of $\mathcal{R}$ that for any $t \in en(m)$ s.t $Lft(t) < \infty$ if in σ for some $\mathrm{i} \in \mathfrak{I}$ we have $clock(\mathrm{i}) + \delta \leq Lft(t)$, then in σ' $clock'(\mathrm{i}) + \delta' \leq Lft(t)$ holds as well, and therefore the time δ' can pass at σ', leading to the state $\sigma' + \delta'$, which satisfies $(\sigma + \delta)\mathcal{R}(\sigma' + \delta')$ in an obvious way.
  - if $en(m)$ contains no transition t with $Lft(t) < \infty$, then we can have either $\delta \leq c_{\mathbf{m1}}$ or $\delta > c_{\mathbf{m1}}$, where by $c_{\mathbf{m1}}$ we mean the value $c_{max}(\mathcal{N}) + 1$. In the first case consider $\delta' = \delta$; it is obvious that such a passage of time at σ' disables no transition and is allowed therefore; it is also easy to see that $(\sigma + \delta)\mathcal{R}(\sigma' + \delta')$. In the case $\delta > c_{\mathbf{m1}}$ assume $\delta' = c_{\mathbf{m1}}$. Again, it is obvious that such a passage of time at σ' disables no transition and due to this is allowed, and that in both the states $\sigma + \delta$ and $\sigma' + \delta'$ we have $clock(\mathrm{i}) > c_{max}(\mathcal{N})$ for all $i \in \mathfrak{I}$, and therefore $(\sigma + \delta)\mathcal{R}(\sigma' + \delta')$.
- the three remaining cases are straightforward.

Extended Detailed Region Graph – Proofs

Below, we provide a proof of Lemma 2:

Proof. We shall show that the relation $\mathcal{R} = \{(\sigma, w) \mid \sigma \in w\}$ is a bisimulation. It is easy to see that $\sigma^0 \mathcal{R} w^0$, and that for each $\sigma \in w$ we have $V_c(\sigma) = V(w)$, since the markings of the related states are equal. Thus, consider $\sigma = (m, clock) \in \Sigma$ and $w = (m, Z) \in W$ such that $\sigma \mathcal{R} w$.

- If $w \xrightarrow{\tau} w'$, where $w' = (m', Z') \in W$, then for each $v \in Z$ (and therefore for that given by $v(x_{\mathrm{i}}) = clock(\mathrm{i})$ for all $\mathrm{i} \in \mathfrak{I}$) there exists $\delta \in [0, c_{\mathbf{m1}}]$ such that $v + \delta \in Z'$. Moreover, the condition $Z' \models inv(m)$ implies that for each $t \in en(m)$ there is $\mathrm{i} \in I\mathcal{V}(t)$ such that $(v + \delta)(x_{\mathrm{i}}) \leq Lft(t)$. Thus, there exists a state $\sigma' \in \Sigma$, given by $\sigma' = (m, clock + \delta)$, satisfying $\sigma \xrightarrow{\delta}_r \sigma'$ and $\sigma' \in w'$ (i.e., $\sigma' \mathcal{R} w'$).

- On the other hand, if $\sigma \xrightarrow{\delta}_r \sigma'$ for some $\sigma' = (m, clock') \in \Sigma$ and $\delta \in [0, c_{\mathbf{m1}}]$, then for each $\sigma_1 = (m, clock_1) \in w$ one can find $\delta' \in [0, c_{\mathbf{m1}}]$ such that the clock valuation v_1' given by $v_1'(x_\mathfrak{i}) = clock_1(\mathfrak{i}) + \delta'$ for all $\mathfrak{i} \in \mathfrak{I}$ is equivalent to the clock valuation v' given by $v'(x_\mathfrak{i}) = clock'(\mathfrak{i})$ for all $\mathfrak{i} \in \mathfrak{I}$[11]. Moreover, from the definition of the time-successor relation we have that for each $t \in en(m)$ there is $\mathfrak{i} \in \mathcal{IV}(t)$ such that $clock'(\mathfrak{i}) \leq Lft(t)$, and therefore from the definition of $\simeq_\mathcal{N}$ it holds also $clock_1(\mathfrak{i}) + \delta' \leq Lft(t)$. Thus, for the extended detailed region $w' = (m, Z')$ such that $\sigma' \in w'$ (and therefore $w'\mathcal{R}^{-1}\sigma'$) we have that for each $v'' \in Z$ there is $\delta'' \in [0, c_{\mathbf{m1}}]$ s.t. $v'' + \delta'' \in Z'$, and we have $Z' \models inv(m)$, which implies $w \xrightarrow{\tau} w'$.
- If $w \xrightarrow{t} w'$ for some transition $t \in T$, where $w' = (m[t\rangle, Z') \in W$, then $t \in en(m)$ and $Z \models fire_t(m) \wedge inv(m)$. Thus, it is easy to see that the transition t can be fired also at the state σ, which leads to $\sigma' = (m', clock') \in \Sigma$, with $m' = m[t\rangle$ and $clock'(\mathfrak{i}) = 0$ for $\mathfrak{i} \in \mathcal{IV}(t)$, and $clock'(\mathfrak{i}) = clock(\mathfrak{i})$ otherwise. Therefore, the clock valuation v' given by $v'(x_\mathfrak{i}) = clock'(\mathfrak{i})$ belongs to the zone $Z[reset(t, m) := 0]$, which implies $\sigma' \in w'$ (and therefore $\sigma'\mathcal{R}w'$).
- If $\sigma \xrightarrow{t}_r \sigma'$ for some transition $t \in T$ and $\sigma' = (m', clock') \in \Sigma$, then $t \in en(m)$, $clock(\mathfrak{i}) \geq Eft(t)$ for every $\mathfrak{i} \in \mathcal{IV}(t)$, and there exists $\mathfrak{i} \in \mathcal{IV}(t)$ such that $clock(\mathfrak{i}) \leq Lft(t)$. Thus, from the definition of $\simeq_\mathcal{N}$ the zone Z satisfies the constraints $fire_t(m)$ and $inv(m)$. Considering $w' = (m', Z')$ such that $\sigma' \in w'$, it is easy to see from the definition of $\simeq_\mathcal{N}$ that $Z' = Z[reset(m, t) := 0]$ (the zone Z collects the clock valuations equivalent to v given by $v(x_\mathfrak{i}) = clock(\mathfrak{i})$ for each $\mathfrak{i} \in \mathfrak{I}$; therefore from $\sigma \xrightarrow{t}_r \sigma'$ and from the definition of $\simeq_\mathcal{N}$ the zone Z' collects the valuations which are like the elements of Z but with the clocks $x_\mathfrak{i}$ with $\mathfrak{i} \in \mathcal{IV}(t)$ set to zero). Moreover, $Z' \models inv(m')$ in an obvious way (we have $m' = m[t\rangle$; if a transition $t' \in en(m')$ became enabled by firing t then there exists $\mathfrak{i} \in \mathcal{IV}(t')$ such that for all $v' \in Z'$ $v'(x_\mathfrak{i}) = 0$ (and therefore $v(x_\mathfrak{i}) \leq Lft(t')$), whereas for all the other transitions $t \in en(m')$ the existence of $\mathfrak{i} \in \mathfrak{I}$ s.t. $v(x_\mathfrak{i}) \leq Lft(t)$ follows from $Z \models inv(m)$, since the values of clocks have not been increased). Thus, for the detailed region w' such that $\sigma' \in w'$ (and therefore $w'\mathcal{R}^{-1}\sigma'$) we have $w \xrightarrow{t} w'$, which ends the proof.

Discretisation – Proofs

Given a distributed time Petri net $\mathcal{N}$ of n processes, and the set of clock $\mathcal{X}$ associated with these processes, let $\mathcal{C}'_\mathcal{X}$ be the set of constraints defined by the grammar

$$\mathfrak{cc} := true \mid x_\mathfrak{i} \sim c \mid x_\mathfrak{i} - x_{\mathfrak{i}_1} \sim c \mid \mathfrak{cc} \wedge \mathfrak{cc},$$

[11] The above fact can be derived from the properties of "standard" detailed region graphs, for which we have that for two equivalent states q_1, q_2, for all $\delta \in \mathbb{R}_+$ whenever some q_1' is a time successor of q_1 on time passage δ, there exists δ_2' and $\delta' \in \mathbb{R}_+$ such that q_2' is the time successor of q_2 on time passage δ', and q_1' is equivalent to q_2' [37]. The equivalence relation $\simeq_\mathcal{N}$ differs from that defining "standard" detailed region in non-involving the maximal constant appearing in the constraints.

where $x_i, x_{i_1} \in \mathcal{X}$, $\sim \in \{<, \leq, =, \geq, >\}$, and $c \in \mathbb{N}$. In order to provide the next proof we recall the following lemmas of [39][12]:

Lemma 6. *Let $\phi \in \mathcal{C}'_{\mathcal{X}}$, $v \in \mathbb{R}^n_+$, and $\delta \in \mathbb{R}_+$. If $v \models \phi$ and $v + \delta \models \phi$, then for each $0 \leq \delta' \leq \delta$ it holds $v + \delta' \models \phi$.*

Lemma 7. *Let $u, v \in \mathbb{R}^n_+$ be clock valuations such that $u \simeq_{\mathcal{N}} v$. For any clock constraint $\phi \in \mathcal{C}'_{\mathcal{X}}$, $u \models \phi \iff v \models \phi$.*

Lemma 8. *Let $u, v \in \mathbb{R}^n_+$ be clock valuations such that for any clock constraint $\phi \in \mathcal{C}'_{\mathcal{X}}$, $u \models \phi \iff v \models \phi$.Then, $u \simeq_{\mathcal{N}} v$.*

Lemma 9. *For every $v \in \mathbb{R}^n_+$ there exists $u \in \mathbb{D}^n$ such that $u \simeq_{\mathcal{N}} v$.*

Lemma 10. *Let $v \in \mathbb{R}^n_+$ be a clock valuation, $\delta \in [0, c_{max}(\mathcal{N}) + 1]$, and $m \in \mathbb{N}$. For each $u \in \mathbb{D}^n_m$ such that $v \simeq_{\mathcal{N}} u$ there exists $\delta' \in \mathbb{E}_{m+1}$ such that $v + \delta \simeq_{\mathcal{N}} u + \delta'$. Moreover, $u + \delta' \in \mathbb{D}^n_{m+1}$.*

Lemma 11. *For a given time Petri net $\mathcal{N}$ the models $M_\Gamma(\mathcal{N}) = (\Gamma(\mathcal{N}), V)$ and $\widetilde{M}_\Gamma(\mathcal{N}) = (\widetilde{\Gamma}(\mathcal{N}), \widetilde{V})$ are bisimulation equivalent.*

A proof of Lemma 3 is as follows:

Proof. We shall show that the relation $\mathcal{R} = \{(\widetilde{w}, w) \mid \widetilde{w} \in w\}$ is a bisimulation (where the definition of $\widetilde{w} \in w$ corresponds to that for concrete states and regions, as $\widetilde{W} \subset \Sigma$). It is obvious that the initial states of both the models are related, and that the related states are of the same valuations. Thus, consider $w = (m, Z) \in W$ and $\widetilde{w} = (m, v) \in \widetilde{W}$ such that $\widetilde{w} \mathcal{R} w$.

- if $w \xrightarrow{\tau} w'$, where $w' = (m, Z') \in W$, then from $(m, Z) \xrightarrow{\tau} (m, Z')$ we have that for each $u \in Z$ (and therefore also for the clock value v of the state $\widetilde{w}$) there exists $\delta \in [0, c_{\mathbf{m1}}]$ such that $u + \delta \in Z'$. From Lemma 10 we have that there is $\delta' \in \mathbb{E}$ such that $v + \delta' \simeq_{\mathcal{N}} v + \delta$ (i.e., $v + \delta' \in Z'$). Moreover, from $Z, Z' \models inv(m)$ we have that $v, v + \delta' \models inv(m)$, which implies that $(m, v) \xrightarrow{\delta'}_d (m, v + \delta')$, and $(m, v + \delta') \mathcal{R} w'$;
- if $\widetilde{w} \xrightarrow{\delta}_d \widetilde{w}'$ for some $\delta' \in \mathbb{E}$, where $\widetilde{w}' = (m, v') \in \widetilde{W}$, then $v' = v + \delta$, and $v, v' \models inv(m)$. From the fact explained in Footnote 11 we have that for any (m, v'') s.t. $v'' \simeq_{\mathcal{N}} v$ there is a time successor $(m, v'' + \delta'')$ for some $\delta'' \in [0, c_{\mathbf{m1}}]$ s.t. $v'' + \delta'' \simeq_{\mathcal{N}} v'$, which implies that there is $w' \in W$ such that $w \xrightarrow{\tau} w'$ and $\widetilde{w}' \in w$;
- if $w \xrightarrow{t} w'$ for some $t \in T$, where $w' = (m[t\rangle, Z') \in W$, then $t \in en(m)$, $Z \models fire_t(m) \wedge inv(m)$, $Z' = Z[reset(m, t) := 0]$ and $Z' \models inv(m[t\rangle)$. Thus, t can be fired at (m, v), leading to a state $(m[t\rangle, v')$ with $v' = v[reset(m, t) := 0]$ and $v' \models inv(m[t\rangle)$, which belongs to w' in an obvious way;

[12] The paper [39] deals with timed automata. However, the proofs do not involve the features of timed automata, so the proofs are not repeated here.

- if $\widetilde{w} \xrightarrow{t}_d \widetilde{w}'$ for some $t \in T$, where $\widetilde{w}' = (m', v')$, then $m' = m[t\rangle$, $v \models fire_t(m) \wedge inv(m)$, $v' = v[reset(m,t) := 0]$ and $v' \models inv(m')$. From Lemma 7 we have that $Z \models fire_t(m) \wedge inv(m)$, and therefore t can be fired also at $w = (m, Z)$. The action successor (m'', Z') satisfies $m'' = m[t\rangle$, $Z' = Z[reset(m,t) := 0]$ and $Z' \models inv(m'')$. Thus, $v \in Z'$.

Testing Reachability – Technical Details

Consider a distributed time Petri net $\mathcal{N}$ of n processes, and with the set of places P. A k-path π is a *special k-path* iff for each even i ($0 \leq i < k$) the transition $\pi(i) \to \pi(i+1)$ is a time transition, and for each odd i ($0 < i < k$) the transition $\pi(i) \to \pi(i+1)$ is an action transition. It is easy to see that a marking is reachable in $M_c(\mathcal{N})$ (respectively in $\widetilde{M}_\Gamma(\mathcal{N})$) iff it is reachable on a special k-path in $M_c(\mathcal{N})$ (respectively in $\widetilde{M}_\Gamma(\mathcal{N})$). Let $h(m) = \lfloor \frac{m+1}{2} \rfloor$. Moreover, let $(m, clock)$, $(m', clock')$ be two states and π, π' be two k-paths. We shall write $(m, clock) \simeq_\mathcal{N} (m', clock')$ iff $m = m'$ and $clock \simeq_\mathcal{N} clock'$. We shall also write $\pi \simeq_\mathcal{N} \pi'$ if for every $0 \leq m \leq k$ it holds $\pi(m) \simeq_\mathcal{N} \pi'(m)$.

A *normalised special k-path* (*normalised k-path* for short) is a special k-path s.t. all the clock values of $\pi'(m)$ ($m = 0, 1, \ldots, k$) belong to $\mathbb{D}_{h(m)}$, and for each even $m < k$ the label of the transition $\pi'(m) \xrightarrow{\delta} \pi'(m+1)$ belongs to $E_{h(m)+1}$. We have the following lemma (analogous to that in [39]):

Lemma 12. *For each $k \in \mathbb{N}$, and for each special k-path in $\widetilde{M}_\Gamma(\mathcal{N})$ there is a normalised special k-path π' in $\widetilde{M}_\Gamma(\mathcal{N})$ such that $\pi \simeq_\mathcal{N} \pi'$.*

The proof is analogous to the proof of Lemma 3.3 in [39]. So, we get that a marking is reachable iff it is reachable on some normalised special k-path in $\widetilde{M}_\Gamma(\mathcal{N})$.

Since the number of time transitions of a normalised k-path is equal to $\lfloor \frac{k+1}{2} \rfloor$, we get that all the clock values of a normalised k-path are bounded by $\lfloor \frac{k+1}{2} \rfloor \cdot c_{\mathbf{m1}}$. This fact is useful when computing the length of a bit vectors encoding the states of a k-path. More precisely, the m-th state of a normalised k-path can be represented by a bit vector of the length $r(m) = \lceil \log_2(|P|) \rceil + |\mathfrak{I}| \cdot (\lceil \log_2(\lfloor \frac{k+1}{2} \rfloor \cdot c_{\mathbf{m1}}) \rceil) + 1 + h(m))$ (the details can be found in [39]).

Testing Unreachability – Technical Details

Again, consider a distributed time Petri net $\mathcal{N}$ of n processes, and with the set of places P. In order to test unreachability we consider *free normalised special k-paths*. A free special k-path π is called a free normalised special k-path (*free normalised k-path* for short) if all the clock values of $\pi(m)$, for $m = 0, \ldots, k$, belong to $\mathbb{D}_{h(m)}$, all the clock values of $\pi(0)$ are not greater than $n \cdot c_{\mathbf{m1}}$, and for each even $m < k$ the label δ of $\pi(m) \xrightarrow{\delta}_d \pi(m+1)$ belongs to $\mathbb{E}_{h(m)+1}$. Let $g(n) = \lceil \log_1(n+1) \rceil$. We have the following lemma:

Lemma 13. *For each $k \in \mathbb{N}$, and for each free special k-path in $\widetilde{M}_\Gamma(\mathcal{N})$ there exists a free normalised special k-path π' in $\widetilde{M}_\Gamma(\mathcal{N})$ such that $\pi \simeq_\mathcal{N} \pi'$.*

The proof is analogous to that of Lemma 3.6 in [39]. So, we get that a marking is reachable on a free path iff it is reachable on some free normalised special path in $\widetilde{M}_{\Gamma}(\mathcal{N})$.

Since the number of time transitions in a free normalised k-path is equal to $\lfloor \frac{k+1}{2} \rfloor$, we get that all the clock values of a free normalised k-path are bounded by $(\lfloor \frac{k+1}{2} \rfloor + n) \cdot (c_{max}(\mathcal{N}) + 1)$. This fact is useful when computing the length of a bit vector encoding the states of a free normalised k-path. More precisely, the m-th state of a normalised k-path can be represented by a bit vector of the length $r(m) = \lceil \log_2(|P|) \rceil + |\mathfrak{I}| \cdot (\lceil \log_2(\lfloor (\frac{k+1}{2} \rfloor + n) \cdot c_{\mathbf{m1}}) \rceil) + 1 + g(n) + h(m))$ (the details can be found in [39]).

Parametric Model Checking with VerICS*

Michał Knapik[1], Artur Niewiadomski[2], Wojciech Penczek[1,2], Agata Półrola[3], Maciej Szreter[1], and Andrzej Zbrzezny[4]

[1] Institute of Computer Science, PAS, Ordona 21, 01-237 Warszawa, Poland
{Michal.Knapik,penczek,mszreter}@ipipan.waw.pl
[2] Siedlce University, ICS, 3 Maja 54, 08-110 Siedlce, Poland
artur@ii.uph.edu.pl
[3] University of Łódź, FMCS, Banacha 22, 90-238 Łódź, Poland
polrola@math.uni.lodz.pl
[4] Jan Długosz University, IMCS, Armii Krajowej 13/15, 42-200 Częstochowa, Poland
a.zbrzezny@ajd.czest.pl

Abstract. The paper presents the verification system VerICS, extended with the three new modules aimed at parametric verification of Elementary Net Systems, Distributed Time Petri Nets, and a subset of UML. All the modules exploit Bounded Model Checking for verifying parametric reachability and the properties specified in the logic PRTECTL – the parametric extension of the existential fragment of CTL.

1 Introduction

VerICS is a model checker for high-level languages as well as real-time and multi-agent systems. Depending on the type of a considered system, the verifier enables to test various classes of properties - from reachability of a state satisfying certain conditions to more complicated features expressed with formulas of (timed) temporal, epistemic, or deontic logics. The implemented model checking methods include SAT-based ones as well as these based on generating abstract models for systems.

The architecture of VerICS is depicted in Fig. 1. At its right-hand side there are visualized the model checking methods offered for real-time systems: bounded model checking (BMC) for proving reachability in Time Petri Nets (TPN) and in Timed Automata (TA) (including TADD - TA with Discrete Data) as well as for testing TECTL (Timed Existential CTL) formulas for TA, unbounded model checking (UMC) for proving CTL properties for slightly restricted TA, and splitting for testing reachability for TA. The modules implementing the above methods are described in [8,17] and [18]. In the boxes with rounded corners the input formalisms are depicted: both the low-level (TPN, TA) and high-level languages (Java, Promela, UML, Estelle). The languages for expressing properties to be verified are depicted in ovals. Considering multi-agent systems, VerICS implements UMC for CTLpK (Computation Tree Logic with knowledge and past

* Partly supported by the Polish Ministry of Science and Higher Education under the grants No. N N206 258035 and N N516 370436.

K. Jensen, S. Donatelli, and M. Koutny (Eds.): ToPNoC IV, LNCS 6550, pp. 98–120, 2010.

operators) and BMC for ECTLKD (the existential fragment of CTL extended with knowledge and deontic operators) as well as TECTLK (the existential fragment of timed CTL extended with knowledge operators). All these modules are covered in [17]. Moreover, our verifier offers also SAT-based model checking for high-level languages like UML [27], Java [13], and Promela [14]. The details can be found in [18].

In this paper we present the three new modules of VerICS, aimed at parametric verification. These are BMC4EPN, BMC4TPN, and BMC4UML displayed in the VerICS' architecture diagram in Fig. 1 (the right upper corner). The modules allow for checking properties, expressed in the PRTECTL logic [12,19], of systems modelled as Elementary Net Systems, Distributed Time Petri Nets, and in a subset of UML, respectively.

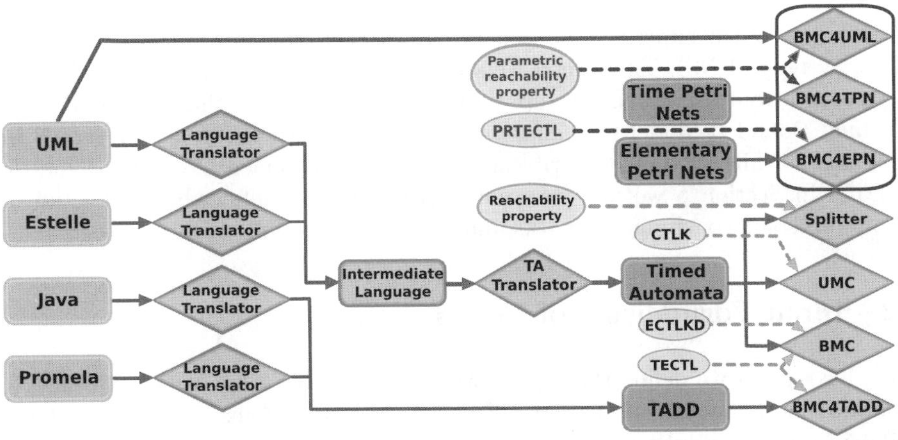

Fig. 1. Architecture of VerICS

Below, we give a short overview of some well-known tools for Petri Nets. Tina [4] is a toolbox for analysis of (Time) Petri Nets, which constructs state class graphs (abstract models) and exploits them for LTL, CTL, or reachability verification. Romeo [22] is a tool for analysis of Time Petri Nets. It provides several methods for translating TPN to TA and for computing state class graphs. CPN Tools [6] is a software package for modelling and analysis of both timed and untimed Coloured Petri Nets, enabling their simulation, generating occurrence (reachability) graphs, and analysis by place invariants.

There have been a lot of attempts to verify UML state machines - all of them based on the same idea consisting in translation of a UML specification to the input language of some model checker, and then performing verification using the model checker. Some of the approaches [16,21] translate UML to the Promela language and then make use of the Spin [14] model checker. Other [10,20] exploit timed automata as an intermediate formalism and employ the UPPAAL [3] for verification. The third group of tools (e.g., [11]) applies the symbolic model checker NuSMV [7] via translating UML to its input language. One of the modules of VerICS follows this idea. A UML subset is translated to the Intermediate Language (IL) of VerICS. However, we have developed also a symbolic model checker that deals directly with UML specifications by avoiding any intermediate translations. The method is implemented as the module BMC4UML.

There are only a few tools designed for parametric verification. One of UPPAAL's modules offers a possibility to verify some properties of Parametric Timed Automata [15] – namely, reachability with additional time constraints; LPMC [33] (a module of the TVS toolset) offers parametric verification of Timed Automata based on partition refinement; Moby/DC [9] implements model checking algorithms for Phase Automata; the Romeo tool contains a module aimed at parametric verification of Time Petri Nets with stopwatches [34]. To our best knowledge, there are no tools dealing with parametric verification of UML.

The rest of the paper is organised as follows. Section 2 introduces Elementary Net Systems (ENS), Time Petri Nets (TPN) (both restricted to 1-safe nets, as required by our tool), and the subset of UML recognized by the tool. Main ideas behind Bounded Model Checking and parametric verification are presented in Section 3, while Section 4 describes major steps of implementation of parametric BMC. In Section 5 we present some experimental results, whereas Section 6 contains some concluding remarks and discusses directions of future work.

2 Input Formalisms of VerICS

In this section we define the input formalisms of VerICS, for which parametric verification is available. These are Elementary Net Systems, Distributed Time Petri Nets, and a subset of UML.

2.1 Elementary Net Systems (ENS)

Elementary Net Systems (called also Elementary Petri Nets) are one of the formalisms used to specify concurrent systems. An *elementary net system* is a 4-tuple $EN = (P, T, F, m^0)$, where P (the *places*) and T (the *transitions*) are finite sets s.t. $P \cap T = \emptyset$, the *flow relation* $F \subseteq (P \times T) \cup (T \times P)$ has the property that for every $t \in T$ there exist $p, p' \in P$ s.t. $(p, t), (t, p') \in F$, and $m^0 \subseteq P$ is the *initial marking* (*initial configuration*). For each transition $t \in T$ we define the set of ingoing places $pre(t) = \{p \in P \mid (p, t) \in F\}$, and the set of outgoing places $post(t) = \{p \in P \mid (t, p) \in F\}$. A state (configuration) of the system EN is given by a *marking* of N, i.e., by a set of places $m \subseteq P$, represented graphically as containing "tokens". We consider 1-*safe* nets only, i.e., these in which each place can be marked by at most one token. Let $m \subseteq P$ be a configuration. If t is a transition, $pre(t) \subseteq m$ and $(post(t) \setminus pre(t)) \cap m = \emptyset$, then we say that the transition t is *enabled* in m (denoted by $m[t\rangle$). Let $m, m' \subseteq P$ be two configurations. A transition t *fires* from m to m' (denoted by $m[t\rangle m'$) if $m[t\rangle$ and $m' = (m \setminus pre(t)) \cup post(t)$. A configuration $m \subseteq P$ is *reachable* if there

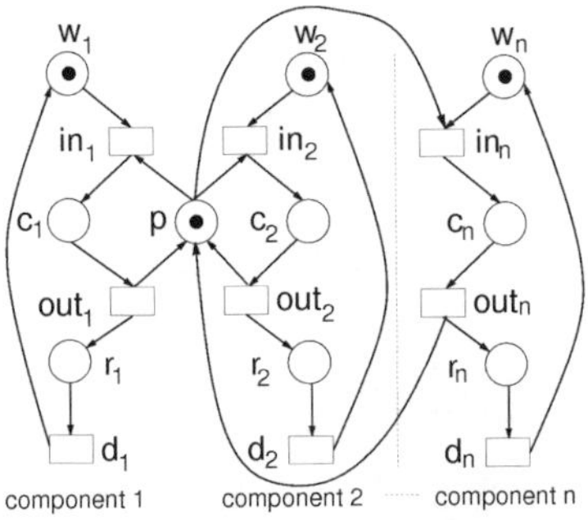

Fig. 2. Elementary net system for a mutual exclusion protocol

are configurations $m_0, m_1, \ldots, m_n \subseteq P$ with $m_0 = m^0, m_n = m$, and transitions $t_0, t_1, \ldots, t_n \in T$ such that $m_{i-1}[t_i\rangle m_i$ for all $1 \leq i \leq n$. We denote the set of all the reachable configurations of EN by M_{EN}.

An example of an elementary net system with $P = \{w_i, c_i, r_i, p\}$ and $T = \{in_i, out_i, d_i\}$, for $i = 1, \ldots, n$ (modelling a mutual exclusion protocol) is presented in Fig. 2.

2.2 Time Petri Nets

The tool VerICS accepts also an input in the form of Time Petri Nets, which are one of the formalisms for specifying real-time systems. A Time Petri Net is a tuple $N = (P, T, F, m^0, Eft, Lft)$, in which the elements P, T, F, and m^0 are the same as in an ENS, while $Eft : T \to \mathbb{N}$ and $Lft : T \to \mathbb{N} \cup \{\infty\}$, satisfying $Eft(t) \leq Lft(t)$ for each $t \in T$, are functions which assign to the transitions their *earliest* and *latest firing times*. The values of these functions are represented graphically as intervals annotating the transitions. In the current version of VerICS, we consider **Distributed Time Petri Nets** [29] only[1]. A Distributed Time Petri Net consists of a set of 1-safe sequential[2] TPNs (called *processes*), of pairwise disjoint sets of places, and communicating via joint transitions. Moreover, the processes are required to be *state machines*, which means that each transition has exactly one input place and exactly one output place in each process it belongs to. A state of the system considered is given by a marking of the net and by the values of the clocks associated with the processes (a detailed description of the nets as well as their semantics can be found in [30]). An example of a distributed TPN (Fischer's mutual exclusion

[1] The restriction follows from efficiency reasons: the distributed form allows to reduce the size of the timed part of the concrete states of nets by assigning clocks to the processes (instead of assigning them to the transitions like in the standard case), which is important for optimising the implementation. Similarly, 1-safety allows to reduce the size of the information stored in the marking part of concrete states.

[2] A net is sequential if none of its reachable markings concurrently enables two transitions.

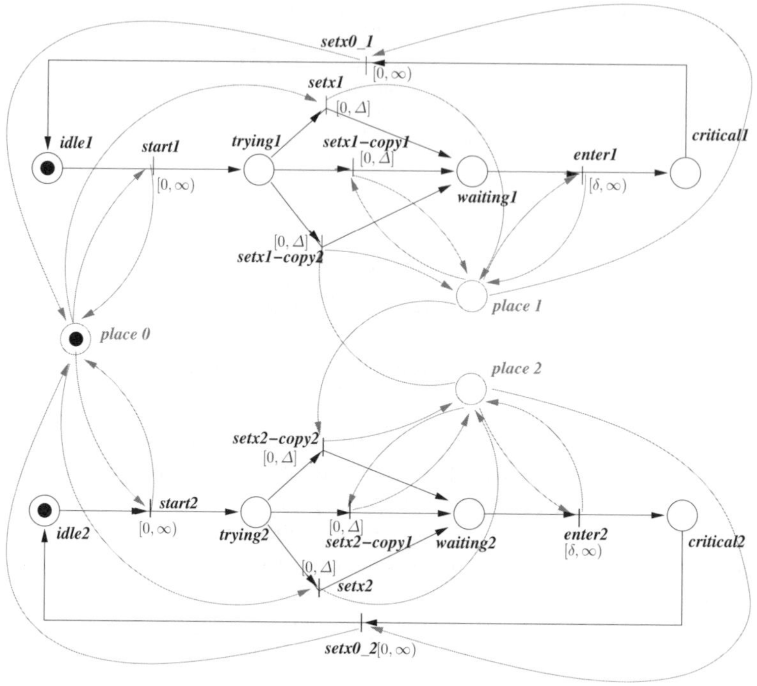

Fig. 3. A net for Fischer's mutual exclusion protocol for $n = 2$

protocol[3]) is shown in Fig. 3. The net consists of three communicating processes with the sets of places $P_i = \{idle_i, trying_i, enter_i, critical_i\}$ for $i = 1, 2$, and $P_3 = \{place0, place1, place2\}$. All the transitions of the process N_1 and all the transitions of the process N_2 (i.e., of the nets modelling the competing processes) are joint with the process N_3 (modelling the process aimed at coordinating the access).

2.3 UML

Another language handled as an input by our tool - a subset of UML - is sketched below. The syntax is illustrated with the diagrams of the Generalised Railroad Crossing (GRC) system, which is also used as a benchmark in Section 5. Due to the space limitations we give only intuitive explanations, but all the remaining details and formal definitions can be found in the papers [24,25].

The systems considered are specified by a single class diagram, which defines k classes (e.g. see Fig. 4(a)), a single object diagram which defines n objects

[3] The system consists of n processes (here $n = 2$) trying to enter their critical sections, and one process aimed at coordinating their access. The system is parameterised by the time-delay constants δ and Δ, whose relationship influences preservation of the mutual exclusion property.

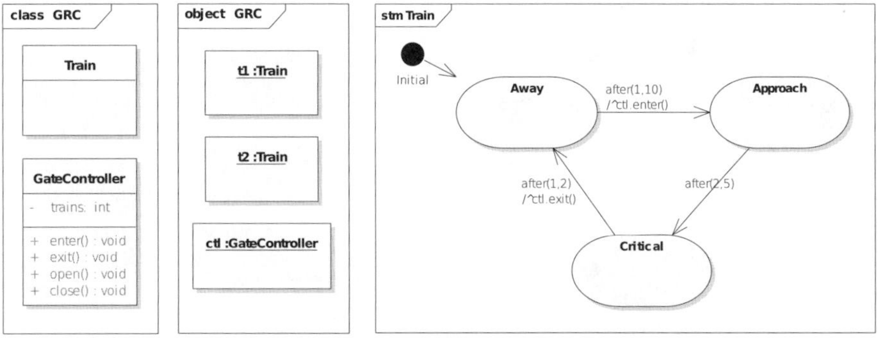

(a) Class and object diagrams (b) State machine diagram of class Train

Fig. 4. Specification of GRC system

(e.g. in Fig. 4(a)), and k state machine diagrams (e.g. in Fig. 4(b), 5), each one assigned to a different class of the class diagram.

The class diagram defines a list of attributes and a list of operations (possibly with parameters) for each class. The object diagram specifies the instances of classes (objects) and (optionally) assigns the initial values to variables. All the objects are visible globally. Moreover the set of objects is constant during the life time of the system and therefore dynamic object creation and termination is not allowed. Each object is assigned an instance of a state machine that determines the behaviour of the object. A state machine diagram typically consists of states, regions and transitions connecting source and target states. We consider several types of states, namely: simple states (e.g., *Away* in Fig. 4(b)), composite states, (e.g., *Main* in Fig. 5), final states, and initial pseudo-states, (e.g., *Initial* in Fig. 5). The areas filling the composite states are called *regions*. The regions contain states and transitions, and thus introduce a *hierarchy* of state machines. The labels of transitions are expressions of the form $trigger[guard]/action$, where each of these components can be empty. The transitions with non-empty trigger are called *triggered transitions*. A transition can be fired if the source state is *active*, the guard (a Boolean expression) is satisfied, and the trigger matching event occurs. An event can be of the following three types: an *operation call*, a *completion event*, or a *time event*. The operation calls coming to the given object are put into the *event queue* of the object, and then, one at a time, they are handled. The completion events and the time events are processed without placing them in queues.

The highest priority is bound to completion events. A completion event occurs for a state, when all internal activities of the state terminate. Then the completion event is discarded (when it cannot fire any transition – level 1 of the hierarchy), or it fires a transition and is consumed (level 2). If none of the above cases holds, triggered transitions are considered. The event from the head of the queue, or a time event possibly fires a transition (level 3), and is consumed. If the event from the head of the queue cannot fire any transition and

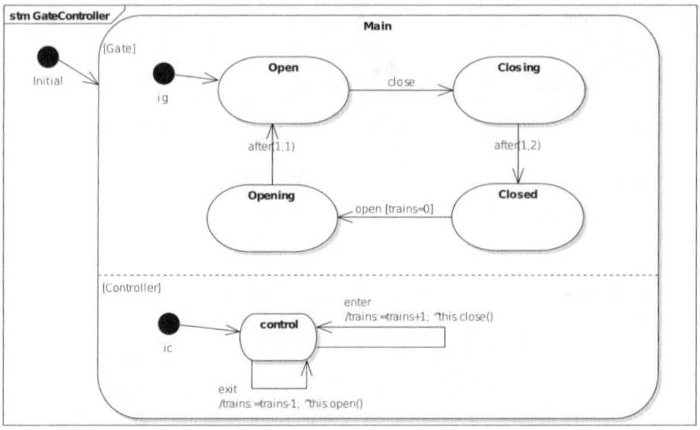

Fig. 5. Specification of GRC system - state machine diagram of class GateController

the matching trigger is *deferred* in the current state, then the event is deferred (level 4), i.e., it will be processed later. Otherwise, the event is discarded (level 5). We refer to the processing of a single event from the queue or a time event as the *Run-To-Completion (RTC) step*. Next, an event can be handled only if the previous one has been fully processed, together with all the completion events which eventually have occurred.

The execution of the whole system follows the interleaving semantics, similar to [10]. During a single step only one object performs its RTC step. If more than one object can execute such a step, then an object is chosen in a non-deterministic way. However, if none of the objects can perform an *untimed action*, then the time flows (level 6).

3 Bounded Model Checking methodology

In this section we present some basic ideas behind Bounded Model Checking and parametric verification.

3.1 SAT-Based Bounded Model Checking

Bounded Model Checking (BMC) is a symbolic method aimed at verification of temporal properties of distributed (timed) systems. It is based on the observation that some properties of a system can be checked using only a part of its model.

In order to apply SAT-based BMC to testing whether a system satisfies a certain (usually undesired) property, we unfold the transition relation of a given system up to some depth k, and encode this unfolding as a propositional formula. Then, the formula expressing a property to be tested is encoded as a propositional formula as well, and satisfiability of the conjunction of these two formulas is checked using a SAT-solver. If the conjunction is satisfiable, one can conclude that a witness was found. Otherwise, the value of k is incremented. The above process can be terminated when the value of k is equal to the diameter of the system, i.e., to the maximal length of a shortest path between its two arbitrary states.

All the above processes are performed fully automatically and do not require any assistance from the user.

3.2 Parametric Verification

The parametric verification performed in our system is of two kinds. In the case of systems modelled by Elementary Petri Nets, BMC is applied to verification of properties expressed in the existential fragment of the logic PRTCTL [12], i.e., PRTECTL. The logic PRTCTL is an extension of Computation Tree Logic (CTL), which allows to formulate properties involving lengths of paths in a model. Informally, the fragment of PRTCTL we consider consists of all the existential CTL formulas, these formulas augmented with superscripts of the form $\leq c$ (where $c \in \mathbb{N}$) restricting the length of the path of interest, and the formulas as above, but with c replaced by a linear expression over a set of natural-valued parameters, preceded by the existential or universal quantifier over (possibly bounded) valuations of these parameters. As to give an example, consider $\mathrm{EG}^{\leq 3}p$, which expresses that there is a path such that in the first four states of this path p holds. Another example is $\forall_{\Theta_1 \leq 1} \exists_{\Theta_2 \leq 2} \mathrm{EF}^{\leq \Theta_1 + \Theta_2} p$, which expresses that for each value of the parameter Θ_1 not greater than 1 there is a value of the parameter Θ_2 not exceeding 2 s.t. for some path we can reach p while visiting not more than $\Theta_1 + \Theta_2 + 1$ first states of that path. The propositions appearing in these formulas correspond to the places of the net considered. To the aim of verification using BMC, the qualitative properties expressed in PRTECTL are directly encoded as propositional formulas. Using some basic features of the considered logic, we introduce bounds on the parameters where not present, and replace the universal and existential quantifiers with, respectively, conjunctions and disjunctions.

Parametric BMC for PRTECTL. The verification of PRTECTL is performed by a translation of a part of a model, together with a property to be checked, to a propositional formula. We have proved in [19] that the method is correct and theoretically complete, albeit in practice translated formulas might be too complex for current SAT-solvers – that is often the case, when the depth of the unwinding is close to the size of a model. We use the Kripke structures induced by Petri nets (i.e., the marking graphs) as the models for PRTECTL logic, where the transitions are assumed to take one unit of time. Such an approach has several benefits listed below.

1. Our choice of parameterized logic is practical, as it is known that the parameterized extensions of temporal logics tend to be difficult problems in model-checking. For example, the joint complexity of verification of the existential fragment of TCTL, is 3EXPTIME [5], which is due to the presence of satisfiability in Presburger Arithmetics as a subproblem.

2. It is shown in [12] that the complexity of model-checking of a PRTCTL formula ϕ containing k parameters, over a Kripke model M, is $O(|M|^{k+1} \cdot |\phi|)$, where $|M|$ stands for the size of M and $|\phi|$ stands for the length of ϕ. Notice, however, that the Kripke structures induced by Petri nets tend to be very large (exponential in the size of the nets), hence the general verification problem may be untractable for many real-life systems. The BMC approach allows for checking some of difficult properties in a part of the model, giving a chance to succeed where the explicit approaches fail.
3. The PRTECTL logic can be model-checked by means of the standard BMC, using an extension of the efficient translation proposed in [37]. This is a serious advantage as the encoding employs an adequate set of symbolic paths for each subformula of a given formula.

A detailed description of the method can be found in [19].

Parametric Reachability. Parametric verification of Time Petri Nets and systems specified in UML is restricted to testing parametric reachability only. Again, the propositions used to build the properties tested correspond to the places of the nets. Besides "ordinary" reachability verification, VerICS enables searching for the minimal time $c \in \mathbb{N}$ in which a state satisfying p can be reached, or finding the minimal time $c \in \mathbb{N}$ after which p does not hold. This is formally expressed respectively as finding the minimal c such that $\mathrm{EF}^{<c}p$ (or $\mathrm{EF}^{\leq c}p$) holds, and finding a maximal c such that $\mathrm{EF}^{>c}p$ (or $\mathrm{EF}^{\geq c}p$) holds. To this aim, *parametric reachability checking* is used. The algorithm for finding the minimal $c \in \mathbb{N}$ such that $EF^{\leq c}p$ holds is as follows:

1. Using the standard BMC approach, find a reachability witness of minimal length[4],
2. Read from the witness the time required to reach p (denoted x). Now, we know that $c \leq \lceil x \rceil$ (where $\lceil \cdot \rceil$ is the *ceiling* function),
3. Extend the verified TPN with a new process N, which is composed of one transition t s.t. $Eft(t) = Lft(t) = n$, and two places p_{in}, p_{out}, where p_{in} is the input place and p_{out} is the output place of t,
4. Set n to $\lceil x \rceil - 1$,
5. Run BMC to test reachability of a state satisfying $p \wedge p_{in}$ in the extended TPN,
6. If such a state is reachable, set $n := n - 1$ and go to 5,
7. If such a state is unreachable, then $c := n + 1$, STOP.

The algorithms for other cases are similar. The details can be found in [30].

Concerning the systems specified in UML, VerICS offers similar options as in the case of Time Petri Nets, i.e., reachability and parametric reachability verification. However, in this case we are restricted to searching for the minimal integer c s.t. $EF^{\leq c}p$ holds in the model. The algorithm is based on the same idea as before. The main differences can be formulated as follows:

[4] If we cannot find such a witness, then we try to prove unreachability of p.

- instead of the additional process we introduce an additional clock that is never reset,
- the values of the clocks can take only natural numbers.

The details of the verification method can be found in [25].

4 The Implementation

Our goal is to symbolically represent all the possible computations of a fixed length k of a given system. In all the cases, i.e., for ENS, TPN, and UML, the main idea is similar: we represent a set of global states (configurations) as a single *symbolic state*, i.e., as a vector of propositional variables $\mathbf{w}$ (called a *state variable vector*). Then, $k+1$ state variable vectors stand for a symbolic k-path, where the first symbolic state encodes the initial state of the system, and the last one corresponds to the last states of the k-paths. Next, we encode the transition relation over the symbolic k-path as a propositional formula, and compute a formula encoding the property tested. Hence, in the general case, the formula encoding the symbolic k-path is defined as follows:

$$path_k(\mathbf{w}^0, \ldots, \mathbf{w}^k) = \mathfrak{I}(\mathbf{w}^0) \wedge \bigwedge_{i=0}^{k-1} \mathfrak{T}(\mathbf{w}^i, \mathbf{w}^{i+1}) \tag{1}$$

where $\mathfrak{I}(\mathbf{w}^0)$ encodes the initial state of the system, and $\mathfrak{T}(\mathbf{w}^i, \mathbf{w}^{i+1})$ encodes a transition between symbolic states represented by the global state vectors $\mathbf{w}^i$ and $\mathbf{w}^{i+1}$.

In what follows we shortly describe how to define $\mathfrak{T}(\mathbf{w}^i, \mathbf{w}^{i+1})$ for ENS, TPN, and systems in UML.

4.1 Implementation for ENS

Consider an Elementary Net System $EN = (P, T, F, m^0)$, where the places are denoted with the integers smaller or equal than $n = |P|$. We use the set $\{p_1, \ldots, p_n\}$ of propositions, where p_i is interpreted as the presence of a token in the place i. We define the model $M = (S, \rightarrow, \mathcal{L})$ for ENS, where $S = M_{EN}$ is the set of the reachable configurations, $s \rightarrow s'$ iff there exists $t \in T$ such that $s[t\rangle s'$ for $s, s' \in S$, and $p_i \in \mathcal{L}(s)$ iff $i \in s$. The states of S are encoded by valuations of a vector of state variables $\mathbf{w} = (\mathbf{w}[1], \ldots, \mathbf{w}[n])$, where $\mathbf{w}[i] = p_i$ for $0 \leq i \leq n$. The initial state and the transition relation $\rightarrow$ are encoded as follows:

- $I_{m^0}(w) := \bigwedge_{i \in m^0} w[i] \wedge \bigwedge_{i \in P \setminus m^0} \neg w[i]$,
- $\mathfrak{T}(\mathbf{w}, \mathbf{v}) := \bigvee_{t \in T} \big(\bigwedge_{i \in pre(t)} \mathbf{w}[i] \wedge \bigwedge_{i \in (post(t) \setminus pre(t))} \neg \mathbf{w}[i] \wedge \bigwedge_{i \in (pre(t) \setminus post(t))} \neg \mathbf{v}[i]$ $\wedge \bigwedge_{i \in post(t)} \mathbf{v}[i] \wedge \bigwedge_{i \in (P \setminus (pre(t) \cup post(t))) \cup (pre(t) \cap post(t))} \mathbf{w}[i] \iff \mathbf{v}[i] \big)$.

As to give an outline of the encoding of the PRTECTL formulas, consider the formula $\beta = \exists_{\Theta \leq c} \alpha(\Theta)$, where $\alpha(\Theta)$ is a PRTECTL formula containing free variable Θ, and $c \in \mathbb{N}$. For a given depth k of the unfolding let $d = min(c, k)$. We define the translation of β in m–th symbolic state of n–th symbolic path, using the set of indices of symbolic k–paths A, as follows:

$$[\beta]_k^{[m,n,A]} := [\alpha(d)]_k^{[m,n,\hat{g}_L(A,f_k(\alpha(d)))]} \vee [\exists_{\Theta \leq d-1}\alpha(\Theta)]_k^{[m,n,\hat{g}_L(A,f_k(\exists_{\Theta \leq d-1}\alpha(\Theta)))]},$$

where f_k a function returning the number of k–paths sufficient to perform the translation of a given formula, and $\hat{g}_L(A, b)$ returns the subset of b least elements of A. The f_k function is an extension of its counterpart for ECTL from [31].

Similarly, consider the formula $\gamma = \forall_{\Theta \leq c}\alpha(\Theta)$. The translation of γ is defined as follows:

$$[\gamma]_k^{[m,n,A]} := [\alpha(c)]_k^{[m,n,\hat{g}_L(A,f_k(\alpha(c)))]} \wedge [\forall_{\Theta \leq c-1}\alpha(\Theta)]_k^{[m,n,\hat{g}_R(A,f_k(\forall_{\Theta \leq c-1}\alpha(\Theta)))]},$$

where $\hat{g}_R(A, b)$ returns the subset of b greatest elements of A.

The consecutive application of any of the above rules leads to the conjunction of $d + 1$ propositional formulas containing no existential quantifiers. These formulas are in turn translated using the efficient translation inspired by its counterpart for ECTL (see [37]), where $\hat{g}_L$ and $\hat{g}_R$ are introduced along with several other methods for an optimal path selection.

A more detailed description and the encoding of the formulas of PRTECTL can be found in [19].

4.2 Implementation for TPN

The main difference between symbolic encoding of the transition relation of ENS and TPN consists in the time flow. A current state of a TPN $\mathcal{N}$ is given by its marking and the time passed since each of the enabled transitions became enabled (which influences the future behaviour of the net). Thus, a *concrete state* σ of $\mathcal{N}$ can be defined as an ordered pair $(m, clock)$, where m is a marking, and $clock : \mathfrak{I} \to \mathbb{R}_+$ is a function, which for each index $\mathfrak{i}$ of a process of $\mathcal{N}$ gives the time elapsed since the marked place of this process became marked most recently [32].

Given a set of propositional variables PV, we introduce a *valuation function* $V_c : \Sigma \to 2^{PV}$, which assigns the same propositions to the states with the same markings. We assume the set PV to be such that each $q \in PV$ corresponds to exactly one place $p \in P$, and use the same names for the propositions and the places. The function V_c is defined by $p \in V_c(\sigma) \Leftrightarrow p \in m$ for each $\sigma = (m, \cdot)$. The structure $M_c(\mathcal{N}) = ((T \cup \mathbb{R}_+, \Sigma, \sigma^0, \to_c), V_c)$ is called a *concrete (dense) model of* $\mathcal{N}$. It is easy to see that concrete models are usually infinite.

In order to deal with countable structures instead of uncountable ones, we introduce *extended detailed region graphs* for distributed TPNs. They correspond to the well-known graphs defined for timed automata in [1] and adapted for Time Petri Nets [26,35], but involve disjunctions of constraints, the reflexive transitive closure of the time successor of [1], and make no use of the maximal constant appearing in the invariants and enabling conditions. To do this, we assign a clock to each of the processes of a net.

To apply the BMC approach to verification of a particular distributed Time Petri Net $\mathcal{N}$, we deal with a model obtained by a *discretisation* of its extended detailed region graph. The model is of an infinite but countable structure, which, however, is sufficient for BMC (which deals with finite sequences of states only). Instead of dealing with the whole extended detailed region graph, we *discretise* this structure, choosing for each region one or more appropriate representatives. The discretisation scheme is based on the one for timed automata [36], and preserves the qualitative behaviour of the underlying system. The details and the formal definitions can be found in [30].

4.3 Implementation for UML

Symbolic semantics. Below we sketch a symbolic encoding of the operational semantics introduced in [24,25].As usual, the global states are represented by state variable vectors. However each global state g is represented by n subvectors, where each one stands for a state of one object (n is the number of objects in the system). The representation of a state of a single object consists of five components that encode respectively a set of active states, a set of completed states, a contents of the event queue, a valuation of the variables, and a valuation of the clocks.

Moreover, according to the OMG semantics, the transition relation is *hierarchical*, i.e., we distinguish between 6 levels (types) of transitions, where the ordering follows their priorities. Therefore, we ensure that a transition of each level becomes enabled only if the transitions of the preceding levels cannot be executed, by nesting the conditions for the consecutive levels [24,25].

Symbolic encoding. The implementations described above for Timed Petri Nets were closely following the general idea of implementing formalisms based on transitions systems, e.g., with symbolic states capable of representing every part of system states, and Boolean constraints added for transitions with respective guards, invariants, etc. While the symbolic operational semantics of UML could be expressed in terms of timed automata or Petri nets, the resulting translation would be highly complex because of the need for representing by means of automata every language construct, most of which are semantically not a close match with this formalism. We have tried another way by encoding these constructions directly into propositional logic, without introducing any intermediate transition systems. The general idea can be described as follows: states of state machines are encoded directly, by assigning boolean variables in symbolic vectors representing system states. Then, propositional formulas are defined for encoding every transition type. Finally, these formulas are structured according to the hierarchy of corresponding transitions (see Section 2.3, page 103), giving as a result the formula encoding the transition relation.

We define propositional formulas $EOi(o, \mathbf{w})$ for transitions of types $1 \leq i \leq 5$ that encode their preconditions over the vector $\mathbf{w}$ for the object o. Also we define the propositional formulas $XOi(o, \mathbf{w}, \mathbf{v})$ for $1 \leq i \leq 5$ encoding an execution of these transitions over the vectors $\mathbf{w}, \mathbf{v}$ for the object o and the formula $X6(\mathbf{w}, \mathbf{v})$ encoding the time flow.

The transitions of types 1–5 are called *local* as their execution does not depend on the type of a transition that can be fired by other objects. The execution of local transitions for object o over the vectors of the state variables $\mathbf{w}$ and $\mathbf{v}$ is recursively encoded as:

$$\begin{aligned} f_5(o,\mathbf{w},\mathbf{v}) &= EO5(o,\mathbf{w}) \wedge XO5(o,\mathbf{w},\mathbf{v}) \\ f_i(o,\mathbf{w},\mathbf{v}) &= EOi(o,\mathbf{w}) \wedge XOi(o,\mathbf{w},\mathbf{v}) \\ &\quad \vee \neg EOi(o,\mathbf{w}) \wedge f_{i+1}(o,\mathbf{w},\mathbf{v}) \texttt{ for } i \in \{1,2,3,4\}, \end{aligned} \tag{2}$$

and we denote $f_1(o,\mathbf{w},\mathbf{v})$ by $XO(o,\mathbf{w},\mathbf{v})$.

We ensure that a transition of each level becomes enabled only if the transitions of the preceeding levels cannot be executed, by nesting the conditions for the consecutive levels. All the components of the encoded model are represented by propositional formulas. For example, an event queue is encoded along with the corresponding operations of inserting and removing an event, testing if a queue is empty or full and so on. A queue is modeled by a circular buffer, with indices pointing to first deferred event, an event to be processed next, and the first free position of the queue (a place for inserting new events).

Then, iterating over the objects of class c, we encode the execution of the local transitions for the class c:

$$XC(c,\mathbf{w},\mathbf{v}) = \bigvee_{o \in Objects(c)} XO(o,\mathbf{w},\mathbf{v}). \tag{3}$$

Now, we are ready to give the encoding of the transition relation:

$$\mathfrak{T}(\mathbf{w},\mathbf{v}) = \bigvee_{c \in Classes} XC(c,\mathbf{w},\mathbf{v}) \vee E6(\mathbf{w}) \wedge X6(\mathbf{w},\mathbf{v}), \tag{4}$$

where $E6(\mathbf{w})$ encodes the enabling conditions of the time flow transition.

In this way we have managed to deal with the hierarchical structure of the transition relation simply by nesting the appropriate formula encoding every level of the hierarchy.

5 Experimental Results

We present some experimental results for parametric verification of systems specified as ENS, Distributed TPN, or in our subset of UML. We deal with standard benchmarks, i.e., timed and untimed versions of the mutual exclusion protocol and the Generalised Railroad Crossing system as well as with timed and untimed versions of Generic Pipeline Paradigm model [28].

Our motivation for presenting the results is to give an idea about the overall performance and about typical problems the tool deals with. To the best of our knowledge there are no other tools performing parametric model checking for a similar input, so we cannot follow a common pattern of comparing several tools for the same input. However, we provide some comparisons with other tools for non-parametric problems in order to give a hint about the efficiency of VerICS.

5.1 Elementary Net Systems

In the case of Elementary Petri Nets we have tested two models. The first one is a system which models the well-known mutual exclusion problem, shown in Fig. 2. The system consists of $n+1$ processes (where $n \geq 2$) of which n processes compete for the access to the shared resource, while one process guards that no two processes use the resource simultaneously. The presence of a token in the place labelled by w_i means that the i-th process is waiting for the access to the critical section while the token in c_i means that the i-th process has acquired the permission and entered the critical section. The place r_i models the unguarded part of the process and the presence of the token in the place p indicates that the resource is available.

We have explored the validity of the formula $\varphi_1^b = \forall_{\Theta \leq b} EF(\neg p \wedge EG^{\leq \Theta} c_1)$ with respect to the value of b. Intuitively, φ_1^b expresses that for each parameter valuation Θ bounded by b, there exists a future state such that the first process stays in the critical section for at least Θ time steps. It is quite obvious that the non-parameterized counterpart of the formula φ_1, i.e., $EF(\neg p \wedge EGc_1)$ does not hold in our model as no process can stay in the critical section forever. The experimental results for the protocol are presented in Table 1.

formula	n	k	PBMC				MiniSAT	SAT?
			vars	clauses	sec	MB	sec	
φ_1^1	3	2	1063	2920	0.01	1.3	0.003	NO
φ_1^1	3	3	1505	4164	0.01	1.5	0.008	YES
φ_1^2	3	4	2930	8144	0.01	1.5	0.01	NO
φ_1^2	3	5	3593	10010	0.01	1.6	0.03	YES
φ_1^2	30	4	37825	108371	0.3	7.4	0.2	NO
φ_1^2	30	5	46688	133955	0.4	8.9	0.52	YES
φ_1^3	4	6	8001	22378	0.06	2.5	0.04	NO
φ_1^3	4	7	9244	25886	0.05	2.8	0.05	YES

Table 1. Elementary Net Systems: Mutual exclusion, testing the formula φ_1^b

The Generic Pipeline Paradigm modelled by an Elementary Petri Net is the second system we have tested. The model consists of three parts, namely: the Producer which is able to produce data ($ProdReady$), the Consumer being able to receive data ($ConsReady$) and a chain of n intermediate Nodes – having capabilities of data receiving ($Node_i Ready$), processing ($Node_i Proc_j$), and sending ($Node_i Send$). Notice that the example is scalable in two ways: firstly – the number n of the processing Nodes can be increased in order to modify the length of the pipeline chain, secondly – the length m of the processing queue in each intermediate Node can be incremented, which may be interpreted as modifying the time spent on internal calculations. In the experiments we explore how these changes affect the validity of the formula tested and the tool performance.

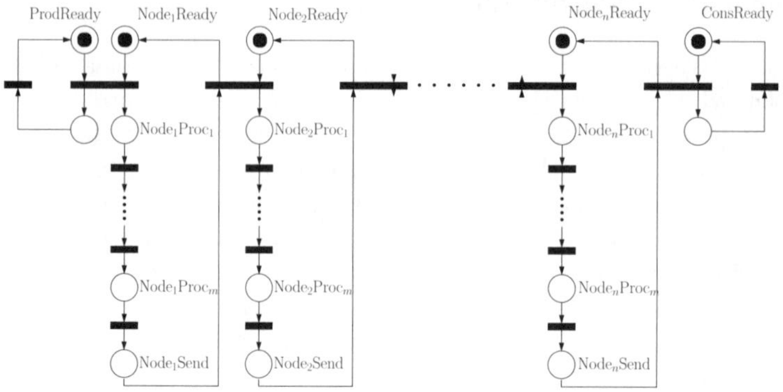

Fig. 6. Elementary Net Systems: Generic Pipeline Paradigm

We have tested the following property:

$$\varphi_4^{n,m} = \forall_{\Theta \leq nm-1} EFEG^{\leq \Theta}(\neg ProdReady \wedge \neg ConsReady \wedge \bigvee_{i=1}^{n} \neg Node_i Ready).$$

The intuitive meaning of $\varphi_4^{n,m}$ is that it is possible that for some state of the system, during some time (bounded by $nm - 1$) neither Producer is able to produce, nor Consumer is able to receive, while the intermediate Node chain is processing or transferring data. The experimental results for the Generic Pipeline Paradigm modelled by an Elementary Petri Net are presented in Table 2.

Table 2. Elementary Net Systems: Generic Pipeline Paradigm, testing the formula $\varphi_4^{n,m}$

formula	n	m	k	PBMC				MiniSAT	SAT?
				vars	clauses	sec	MB	sec	
$\varphi_4^{2,1}$	2	1	6	4086	11315	0.03	2.07	0.008	NO
$\varphi_4^{2,1}$	2	1	7	4696	13079	0.036	2.7	0.02	YES
$\varphi_4^{2,2}$	2	2	8	5980	16811	0.06	2.6	0.01	NO
$\varphi_4^{2,2}$	2	2	9	13484	37927	0.08	2.7	0.06	YES
$\varphi_4^{2,3}$	2	3	10	8844	24873	0.07	2.9	0.02	NO
$\varphi_4^{2,3}$	2	3	11	9776	27509	0.08	3.1	0.2	YES
$\varphi_4^{3,1}$	3	1	8	7416	20739	0.04	2.6	0.01	NO
$\varphi_4^{3,1}$	3	1	9	8292	23207	0.03	2.7	0.07	YES
$\varphi_4^{3,2}$	3	2	11	20025	56568	0.12	4.6	0.04	NO
$\varphi_4^{3,2}$	3	2	12	21768	61517	0.14	4.7	0.43	YES
$\varphi_4^{10,1}$	10	1	24	74488	212315	0.4	13.2	0.43	NO
$\varphi_4^{10,1}$	10	1	25	77548	221055	0.52	13.6	19.2	YES
$\varphi_4^{10,2}$	10	2	32	111844	320863	1.6	37.3	0.98	NO
$\varphi_4^{10,2}$	10	2	33	230812	662175	1.64	38.4	23.1	YES

The experiments were performed on a Linux machine with dual core 1.6 GHz processor; satisfiability was tested using the MiniSAT solver [23].

5.2 Distributed Time Petri Nets

We have tested Distributed Time Petri Nets specifying the standard (timed) *Fischer's mutual exclusion protocol* (mutex) [2] and a timed version of Generic Pipeline Paradigm.

The mutex model consists of N Time Petri Nets, each one modelling a process, together with one additional net used to coordinate their access to the critical sections. A distributed TPN modelling the system for $n = 2$ is shown in Fig. 3. *Mutual exclusion* means that no two processes can reach their critical sections at the same time. The preservation of this property depends on the relative values of the time-delay constants δ and Δ parametrizing the system: they correspond to the earliest firing time of the the transition entering the critical section and the latest firing time of the transition entering the waiting section, respectively. In particular, the following property holds: "*Fischer's protocol ensures mutual exclusion iff* $\Delta < \delta$".

We have searched for the minimal c such that $\mathrm{EF}^{\leq c}p$ holds. The results are presented in Table 3 (see the table denoted with **Tb**). We considered the case, where $\Delta = 2$ and $\delta = 1$, and the net of 25 processes. The witness was found for $k = 12$, while the time of the path found was between 8 and 9. The column marked with n shows the values of the parameter in the additional component. For $n = 1$ and $k = 12$ unsatisfiability was returned. Testing the property on a longer path could not be completed in a reasonable time.

Comparing the last two rows of Table **Tb** one can see the typical behaviour of SAT testers, namely that diagnosing unsatisfiability is usually much harder than satisfiability given formulas of similar size.

We have compared the efficiency of VerICS with the tool Romeo [22], using exactly the same mutex benchmark and testing the same property. The left part (denoted with **Ta**) of Table 3 contains the results, where N is the number of processes.

The Generic Timed Pipelining Paradigm modelled by a Distributed Time Petri Net has a structure similar to its untimed version. Again, the system consists of Producer, Consumer, and a chain of n intermediate Nodes. As previously,

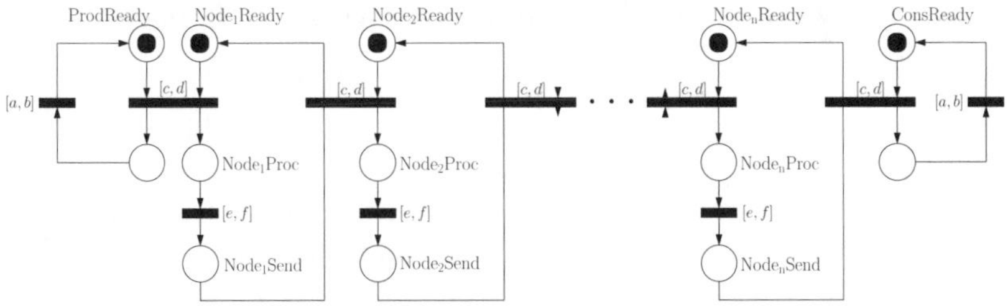

Fig. 7. Distributed Time Petri Nets: Generic Timed Pipelining Paradigm

Table 3. Distributed Time Petri Nets: Results for mutex, $\Delta = 2$, $\delta = 1$, mutual exclusion violated. Left: comparison with Romeo. Right: details of verification with VerICS for 25 processes. The tpnBMC column shows the results for the part of the tool used to represent the problem as a propositional formula (a set of clauses); the column RSat displays the results of running the RSat solver for the set of clauses obtained from tpnBMC.

Ta	Romeo		VerICS	
N	sec	MB	sec	MB
2	0.1	1	0.65	3
3	0.14	6	2.65	4
4	0.61	9	1.92	5
5	4.99	38	2.93	6
6	44.76	364	6.02	7
7	>360	>2000	8.63	9
8	-	-	12.67	12
9	-	-	20.74	15
10	-	-	30.28	23
12	-	-	43.72	32
15	-	-	136.78	92
20	-	-	551.64	299
25	-	-	1304.2	538

Tb		tpnBMC				RSat		
k	N	variables	clauses	sec	MB	sec	MB	sat
0	-	840	2192	0.02	1.688	0	1.4	NO
2	-	16263	47705	0.31	3.621	0	4.9	NO
4	-	33835	99737	0.66	5.805	0.3	9.1	NO
6	-	51406	151697	1.04	8.113	0.8	13.8	NO
8	-	72752	214851	1.49	10.81	8.5	27.7	NO
10	-	92629	273489	1.95	13.27	152.3	200.8	NO
12	-	113292	334355	2.4	15.84	6.7	39.0	YES
12	8	120182	354944	2.57	16.74	13.8	47.9	YES
12	7	120254	355178	2.67	16.74	5.7	38.3	YES
12	3	115675	341405	2.52	16.22	12.7	49.0	YES
12	2	115669	341387	2.56	16.23	3.3	32.3	YES
12	1	115729	341579	2.54	16.23	1100.1	538.4	NO
sum for all rows:				20.73	16.23	1304.2	538.4	

the length of the chain is scalable, this time however we are able to manipulate the time properties of all the parts by means of parameters a, b, c, d, e, and f. In this way we can specify, for example, the maximal idle time allowed for Producer or Consumer. We have tested the following formula:

$$\varphi_5 := EF^{\leq \Theta}(\neg ProdReady \wedge \neg ConsReady).$$

Intuitively, it expresses that the system can reach, in the time smaller or equal than some value Θ, such a state that Producer is not able to produce, and Consumer receiving abilities are disabled. The aim of the experiment was to synthesize the smallest Θ value for which φ_5 holds, using parametric reachability methods. We have checked the property for various instances of Generic Timed Pipelining Paradigm, by setting some arbitrary values of the chain length n, and the time constraint parameters a, b, c, d, e, and f. The results can be found in Table 4.

The experiments were performed on the computer equipped with Intel Pentium Core 2 Duo CPU (2.40 GHz), 2 GB main memory and the operating system Linux 2.6.28.

5.3 UML

The UML specification tested is a variant of the well known Generalised Railroad Crossing (GRC) benchmark (Fig. 4, 5). The system, operating a gate at a railroad crossing, consists of a gate, a controller, and N tracks which are occupied by trains. Each track is equipped with sensors that indicate a position of a train and send an appropriate message to the controller. Depending on the track occupancy

Table 4. Distributed Time Petri Nets: Testing the formula φ_5. Memory in megabytes, time in seconds.

n	k	time params						PBMC				RSat		synth. Θ
		a	b	c	d	e	f	clauses	vars	time	mem	time	mem	
1	10	1	1	1	3	1	3	19686	6915	0.25	2.203	0.1	2.8	6
1	10	1	3	3	4	3	5	22928	7974	0.3	2.332	0.1	3.1	12
2	14	1	2	1	3	2	4	41467	14378	0.77	3.105	0.5	4.6	7
2	14	1	1	2	4	2	5	44191	15306	0.57	3.234	0.4	4.8	10
3	18	1	4	2	2	1	5	73913	25554	0.94	4.52	1.9	7.2	11
3	26	1	2	1	3	2	5	133423	46028	1.7	7.098	19.3	13.9	10
4	30	1	4	2	2	1	5	109339	37923	1.82	6.059	3.4	10	11
4	22	2	3	1	2	1	3	115001	29661	1.47	6.289	5.2	10.4	9
5	34	1	4	2	2	1	5	92628	268942	3.74	12.75	93.7	28.8	17
5	36	1	3	1	2	2	3	291710	100530	4.09	13.66	61.8	27	16
6	30	2	3	1	4	0	1	235115	81118	3.82	11.34	27.8	21.6	7
6	38	1	4	2	2	1	5	354108	121937	4.64	16.36	92.2	34.1	20
7	34	2	3	1	4	0	1	311252	107432	4.78	14.56	31.8	26.3	8
7	54	1	4	2	2	1	5	687242	236971	11.17	30.41	2565.0	177.2	23

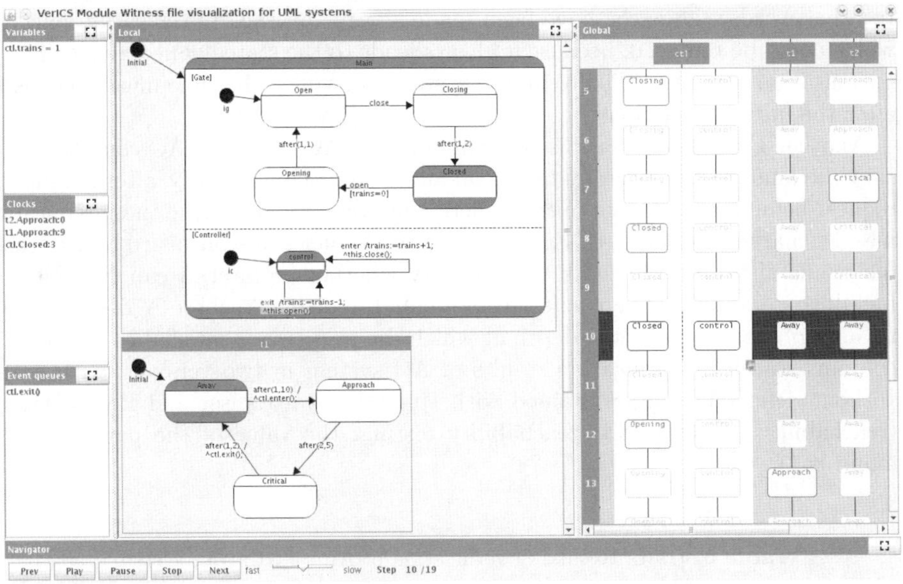

Fig. 8. GUI screenshot: Simulation of a UML witness

the controller can either open or close the gate. We check whether a train can cross the road while the gate is not closed. The tests have been performed on the computer equipped with Pentium M 1.73 GHz CPU and 1.2 GB RAM running Linux.

Table 5. UML: The results of verification of GRC

N	Hugo & Uppaal[s]	BMC4UML[s]			BMC4UML*[s]		
		k	reachability	par.reach.	k	reachability	par.reach.
3	2.89	24	86.07	140.9	18	40.44	27.51
4	175.41	25	139.4	83.45	18	50.41	85.01
5	>2500	26	221.4	240.9	18	59.90	131.5
6	—	27	1354.9	365.4	18	75.21	175.6
7	—	—	—	—	18	92.60	191.5
20	—	—	—	—	18	448.6	620.7

Table 5 presents the results of verification, where N denotes the number of trains, and k - the depth of a symbolic path at which the tested property is satisfiable. The next columns show the time consumed by Hugo/Uppaal toolset, and our BMC4UML tool (reachability and parametric reachability testing). The minimal time in which property can be reached (as introduced in Section 3.2, p. 106) was found to be 6. The results in the column marked with the asterisk concern the symbolic paths of length 18 that do not start from the initial state of the GRC system, but from the state where all the trains are in the states *Away* and the object *ctl* is in the states *Main*, *Open*, and *control* (see Fig. 4, 5). In other words, the paths have been made shorter by the "initialisation part", which could be removed, because it always leads to the state defined above. This optimisation can be applied to all the systems for which the time must flow just after the initial transitions.

Another UML benchmark is Aircraft Carrier (AC - Fig. 9). AC consists of a ship and a number of aircrafts taking off and landing continuously, after issuing a request being accepted by the controller. The events of answering these requests may be marked as deferred. Each aircraft refills fuel while on board and burns fuel while airborne. We check the property whether an aircraft can run out of fuel during its flight. The results are presented in Table 6, where N denotes the number of planes, and k the depth at which the property is satisfiable. The next columns stand for verification results of AC system in two versions: with and without deferred events, obtained with Hugo/Uppaal toolset and BMC4UML (reachability + parametric reachability testing, the value of the parameter c found is 4).

Table 6. UML: Results of verification of Aircraft Carrier system

N	k	Hugo+Uppaal [s]		BMC4UML [s]	
		deferred	no defer	deferred	no defer
3	19	1.32	1.25	67.59 + 31.34	51.26 + 22.64
4	20	13.15	11.41	101.58 + 45.44	81.28 + 42.38
5	21	147.43	95.67	155.63 + 60.49	132.34 + 37.01
6	22	Out of mem		257.08 + 52.23	216.42 + 75.08
7	23	—		686.06 + 101.86	421.85 + 199.09

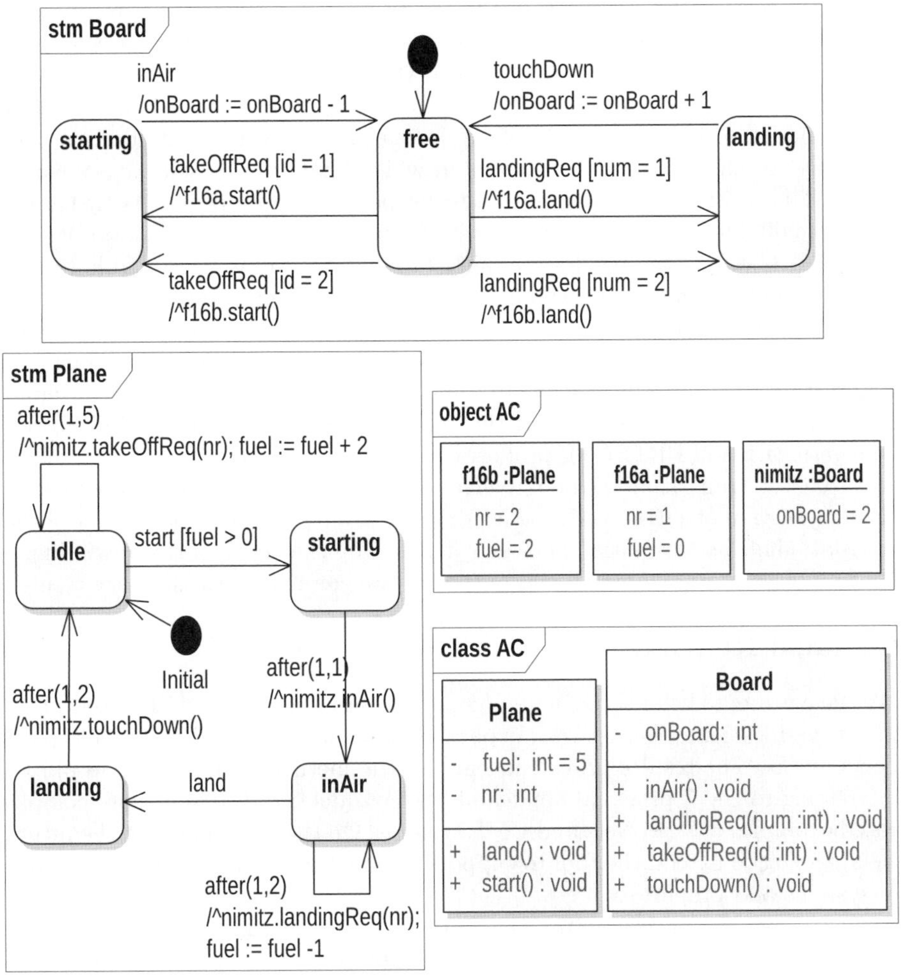

Fig. 9. UML diagrams of Aircraft Carrier

Finally, if the tested property is satisfiable, then it can be visualised and simulated with the VerICS graphical user interface (see Fig. 8).

5.4 Analysis of the Results

The experiments have confirmed the well-known fact that BMC is a method of falsification rather than verification. The method performs best when a counterexample is found before the resources are exhausted when increasing the depth of the unfolding. The parametric features seem to work best within the range of successful BMC applications.

Our general observation on the non-parametric features is that we have obtained the efficient state representations and the compact encoding of the transition relation for all the types of the presented systems. The overall performance is determined by the characteristics of the method to which these representations and encodings are applied (BMC in this case).

Concerning our parametric extensions, our motivation was to show that they can be added to the framework relatively easily. We learned that the best performance is achieved for the scenarios in which BMC works well, i.e., on short paths. The overhead introduced by testing parametric properties is then relatively small. The parameter synthesis in the parametric reachability problem is a difficult task, yet the results are quite promising – we have been able to test simple models in matter of seconds or minutes, however the verification of some properties in the large networks (e.g., Generic Timed Pipelining Paradigm with 7 nodes, $a = 1$, $b = 4$, $c = d = 2$, $e = 1$, $f = 5$) took a large amount of time (see Figure 4). The latter is mostly due to the size of the tested propositional formulas and may heavily depend on heuristics implemented in the applied SAT-solver. The verification of PRTECTL properties seems to be quite efficient, despite the fact that the translation of the universal quantifier bounded with b results with the conjunction of length $b+1$. Notice that the disjunction being the result of the translation of the existential quantifier depends on the depth of the unwinding – hence in case of purely existential properties we can expect satisfactory results.

6 Final Remarks

We have presented the three new modules of VerICS aimed at SAT-based parametric verification, together with experimental results obtained for some typical benchmarks. The results prove efficiency of the method. However, it would be interesting to check practical applicability of parametric BMC for more complicated examples of Petri Nets and UML systems. On the other hand, in the future we are going to extend the tool to support parametric verification of other kinds of systems and properties.

As far as a comparison with other tools is concerned, in this paper we compared VerICS with Hugo (see Table 5) and Romeo (see Table 3). It seems that both these tools suffer from the exponential explosion for large systems, while VerICS can still deal with k-models for some small values of k.

The VerICS parametric toolset described in the paper can be downloaded from the site `http://verics.ipipan.waw.pl/parametric` together with all the benchmarks presented. All the input files for running experiments with Romeo, Hugo, and UppAal tools are available at `http://ii.uph.edu.pl/~artur/topnoc`.

References

1. Alur, R., Courcoubetis, C., Dill, D.: Model checking for real-time systems. In: Proc. of the 5th Symp. on Logic in Computer Science (LICS 1990), pp. 414–425. IEEE Computer Society Press, Los Alamitos (1990)
2. Alur, R., Courcoubetis, C., Dill, D., Halbwachs, N., Wong-Toi, H.: An implementation of three algorithms for timing verification based on automata emptiness. In: Proc. of the 13th IEEE Real-Time Systems Symposium (RTSS 1992), pp. 157–166. IEEE Computer Society Press, Los Alamitos (1992)

3. Bengtsson, J., Larsen, K.G., Larsson, F., Pettersson, P., Yi, W., Weise, C.: New generation of UPPAAL. In: Proc. of the Int. Workshop on Software Tools for Technology Transfer (1998)
4. Berthomieu, B., Ribet, P.-O., Vernadat, F.: The tool TINA - construction of abstract state spaces for Petri nets and time Petri nets. International Journal of Production Research 42(14) (2004)
5. Bruyére, V., Dall'Olio, E., Raskin, J.-F.: Durations and parametric model-checking in timed automata. ACM Transactions on Computational Logic 9(2) (2008)
6. Christensen, S., Jørgensen, J., Kristensen, L.: Design/CPN - a computer tool for coloured Petri nets. In: Brinksma, E. (ed.) TACAS 1997. LNCS, vol. 1217, pp. 209–223. Springer, Heidelberg (1997)
7. Cimatti, A., Clarke, E., Giunchiglia, E., Giunchiglia, F., Pistore, M., Roveri, M., Sebastiani, R., Tacchella, A.: NuSMV 2: An openSource tool for symbolic model checking. In: Brinksma, E., Larsen, K.G. (eds.) CAV 2002. LNCS, vol. 2404, pp. 359–364. Springer, Heidelberg (2002)
8. Dembinski, P., Janowska, A., Janowski, P., Penczek, W., Półrola, A., Szreter, M., Woźna, B., Zbrzezny, A.: VerICS: A tool for verifying timed automata and Estelle specifications. In: Garavel, H., Hatcliff, J. (eds.) TACAS 2003. LNCS, vol. 2619, pp. 278–283. Springer, Heidelberg (2003)
9. Dierks, H., Tapken, J.: MOBY/DC - A tool for model-checking parametric real-time specifications. In: Garavel, H., Hatcliff, J. (eds.) TACAS 2003. LNCS, vol. 2619, pp. 271–277. Springer, Heidelberg (2003)
10. Diethers, K., Goltz, U., Huhn, M.: Model checking UML statecharts with time. In: Proc. of the Workshop on Critical Systems Development with UML (CSDUML 2002), Technische Universität München, pp. 35–52 (2002)
11. Dubrovin, J., Junttila, T.: Symbolic model checking of hierarchical UML state machines. Technical Report HUT-TCS-B23, Helsinki Institute of Technology, Espoo, Finland (2007)
12. Emerson, E.A., Trefler, R.: Parametric quantitative temporal reasoning. In: Proc. of the 14th Symp. on Logic in Computer Science (LICS 1999), July 1999, pp. 336–343. IEEE Computer Society Press, Los Alamitos (1999)
13. Gosling, J., Joy, B., Steele, G., Bracha, G.: The Java Language Specification, 3rd edn. Addison-Wesley, Reading (2005)
14. Holzmann, G.J.: The model checker SPIN. IEEE Trans. on Software Eng. 23(5), 279–295 (1997)
15. Hune, T., Romijn, J., Stoelinga, M., Vaandrager, F.: Linear parametric model checking of timed automata. In: Margaria, T., Yi, W. (eds.) TACAS 2001. LNCS, vol. 2031, pp. 189–203. Springer, Heidelberg (2001)
16. Jussila, T., Dubrovin, J., Junttila, T., Latvala, T., Porres, I.: Model checking dynamic and hierarchical UML state machines. In: Proc. of the 3rd Int. Workshop on Model Design and Validation (MoDeVa 2006), pp. 94–110. CEA (2006)
17. Kacprzak, M., Nabiałek, W., Niewiadomski, A., Penczek, W., Półrola, A., Szreter, M., Woźna, B., Zbrzezny, A.: VerICS 2007 - a model checker for knowledge and real-time. Fundamenta Informaticae 85(1-4), 313–328 (2008)
18. Kacprzak, M., Nabiałek, W., Niewiadomski, A., Penczek, W., Półrola, A., Szreter, M., Woźna, B., Zbrzezny, A.: VerICS 2008 - a model checker for time Petri nets and high-level languages. In: Proc. of Int. Workshop on Petri Nets and Software Engineering (PNSE 2009), pp. 119–132. University of Hamburg (2009)
19. Knapik, M., Szreter, M., Penczek, W.: Bounded Parametric Model Checking for Elementary Net Systems. In: Jensen, K., Donatelli, S., Koutny, M. (eds.) ToPNoC IV. LNCS, vol. 6550, pp. 42–71. Springer, Heidelberg (2010)

20. Knapp, A., Merz, S., Rauh, C.: Model checking - timed UML state machines and collaborations. In: Damm, W., Olderog, E.-R. (eds.) FTRTFT 2002. LNCS, vol. 2469, pp. 395–416. Springer, Heidelberg (2002)
21. Lilius, J., Paltor, I.: vUML: A tool for verifying UML models. In: Proc. of the 14th IEEE Int. Conf. on Automated Software Engineering (ASE 1999), pp. 255–258. IEEE Computer Society Press, Los Alamitos (1999)
22. Lime, D., Roux, O.H., Seidner, C., Traonouez, L.-M.: Romeo: A parametric model-checker for petri nets with stopwatches. In: Kowalewski, S., Philippou, A. (eds.) TACAS 2009. LNCS, vol. 5505, pp. 54–57. Springer, Heidelberg (2009)
23. MiniSat (2006), `http://www.cs.chalmers.se/Cs/Research/FormalMethods/MiniSat`
24. Niewiadomski, A., Penczek, W., Szreter, M.: A new approach to model checking of UML state machines. Fundamenta Informaticae 93(1-3), 289–303 (2009)
25. Niewiadomski, A., Penczek, W., Szreter, M.: Towards checking parametric reachability for UML state machines. In: Pnueli, A., Virbitskaite, I., Voronkov, A. (eds.) PSI 2009. LNCS, vol. 5947, pp. 319–330. Springer, Heidelberg (2010)
26. Okawa, Y., Yoneda, T.: Symbolic CTL model checking of time Petri nets. Electronics and Communications in Japan, Scripta Technica 80(4), 11–20 (1997)
27. OMG. Unified Modeling Language (2007), `http://www.omg.org/spec/UML/2.1.2`
28. Peled, D.: All from one, one for all: On model checking using representatives. In: Courcoubetis, C. (ed.) CAV 1993. LNCS, vol. 697, pp. 409–423. Springer, Heidelberg (1993)
29. Penczek, W., Półrola, A., Woźna, B., Zbrzezny, A.: Bounded model checking for reachability testing in time Petri nets. In: Proc. of the Int. Workshop on Concurrency, Specification and Programming (CS&P 2004). Informatik-Berichte, vol. 170(1), pp. 124–135. Humboldt University (2004)
30. Penczek, W., Pòłrola, A., Zbrzezny, A.: SAT-Based (Parametric) Reachability for a Class of Distributed Time Petri Nets. In: Jensen, K., Donatelli, S., Koutny, M. (eds.) ToPNoC IV. LNCS, vol. 6550, pp. 72–97. Springer, Heidelberg (2010)
31. Penczek, W., Woźna, B., Zbrzezny, A.: Bounded model checking for the universal fragment of CTL. Fundamenta Informaticae 51(1-2), 135–156 (2002)
32. Półrola, A., Penczek, W.: Minimization algorithms for time Petri nets. Fundamenta Informaticae 60(1-4), 307–331 (2004)
33. Spelberg, R.L., Toetenel, H., Ammerlaan, M.: Partition refinement in real-time model checking. In: Ravn, A.P., Rischel, H. (eds.) FTRTFT 1998. LNCS, vol. 1486, pp. 143–157. Springer, Heidelberg (1998)
34. Traonouez, L.-M., Lime, D., Roux, O.H.: Parametric model-checking of time petri nets with stopwatches using the state-class graph. In: Cassez, F., Jard, C. (eds.) FORMATS 2008. LNCS, vol. 5215, pp. 280–294. Springer, Heidelberg (2008)
35. Virbitskaite, I.B., Pokozy, E.A.: A partial order method for the verification of time petri nets. In: Ciobanu, G., Păun, G. (eds.) FCT 1999. LNCS, vol. 1684, pp. 547–558. Springer, Heidelberg (1999)
36. Zbrzezny, A.: SAT-based reachability checking for timed automata with diagonal constraints. Fundamenta Informaticae 67(1-3), 303–322 (2005)
37. Zbrzezny, A.: Improving the translation from ECTL to SAT. Fundamenta Informaticae 85(1-4), 513–531 (2008)

Schedule-Aware Workflow Management Systems

Ronny S. Mans[1,3], Nick C. Russell[2], Wil M.P. van der Aalst[1], Arnold J. Moleman[3], and Piet J.M. Bakker[3]

[1] Department of Information Systems, Eindhoven University of Technology, P.O. Box 513, NL-5600 MB, Eindhoven, The Netherlands
{r.s.mans,w.m.p.v.d.aalst}@tue.nl

[2] Carba-Tec Pty Ltd, 128 Ingleston Rd, Wakerley QLD 4154, Australia
nrussell@carbatec.com.au

[3] Department of Quality Assurance and Process Innovation, Academic Medical Center, University of Amsterdam, P.O. Box 2260, NL-1100 DD, Amsterdam, The Netherlands
{a.j.moleman,p.j.bakker}@amc.uva.nl

Abstract. Contemporary workflow management systems offer work-items to users through specific work-lists. Users select the work-items they will perform without having a specific schedule in mind. However, in many environments work needs to be scheduled and performed at particular times. For example, in hospitals many work-items are linked to appointments, e.g., a doctor cannot perform surgery without reserving an operating theater and making sure that the patient is present. *One of the problems when applying workflow technology in such domains is the lack of calendar-based scheduling support.* In this paper, we present an approach that supports the seamless integration of unscheduled (flow) and scheduled (schedule) tasks. Using CPN Tools we have developed a specification and simulation model for schedule-aware workflow management systems. Based on this a system has been realized that uses YAWL, Microsoft Exchange Server 2007, Outlook, and a dedicated scheduling service. The approach is illustrated using a real-life case study at the AMC hospital in the Netherlands. In addition, we elaborate on the experiences obtained when developing and implementing a system of this scale using formal techniques.

Keywords: workflow management, healthcare, software development, scheduling.

1 Introduction

Healthcare is a prime example of a domain where the effective execution of tasks is often tied to the availability of multiple scarce resources, e.g. doctors. In order to maximize the effectiveness of individual resources and minimize process throughput times, an appointment-based approach is typically utilized when scheduling the tasks performed by these resources. However, the scheduling of these appointments is often undertaken on a manual basis and its effectiveness

K. Jensen, S. Donatelli, and M. Koutny (Eds.): ToPNoC IV, LNCS 6550, pp. 121–143, 2010.

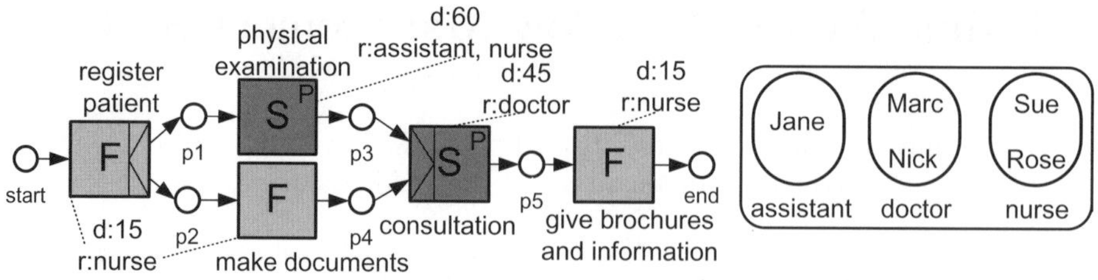

Fig. 1. Running example showing schedule (S) and flow (F) tasks. The prefix "d:" indicates the average time needed for performing the task and prefix "r:" indicates which roles are necessary to perform the task. From each associated role, exactly one person needs to be assigned to the task. For both schedule tasks, indicated by the character "P" in the top-right corner of the task, the patient is also required to be present.

is critically dependent on preceding tasks being performed on-time in order to prevent the need for subsequent rescheduling.

To illustrate the importance of the afore-mentioned issue, consider the small hospital process for diagnosing a patient shown in Figure 1. The first step is to register the patient. Next, a physical examination (task "physical examination") of the patient takes place which is done by an assistant and a nurse. In parallel, a nurse prepares the documents for the patient (task "make documents"). When these tasks have been completed, a doctor evaluates the result of the test (task "consultation") and decides about the information and brochures that need to be provided by the nurse (task "give brochures and information"). Figure 1 also shows the corresponding organizational model which indicates the roles being played by various people in the organization.

From this example, it can be seen that a distinction can be made between two kinds of tasks. The tasks annotated with an "F" in the figure, can be performed at *an arbitrary point in time when a resource becomes available* and are called *flow tasks*. However, the tasks "physical examination" and "consultation", annotated with an "S" in the figure, can only be performed when the required room is reserved, the patient is present, and the necessary medical staff are available to perform the specific task, i.e. these tasks need to be scheduled and performed at particular times. Therefore, we call these kinds of tasks *schedule tasks* as they are performed *by one or more resources at a specified time*.

For the consultation task in the figure, it is often the case that a doctor finds out at the actual appointment that some results from required diagnostic tests are missing. This leads to wasted time for the doctor as a new appointment needs to be scheduled. Therefore, for the effective performance of schedule tasks it is vital that the whole workflow is taken into account in order to guarantee that preceding tasks are performed on-time thereby preventing the need for rescheduling and avoiding unproductive time for resources as a result of canceled appointments.

Workflow technology presents an interesting vehicle with which to support healthcare processes. Based on a corresponding process definition, Workflow

Management Systems (WfMSs) support processes by managing the flow of work such that individual work-items are done at the right time by the proper person [2]. Contemporary WfMSs offer work-items through so-called work-lists. At an arbitrary point in time, a user can pick a work-item from this list and perform the associated task.

If we consider the implementation of this process in the context of a WfMS, we find that a significant dichotomy exists in that people are used to working in a scheduled way, but this is not supported by current WfMSs. In contrast to administrative processes, healthcare processes invoke the coordination of expensive resources which have scarce availability. Therefore, it is of the utmost importance that the scheduling of appointments for these resources is done in an efficient way that is suitable both for the medical staff and also for the patients being treated. To summarize, there is a *need to integrate workflow management systems with scheduling facilities*.

In this paper, we present the design and implementation of a WfMS supporting both schedule and flow tasks. In addition to the classical work-list functionality generally associated with workflow systems, the concept of a calendar is also introduced in order to present appointments for scheduled work-items to the people involved. Unlike traditional workflow implementations, a specific contribution of this paper is on *how WfMSs can be fully extended with scheduling facilities* rather than simply extending the functionality of a WfMS or a scheduling system (e.g. a scheduling algorithm). In other words, we investigate the general problem of adding scheduling facilities to workflow systems. Note that our results are not limited to the healthcare domain. Any process in which tasks are linked to appointments can be supported by our approach.

An interesting problem in this context lies in the actual development approach taken to extending a WfMS with scheduling facilities. Our strategy for this is based on the use of CPN Tools, a widely used modeling and execution tool for Colored Petri Nets (CP Nets) [21], with which we developed a *comprehensive conceptual model capable of serving both as a specification and simulation model for the application domain.* Formalizing such a system using CP Nets offers several benefits. First of all, building such a net allows for *experimentation.* So, the model or parts of it can be executed, simulated, and analyzed which leads to important insights about the design and implementation of the system. Second, the hierarchical structuring of CP Nets allows for the modeling of large complex systems at different levels of abstraction. That is, CP Nets can be structured into a set of components which interact with each other through a set of well-defined interfaces, in a similar way to the components in a modular software architecture.

In this way, we were able to use the conceptual model as a *specification* for the subsequent realization of the system. In order to realize the functionality contained in the conceptual model, we *incrementally* mapped it to an operational system based on widely available open-source and commercial-off-the-shelf (COTS) software. Although the conceptual model is detailed, it remains abstract enough, such that its components can be concretized in many different ways.

We choose an approach based on the reuse of existing software. In total, the conceptual model consists of 30 nets, 238 transitions, 625 places, and in excess of 1000 lines of ML-code illustrating the overall complexity of the system. For the concrete realization of the system we used the open-source, service-oriented architecture of YAWL and Microsoft Exchange Server 2007 as the implementation platform.

A second contribution of this paper lies in the development approach followed for the design and subsequent implementation of a newly system. Moreover, from a software engineering point of view, we also elaborate on the experiences associated with developing and implementing a system of this scale using formal techniques.

The remainder of the paper is organized as follows. In Section 2 we explain how a workflow language can be augmented with information relevant for scheduling. In Section 3, we present the approach followed for designing and implementing a WfMS integrated with scheduling facilities together with a general overview of the architecture of the conceptual model and the resulting system. Next, in Section 4, the individual components of the system are discussed in more detail. In Section 5 a concrete application of the realized system is presented. Section 6 discusses related work and finally Section 7 concludes the paper.

2 Flow and Schedule Tasks

In order to allow for the extension of a WfMS with scheduling functionality some concepts need to be introduced. It is assumed that the reader is familiar with basic workflow management concepts, like case, role, and so on [2]. Using the process shown in Figure 1, we will elaborate on how a workflow language can be integrated with scheduling functionality.

2.1 Concepts

We can distinguish between two distinct types of tasks. Flow tasks are performed at an arbitrary point in time when a resource becomes available. As only one resource is needed, it is sufficient to define only *one* role for each of them[1]. Consequently, these tasks can be presented in an ordinary *work-list*. For example, for the flow task "make documents" the work may either be performed by "Sue" or "Rose".

Conversely, schedule tasks are performed by one or more resources at a specified time. As multiple resources can be involved, with differing capabilities, it is necessary to specify which kinds of resources are needed to participate in completing the task. To this end, multiple resources may be defined for a schedule task where for each role specified, only *one* resource may be involved in the actual performance of the task. For example, in Figure 1, the schedule task "physical examination" may be performed by "Jane" and "Rose", but not by "Sue" and

[1] There also exist approaches for which more roles may be defined, but this is not the focus of our work.

"Rose". Note that a resource involved in the performance of a schedule task may also be a physical resource such as medical equipment or a room. Furthermore, for the schedule tasks the patient may be involved which means that the patient is also a required resource for these tasks. Note that the patient is not involved in the actual execution of the task but is a passive resource who needs to be present whilst it is completed. For this reason, the patient is not added to any of the roles for the task, nor are they defined in terms of a separate role. Instead, schedule tasks for which the patient needs to be present are specifically identified.

For presenting the appointments made for schedule tasks to users, the concept of a *calendar* will be used. More specifically, each resource will have its own calendar in which appointments can be booked. Note that each patient also has his / her own calendar. An appointment either refers to a schedule task which needs to be performed for a specific case or to an activity which is not workflow related. So, an appointment appears in the calendars of all resources that are involved in the actual performance of the task. An appointment for a schedule task, for which a work-item does not yet exist, can be booked into the calendar of a resource. However, when the work-item becomes available it has already been determined when it will be performed and by whom. Note that sometimes work-items need to be rescheduled because of anticipated delays in preceding tasks.

In order to be able to determine at runtime the earliest time that a schedule task can be started, information about the duration of every task needs to be known. For example, in Figure 1, for each task the average duration is indicated by prefix "d:". For example, one block represents one minute, which means that the task "physical examination" takes on average 60 minutes to complete.

2.2 Formalization

Based on the informal discussion in the previous section, we now formalize the augmented workflow language. The definition of our language is based on WF-nets [2]. Note that our results are in no way limited to WF-nets and can be applied to more complex notations (BPMN, EPCs, BPEL, etc). Note that WF-nets are the most widely used formal representation of workflows. A WF-net is a tuple $N = (P, T, F)$ defined in the following way:

- P is a non-empty finite set of *places*;
- T is a non-empty finite set of *tasks* ($P \cap T = \emptyset$);
- $F \subseteq (P \times T) \cup (T \times P)$ is a set of arcs (flow relation);
- There is one initial place $i \in P$ and one final place $o \in P$ such that every place or transition is on a directed path from i to o.

A WF-net can be extended in the following way, called a *scheduling WF-net* (sWF-net). A *sWF*-net is a tuple $N = (P, T_f, T_s, F, CR, Res, Role, R, Rtf, Rts, D)$, where:

- T_f is a finite set of *flow tasks*;
- T_s is a finite set of *schedule tasks*;
- $T_f \cup T_s = T$ and $T_f \cap T_s = \emptyset$, i.e., T_s and T_f partition T. So, a task is either a flow task or a schedule task, but not both;
- (P, T, F) is a WF-net;
- $CR \subseteq T_s$ is the set of schedule tasks for which the human resource for whom the case is being performed is also required to be present.
- Res is a non-empty finite set of *resources*;
- $Role$ is a non-empty finite set of *roles*;
- R: $Res \rightarrow \mathcal{P}(Role)$ is a function which maps resources on to sets of roles;
- Rtf: $T_f \nrightarrow Role$ is a partial function which maps flow tasks on to roles;
- Rts: $T_s \rightarrow \mathcal{P}(Role)\backslash\{\emptyset\}$ is a function which maps schedule tasks on to at least one role;
- D: $T \rightarrow \mathbb{N}_0$ is a function which maps tasks onto the number of blocks that are needed for the execution of the task.

Note that Figure 1 fully defines a particular sWF-net.

3 Design of a Schedule-Aware WfMS

In this section, we present the approach followed for designing and implementing a WfMS integrated with scheduling facilities. A general overview of the architecture of the conceptual model and the resultant system is also provided.

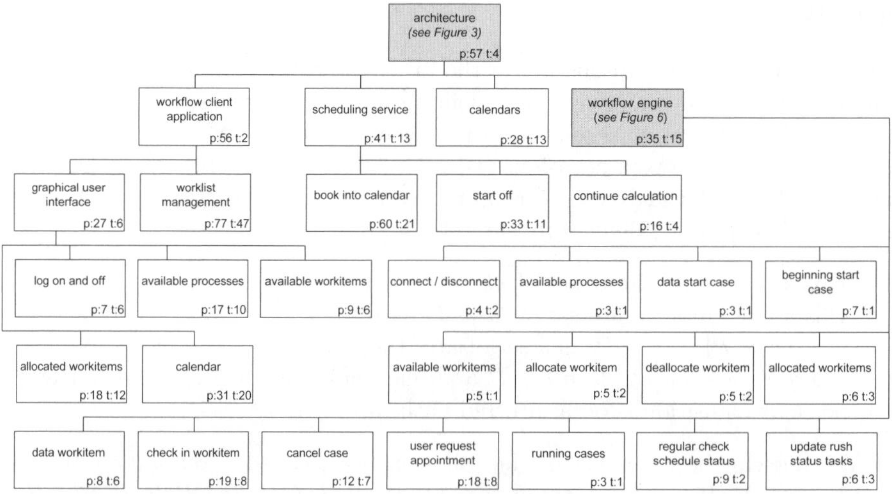

Fig. 2. CP Net hierarchy of the conceptual model: each square represents a (sub)net containing places and transitions

3.1 Approach

Contemporary WfMSs provide a wide range of functions. In order to determine prior to the implementation phase how scheduling facilities can be integrated with such a system, one needs to identify how the new scheduling capabilities should be incorporated into existing functionality. To this end, *Colored Petri Nets (CP Nets)* have been chosen as the mechanism to identify and formalize the behavior of the system. CP Nets provide a well-established and well-proven language suited to describe the behavior of systems exhibiting characteristics such as concurrency, resource sharing, and synchronization.

Formalizing a system using CP Nets offers several benefits. First of all, building such a net allows for *experimentation*. So, the model or parts of it can be executed, simulated and analyzed which leads to insights about the design and implementation of the system. Since the model is executable, it is possible to evaluate and test various design decisions much earlier than would normally be the case during the development process. In this way, where suboptimal design decisions or design flaws are revealed, the cost of rectifying them is significantly less than would be the case later in the development lifecycle. It also facilitates a better understanding of the problem domain.

Second, a complete model of the system allows for *testing* parts of the system that have been implemented. As a CP Net consists of several components, we can "replace" one or more components in the CP Net with the concrete implementation of these components by establishing connections between the CP Net model and components in the actual system. As the CP Net is an executable model this allows for the testing of numerous scenarios facilitating the discovery of potential flaws in both the architecture and the corresponding implementation.

Another important benefit of having a CP Net consisting of several components, is that it provides precise guidance in the configuration of software products, thereby allowing for the use of existing software. As will become clear in subsequent parts of the paper, whilst the specification model is detailed, it remains abstract enough to allow components to be concretized in various ways.

Note that other approaches exist for developing large and complex systems. However, we believe that none of them can deliver the benefits that are provided by the CP Nets and CPN Tools combination discussed above. For example, formal methods such as π-calculus and process algebra as well as software-oriented specification formalisms such as Z and VDM lack a graphical representation. As a consequence, the visualization and assessment of specific design choices is difficult.

In addition to the above mentioned advantages, the development of a large and complex CPN model also has its limitations. Perhaps the most significant limitation is that no meaningful verification of the CP Net is possible due to its size and complexity. Furthermore, as an unlimited number of business process models and users can be represented, state space analysis is impossible for the general case.

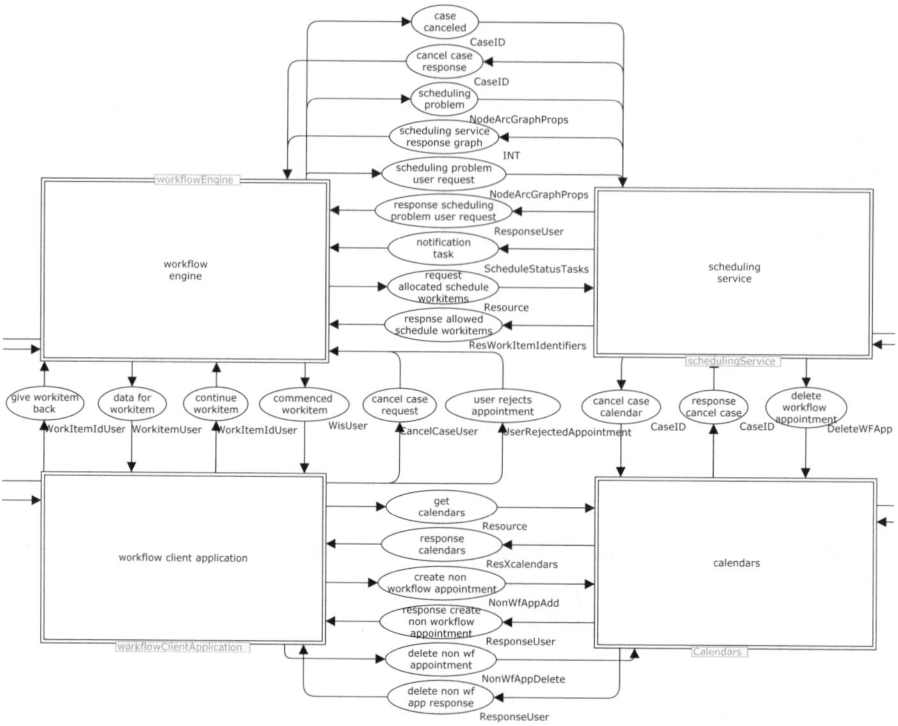

Fig. 3. The topmost model of the conceptual model realized in terms of CP Nets

3.2 Conceptual Model

The complete conceptual model, defining the precise behavior of a workflow management system augmented with scheduling facilities, consists of a series of CP Nets in which several layers can be distinguished. Figure 2 shows the hierarchy of CP Nets in the CP Net model, together with the relationships between them. In total, there are 30 distinct CP Nets. An indication of the complexity of each net is expressed by the p and t values included for each of them, which show the number of places and transitions they contain. In total, the whole CP Net consists of 238 transitions, 625 places and in excess of 1000 lines of ML code. The construction of the complete model required more than three months of work. This underscores the fact that it is a complex system. In order to illustrate the use of CP Nets in the development approach, the grey shaded blocks in Figure 2 will be discussed in more detail.

Figure 3 shows the topmost net in the CP Net model and gives an idea of the main components in the system and the interfaces between them. It can be seen in the figure that there are four substitution transitions. They represent the major functional units in the system and are explained in detail in the next section. Each place which connects two components forms part of the interface between those two components. Additionally, for each place which forms part of the interface, the direction of the arcs between the place and the two connected components indicates the sending (tail) and the receiving component (head) for a specific message.

3.3 Architecture

In this section, we give a global overview of the architecture of a WfMS integrated with scheduling facilities. As Figure 3 only provides a snippet of the complete conceptual model (it only shows 22 places of the 57 places that are part of an interface), Figure 4a provides a more comprehensive depiction of the architecture of the conceptual model together with an illustration of the interfaces between the components (shown as clouds). The concrete implementation of the system architecture is shown in Figure 4b. Both architectures illustrate that the system is defined in a service oriented way. The components are loosely coupled and the interfaces are kept as compact and simple as possible. As the interfaces share the same numbering, it is easy to compare the two sets of interfaces.

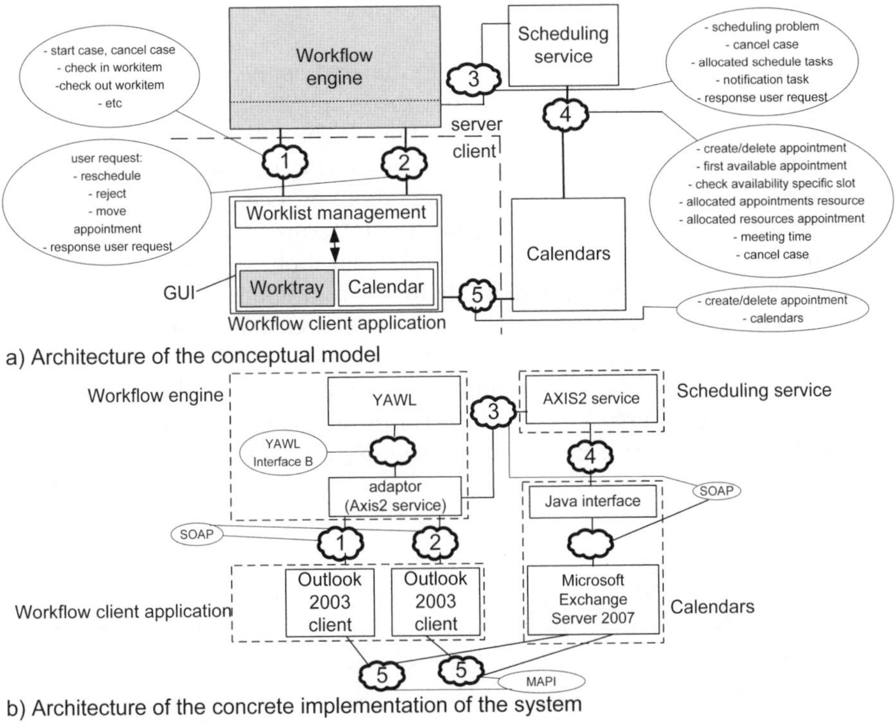

Fig. 4. Architectures of both the conceptual model and the concrete implementation of the system. There are four main components: (I) workflow engine, (II) scheduling service, (III) workflow client application, and (IV) calendars. The individual interfaces are indicated by numbers.

The architecture consists of four components. First of all, the *workflow engine* routes cases through the organization. Based on the business process definition for a case, tasks are carried out in the right order and by the right people. Once a task in a case becomes available for execution, the corresponding work-item is communicated to users via the *workflow client application* allowing it to be selected and performed by one of them. The scheduling service and the workflow client application communicate with the *Calendars* component in order to obtain a view on users' calendars and to manipulate their contents. Note that users can add / remove appointments that are possibly unrelated to the workflow.

As our focus is on how a WfMS can be *integrated* with scheduling facilities, we want to completely separate the scheduling facilities provided by the system from the engine. As a consequence, we have a separate *scheduling service* component which is responsible for providing scheduling facilities to the system (e.g. (re)scheduling of tasks). In order for the scheduling service to function correctly, all scheduling constraints imposed by the engine (which might be relevant to a scheduling decision) need to be sent to the scheduling service. To be more precise, the scheduling service receives a *scheduling problem*, which contains all relevant constraints for one case only. Based on these constraints, the scheduling service makes decisions with regard to the scheduling of schedule tasks for the case.

Informally, the scheduling problem is formulated as a *graph* which has *nodes* and *arcs* between nodes. Nodes, arcs and the graph itself may have properties which are represented as name-value attributes. The rationale for representing the scheduling problem using this data structure is that any information which is deemed relevant can be included in the graph. For a case, which is in a given state, we map the process definition, defined in terms of the formal definition given in Section 2.2, to the graph (e.g. tasks, duration, split/join semantics of a node, roles). Where a work-item exists for a given node, a property is added to that node indicating the state the work-item is currently in. For a user to reschedule an appointment, additional information is added, such as the name of the requester. Moreover, if the human resource for which the case is being performed is also required in order to perform any task, then the name of the calendar for this resource is also included together with the names of the relevant schedule tasks.

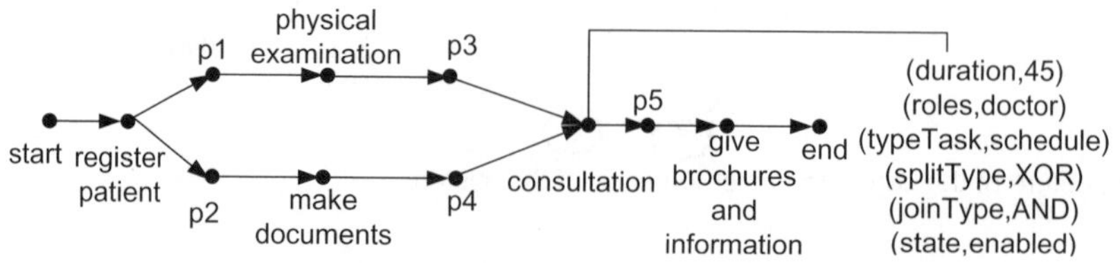

Fig. 5. Scheduling graph for the running example of Figure 1 in which the task "consultation" is enabled

An example of a scheduling graph is given in Figure 5. In this figure, we see how the process definition shown in Figure 1 is mapped to the graph. In order to simplify the graph, the figure only shows the properties for the "consultation" node. For this node it is indicated that the average duration is 45 minutes, only a doctor is allowed to perform the task, the task is a schedule task, the node has XOR-split semantics, AND-join semantics, and a work-item exists for it which is in the enabled state.

4 Modeling and Implementing the Components

In sections 4.1 to 4.4 the individual components in the architecture are discussed in more detail. For each component a description of the main functionality is provided together with a discussion on its interactions with other components. Note that, due to space limitations, only the most important interface methods will be discussed. For each component, three distinct aspects are discussed. Under the "model" heading, details are provided about the role of the component in the conceptual model. Under the "implementation" heading, there is a discussion on how the component has been realized. Finally, under the "findings" heading there is a reflection on how the use of the conceptual model has benefited the realization and the subsequent implementation of the component. For both the "workflow engine" and the "scheduling service" components we have replaced the component in the conceptual model by establishing connections between the CP Net model and the concrete implementation allowing for the systematic testing of the component [24]. For both of them we also present some of the findings resulting from this research.

4.1 Workflow Engine

A workflow engine is responsible for the routing of cases. In addition to the standard facilities an engine should provide [2], the following features are added in order to integrate scheduling capabilities.

The engine is responsible for sending a scheduling problem to the scheduling service in order to determine whether appointments need to be (re)scheduled, or if limited time remains in which to finish work-items for tasks preceding an appointment. As a consequence of our choice to completely separate the scheduling facilities from the engine, a scheduling problem for a case is sent when the following situations occur: (1) a case is started; (2) a work-item is finished; (3) a user wants to reschedule an appointment; and (4) at regular time intervals. The fourth option is necessary as it may be the case that no work-items are completed in a given period, but that some appointments need to be rescheduled due to the passing of time. Obviously, the graph is sent the least number of times possible.

As a consequence of the execution of the scheduling service, the engine is informed about appointments for which limited time is left in which to finish work-items of preceding tasks. For these work-items, a warning is sent to the workflow client to indicate that limited time remains.

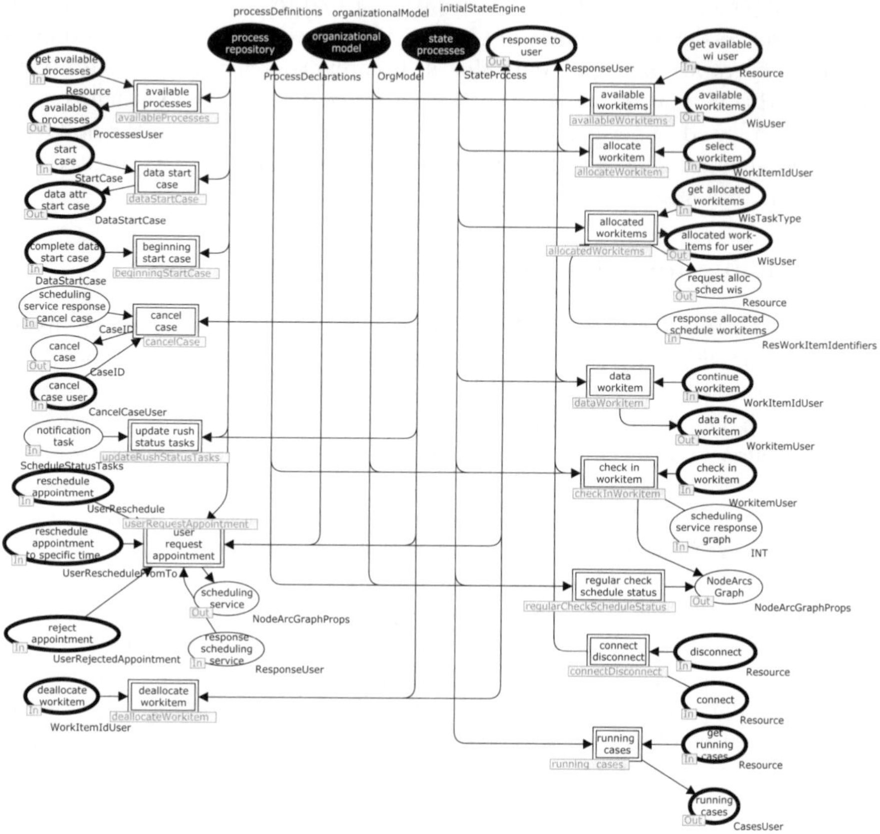

Fig. 6. CP Net component for the workflow engine component

Model
The complete CP Net for the workflow engine component is depicted in Figure 6. The places with an input or output port tag (shown by a rectangle with the text "In" or "Out" respectively) are part of the interface of the engine. More specifically, the white colored places with a thick black line are part of the interface of the workflow client application. The white colored places with a thin black line are part of the interface of the scheduling service and the black colored places are places which retain internal engine information.

The substitution transitions have been defined such that each of them corresponds to specific functionality provided by the engine. For example, the "cancel case" substitution transition models the actions taken by the engine when a case is canceled. A cancelation request is received via the "cancel case user" place. This causes the corresponding case information to be removed from the "state cases" place which contains the state information for all cases. After this, the scheduling service is informed, via the "cancel case" place, so that any appointments made for the case are deleted. As an indication of the complexity of the engine it is worth mentioning that the flattened substitution transition comprises 63 transitions and 151 places.

Implementation
The Engine component in the CP Net model can be replaced by a concrete implementation which allows it to be tested. The workflow component is realized (see Figure 4b) using the open-source WfMS YAWL [1] and a service which acts as an adaptor in-between YAWL and the workflow client application. The adaptor service communicates with YAWL via "Interface B" [1]. The adaptor also communicates with the scheduling service using SOAP messages. The adaptor and the YAWL system are tightly coupled as large volumes of work-item and process related information are exchanged.

Findings
With regard to the separation of the scheduling facilities from the engine, the development of the conceptual model provided several important insights related to this design decision. For example, when sending the scheduling problem to the scheduling service it proved to be advantageous to deploy a single method in which a scheduling graph is sent which contained all required information, instead of having multiple methods in which parts of the scheduling problem were communicated.

From an implementation standpoint it was obvious that many of the functions of the workflow engine component could be provided by contemporary WfMSs. The workflow engine component of the conceptual model provided guidance in the following way. For the functionality that needed to be provided by the selected WfMS corresponding interface methods needed to be found (e.g. checking in a work-item and retrieving the current state of work-items for a case). For the functionality that was not provided by the selected WfMS, the workflow engine component of the conceptual model served as a blueprint for the realization of this functionality.

As part of the strategy to replace components in the conceptual model with their implemented counterparts [24], several errors were identified in the adaptor component of the engine. Surprisingly also some errors in the design of the "workflow engine" component of the conceptual model were uncovered. A serious design flaw had been discovered which necessitated changes to the interface between the engine and the scheduling service. This was due to the fact that first a scheduling problem for a certain case was sent to the scheduling service followed by a request for the cancelation of the same case. However, first the cancelation of the case was dealt with, immediately followed by the scheduling problem. This caused the scheduling service to crash. The interface was changed such that the successful completion of a scheduling problem is now acknowledged which did not happen previously.

4.2 Workflow Client Application

Users working with the WfMS do so via the workflow client application which delivers the basic user interaction facilities expected of this facility [2].

The component consists of a GUI and a work-list management component. The work-list management component serves as a connection layer between the engine and the GUI and takes care of the communication between them. The GUI component consists of a "worktray" and a "calendar" component where the "worktray" provides the same facilities as a classical worktray. That is, work-items for flow tasks are advertised and performed via the worktray. The appointments that are created for schedule tasks are advertised via the calendar. Once a work-item becomes available for such an appointment, it can be performed via the calendar. In principle, both the "worktray" and "calendar" components provide the same facilities for the execution of a work-item. However, unlike work-items for flow tasks, work-items for schedule tasks can not be selected as an appointment already exists for them. As a result, work-items for schedule tasks are immediately checked out by the engine once they are created. Furthermore, in our approach, only one user can interact with the WfMS to indicate the completion of a work-item. This prevents concurrency issues should multiple users want to complete the same work-item.

For appointments that are made for schedule tasks, users are able to express their dissatisfaction with the nominated scheduling by requesting: (1) the rescheduling of the appointment, (2) the rescheduling of the appointment to a specified date and time, or (3) the reassignment of the appointment to another employee. Such a user request can be done as a single action and is the only supported means of rescheduling appointments by users. In addition, the workflow client also indicates whether limited time is left in which to undertake work-items in order to meet the schedule. Moreover, users are also allowed to add appointments to the calendar which are not workflow related (e.g. having dinner with friends).

As can be seen in Figure 4a, two interfaces are defined for the communication between the workflow client application and the engine. The interface with number "1" defines the standard communication that takes place between an engine and a workflow client application. The interface with number "2" defines methods added as a consequence of the scheduling facilities developed for the system. For this interface, nothing is stored in the engine when these methods are called.

Model

The corresponding CP Net model for the work-list management component is relatively complex (and is not shown here): the component's model contains 109 transitions and 239 places. However, in order to allow for experimentation, we also included some user behavior, such as selection of a work-item and so on, which is unrelated to the actual behavior of the system and only utilized for testing purposes.

Implementation

The workflow client application component of the CP Net was replaced by a concrete implementation. Once the Exchange Server was in place we could easily use the Microsoft Outlook 2003 client to obtain a view of a user's calendar.

Furthermore, the Outlook client can be configured in such a way that it can act as a full workflow client application which can communicate with the WfMS via an adaptor service through the exchange of SOAP messages.

Findings
Work-items for flow tasks are performed via the worktray whereas work-items for schedule tasks are performed via the calendar. The conceptual model proved beneficial in establishing a clear separation between the worktray and the calendars allowing them to be presented via their own GUIs. Additionally, common functionality could be identified (e.g. the checking in of a work-item) ensuring that the number of interfaces required for communicating with the engine was minimized and that each interface provided distinct functionality.

The existence of the "workflow client application" component in the conceptual model allowed us to focus only on how it could be realized. The configuration of Outlook clients, the places in between the "workflow engine" component and the "workflow client application" component, together with their associated types, served as a blueprint for the tooling that was used to automatically generate the code for the interface between the Outlook client and the workflow engine (see [14] for more specific details about the tooling used). Furthermore, based on the transitions and functions defined in the "workflow client application" component, it was relatively straightforward to generate Visual Basic code that realized the desired functionality.

4.3 Scheduling Service

The scheduling service is responsible for providing scheduling facilities to the WfMS. Scheduling is done sequentially on a case-by-case base. Once a scheduling problem is received, the scheduling service needs to determine whether some of the schedule tasks need to be (re)scheduled. Moreover, several distinct issues need to be addressed of which we will discuss the most important ones of these below.

First of all, the actual scheduling of tasks needs to occur in the same order as the sequence of schedule tasks in the accompanying process definition for the case. Moreover, there should be sufficient time between two scheduled tasks. Also, when rescheduling appointments, any preceding constraints need to be satisfied. For example, in Figure 1, it needs to be guaranteed that first the "physical examination" task is scheduled, followed by the "consultation" task which needs to occur at a later time.

Second, for the actual scheduling of an appointment multiple roles can be specified for a schedule task. For each role specified a resource needs to be selected, i.e., the number of roles determines the number of resources involved in the actual performance of the task. If the patient for which the case is performed also needs to be present at an appointment, then this also needs to be taken into account. The scheduling service only books an appointment in the calendars of these resources who need to be present during the performance of the task (i.e. the performers of the task and the patient (if needed)).

Third, the scheduling service is also responsible for determining whether limited time is left for performing work-items preceding scheduled tasks. In such a situation, the engine needs to be informed. Moreover, the scheduling service is also informed about the cancelation of a case, so that all appointments related to the case can be removed from schedules. When too little time is left for performing work-items preceding a schedule task, the corresponding appointment is automatically rescheduled which in this context can be seen as the most straightforward recovery action. However, different strategies can also be conceived for dealing with such situations. Potential solutions can be found in [4].

In this paper, we focus on integration aspects instead of devising new scheduling algorithms. Nevertheless, to demonstrate the approach that is used for the scheduling of appointments, we will briefly examine the implemented 'naive' scheduling algorithm. Of course it can be envisaged that more advanced scheduling strategies are possible, for example, minimizing the total time and the number of times a patient has to be at the hospital.

The (re)scheduling of appointments is done automatically, and does not require any user involvement. Starting with the tasks in the graph for which a work-item exists, it is determined which schedule tasks need to be (re)scheduled. Once we know that tasks are able to be scheduled, they are scheduled. Moreover, these tasks are scheduled on a sequential basis in order to avoid conflicts involving shared resources. However, we do not schedule any tasks which occur after a choice in the process as this can lead to unnecessary usage of available slots in the calendar. Moreover, we do not take loops into account.

For the actual scheduling of an appointment, a search is started for the first opportunity where one of the resources of a role can be booked for the respective work-item. If found, an appointment is scheduled in the calendar of the resource. If the patient for which the case is performed also needs to be present at the appointment, then this is also taken into account. For example, for Figure 1, if a case is started, an appointment is created for task "physical examination" in the calendars of "Jane", "Sue", and the patient, or "Jane", "Rose" and the patient.

Model
The CP Net model which models the scheduling service consists of 49 transitions and 150 places. Modeling the scheduling behavior necessitated writing a significant volume of ML code.

Implementation
The concrete implementation of this component of the CP Net is shown in Figure 4b. Here we see that the component is implemented in Java as a service which communicates with the WfMS via SOAP messages. However, in order to get a view of and to manipulate the calendar, the service also communicates via a Java interface with the Exchange Server which in turn exchanges information via SOAP messages.

Findings
For the scheduling service, the conceptual model was crucial for identifying the functionality that needed to be provided by such a service, the necessary

information for the service to function correctly, and the interactions required with a calender system. For example, the model showed which actions occurring in the context of a WfMS require interactions with the scheduling service. For checking out a work-item no interaction is needed, whereas for checking in a work-item a scheduling problem needs to be sent which subsequently requires several interactions with the calendar system.

In a similar fashion to the workflow client application, the places between the "workflow engine" component and the "scheduling service" component served as blueprint for the tooling used for the automatic generation of the code required for the interface between them (see [19] for more details about the tooling used). Moreover, based on the transitions and functions defined in the "scheduling service" component, Java code could be written relatively quickly that realized the desired functionality. In general, the types of places correspond with data types that are defined whereas for the transitions and their associated functions, corresponding Java classes and methods need to be crafted.

When replacing the scheduling service component in the conceptual model by its implementation [24], several flaws have been identified ranging from simple implementation errors to more serious design errors. For example, it appeared that in the process of scheduling appointments it was necessary to lock the calendars so that non-workflow related appointments can not be scheduled.

4.4 Calendars

The Calendars component is responsible for providing a view on the calendars of users and for manipulating their contents. It is possible to create / delete appointments or to get information about appointments that have been made. Moreover, the interface contains some convenience methods for deleting cases and finding the first available slot for a schedule task. Otherwise, large volumes of low-level information need to be exchanged whereas now only one call is necessary.

Model

The CP Net model which models the scheduling service consists of 13 transitions and 28 places. It is relatively simple model.

Implementation

For the Calendars component we selected Microsoft Exchange Server 2007 as the system for storing the calendars of users. This system provides several advantages including widespread usage and the fact that it offers several interfaces for viewing and manipulating calendars.

Findings

A calendar system can be used for many different purposes. In order to augment WfMSs with scheduling facilities it is important that appointments made for work-items of schedule tasks are clearly separated from non-workflow related appointments. Moreover, in order for the whole system to work properly it is important that there is a single system keeping track of the calendars of the users and that it is up-to-date.

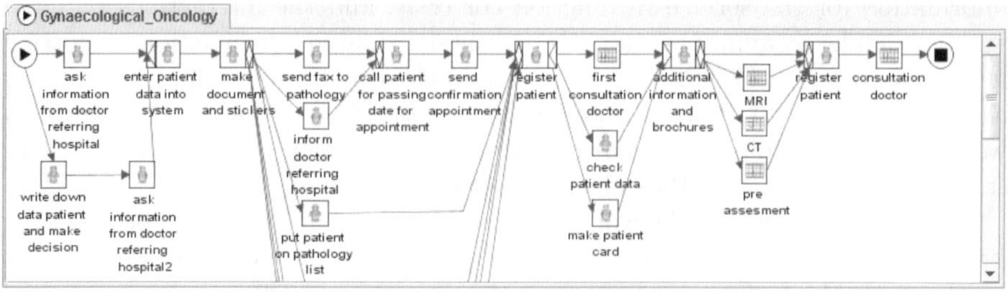

Fig. 7. Screenshot of the YAWL editor showing the initial stages of the gynecological oncology healthcare process. The flow tasks are indicated by a person icon and the schedule tasks are indicated by a calendar icon.

Via a SOAP interface, the Microsoft Exchange Server 2007 offers a wide range of (advanced) facilities for booking appointments and viewing the contents of calendars [28,13]. By means of the conceptual model, we only needed to realize the functionality described in the "calendars" component.

5 Application

In this section, we demonstrate our approach and the supporting software in the context of a real-life healthcare scenario from the AMC hospital, a large academic hospital in the Netherlands. Subsequently, we elaborate on the benefits that can be derived when the system is ultimately applied in the hospital.

To evaluate our approach, we have taken the diagnostic process of patients visiting the gynecological oncology outpatient clinic at the AMC hospital. This healthcare process deals with the diagnostic process that is followed by a patient who is referred to the AMC hospital for treatment, up to the point where the patient is diagnosed. However, for our scenario we will only focus on the initial stages of the process shown in Figure 7.

At the beginning of the process, a doctor in a referring hospital calls a nurse or doctor at the AMC hospital resulting in an appointment being made for the first visit of the patient. Several administrative tasks need to be requested before the first visit of the patient (e.g. task "first consultation doctor"). At the first consultation, the doctor decides which diagnostic tests are necessary (Magnetic Resonance Imaging (MRI), Computed Tomography (CT), or pre-assessment) before the next visit of the patient (task "consultation doctor"). Note that for the MRI, CT and pre-assessment tasks we do not show the preceding tasks at the respective departments that need to performed in order to simplify the model presented.

For this scenario, we assume that the task "additional information and brochures" has been performed. Moreover, at the first consultation with the doctor it has been decided that an MRI and a pre-assessment are needed for the patient. So, by looking at the process model it becomes clear that the tasks "MRI", "pre-assessment" and "consultation doctor" need to be scheduled. The result of the scheduling performed by the system for these tasks is shown in Figure 8a. Note

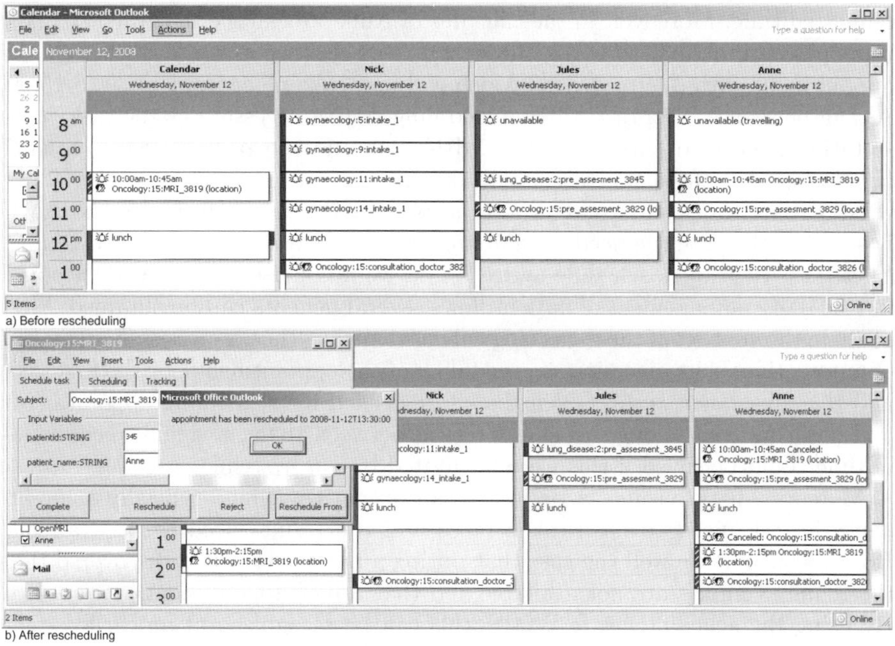

Fig. 8. Screenshot of the calendars for the "MRI", "first consultation doctor", and the "pre-assessment" tasks before and after rescheduling

that our case has "Oncology" as its process identifier and has "15" as its case identifier. Moreover, for the "consultation doctor", "pre assessment", and "MRI" examination, a doctor, an anesthetist, and MRI machine are needed respectively. Moreover, the patient is also required to be present.

In Figure 8a we can see that the "MRI" has been scheduled for 10:00 to 10:45 (see first column), the consultation with the doctor has been scheduled for 13:00 to 13:30 in the calendar of doctor "Nick" (see second column), and that the pre-assessment has been scheduled for 11:00 to 11:30 in the calendar of anesthetist "Jules" (see third column). At the far right, we can see the calendar of patient Anne who also needs to be present for the work-items mentioned, which explains why the previously mentioned appointments are also present in her calendar. For Anne we see that she is not available till 10 'o clock which has influenced the actual scheduling. This is due to the fact that she can not manage to be at the hospital before 10 'o clock by public transport. However, it is important that the "consultation doctor" task is scheduled after the "MRI" and "pre-assessment" task, which is also consistent with the corresponding process definition.

Now, let us assume that some unexpected maintenance for the MRI machine is necessary on that day, which will take until 13:30 hours to complete. Consequently, the MRI appointment needs to be rescheduled to 13:30 hours. The effect of this specific rescheduling request can be seen in Figure 8b. In this figure, the message box indicates that the MRI has been successfully rescheduled to the requested time. Moreover, in the calendar of Anne we can see that the MRI now takes place from 13:30 to 14:15. However, it was also necessary to reschedule the appointment with doctor "Nick" which will now take place from 14:30 to 15:00. As can be seen in Figure 7, this rescheduling step is necessary as the task "consultation doctor" occurs after the "MRI" task and the task "register patient" falls in between these two tasks and takes 15 minutes.

Note that the results and prototype presented were realized for the AMC hospital as they see the need for unifying workflow management and scheduling. In case the developed schedule-aware WfMS would be used in the AMC hospital for the daily management of patient flows several benefits can be obtained. First of all, in the context of the gynecological oncology healthcare process, a great deal of nurse's time is involved in the scheduling of the appointments for the first visit and the subsequent tests. Given the effort needed for scheduling appointments and ensuring that enough time is reserved between them, a significant amount of time could be saved if this were facilitated by our system.

Moreover, for a visit of a patient to an outpatient clinic, typically some diagnostic tests need to have taken place and the results need to be available. However, it may be well the case that during a patient visit it is discovered that the required inputs are not available and that a new appointment is necessary. By using the schedule-aware WfMS, this can be recognized at an earlier stage and action can be taken in order to avoid the need for any rescheduling.

6 Related Work

Analysis of the healthcare research shows that significant work has been done on the problem of appointment scheduling. Examples of such research efforts are appointment scheduling of outpatient services [10,20] and operating room scheduling [9]. However, most of these studies focus on a single unit instead of situations in which a patient passes through multiple facilities. Another approach is described in [30] in which the problem of scheduling multiple appointments on a single day is handled for outpatients by only considering the appointments which actually need to be scheduled. In our research, we take the scheduling of work-items for the whole workflow into account together with the current state of a case.

Our work is also related to time management in workflows. For example, in [25,17] the authors focus on the satisfiability of time constraints and the enforcement of these at run-time. In addition, there is also research on the problem of the scheduling of tasks by WfMSs. For example, [7,12,27,29] present algorithms for the scheduling of tasks. In contrast, we focus on the augmentation of a WfMS with scheduling facilities instead of just presenting new scheduling algorithms.

The work presented in [11] is somewhat similar to ours as it presents different architectures for a WfMS in which temporal aspects are explicitly considered. However, the temporal reasoning facilities are added as core functionality to the engine. In this paper, we propose a different approach where this kind of functionality is realized through a separate service in the system. In this way, loose coupling is guaranteed which means that our approach can be generalized to any WfMS (or even to multiple engines at the same time).

Multiple people can be involved in the actual performance of a schedule task. However, in our approach, only one user can interact with the WfMS with respect to the completion of a work-item. In [3,8,16] reference models to extend the organizational meta model with a team concept allowing for the distribution of work to teams are proposed. By doing so, advanced mechanisms are offered for the performance of work by such a team. Additionally, in [3,8] a language is discussed for defining work allocation requirements to people.

For various systems, CP Nets have been used to formalize and validate functional requirements. A good overview can be found in [15]. For example: formalizing the design of the so-called worklet service, which adds flexibility and exception handling capabilities to the YAWL workflow system [5]; formalizing the implementation of a healthcare process in a workflow management system [23]; presenting a model-based approach to requirements engineering for reactive systems [18]; expressing architectural requirements; assessing middleware support in terms of decoupling [6]; and formalizing the implementation of a patient record system by modeling task descriptions [22]. Related to this is [26], in which CP Nets are used for specifying the operational semantics of newYAWL, a business process modeling language founded on the well-known workflow patterns. To the best of our knowledge we are not aware of any work in which a comprehensive conceptual model of similar size and complexity is used for the specification and subsequent implementation of a newly developed system. Moreover, the specific component-based construction of the conceptual model allowed for the incremental mapping of the functionality contained in the conceptual model to an operational system based on widely available open-source and COTS software.

7 Conclusions and Future Work

In this paper, we have presented the design and implementation of a WfMS augmented with calendar-based scheduling facilities. Instead of just offering work-items via a work-list, as is the case in most existing WfMSs, they can also be offered as a concrete appointment in a calendar taking into account which preceding tasks are necessary and whether they have been performed. For the system developed, we have also elaborated on the experiences associated with developing and implementing a system of this scale.

Our approach demonstrates that the use of CP Nets for constructing a conceptual model of a system prior to its realization, provides valuable insights in terms of understanding the problem domain and clarifying the overall behavior of the system. Moreover, the same conceptual model provides a comprehensive specification on which to base the ultimate realization of the required functionality. We have incrementally mapped it to an operational system using widely available open-source and commercial-off-the-shelf (COTS) software. For the concrete realization of the system we used YAWL (as a workflow engine) and Microsoft Exchange Server 2007 / Outlook (as the platform providing calendar and user interaction). This demonstrates that although the specification model is detailed, it remains at a sufficient level of abstraction to allow its constituent components to be concretized in various ways. Moreover, it also shows that our ideas can, for example, be applied to a variety of WfMSs and scheduling systems.

Finally, to test the feasibility of our approach, we plan to evaluate the operational effectiveness of our resultant system in a real-life scenario at the AMC hospital.

References

1. van der Aalst, W.M.P., Aldred, L., Dumas, M., ter Hofstede, A.H.M.: Design and Implementation of the YAWL System. In: Persson, A., Stirna, J. (eds.) CAiSE 2004. LNCS, vol. 3084, pp. 142–159. Springer, Heidelberg (2004)
2. van der Aalst, W.M.P., van Hee, K.M.: Workflow Management: Models, Methods, and Systems. MIT Press, Cambridge (2002)
3. van der Aalst, W.M.P., Kumar, A.: A Reference Model for Team-Enabled Workflow Management Systems. Data and Knowledge Engineering 38(3), 335–363 (2001)
4. van der Aalst, W.M.P., Rosemann, M., Dumas, M.: Deadline-based Escalation in Process-Aware Information Systems. Decision Support Systems 43(2), 492–511 (2007)
5. Adams, M.J.: Facilitating Dynamic Flexibility and Exception Handling for Workflows. PhD thesis, Faculty of Information Technology, Queensland University of Technology (2007)
6. Aldred, L., van der Aalst, W.M.P., Dumas, M., ter Hofstede, A.H.M.: On the notion of coupling in communication middleware. In: Meersman, R., Tari, Z. (eds.) OTM 2005. LNCS, vol. 3761, pp. 1015–1033. Springer, Heidelberg (2005)
7. Bettini, C., Wang, X.S., Jajodia, S.: Temporal Reasoning in Workflow Systems. Distributed and Parallel Databases 11(3), 269–306 (2002)
8. Cao, J., Zhang, S., Zhang, X.: Team Work Oriented Flexible Workflow Management System. In: Meng, X., Su, J., Wang, Y. (eds.) WAIM 2002. LNCS, vol. 2419, pp. 189–200. Springer, Heidelberg (2002)
9. Cardoen, B., Demeulemeester, E., Beliën, J.: Operating room planning and scheduling: A literature review. To appear in European Journal of Operational Research (2009)
10. Cayirli, T., Veral, E.: Outpatient Scheduling in Health Care: A Review of Literature. Product Operations Management 12(4), 519–549 (2003)
11. Combi, C., Pozzi, G.: Architectures for a Temporal Workflow Management System. In: Haddad, H., Omicini, A., Wainwright, R.L., Liebrock, L.M. (eds.) Proc. of the 2004 ACM Symposium on Applied Computing, pp. 659–666 (2004)
12. Combi, C., Pozzi, G.: Task Scheduling for a Temporal Workflow Management System. In: Thirteenth International Symposium on Temporal Representation and Reasoning (TIME 2006), pp. 61–68 (2006)
13. Microsoft Corporation. Microsoft Exchange Server 2007 Web Services Reference, `http://msdn.microsoft.com/enus/library/aa566050EXCHG.80.aspx` (accessed on 23-03-2010)
14. Microsoft Corporation. Microsoft Office 2003 Web Services Toolkit 2.01, `http://www.microsoft.com/downloads/en/details.aspx?familyid=FA36018A-E1CF-48A3-9B35-169D819ECF18&displaylang=en` (accessed on 23-03-2010)
15. CPN Group, Aarhus. Overview of projects documenting the large-scale practical use of CP-nets and their tools, `http://cs.au.dk/cpnets/industrial-use/`

16. Cui, L., Wang, H.: Research on Cooperative Workflow Management Systems. In: Shen, W.-m., Lin, Z., Barthès, J.-P.A., Li, T.-Q. (eds.) CSCWD 2004. LNCS, vol. 3168, pp. 359–367. Springer, Heidelberg (2005)
17. Eder, J., Panagos, E., Rabinovich, M.: Time Constraints in Workflow Systems. In: Jarke, M., Oberweis, A. (eds.) CAiSE 1999. LNCS, vol. 1626, pp. 286–300. Springer, Heidelberg (1999)
18. Fernandes, J.M., Jørgensen, J.B., Tjell, S.: Requirements Engineering for Reactive Systems: Coloured Petri Nets for an Elevator Controller. In: Proceedings of the 13th Asia-Pacific Software Engineering Conference (APSEC 2007), pp. 294–301. IEEE Computer Society Press, Los Alamitos (2007)
19. The Apache Software Foundation. Apache Axis2 User's Guide - Creating Clients, `http://ws.apache.org/axis2/1_5/userguide-creatingclients.html` (accessed on 23-03-2010)
20. Gupta, D., Denton, B.: Appointment scheduling in health care: Challenges and opportunities. IIE Transactions 40(9), 800–819 (2008)
21. Jensen, K., Kristensen, L.M., Wells, L.: Coloured Petri Nets and CPN Tools for Modelling and Validation of Concurrent Systems. International Journal on Software Tools for Technology Transfer 9(3-4), 213–254 (2007)
22. Jørgensen, J.B., Lassen, K.B., van der Aalst, W.M.P.: From task descriptions via colored Petri nets towards an implementation of a new electronic patient record workflow system. International Journal on Software Tools for Technology Transfer (STTT) 10(1), 15–28 (2007)
23. Mans, R.S., van der Aalst, W.M.P., Russell, N.C., Bakker, P.J.M., Moleman, A.J., Lassen, K.B., Jørgensen, J.B.: From requirements via colored workflow nets to an implementation in several workflow systems. In: Jensen, K., Billington, J., Koutny, M. (eds.) Transactions on Petri Nets and Other Models of Concurrency III. LNCS, vol. 5800, pp. 25–49. Springer, Heidelberg (2009)
24. Mans, R.S., van der Aalst, W.M.P., Russell, N.C., Bakker, P.J.M., Moleman, A.J.: Model-based Development and Testing of Process-Aware Information Systems. In: Alimohammad, A., Meixner, A., Popescu, M. (eds.) Proceedings of The First International Conference on Advances in System Testing and Validation Lifecycle (VALID 2009), pp. 129–134. IEEE Computer Society Press, Los Alamitos (2009)
25. Marjanovic, O., Orlowska, M.: On Modeling and Verification of Temporal Constraints in Production Workflows. Knowledge and Information Systems 1(2), 157–192 (1999)
26. Russell, N.C., van der Aalst, W.M.P., ter Hofstede, A.H.M.: Designing a Workflow System Using Coloured Petri Nets. In: Jensen, K., Billington, J., Koutny, M. (eds.) Transactions on Petri Nets and Other Models of Concurrency III. LNCS, vol. 5800, pp. 1–24. Springer, Heidelberg (2009)
27. Senkul, P., Toroslu, I.H.: An Architecture for Workflow Scheduling under Resource Allocation constraints. Information Systems 30(5), 399–422 (2005)
28. Sterling, D., Spain, B., Mainer, M., Taylor, M., Upshall, H.: Inside Microsoft Exchange Server 2007 Web Services. Microsoft Press, Redmond (2007)
29. Tramontina, G.B., Wainer, J., Ellis, C.A.: Applying Scheduling Techniques to Minimize the Number of Late Jobs in Workflow Systems. In: Proc. of the 2004 ACM Symposium on Applied Computing, pp. 1396–1403 (2004)
30. Vermeulen, I., La Poutré, H., Bohte, S.M., Elkhuizen, S.G., Bakker, P.J.: Decentralized Online Scheduling of Combination-Appointments in Hospitals. In: Proceedings of ICAPS-2008, the International Conference on Automated Planning and Scheduling, Sydney, Australia. AAAI Press, Menlo Park (2008)

On-the-Fly Auditing of Business Processes

Kees van Hee[1], Jan Hidders[2], Geert-Jan Houben[2], Jan Paredaens[3], and Philippe Thiran[4]

[1] Department of Mathematics and Computer Science
Eindhoven University of Technology
k.m.v.hee@tue.nl
[2] Department of Electrical Engineering, Mathematics and Computer Science
Delft University of Technology
{a.j.h.hidders,g.j.p.m.houben}@tudelft.nl
[3] Department of Mathematics and Computer Science
University of Antwerp
jan.paredaens@ua.ac.be
[4] Faculty of Computer Science
University of Namur
philippe.thiran@fundp.ac.be

Abstract. Information systems supporting business processes are usually very complex. If we have to ensure that certain business rules are enforced in a business process, it is often easier to design a separate system, called a monitor, that collects the events of the business processes and verifies whether the rules are satisfied or not. This requires a business rule language (BRL) that allows to verify business rules over finite histories. We introduce such a BRL and show that it can express many common types of business rules. We introduce two interesting properties of BRL formulas: the future stability and the past stability. The monitor should be able to verify the business rules over the complete history, which is increasing over time. Therefore we consider *abstractions* of the history. Actually we generate from a set of business rules a labeled transition system (with countable state space) that can be executed by the monitor if each relevant event of the business process triggers a step in the labeled transition system. As long as the monitor is able to execute a step, the business rules are not violated. We show that for a sublanguage of BRL, we can transform the labeled transition system into a colored Petri net such that verification becomes independent of the history length.

1 Introduction and Motivation

In the past business information systems (BIS) were mainly used to support people in executing tasks in the business processes of an organization. Today we see that BIS have a much more responsible task: they execute large parts of the business process autonomously. So organizations become more and more dependable on their BIS. Business processes prescribe the order in which activities have to be executed. On top of that, there are often several other *business*

K. Jensen, S. Donatelli, and M. Koutny (Eds.): ToPNoC IV, LNCS 6550, pp. 144–173, 2010.

rules that should be met by the execution of business processes. Business rules can be required by any stakeholders, such as management, government (by law), shareholders and business partners (clients and suppliers).

It is practically impossible to verify whether a BIS is satisfying the business rules. So we have to live with the fact that systems can always have some errors that may violate business rules. Normally *auditors* check periodically whether the business rules are satisfied in the past period by inspecting an *audit trail* of the business process, which is actually a log file with past events. Not all business rules can be verified only from the past. For instance the rule: "All invoices should be paid", cannot be verified over the past in general, because there might be an unpaid invoice for which we cannot conclude that it will never be paid. So *auditing* concerns only business rules that can be verified over the past. In particular we are looking for rules that have the property that they hold for an empty log and that if they are false for the current log then they stay false for every future extension of that log. We call them *past stable* formulas. The example can be modified into "All invoices should be paid within 30 days" which can be audited. In this paper we assume that a BIS may have some unknown errors and that the system is for all stakeholders a black box. Instead of a human auditor we propose here an approach where the BIS is extended by an independent *monitor system* that checks the essential business rules *on the fly* and that reports violations of business rules (detective mode) or that interrupts the BIS to prevent the occurrence of a violation (preventive mode). We may consider the BIS extended with the monitor system as a new BIS. This BIS has a better chance of preserving the business rules than the original one. The main reason is that the monitor system is an independent subsystem dedicated to the verification of the business rules.

We introduce a powerful language to express common business rules. Note that business rules often require summation and other computations. To illustrate its power we express common business rules in this language.

Our approach is to generate from a set of business rules a process model, i.e., a labeled transition system, that can be executed by the monitor, in such a way that relevant events in the BIS are transferred to the monitor and that the monitor will try to execute the event as a transition in the process model. As long as the monitor is able to perform the transitions, no violation of business rules should have happened, and if a step is not executable this means the violation of a rule. We do not consider here how the monitor is reset to continue after a violation. In fact, the process model of the monitor can be seen as an *abstraction* of the real business process, reflecting only the details relevant for the business rules. For on-the-fly auditing it is essential that the time to verify the rules is not increasing with the size of the log. Therefore the state space of the process model should contain all relevant information of the history to verify the business rules, therefore it is an *abstraction* of the history a the process. If the abstraction has a finite state space we are done, but in realistic situations that is not possible. The challenge is to find process models with *states* that are *bounded* in size, i.e., they should not grow with the size of the log and that have computation times dependent of the size of the states only. We first consider a standard labeled transition system, but later we transform it for a sublanguage of BRL into a colored Petri net with bounded size of tokens and the number of tokens does not depend on the history length.

In Section 2 we give the necessary concepts for the approach and a set of characteristic business rules. In Section 3 we define BRL. In Section 4 we express some characteristic business rules in BRL. In Section 5 we first introduce two interesting properties of formulas in BRL: future stability and past stability. Then we consider the generation of a labeled transition system from the business rules. In Section 6 we show how colored Petri nets, can be used to model the labeled transition system of the monitor for sublanguages of BRL. This gives us the opportunity to use existing tools to realize the monitor.

2 Basic Concepts

Organizations perform *business processes* (also called *workflows*) in order to meet their *objectives* within the limits of a set of *business rules*. Business processes are sets of *tasks* with some precedence relationship. A business processes can have many concurrent instances. An instance of a business process is called a *case*. In a BIS many cases may be active concurrently. Tasks are executed for a case. They can be *instantaneous*, in which case the task execution is an *event*, or the execution of a task takes time, in which case we distinguish a *start event* and an *stop event*. Tasks are executed by *agents*, which can be humans or automated parts of the information system. An agent has one or more *roles* and is only allowed to execute a task if it has a role that is assigned to that task. Agents can be *authorized* by other agents to fulfill a role. We consider authorization as a special kind of task that is not case related.

Tasks manipulate objects called *resources*. Resources are created, deleted, used or transformed during a task execution. In the business process resources can be for instance materials, components, final products, energy, information or money. In a BIS the resources are always represented as data. Note that we follow the terminology that is used in the domain of *accounting information systems* where the REA datamodel is used frequently. REA stands for Resource, Event and Agent, concepts with the same meaning as we gave them. The REA datamodel is an Entity Relationship model for accounting information systems [1,2,3].

For the enforcement of the business rules we propose a *monitor system* that *detects* and *reports* violations of the business rules or that *prevents* violations by interrupting the BIS and triggering an exception handler. In order to do so the monitor system *records* relevant *events*, i.e., task executions of the original BIS. So the monitor is "hooked on" the original BIS and it intervenes the execution of it.

Nature of Business Rules. Examples of business rules are the famous Sarbanes-Oxley [4] rules and the International Accounting Standards [5]. The business rules that we encounter in practice mostly are of the following nature:

- *Task-order* rules. Rules that prescribe or forbid certain task orders in a case, such as: task A should always precede task B if task C has been executed.
- *Authorization* rules. Rules that prescribe or forbid certain assignments of tasks to agents or roles, such as: two specific tasks in the same case are not allowed to be executed by the same agent. This rule is known by auditors as the *four-eyes principle*. Other examples are rules that allow agents to delegate certain roles to other agents, such as an agent can only be given a certain role to another agent if he has that role himself. We call this the *delegation principle*. Other authorization rules prescribe that agents having a certain role are needed for a task.
- *Resource balancing* rules. Rules concerning the use of resources and in particular these resources that are balancing in some way. An example is the *three-way matching rule* that prescribes that the number of items of a certain resource in an invoice should be equal to the number of items in a delivery and the number of items in the order. This rule is well-known by financial auditors. Another example is that the amount of resources of a certain type has always to be within bounds.

Combinations of them are possible as well. Note that the task-order rules should hold for each case separately. There are case independent authorization rules as well as case dependent ones and the resource balancing rules could involve all cases.

Informal Examples of Business Rules. For illustrating the business rules, we adopt a simplified version of a business process in a bakery. Here we specify the domain specific concepts. The process describes the procurement of three products, i.e., resources: $\mathbf{butter}, \mathbf{bread}, \mathbf{salmon}$. The procurement consists of the execution of the six following tasks: buy, packaging, packaging − grant, delivery, pay and use. The first and the last two tasks are carried out by the agent customer while the other ones are taken in charge by the agent baker. By packaging − grant, the agent baker can delegate the task packaging to his assistant (the agent assistant).

For this simple scenario, we give informal examples of each nature of business rules:

- *Task-order* rules: "for every case, the tasks buy, packaging, delivery, pay and use happen in that order"
- *Authorization* rules: "an agent with role manager can assign the role assistant to the task packaging" and "for every case, the execution of the task buy is assigned to agent customer by agent baker", which actually means that the bakery is open;
- *Resource balancing* rules: "at each moment the total amount of used bread does not exceed the amount of previously delivered bread" or "if bread is bought then it has to be delivered in the same quantity".

These examples will be used for illustrating the next sections.

3 Business Rule Language

In this section we define the language BRL to formulate business rules. Business processes are described in terms of events, which are defined in the following. An event is characterized by the task that is performed, at a certain time, by an agent in a certain role and often for a certain case. Events can have more properties, this dependents on the task.

3.1 Postulated Sets and Concepts

We postulate the set $\mathbb{Q}$ of rational numbers together with the usual operations of addition (+), multiplication ($\cdot$) and a strict linear order (<). We let $X \rightharpoonup Y$ denote the set of partial functions from X to Y. For a partial function $f : X \rightharpoonup Y$ we let $\mathbf{dom}(f)$ denote the subset of X for which f is defined. The property types set is $\Theta = \{\mathbf{Time}, \mathbf{Case}, \mathbf{Task}, \mathbf{TaskType}, \mathbf{Agent}, \mathbf{Role}, \mathbf{Quantity}, \mathbf{Boolean}\}$.

Process Schema. A *process schema* is defined as $S = (C, T, A, R, \mathcal{P}, \theta, \pi)$ where C is a countably infinite set of case identifiers, T is a finite set of *tasks*, A a finite set of *agents*, R a finite set of *roles* for agents, $\mathcal{P}$ a finite set of *properties*, $\theta : \mathcal{P} \to \Theta$ is the *type assignment* for the properties in $\mathcal{P}$ and $\pi : T \to 2^{\mathcal{P}}$ is the *property-set function* which gives the applicable set of properties for each task.

The set $\mathcal{P}$ contains at least the properties **time**, **case**, **task**, **tasktype**, **agent**, **to** and **role**, such that $\theta(\mathbf{time}) = \mathbf{Time}$, $\theta(\mathbf{case}) = \mathbf{Case}$, $\theta(\mathbf{task}) = \mathbf{Task}$, $\theta(\mathbf{tasktype}) = \mathbf{TaskType}$, $\theta(\mathbf{agent}) = \mathbf{Agent}$, $\theta(\mathbf{to}) = \mathbf{Agent}$ and $\theta(\mathbf{role}) = \mathbf{Role}$.

The set $[\![\mathbf{TaskType}]\!] = \{\text{open}, \text{close}, \text{grant}, \text{retract}, \text{engage}, \text{release}, \text{use}\}$ is the set of task types. The task-types have the following meaning: "open" means that the task starts a case and "close" that the task closes a case, "grant" is a task of giving an agent a certain role, i.e., the right to fulfill that role, and "retract" is the inverse. Further "engage" means that an agent is engaged for a case and "release" that it is freed. A task of type "use" is only allowed to use an agent that is engaged for the case. In this way we can model that activities take time: so an activity may start with an engage task, then a use task is executed and it ends with a release task. The time between the engage task and the release task is the time the agent is busy. With "engage" and "release" we can also model more complex structures.

For all $t \in T : \{\mathbf{time}, \mathbf{task}, \mathbf{tasktype}, \mathbf{agent}, \mathbf{role}\} \subseteq \pi(t)$. We sometimes have "dummy" tasks, called "dummy" for instance when we open or close a case. Such tasks are characterized by their task type and they have no additional properties. Note that the elements of the sets C and A never occur in business rules: we only use quantifications over these sets.

We distinguish a set $Res \subseteq \mathcal{P} \backslash \{\mathbf{time}, \mathbf{case}, \mathbf{task}, \mathbf{tasktype}, \mathbf{role}, \mathbf{agent}, \mathbf{to}\}$, which is used to represent *resources* and $\forall r \in Res : \theta(r) = \mathbf{Quantity}$.

The tasks with the **case** property describe the type of events that may occur in the run of a workflow, such as *place order*, *contact client*. They are domain specific and we call them *case tasks*. The property **case** indicates the case to which an event belongs. The property **time** denotes the timestamp of the event, i.e., when it happened. The property **task** describes the task that is performed by the event and since it defines type of the event we use the task as the name of the event. The property **agent** says which agent performed the event and **role** in which role the agent acts. Finally property **to** says to which agent a role is delegated. In the execution of a case there can be more than one instance of a certain task. We require that each event is executed by a certain agent.

In the following definitions of this section we assume a fixed process schema $S = (C, T, A, R, \mathcal{P}, \theta, \pi)$.

Schema-Dependent Concepts. Based on the process schema we define several derived notions. We let $V = C \cup T \cup A \cup R \cup \mathbb{Q}$ denote the set of all possible *property values*. The semantics of the types is defined such that $[\![\mathbf{Time}]\!] = \mathbb{Q}$, $[\![\mathbf{Case}]\!] = C$, $[\![\mathbf{Task}]\!] = T$, $[\![\mathbf{Agent}]\!] = A$, $[\![\mathbf{Role}]\!] = R$, $[\![\mathbf{Quantity}]\!] = \mathbb{Q}$ and $[\![\mathbf{Boolean}]\!] = \{1, 0\} \subseteq \mathbb{Q}$. Note that $[\![\mathbf{TaskType}]\!]$ is already defined.

Event. We define an *event* as a partial function $ev : \mathcal{P} \rightharpoonup V$ that maps properties to their value such that (i) at least the property **task** which indicates the executed task has a value, i.e., $\mathbf{task} \in \mathbf{dom}(ev)$, (ii) exactly all properties that are associated with the task of the event have a value, i.e., if $t = ev(\mathbf{task})$ then $\mathbf{dom}(ev) = \pi(t)$ and (iii) the value of each property is in the semantics of the type of that property, i.e., $ev(p) \in [\![\theta(p)]\!]$ for all $p \in \pi(t)$. The set of all events is denoted as $\mathcal{E}$. So an $ev \in \mathcal{E}$ can be seen as a record of an event that occurred in the BIS.

Event Log. A *event log* α is defined as a finite set of events. We use variables such as α and β to denote such event logs. Note that although they are sets, event logs can be thought of as ordered sets where the events are ordered by their timestamp.

3.2 Core Business Rule Language

We now proceed with defining the language BRL (Business Rule Language). Given a process schema, BRL is the language in which we specify the business rules. A business rule expresses a property of the event logs.

We start by postulating a countably infinite set of variables $\mathcal{X}$ that will be used to refer to events. We then define the sets of expressions E with the following abstract syntax:

$$E ::= \neg E \mid (E \wedge E) \mid \mathcal{X}.\mathcal{P} \mid (E = E) \mid (E < E) \mid (\mathcal{X} = \mathcal{X}) \mid \\ \mathbb{Q} \mid A \mid T \mid \Sigma(\mathcal{X} : E)\ E \mid (E + E) \mid (E \cdot E).$$

We briefly and informally describe the semantics here, and give a full formal semantics in Appendix A. The expressions $\neg e_1$ and $(e_1 \wedge e_2)$ denote the logical operations over booleans. The expression $x.p$ denotes the value of property p of event x. The expression $(e_1 = e_2)$ denotes the equality operator, and $(e_1 < e_2)$

the comparison as defined by the strict linear order $<$ of $\mathbb{Q}$ which is used to represent both quantities and time. The equation $(x_1 = x_2)$ is true if x_1 and x_2 refer to the same event. The numbers $q \in \mathbb{Q}$, agents $a \in A$ and tasks $t \in T$ all denote themselves. The expression $\Sigma(x : e_1)\ e_2$ denotes the summation of the value of e_2 for each event x in the event log that satisfies formula e_1. For example, $\Sigma(x : x.\mathbf{task} = \mathit{order})\ x.\mathbf{amount}$ computes the sum of all amounts x that were ordered. Finally, the expressions $(e_1 + e_2)$ and $(e_1 \cdot e_2)$ express the addition and multiplication over $\mathbb{Q}$. In order to avoid expressions that have no well-defined result, such as boolean operations over non-boolean values, there is a typing regime that defines when an expression is *well-typed*, which is formally defined in Appendix A.

3.3 Syntactic Short-Hands

We introduce syntactic short-hands for the booleans: $\mathbf{true} \equiv (1 = 1)$ and $\mathbf{false} \equiv (1 = 0)$. Moreover, we allow simultaneous quantification over several variables, i.e., we allow expressions $\Sigma(x_1, x_2, \ldots, x_n : e_1)\ e_2$ with $n > 1$ and their meaning is defined with induction on n to be equivalent with

$$\Sigma(x_1 : \mathbf{true})\ (\Sigma(x_2, \ldots, x_n : e_1)\ e_2)$$

for $n > 1$. So, for $n = 3$, for example, we get

$$\Sigma(x_1, x_2, x_3 : e_1)\ e_2 \equiv \Sigma(x_1 : \mathbf{true})\ (\Sigma(x_2 : \mathbf{true})\ (\Sigma(x_3 : e_1)\ e_2)).$$

We also introduce the following short-hands for logical disjunction, logical implication, existential quantification and universal quantification: $(\varphi \vee \psi) \equiv \neg(\neg\varphi \wedge \neg\psi)$, $(\varphi \Rightarrow \psi) \equiv (\neg\varphi \vee \psi)$, $\exists x_1, \ldots, x_n(\varphi) \equiv ((\Sigma(x_1, \ldots, x_n : \varphi)\ 1) > 0)$ and $\forall x_1, \ldots, x_n(\varphi) \equiv \neg(\exists x_1, \ldots, x_n(\neg\varphi))$. For expressions that use the short-hands we generalize the notion of well-typedness such that an expression is well-typed iff the expression that is obtained after rewriting all the short-hands is well-typed.

We let $e_1 \leq e_2$ and $e_1 \geq e_2$ denote $\neg(e_1 > e_2)$ and $\neg(e_1 < e_2)$, respectively. We write $e_1\ op_1\ e_2\ op_2\ e_3$ instead of $(e_1\ op_1\ e_2) \wedge (e_2\ op_2\ e_3)$ for $op_1, op_2 \in \{<, \leq, =, >, \geq\}$. Finally we introduce a short-hand to denote an enumeration of possible values. We let $x.p \in \{v_1, \ldots, v_n\}$ denote the formula $x.p = v_1 \vee \ldots \vee x.p = v_n$.

In order to denote the first and the last event in the log, assuming the ordering of events by their timestamp, we define the event expressions **first** and **last** which can be used in a formula anywhere a variable can be used. We then interpret a formula φ that contains **first** as the formula $\neg(\exists x(\mathbf{true})) \vee \exists x(\forall y(y.\mathbf{time} \geq x.\mathbf{time}) \wedge \varphi')$ where x and y are fresh variables and φ' is constructed from φ by replacing all occurrences of **first** with x. Analogously, if φ contains **last** its meaning is defined as $\neg(\exists x(\mathbf{true})) \vee \exists x(\forall y(y.\mathbf{time} \leq x.\mathbf{time}) \wedge \varphi')$ where φ' is constructed from φ by replacing **last** with x.

4 Characteristic Examples of BRL

To illustrate BRL we present some rules from the bakery example of Section 2, but also some generic rules that fit into any business domain. Consider the following process schema $S = (C, T, A, R, \mathcal{P}, \theta, \pi)$ with tasks

$$T = \{\text{buy}, \text{deliver}, \text{pay}, \text{use}, \text{packaging}, \text{dummy}\}$$

Further C, A, R are arbitrary sets and

$$\mathcal{P} = \{\mathbf{time}, \mathbf{case}, \mathbf{task}, \mathbf{tasktype}, \mathbf{agent}, \mathbf{role}, \mathbf{to}, \mathbf{butter}, \mathbf{bread}, \mathbf{salmon}\}$$

The last three are resources. The type assignment is:

$$\begin{aligned}\theta = \{\ &(\mathbf{time}, \mathbf{Time}), (\mathbf{case}, \mathbf{Case}), (\mathbf{task}, \mathbf{Task}), (\mathbf{tasktype}, \mathbf{TaskType}),\\ &(\mathbf{agent}, \mathbf{Agent}), (\mathbf{role}, \mathbf{Role}), (\mathbf{butter}, \mathbf{Quantity}), (\mathbf{bread}, \mathbf{Quantity}),\\ &(\mathbf{salmon}, \mathbf{Quantity}), (\mathbf{to}, \mathbf{Agent})\}\end{aligned}$$

and the property-set function

$$\pi = \{\ (\text{buy}, F), (\text{deliver}, F), (\text{pay}, F), (\text{use}, F), (\text{packaging}, F), (\text{dummy}, G \cup \{to\})\}$$

where the set F is defined as $F = \{\mathbf{case}, \mathbf{butter}, \mathbf{bread}, \mathbf{salmon}\} \cup G$ and $G = \{\mathbf{agent}, \mathbf{role}, \mathbf{time}, \mathbf{task}, \mathbf{tasktype}\}$.

We consider the sets of characteristic examples defined in Section 2. Note that all rules should hold at every moment, so also for every prefix of an event log.

4.1 Task-Order Rules

Rule (a). The rule "no two distinct events for the same case can happen on the same moment" can be formulated as follows:

$$\forall x_1, x_2(\neg(x_1 = x_2) \Rightarrow \neg(x_1.\mathbf{time} = x_2.\mathbf{time}))$$

Rule (b). The rule "for every case the tasks buy, deliver, pay and use happen in that order." would be formulated in BRL as:

$$\begin{aligned}\forall x_1, x_2, x_3(x_1.\mathbf{task} = \text{buy} \wedge x_2.\mathbf{task} = \text{deliver} \wedge x_3.\mathbf{task} = \text{pay} \wedge\\ x_1.\mathbf{case} = x_2.\mathbf{case} = x_3.\mathbf{case}\\ \Rightarrow x_1.\mathbf{time} < x_2.\mathbf{time} < x_3.\mathbf{time})\end{aligned}$$

Rule (c). Task-order rules are very important and therefore we pay special attention to them. We first define a short-hand for counting the number of occurrences of task a in the case of event c:

$$\phi(a, c) := \Sigma(y : y.\mathbf{task} = a \wedge y.\mathbf{case} = c.\mathbf{case})\ 1$$

Note that the variables c and y represent events only. Actually a is a meta variable representing a task and c is representing an arbitrary event used to mark an arbitrary case in the log. Now, consider for example business rules of the form:

$$\forall c(\phi(a, c) + \phi(b, c) \geq \phi(d, c) + \phi(e, c))$$

where a, b, d, e are tasks. These require that for all cases the number of occurrences of tasks a and b is at least the number of occurrences of task d and task e. Because we cannot quantify over case identifiers, we quantify over all events c and we count the number of events y with the same case identifier as c and task equal to a, b, d and e respectively. So we consider c as a dummy variable over the case identifiers. Formally we define a class of similar business rules by

$$E_1 ::= \phi(T, \mathcal{X}) \mid (E_1 + E_1) \mid \mathbb{Q}.$$
$$E_2 ::= (E_1 \geq E_1) \mid (E_2 \vee E_2) \mid (E_2 \wedge E_2) \mid \neg E_2.$$
$$E_3 ::= \forall \mathcal{X}(E_2).$$

In addition we do not allow free variables in E_3. Business rules of type E_3 can express sequences, alternatives, parallel tasks and iterations of tasks. For example $\forall c(\phi(a, c) \geq \phi(b, c))$ means that a always precedes b and $\forall c(\phi(a, c) \geq \phi(b, c) + \phi(d, c))$ that after a single a we may have either a b or a d but not both, while $\forall c(\phi(a, c) \geq \phi(b, c) \wedge \phi(a, c) \geq \phi(d, c))$ implies that after a single a, b and d may occur both together. The fact that multiple occurrences are allowed shows that we may have iterations. Often we require that between two occurrences of two tasks there is an occurrence of another task: $\forall c(\phi(a, c) \geq \phi(b, c) \geq \phi(a, c) - 1)$. In [6] formulas of the type E_3 are called *counting formulas* and formulas of the type $E_1 \geq E_1$ are called *basic counting formulas.*

Rule (d). A typical task order rule uses the *current time*. An example is "for all cases the task 'invoice' should be followed by a task 'payment' within 30 days". We can express this rule as:

$$\begin{aligned}\forall z(\ & z.\textbf{task} = \text{invoice} \Rightarrow \exists z'(\ z'.\textbf{task} = \text{payment} \wedge z'.\textbf{case} = z.\textbf{case} \wedge \\ & \qquad z.\textbf{time} < z'.\textbf{time} \leq z.\textbf{time} + 30) \vee \\ & \qquad (z.\textbf{time} + 30) > \textbf{last}.\textbf{time}))\end{aligned}$$

Recall that **last** refers to the last event in the log.

Rule (e). Cases have a start and a stop event, which is expressed by two task types called "open" and "close". No event for a case is allowed to happen before the start event or after the stop event.

$$\begin{aligned}\forall x(\ & \neg(x.\textbf{tasktype} \in \{\text{open}, \text{close}, \text{grant}, \text{retract}\} \Rightarrow \\ & ((\exists y(y.\textbf{tasktype} = \text{open} \wedge y.\textbf{case} = x.\textbf{case} \wedge y.\textbf{time} \leq x.\textbf{time}))\end{aligned}$$

$$\wedge$$

$$\begin{aligned}\forall x(\ & \neg x.\textbf{tasktype} \in \{\text{open}, \text{close}, \text{grant}, \text{retract}\} \wedge \\ & \exists y(y.\textbf{tasktype} = \text{close} \wedge y.\textbf{case} = x.\textbf{case}) \Rightarrow x.\textbf{time} \leq y.\textbf{time})\end{aligned}$$

4.2 Authorization Rules

Rule (f). The rule "if an agent is acting in a role then it was granted that role earlier on and that grant was not retracted in the meantime" is expressed as:

$$\begin{aligned}\forall x(\ & x.\mathbf{time} > 0 \wedge \exists y(\ y.\mathbf{tasktype} = \text{grant} \wedge y.\mathbf{to} = x.\mathbf{agent}\ \wedge \\ & \quad y.\mathbf{role} = x.\mathbf{role} \wedge y.\mathbf{time} < x.\mathbf{time} \wedge \\ & \quad \neg\exists z(\ z.\mathbf{tasktype} = \text{retract} \wedge z.\mathbf{to} = x.\mathbf{agent}\ \wedge \\ & \qquad z.\mathbf{role} = x.\mathbf{role} \wedge y.\mathbf{time} < z.\mathbf{time} < x.\mathbf{time})))\end{aligned}$$

We assume at time=0 several initial events that grant roles to agents. The agent of these events could be the manager. We do not give these events here.

Rule (g). The *four-eyes principle* can be formulated in general, using two arbitrary tasks T_1 and T_2:

$$\forall x, y(x.\mathbf{task} = T_1 \wedge y.\mathbf{task} = T_2 \wedge x.\mathbf{case} = y.\mathbf{case} \Rightarrow x.\mathbf{agent} \neq y.\mathbf{agent})$$

Note that this is just an example of the four-eyes principle. We may have rules that require that all tasks in some set of tasks should have different agents per case.

Rule (h). The *delegation principle* is formulated by two rules. The first says that an agent can grant a role to another agent only if he has the authorization himself:

$$\begin{aligned}\forall x(\ & x.\mathbf{tasktype} = \text{grant} \Rightarrow \\ & \exists y(\ y.\mathbf{tasktype} = \text{grant} \wedge y.\mathbf{to} = x.\mathbf{agent} \wedge y.\mathbf{role} = x.\mathbf{role}\ \wedge \\ & \quad y.\mathbf{time} < x.\mathbf{time} \wedge \\ & \quad \neg\exists z(\ z.\mathbf{tasktype} = \text{retract} \wedge z.\mathbf{to} = x.\mathbf{agent} \wedge z.\mathbf{role} = x.\mathbf{role}\ \wedge \\ & \qquad y.\mathbf{time} < z.\mathbf{time} < x.\mathbf{time})))\end{aligned}$$

The second rule of the delegation principle says that an agent can retract a role from an agent only if he has granted this role to him before and that agent has not granted another agent:

$$\begin{aligned}\forall x(\ & x.\mathbf{tasktype} = \text{retract} \Rightarrow \\ & \exists y(\ y.\mathbf{tasktype} = \text{grant} \wedge y.\mathbf{to} = x.\mathbf{to} \wedge y.\mathbf{agent} = x.\mathbf{agent}\ \wedge \\ & \quad y.\mathbf{role} = x.\mathbf{role} \wedge y.\mathbf{time} < x.\mathbf{time}\ \wedge \\ & \quad \forall z(\ z.\mathbf{tasktype} = \text{grant} \wedge z.\mathbf{agent} = y.\mathbf{to} \wedge z.\mathbf{role} = y.\mathbf{role}\ \wedge \\ & \qquad y.\mathbf{time} < z.\mathbf{time} < x.\mathbf{time} \Rightarrow \\ & \qquad \exists w(\ w.\mathbf{tasktype} = \text{retract} \wedge w.\mathbf{agent} = z.\mathbf{agent} \wedge w.\mathbf{to} = z.\mathbf{to}\ \wedge \\ & \qquad\quad w.\mathbf{role} = z.\mathbf{role} \wedge z.\mathbf{time} < w.\mathbf{time} < x.\mathbf{time}))))\end{aligned}$$

Rule (i). The *agent engagement principle* says that agents can only be attached to a task for a case if the agent is engaged to the case. The tasks that mark the begin and end of an engagement period have task-type "engage" and "release". An agent can be involved in only one engagement at a time. This is expressed by the first engagement rule:

$$\begin{aligned}\forall x, y(\ & ((x.\mathbf{tasktype} = \text{engage} \wedge y.\mathbf{tasktype} = \text{engage} \wedge x.\mathbf{agent} = y.\mathbf{agent}\ \wedge \\ & \quad x.\mathbf{time} \leq y.\mathbf{time} \wedge x \neq y) \Rightarrow \\ & \quad \exists z(\ z.\mathbf{tasktype} = \text{release} \wedge z.\mathbf{agent} = y.\mathbf{agent}\ \wedge\end{aligned}$$

$$
\begin{aligned}
&x.\mathbf{time} < z.\mathbf{time} < y.\mathbf{time} \wedge x.\mathbf{case} = z.\mathbf{case}))\\
&\wedge\\
&((x.\mathbf{tasktype} = \text{release} \wedge y.\mathbf{tasktype} = \text{release} \wedge x.\mathbf{agent} = y.\mathbf{agent} \wedge\\
&x.\mathbf{time} \leq y.\mathbf{time} \wedge x \neq y) \Rightarrow\\
&\exists z(\ z.\mathbf{tasktype} = \text{engage} \wedge z.\mathbf{agent} = y.\mathbf{agent} \wedge\\
&x.\mathbf{time} < z.\mathbf{time} < y.\mathbf{time} \wedge x.\mathbf{case} = z.\mathbf{case})))
\end{aligned}
$$

The second engagement rule says that a "normal" task can only be performed by an agent that was first engaged and not released for the case.

$$
\begin{aligned}
&\forall x(\ \neg(x.\mathbf{tasktype} \in \{\text{grant}, \text{retract}, \text{open}, \text{close}, \text{engage}, \text{release}\}) \Rightarrow\\
&\quad \exists y(\ y.\mathbf{tasktype} = \text{engage} \wedge y.\mathbf{agent} = x.\mathbf{agent} \wedge x.\mathbf{case} = y.\mathbf{case} \wedge\\
&\quad y.\mathbf{time} < x.\mathbf{time} \wedge \neg\exists z(\ z.\mathbf{tasktype} = \text{release} \wedge z.\mathbf{agent} = x.\mathbf{agent} \wedge\\
&\quad x.\mathbf{case} = z.\mathbf{case} \wedge y.\mathbf{time} < z.\mathbf{time} < x.\mathbf{time})))
\end{aligned}
$$

4.3 Resource Balancing Rules

Rule (j). The rule "at each moment the total amount of used bread does not exceed the amount of previously delivered bread" is a global resource balancing rule and can be formulated as:

$$\Sigma(y : y.\mathbf{task} = \text{use})\ y.\mathbf{bread} \leq \Sigma(y : y.\mathbf{task} = \text{deliver})\ y.\mathbf{bread}$$

Rule (k). The rule "for every case there is at most one delivery of bread" is a local resource balancing rule and can be formulated as:

$$
\begin{aligned}
&\forall x, y(\ x.\mathbf{task} = \text{deliver} \wedge x.\text{bread} > 0 \wedge\\
&\qquad y.\mathbf{task} = \text{deliver} \wedge y.\text{bread} > 0 \wedge x.\mathbf{case} = y.\mathbf{case} \Rightarrow x = y)
\end{aligned}
$$

Rule (l). In general we distinguish two kinds of resource balancing rules: *global resource balancing* rules that hold for each moment and *local resource balancing* rules that hold for each case individually and for each moment. So there are two sets of resources: $Res = Res_1 \cup Res_2$ and $Res_1 \cap Res_2 = \emptyset$, where Res_1 represents all the global resources and Res_2 all the local resources. In general the *resource balancing rules* make use of the formulae ψ_0 for global resource balancing and ψ_1 for local resource balancing rules:

$$
\begin{aligned}
\psi_0(\mathbf{r}) &:= \Sigma(y : \mathbf{true})\ y.\mathbf{r},\ \ \mathbf{r} \in Res_1\\
\psi_1(\mathbf{r}, c) &:= \Sigma(y : y.\mathbf{case} = c.\mathbf{case})\ y.\mathbf{r},\ \ \mathbf{r} \in Res_2
\end{aligned}
$$

In the same way as for the task-order rules we can define a syntax:

$$
\begin{aligned}
&E_1 ::= \psi_0(Res) \mid \psi_1(Res, \mathcal{X}) \mid (E_1 + E_1) \mid \mathbb{Q}.\\
&E_2 ::= (E_1 \geq E_1) \mid (E_2 \vee E_2) \mid (E_2 \wedge E_2) \mid \neg E_2.\\
&E_3 ::= \forall \mathcal{X}(E_2) \mid E_2.
\end{aligned}
$$

Again we also require that the the variable in E_3 is everywhere used in the same position in the parameters of ψ.

5 Generating a Monitor from Business Rules

Our goal is to construct a monitor that gets as input each event that is processed by the system and that notifies the environment as soon as it is sure that some business rule cannot be satisfied anymore in the future. In this case the monitor will interrupt the system or it gives an alarm.

In this section we first introduce two interesting concepts, the future-stability and the past-stability. We then consider a monitor as a labeled transition system. Finally we discuss the special case where the monitor has a finite set of states. In the next section we generalize this to a Petri Net.

5.1 Stable BRL-Formula

Some BRL-formulas have a very special property, namely that once they hold then they will hold always in the future. These BRL-formula are called future-stable. So, once they hold, we do not need to verify them anymore in the future. Some BRL-formula have the property that if they hold now then they held always in the past. These BRL-formula are called past-stable. So, suppose that they have to hold at an infinite number of specified moments, then we know they have to hold always. Let us define these notions exactly.

If α and β are logs, β is called a sublog of α iff $\beta \subseteq \alpha$. β is called a prelog of α, denoted $\beta \subseteq_P \alpha$ iff

- β is a sublog of α
- $\forall e_1 \in \beta \; \forall e_2 \in \alpha - \beta \; (e_1(\mathbf{time}) < e_2(\mathbf{time}))$

Formally the semantics of an expressions $e \in E$ is defined by the proposition $\alpha, \Gamma \vdash e \rightsquigarrow v$ which states that the value of e is v for the process log α and the variable binding Γ. Here a *variable binding* is defined as a partial function $\Gamma : \mathcal{X} \rightharpoonup \mathcal{E}$ which maps variables to events. For the full definition of the syntax and semantics the reader is referred to Appendix A.

The closed BRL-formula φ is called *future-stable* (fs) iff

$$\forall\alpha\forall\beta \; (\beta, \emptyset \vdash \varphi \rightsquigarrow 1 \wedge \beta \subseteq_P \alpha \Rightarrow \alpha, \emptyset \vdash \varphi \rightsquigarrow 1)$$

The closed BRL-formula φ is called *past-stable* (ps) iff

$$\forall\alpha\forall\beta \; (\alpha, \emptyset \vdash \varphi \rightsquigarrow 1 \wedge \beta \subseteq_P \alpha \Rightarrow \beta, \emptyset \vdash \varphi \rightsquigarrow 1)$$

Example 1. Let **prop** the name of a property of type **Quantity** and a an agent.

- $\exists x(x.\mathbf{agent} = a)$ is fs and $\forall x(\neg x.\mathbf{agent} = a)$ is ps;
- $\forall x_1(x_1.\mathbf{time} > 0 \;\Rightarrow \exists x_2(x_2.\mathbf{time} < x_1.\mathbf{time}))$ is ps;
- $\forall x_1(x_1.\mathbf{time} > 0 \;\Rightarrow \exists x_2, x_3(x_3.\mathbf{time} < x_2.\mathbf{time} < x_1.\mathbf{time} \wedge \neg(x_2.\mathbf{prop} = x_3.\mathbf{prop})))$ is ps;
- $\forall x_1 \; \exists x_2(x_1.\mathbf{time} < x_2.\mathbf{time})$ is not ps nor fs.

Corollary 1. *A BRL-formula that is both ps and fs is equivalent with the formula* **true** *or* **false**.

Theorem 1. *φ is fs iff $\neg\varphi$ is ps.*

Proof. Let φ be fs and let $\beta \subseteq_P \alpha$ and $\alpha, \emptyset \vdash \neg\varphi \rightsquigarrow 1$. Then $\alpha, \emptyset \vdash \varphi \rightsquigarrow 0$, so $\beta, \emptyset \vdash \varphi \rightsquigarrow 0$ and $\beta, \emptyset \vdash \neg\varphi \rightsquigarrow 1$, so $\neg\varphi$ is ps. □

Theorem 2. *If φ_1 and φ_2 are fs then $\varphi_1 \vee \varphi_2$ and $\varphi_1 \wedge \varphi_2$ are fs. If φ_1 and φ_2 are ps then $\varphi_1 \vee \varphi_2$ and $\varphi_1 \wedge \varphi_2$ are ps.*

Some BRL-formulas are not past-stable but it is sometimes possible to find a past-stable formula that can be used by the monitor to detect when the first formula becomes definitively false. More formally, we say that formula φ *is checked by* formula ψ if it holds that $\alpha, \emptyset \vdash \psi \rightsquigarrow 0$ iff $\forall_{\beta \supseteq_P \alpha}(\beta, \emptyset \vdash \varphi \rightsquigarrow 0)$. If a formula is not checked by the formula **true** then it can be meaningfully monitored and therefore we say that φ is *quasi-past-stable*. Consider for instance the two following formulas, where x_1 and x_2 are given events:

1. $\forall x_1 \; \exists x_2 (x_1.\mathbf{time} < x_2.\mathbf{time} \leq x_1.\mathbf{time} + 5 \;\wedge\; x_1.\mathbf{prop} = x_2.\mathbf{prop})$
2. $\forall x_1 \; \exists x_2 (x_1.\mathbf{time} < x_2.\mathbf{time} \;\wedge\; x_1.\mathbf{prop} = x_2.\mathbf{prop})$

The first of these formulas is quasi-past-stable since it is checked by

$$\forall x_1 \; \forall x_2 (x_1.\mathbf{time} + 5 \leq x_2.\mathbf{time} \Rightarrow \\ \exists x_3 (x_1.\mathbf{time} < x_3.\mathbf{time} \leq x_1.\mathbf{time} + 5 \;\wedge\; x_1.\mathbf{prop} = x_3.\mathbf{prop})).$$

The second formula is not quasi-past-stable since we always have to wait till the end of the concerned case before we can be sure that it is definitively false, and so it is checked by **true**.

5.2 Monitor Modeled as Labeled Transition System

Let us assume for a moment that we have a set of past-stable BRL-formulas. Their conjunction should hold. We start with a very simple process model for the monitor: a labeled transition system that exactly obeys the BRL-formulas. So if we let the monitor system execute this process model, in the sense that each event of the BIS is the label of a transition that is executed, then we can discover violations as soon as an event occurs that brings the system in a violation state. Since the BRL-formulas are past stable we know that from now on the process is violating the BRL-formulas. We model this as follows. We start with an empty event log ϵ. In fact the log so far is the *state* of the system. We assume that this initial state ϵ is a non-violation state, otherwise the whole process would violate the BRL-formulas, since they are ps. At some point in time the system is in state q. We allow a new event to be executed, leading to new state q'. As long as q' is a non-violation state there is no problem. But if it is a violation state, it indicates that BRL-formulas are not satisfied, and will never be satisfied in the future since they are ps.

Note that the state q of the monitor is increasing *unboundedly* and therefore the transition system can have in general an *infinite* state space Q. Since the monitor has to keep track of the BIS in real time we need a bounded abstraction of the states. In general this is not possible since we might have BRL-formulas that need to keep infinite information of the past events, such as "no two events may occur with the same value for some property p ($p \in \mathcal{P}$)". However there are (non trivial) subsets of BRL-formulas for which bounded abstractions of the log are sufficient. We discuss this later in this section.

We now define the labeled transition system and the verification of a BRL-formula more formally. From now on we suppose that all events in a log have different timestamps. Consider a finite or infinite sequence of events $e_1, e_2, \ldots \in \mathcal{E}$ with $e_{i-1}(\mathbf{time}) < e_i(\mathbf{time})$ for each $i > 0$. Let $\alpha_i = \{e_1, \ldots, e_i\}$ for all $i \geq 0$. We call $M = (\mathcal{E}, Q, q_0, \delta, F)$ a *labeled transition system* where

- $\mathcal{E}$ is the set of labels which are the events.
- Q is the set of states;
- q_0 is the initial state;
- $\delta : Q \times \mathcal{E} \to Q$, the computable transition function;
- $F \subseteq Q$, the set of violation states. $Q - F$ are called the non-violation states.

We say that M *verifies* a given BRL-formula φ iff there is a function $\Psi : \{\alpha_i \mid i \geq 0\} \to Q$ with

- $\Psi(\alpha_0) = q_0$;
- $\alpha_i, \emptyset \vdash \varphi \rightsquigarrow 0 \Leftrightarrow \Psi(\alpha_i) \in F$;
- $\delta(\Psi(\alpha_i), e) = \Psi(\alpha_i \cup \{e\})$, for each event e and $i \geq 0$.

We call Ψ the *abstraction* function.

Note that $\mathcal{E}$ and Q can be infinite sets and that we have a deterministic labeled transition system. In general every BRL-formula, also those that are not ps, can be verified by a labeled transition system. An interesting class of BRL-formulas are those that can be verified by a labeled transition system with a *finite* state space. These BRL-formulas are called *finite-state BRL-formulas.*

Each BRL-formula can be ps or not, fs or not and finite-state or not. So there are 8 possible combinations, from which one is excluded by Corollary 1. The next theorem says that the other possibilities exist:

Theorem 3. *BRL-formula that are ps and fs have to be finite-state. All the other combinations are possible.*

Proof. There are examples of the 7 possible cases: Let a be an agent, **prop** the name of a property of type **Quantity**,

1. past-stable, future-stable, finite-state: 1;
2. past-stable, future-stable, not finite-state: impossible;
3. past-stable, not future-stable, finite-state: $\forall x(\neg x.\mathbf{agent} = a)$;
4. past-stable, not future-stable, not finite-state: $\forall x_1\, \exists x_2(x_2.\mathbf{time} < x_1.\mathbf{time} \wedge x_1.\mathbf{prop} = x_2.\mathbf{prop})$
5. not past-stable, future-stable, finite-state: $\exists x(x.\mathbf{agent} = a)$
6. not past-stable, future-stable, not finite-state: $\exists x_1, x_2(x_2.\mathbf{time} = x_1.\mathbf{time} + 1\ \wedge x_1.\mathbf{prop} = x_2.\mathbf{prop})$

7. not past-stable, not future-stable, finite-state:
   $\forall x_1 \ \exists x_2(x_1.\mathbf{time} < x_2.\mathbf{time} \ \wedge x_1.\mathbf{agent} = x_2.\mathbf{agent})$
8. not past-stable, not future-stable, not finite-state:
   $\forall x_1 \ \exists x_2(x_1.\mathbf{time} < x_2.\mathbf{time} \ \wedge \ x_1.\mathbf{prop} = x_2.\mathbf{prop})$ □

Theorem 4. *If φ_1 and φ_2 are finite-state, so are $\varphi_1 \vee \varphi_2$, $\varphi_1 \wedge \varphi_2$ and $\neg\varphi_1$.*

Given a finite-state BRL-formula, it is easy to verify whether it is fs or ps.

Theorem 5. *Let φ be a finite-state BRL-formula that is verified by the labeled transition system $M = (\mathcal{E}, Q, q_0, \delta, F)$. The formula φ is ps iff $\delta(q, e) \in F$ for every $q \in F$ and $e \in \mathcal{E}$. The formula φ is fs iff $\delta(q, e) \notin F$ for every $q \notin F$ and $e \in \mathcal{E}$.*

5.3 Closed and Open Cases

We further optimize some interesting special past-stable BRL-formulas. We make here the distinction between closed and open cases. A case is closed if we are sure that all the events of the case already happened. If a case is not open we call it closed. In this section we only consider well-behaved logs where for every case there is a task "open" and a possible task "close" and where no event of a case happens before its open-task or after its closed-task, i.e., where the event log satisfies rule (e) (see section 4).

We split well-behaved logs into parts that concern closed cases and parts that concern open cases. For a well-behaved log α we let α_{closed} denote that part that concerns closed cases, i.e., $\alpha_{closed} = \{ev \in \alpha \mid \exists ev' \in \alpha \ (ev'(\mathbf{case}) = ev(\mathbf{case}) \wedge ev'(\mathbf{task}) = \text{close})\}$ and we let α_{open} denote that part that concerns open cases, i.e., $\alpha_{open} = \alpha - \alpha_{closed}$. Based on this we can define a notion of active case formula, which captures the intuition that in order to verify a formula for a certain log we can ignore the closed cases if the formula was satisfied for these cases.

Definition 1. *We call a formula φ an* active case formula *if it holds for all well-behaved logs α that if $\alpha_{closed}, \emptyset \vdash \varphi \rightsquigarrow 1$ then $\alpha, \emptyset \vdash \varphi \rightsquigarrow 1$ iff $\alpha_{open}, \emptyset \vdash \varphi \rightsquigarrow 1$.*

The following theorem says that in some important BRL-formulas we can indeed delete the closed cases from α.

Theorem 6. *Let $\varphi(x)$ be a BRL-formula with one free variable x such that all quantifiers are of the form $\forall y(y.\mathbf{case} = x.\mathbf{case} \wedge ...)$, $\exists y(y.\mathbf{case} = x.\mathbf{case} \wedge ...)$ or $\Sigma(y : y.\mathbf{case} = x.\mathbf{case} \wedge ...)$.... then a BRL-formula of the form $\forall x(\varphi(x))$ is an active case formula.*

6 Monitor Modeled as Colored Petri Nets

In this section we show how we can transform the set of characteristic business rules of Section 4 directly into a colored Petri net. Any labeled transition system can be expressed as a colored Petri net, so that is not remarkable. The advantage of modeling with Petri nets over labeled transitions systems, is that the state is distributed over places and that transitions have only a local effect on the connected places. This makes it easy to refine a model by adding more structural elements, i.e., places and transitions. That is what we do in this section. We start with a colored Petri net that models the state of the labeled transition system of Section 5.2, i.e., the event log, as one token in a place called "event-log". Afterwards we refine the model to represent certain business rules by structural elements of the Petri net. The verification of the business rules is equivalent with firing a transition: each event corresponds to firing a transition in the colored Petri net and if the transition is enabled in the net, then the rules are still valid, if not then at least one rule will be violated. Note that we reduce on-the-fly auditing to simulating a colored Petri net. The resulting colored Petri net might not be very readable, however that is not our goal: it will be generated from the business rules and the monitor should eb a black box for the users.

The time complexity of computing the enabling of a transition and the memory usage depend only on the number and size of tokens in the net. In many practical cases we only have business rules that can be transformed into a colored Petri nets with a bounded number of tokens of a bounded size. So the verification of the corresponding business rules is not increasing with the size of the log, which would be the case if we would apply the brute force verification method suggested by the semantics (cf. Section 3).

6.1 Colored Petri Nets

We use here colored Petri nets for modeling purposes. We refer to the standard literature for more extensive definitions [7]. A *colored Petri net* is a 7-tuple $(P, T, F, \tau, \nu, \mu, m_0)$, where $P \cap T = \emptyset$, P is the set of *places*, T the set of *transitions*, $F \subseteq (P \times T) \cup (T \times P)$ the set of *arcs*, τ is a function with $\mathrm{dom}(\tau) = P$ and for $p \in P : \tau(p)$ is a type called *color set*, ν is a function with $\mathrm{dom}(\nu) = F$ and for each $f \in F : \nu(f)$ is an expression called an *arc inscription*, μ is a function with $\mathrm{dom}(\mu) = T$ and for each $t \in T : \mu(t)$ is a *predicate* over the variables of the arcs of the transition called a *guard* and finally m_0 is the *initial state* (initial marking). A *marking* m is a distribution of tokens over the places, where each token has a value that belongs to the color set of the place. Formally a marking is a function: $m : P \rightarrow (D \rightarrow \mathbb{N})$ where D is the set (domain) of all possible token values, i.e., $D = \bigcup_{p \in P} \tau(p)$, and $\forall (t, v) \in m(p) : v \subseteq \tau(p)$, and we say t is the token and v is its color.

Note that if we discard the functions τ, ν and μ then we have a classical Petri net. In CPN tools (cf. [7]) there is a syntax for color sets, arc inscriptions and guards. We deviate a little from this official syntax since we prefer to use standard mathematical notations for color sets and functions. The arc inscriptions we consider are only *variables*. Note that all arc inscriptions per transition are unique. An arc with double arrowheads is called a bi-flow and actually it stands for two arcs: one input and one output. If x is the variable on a bi-flow then this x belongs to the input arc and we assume (but do not display) the variable x'

on the output arc. The *enabling* rule is as usual: we try to find a binding for all variables on the arcs connected to the transition, such that each input variable is bound to an input token and the output variables are free but of the type of the output places. If a binding that makes the guard true exists, then the transition is enabled and may *fire* with this binding. If it fires the tokens bound to the input variables are consumed and the output variables are transformed into output tokens. We allow to produce more than one token per output variable. So the guard is actually a combination of a *pre-condition* (binding input variables to existing tokens) and a *post-condition* (binding output variables to new tokens). Note that the standard semantics of a colored Petri net is a labeled transition system. The formalization of this semantics is not trivial but well-known, see e.g. [7] and [8] for the approach.

In Fig. 1 we see a transition t with input places a, b and c and output places c and d all with type $\mathbb{Q}$. The guard says that t is enabled if two tokens can be found in a and b such that $x \neq y$ and the result is a (new) token in place c with value equal to the set of all input pairs so far and one new token in place d with value the sum of the input values. In Tables 1 and 2 this is displayed.

We also use the concept of a *workflow net*, a special class of Petri nets (cf. for details see [9,10]). Here we consider a Petri net to be a workflow net if there is exactly one transition without input arcs (called "open"), exactly one transition without output arcs (called "close") and every other place or transition is on a directed path from "open" to "close". We sometimes consider colored Petri nets in which subnets have the structure of a workflow net.

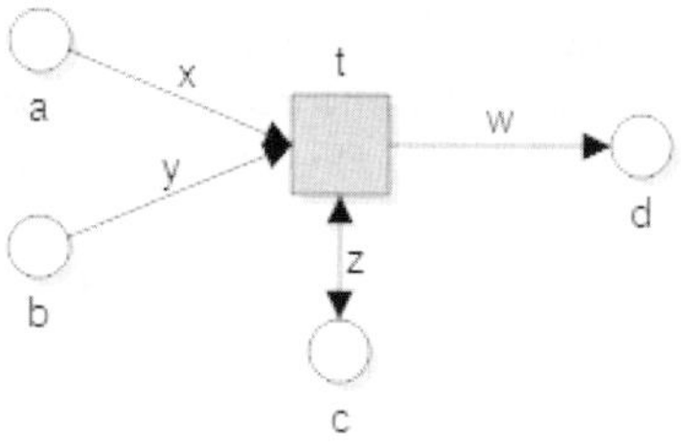

Fig. 1. A transition with arc inscriptions

Table 1. Places of Fig. 1

place	colorset
a	$\mathbb{Q}$
b	$\mathbb{Q}$
c	$\mathcal{P}(\mathbb{Q} \times \mathbb{Q})$
d	$\mathbb{Q}$

Table 2. Transitions of Fig. 1

transition	input	output	guard
t	x, y, z	z', w	$x \neq y \wedge z' = z \cup \{(x, y)\} \wedge w = (x + y)$

6.2 Representing the Labeled Transition System as Colored Petri Net

We start with a straightforward translation of the labeled transition system of Section 5.2 into a colored Petri as shown in Fig. 2. Here we see a colored Petri net with two transitions and six places. We assume that the environment, i.e., the BIS, delivers event tokens in place "event", but only if the place is empty! According to business rule (e) (see section 4) we require that each case starts with a task with type "open" and has no more events after a task with type "close". Transition "event handler" consumes tokens from the input place "event". There are two guards: the time stamp $e.\mathbf{time}$ of a new event e should be greater than as the time in place "time stamp" and the case identifier $e.\mathbf{case}$ must occur in the token from place "current cases" unless the task $e.\mathbf{tasktype} \in \{open, grant, retract\}$. If the task is $e.\mathbf{tasktype} = open$ then the $e.\mathbf{case}$ is inserted in the token from "current cases". So the "event handler" is the gate keeper. If the "event handler" fires the event e is inserted into the token in the "event log" and a colorless (black) token is put in place p. This token is the trigger for transition "BR-evaluator" which has a black token as output for place q. It has a guard which is the conjunction of all business rules. Since the business rules are decidable the guard can be computed. After a token is put in the place "event", the marking displayed in Fig. 2 should be reachable. If so, then the business rules are not violated.

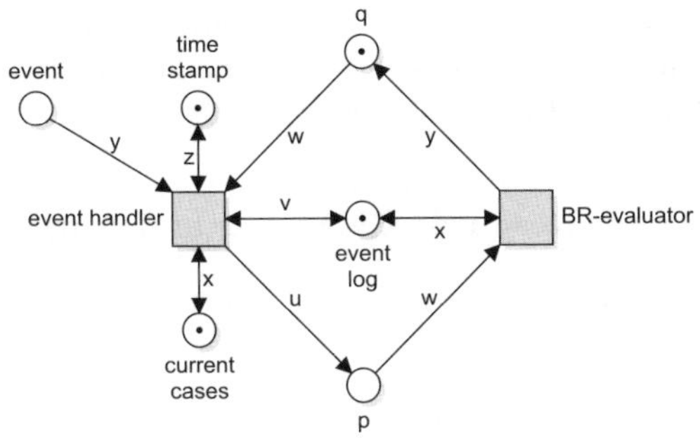

Fig. 2. The basic colored Petri net

Note that colorset $2^{\emptyset}$ only contains the value $\emptyset$ which represents the "black" token of classical Petri nets.

Here BR stands for the conjunction of all business rules and the guard evaluates them. Only if there is a binding in the event log, i.e., variable v, that makes it "true" then the transition will fire.

$$\phi = z < y.\text{time} \wedge (\neg(y.\text{task} \in \{open, grant, retract\} \Rightarrow y.\text{case} \in x) \wedge$$

$$v' = v \cup \{y.\text{case}\} \wedge u = \emptyset \wedge t.\text{task} = open \Rightarrow x' = x \cup \{y.\text{case}\} \wedge$$

$$y.\text{task} = close \Rightarrow x' = x \backslash \{y.\text{case}\} \wedge (t.\text{task} \in \{open, close\} \vee x' = x)$$

Table 3. Places of Fig. 2

place	colorset
event	E
current cases	2^C
time stamp	$\mathbb{Q}$
p	$2^{\emptyset}, (black)$
q	$2^{\emptyset}, (black)$
event log	2^E

Table 4. Transitions of Fig. 2

transition	input	output	guard
event handler	x, y, z, v, w	x', z', v', u	ϕ
BR-evaluator	x, w	x', y	$x \models BR \wedge w = \emptyset \wedge y = w$

Theorem 7. *In the colored Petri net of Fig. 2 the marking with no tokens in places event and p and one token in q is reachable from the initial marking if and only if the business rules are valid until then.*

Note that the colored Petri net of Fig. 2 is not the one we want since the token in "event log" grows unlimited, so verification will take increasing time. Therefore we restrict ourselves to a subset of the business rules and for this set we refine the colored Petri net in the sense that we add more structural Petri net elements (places and transitions) that replaces several formulae in the guard of the BR-evaluator and it will reduce the size of the log.

6.3 First Refinement: Resource Balancing and Authorization Rules

In the first refinement we assume that we only have the following types of formulae:

- resource balancing rule (l) of Section 4.3.
- authorization rules (f),(g),(h) and (i) of Section 4.2.
- arbitrary "active case rules"

In this refinement we still have an event log, but restricted to events belonging to the *current* cases, i.e., cases that have been opened and not yet closed. Later on we restrict the task-order rules and then we develop a second refinement in which we do not need a place that represents an event log any more. The first refined model is displayed in Fig. 3 and is a refinement where the authorization rules and the resource balancing rules are replaced by structural elements. The BR-evaluator is now replaced by a transition called "case rule evaluator" which only works on the "current cases". In order to understand this model we first model the resource balancing and authorization rules in isolation.

We now explain the first refinement model, displayed in Fig. 3. We add places and transitions. Actually the tokens in these places can be seen as abstractions

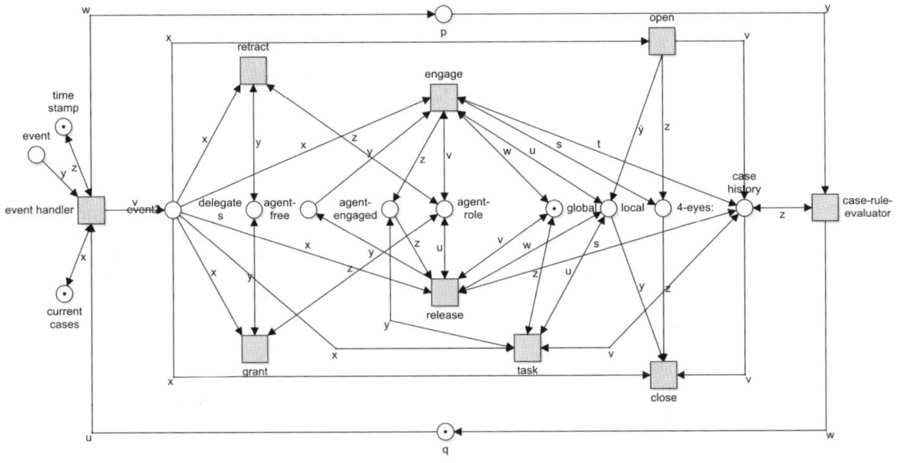

Fig. 3. The first refinement

from the event log. The refined model is constructed from the basic model in Fig. 2 by adding representations of the different rules: the resource balancing rules, the delegation rules, the four-eyes principle and the agent engagement rules in that order. This is explained in the following paragraphs. We do not distinguish different tasks, but only different task-types. Note that we do not specify the transition guards in detail, because they depend on the specific business rules. We start with the resource balancing rules. The color sets of the places are either the ones defined for

Resource Balancing Rules. There are two kinds of resource balancing rules, global and local resource balancing rules. They will be modeled by embedding Fig. 4 (i) into Fig. 2. We create one place for all the global resources and one for all the local resources, in Fig. 4 (i) called "global" and "local". The color set of "global" is a finite subset of $Res_1 \to \mathbb{Q}$ and the color set of "local" is a finite subset of $C \times (Res_2 \to Q)$, where $Res = Res_1 \cup Res_2$ and $Res_1 \cap Res_2 = \emptyset$, where Res_1 represents all the global resources and Res_2 all the local resources. The global resource place contains always one token, representing the current status of all the global resources. In the initial state it has the initial values of the resources. Each transition is allowed to manipulate the resources: by additions or subtractions. So we connect each case task to these two resources places with an input and an output arc so that each transition can update the resources. The local resource place has type $C \times (Res_2 \to \mathbb{Q})$. For the local resource place we have two more connections: one input arc from the "open" transition and one output arc to the "close" transition. This is because the local resources are case-specific and as soon as the case is closed this token is not necessary any more. The "open" transition creates for a new case one token in the "local res" with an initial value for each local resource. Now we have modeled the updating of the resources. The only thing that remains is the modeling of the resource balancing rules. We take them out of the guard of the "BR-evaluator" and put them in the guard of the case task transitions, because they are the only ones who could make them invalid.

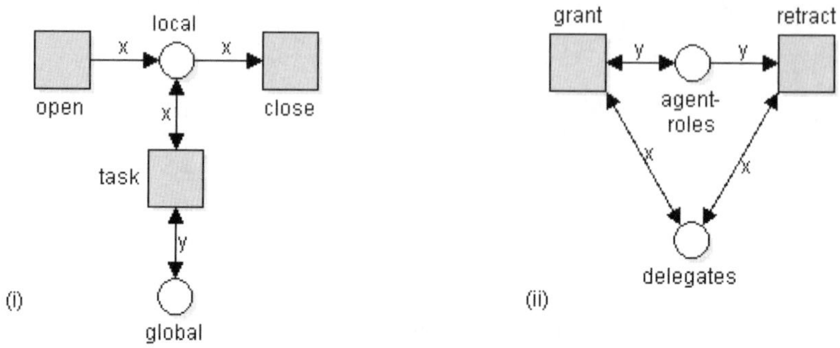

Fig. 4. Resource rules (i) and delegation rules (ii)

Next we consider the *authorization* rules.

Delegation Rules. The delegation rules will be modeled by embedding Fig. 4 (ii) into Fig. 2. In Fig. 4 (ii) we see a subnet of Fig. 3 with two tasks "grant" and "retract" and two places "agent-roles" and "delegates" with one token each with color sets $2^{A\times R\times A}$ and $2^{A\times R\times \mathbb{N}}$ respectively. These sets are always bounded since we assume the sets A and R to be fixed. The meaning of this is that in "agent roles" the token is a set containing for each role an agent and the agent from whom it was obtained in the current state. In "delegates" the token is a set that contains for each role an agent together with the amount of delegates it has created for this role.

Table 5. The guard of of "grant" in Fig. 4 (ii)

guard of grant
$(b,r,c) \in y \wedge y' = y \cup \{(a,r,b)\} \wedge (b,r,n) \in x \wedge x' = (x \backslash \{(b,r,n)\}) \cup \{(b,r,n+1)\}$

Table 6. The guard of "retract" in Fig. 4 (ii)

guard of retract
$(a,r,b) \in y \wedge \{(b,r,n),(a,r,0)\} \subseteq x \wedge x' = (x \backslash \{(b,r,n)\}) \cup \{(b,r,n-1)\}$

The guards explain the working: if "grant" fires it adds a triple with value (a, r, b) meaning that agent a receives from agent b the role r. (Note that the a is coming from another input that we did not display here). In order to be able to do so the triple (b, r, c) should be available, meaning that agent b has been granted role r by some agent c. The pre-condition is that he triple (b, r, n) is in the token of place "delegates" meaning that agent b has granted role r to other agents already n times. Finally the token is update by replacing the triple by $(b, r, n + 1)$. The working of task "retract" a similar. In the initial state we need at least for each role one token in place "agent-roles" with an agent that has that role (for example a role "manager" that has all roles). In the token of place "agent-delegate" we have in the initial state as many tokens as there are agents.

It is easy to see that agents only are granted a role by somebody who has that role, and that roles are only retracted from agents that have no outstanding grants of that role for other agents. This expresses that the agent in that role is needed for the task. Note that we assume that an agent can have more than one role at the same time.

Four-Eyes Principle. Next we show how the *four-eyes principle* can be represented. We generalize the four eyes principle in the sense that there can be a set of tasks for which the all agents should be different per case. In order to model this we added one place called "4-eyes" (see Fig. 3) with color set $C \times 2^{T \times A}$. So the place stores, per current case, the set of all pairs of a task and an agent that occurred in a case so far. This place is connected to transition "engage" with a bi-flow in order to enable this transition to update the token. Transition "open" is input for this place and transition "close" is output for it, they create and destroy the token per case. The business rule that checks the four-eyes principle is a guard for the transition "engage", because this transition is the only one that can make the rule invalid.

Agent Engagement Rules. Next we consider the *agent engagement* rules. These rules say that an agent can be engaged in only one case at a time. So in order to engage an agent it should be free. We model this in Fig. 3 with the places "agent-free" and "agent-engaged", with color sets A and $A \times C$. Initially the first one contains all agents and the second one is empty. In the "agent-engaged" place we record to which case the agent is engaged. These places are connected to transitions "engage" and "release" in the obvious way: "agent-engaged" is input for "release" and output for "engage" and similarly "agent-free" is input for "engage" and output for "release". For all other tasks there is one transition "normal-task" that checks whether the agent it needs is engaged for the case and which updates the "case-history" like all other transitions.

Finally we note that we have restricted the other business rules to *single-case* rules, which means that we only need the current cases to check them. That is done in Fig. 3 by transition "case-rule-evaluator" using the place "case-history". Per current case there is one token in this place, created by "open" and removed by "close". the transitions "engage" and "release" update these tokens. So we may formulate the following theorem.

Theorem 8. *In the colored Petri net of Fig. 3 the* final *marking with no tokens in places event and p and one token in place q is reachable from the initial marking if and only if the business rules are valid until then.*

We summarize the places and their color sets of the model of Fig. 3

Table 7. Places of Fig. 3

place	colorset
event	E
event2	E
current cases	2^C
time stamp	$\mathbb{Q}$
p	$2^{\emptyset}(black)$
q	$2^{\emptyset}(black)$
delegates	$2^{A\times R\times A}$
agent-roles	$2^{A\times R\times \mathbb{N}}$
global	$Res_1 \rightarrow \mathbb{Q}$
local	$C \times (Res_2 \rightarrow \mathbb{Q})$
agent-free	A
agent-engaged	$A \times C$
4-eyes	$C \times 2^{T\times A}$
case history	2^E

6.4 Second Refinement: Task-Order Rules

In the former refinement we had for each task-type a transition. In the second refinement we introduce transitions for all the tasks and places for the basic counting formula. The model is displayed in Fig. 5. The color sets are as in Table 7.

In this section we consider a refinement for task-order rules. We assume that the task-order rules are only formulated as (a conjunction of) *basic counting formula* as defined by rule (c) in Section 4.1. If we restrict the task-order rules in this way we can remove from Fig. 3 the place "event-history" and transition "case-rule-evaluator" by adding more structure. The transition in Fig. 5, with name "subnet" and displayed with an eye glass symbol, will be filled by a task-order specific subnet. As an example consider the counting formula:

$$\forall c(\ \phi(a,c)+\phi(b,c) \geq \phi(d,c)+\phi(e,c)\ \wedge\ \phi(b,c) \geq \phi(g,c)\ )$$

where a, b, d, e, g are tasks. As explained in [6] each such a rule puts a restriction on the firing of transitions which can be expressed by a place.

The construction rule says that we create for each basic counting formula a place that is an *output* place of all transitions on the left hand side and an *input* place for all transitions on the right-hand side of the $\geq$ sign. In Fig. 6 we see the

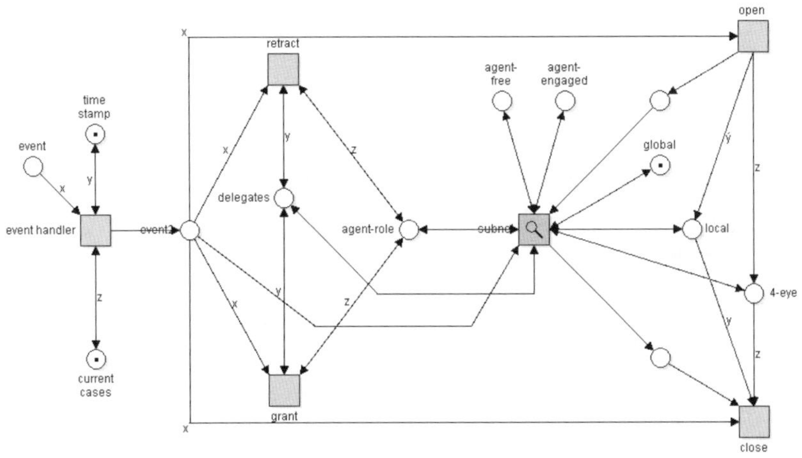

Fig. 5. Expressing the task-order rules

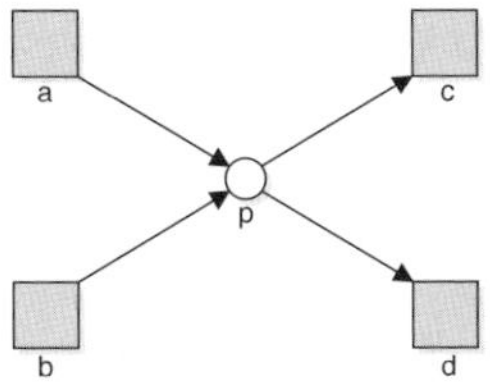

Fig. 6. Transformation of a basic counting formula

transformation of $\forall c(\phi(a,c) + \phi(b,c) \geq \phi(d,c) + \phi(e,c))$ into the Petri net with one place called p and four transitions $\{a, b, d, e\}$.

We may reduce such a business rule by eliminating *implicit places* (cf. [11]). Instead of using such standard Petri nets techniques for this elimination we can eliminate basic counting formula. Reduction means that if we have a subformula φ in the conjunction that is implied by one or more other subformula, then we delete φ. For example if we have $\forall c, t((\phi(a,c,t) \geq \phi(b,c,t) \wedge \phi(b,c,t) \geq \phi(d,c,t) \wedge \phi(a,c,t) \geq \phi(d,c,t))$ then we delete $\phi(a,c,t) \geq \phi(d,c,t)$. Another example of reduction is $\forall c(\ \phi(a,c)+\phi(b,c) \geq \phi(d,c) \wedge \phi(b,c) \geq \phi(d,c)+\phi(e,c)\ )$ then we delete $\phi(a,c)+\phi(b,c) \geq \phi(d,c)$. So the reduction rule keeps the formula with the *minimal* number of terms on the left-hand side of the $\geq$ sign and the *maximal* number of terms on the right-hand side of the $\geq$ sign. We assume that the task-order rules are in the normal form described above and are irreducible.

Note that in the language-based based theory of regions and in process discovery the same idea of transforming a set of equations over firing sequences into a place is used (cf. [12,13]).

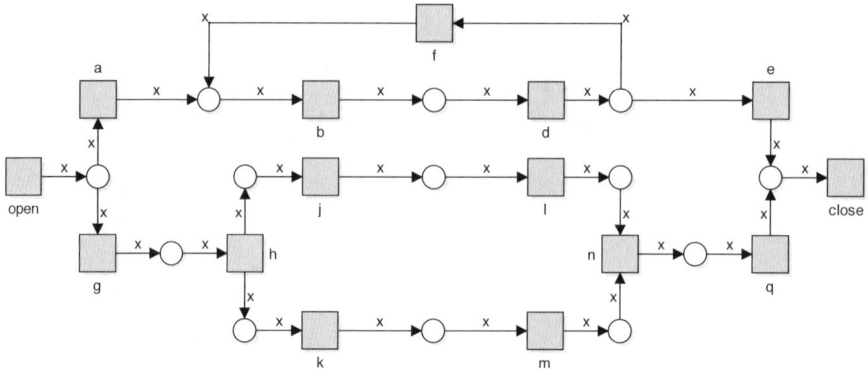

Fig. 7. Example of a workflow net with two case types

If we have a business rule that is a conjunction of a set of basic counting formulas then we repeat this construction and so we obtain a Petri net. Note that since we consider only the conjunction of business rules we may combine the task-order rules into one business rule. As an example consider the formula:

$$\forall c(\phi(open, c) \geq \phi(a, c) + \phi(g, c) \wedge \phi(a, c) + \phi(f, c) \geq \phi(b, c) \wedge$$
$$\phi(b, c) \geq \phi(d, c) \wedge \phi(d, c) \geq \phi(e, c) + \phi(f, c) \wedge$$
$$\phi(e, c) + \phi(q, c) \geq \phi(close, c) \wedge$$
$$\phi(g, c) \geq \phi(h, c) \wedge \phi(h, c) \geq \phi(j, c) \wedge \phi(h, c) \geq \phi(k, c) \wedge$$
$$\phi(j, c) \geq \phi(l, c) \wedge \phi(k, c) \geq \phi(m, c) \wedge \phi(l, c) \geq \phi(n, c) \wedge$$
$$\phi(m, c) \geq \phi(n, c) \wedge \phi(n, c) \geq \phi(q, c))$$

Applying the construction rules we obtain the (classical) Petri net in Fig. 7. This classical Petri net is a *workflow* net and is *sound* (cf. [10]). This means that transition "close" always eventually can fire and that no tokens are left if it fires.

In case the task-order rules do not determine a sound workflow net we still can transform them into a Petri net. In Fig. 8 we show this construction for the simple case where the rule of Fig. 6 is the only task-order rule. Here we considered only one basic counting formula, namely the same as in Fig. 6, but the construction for more is obvious. We use here a *reset arc* (cf. [11]) to all places introduced by the basic counting formula and the "close" transition. A transition removes all tokens from the places its connected to by a reset arc. This also guarantees that after firing "close" no tokens are left. In Fig. 8 the arc between place p and transition "close" is a reset arc.

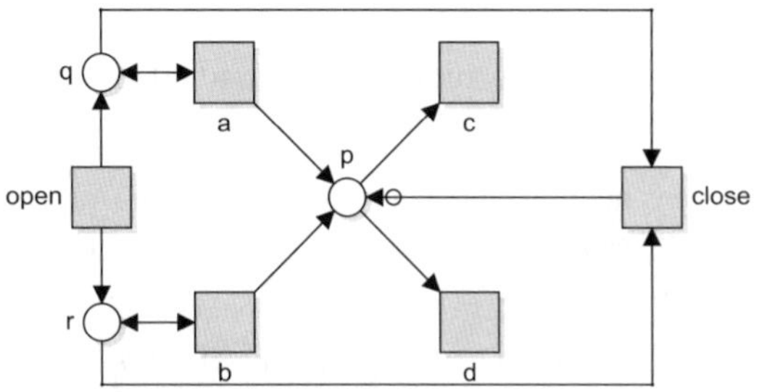

Fig. 8. A Petri net for non-worklfow situations

Adding Color to the Classical Subnet. So far we translated the task-order rules into a classical Petri net. Next we augment our net with color and then we embed it into the net of Fig. 5:

- All places in this net obtain the case identifiers, i.e., C, as color set.
- All transitions have arc inscriptions with the same variable (from C) which means that transitions can only fire if they consume tokens with the same case identifier and that they produce tokens with the same case identifier.
- Reset arcs will be color sensitive, i.e., they will only remove tokens with the same value (case identifier) as one of the other inputs. The guard requires that there is only one case identifier in the other input.
- Transitions of the subnet are connected to the places in Fig. 5 as is done for transitions in Fig. 3 with the corresponding task type.

Expressing this for a colored Petri net tool like CPN-tools (cf. [7])is straightforward.

Theorem 9. *The task-order rules are valid if and only if the firing sequence from the event log is executable on the constructed Petri net.*

Since we have now translated both the task-order rules as well as the resource balancing and authorization rules we have the following corollary.

Corollary 2. *For all translated rules it holds that they are valid if and only if the firing sequence from the event log is executable on the constructed Petri net.*

6.5 Limits on Memory Usage and Computing Time

In this subsection we show that the token in "case history" is *probabilistically* bounded. We make the following assumptions:

- new case arrive with a frequency λ
- the time between the arrival of an "open" event and a "close" event for a case is on average w

- the number of events of case i is a random variable M_i. The expected value of M_i is $\mathbb{E}[M_i] = m$
- the random variables M_i are independent and identically distributed and also independent of L.

The amount of memory needed and the evaluation time of guards is a proportional to the amount of events stored. So we have to determine a bound on the number of events in the model.

Theorem 10. *Let L be a random variable expressing the number of active cases in the stable situation, let M_i be the random number of events of case i in the active cases. Then the probability that the number of cases in the case history exceeds b is bounded by:*

$$\mathbb{P}[\sum_{i=1}^{L} M_i \geq b] \leq l.m/b$$

Proof. By Little's formula the expected value of L is $\mathbb{E}[L] = \lambda.w$. By Markov's inequality we have: $\mathbb{P}[\sum_{i=1}^{L} M_i \geq b] \leq \mathbb{E}[\sum_{i=1}^{L} M_i]/b$. By Wald's formula we have $\mathbb{E}[\sum_{i=1}^{L} M_i] = \mathbb{E}[L].m$. For a derivation of the used formula see [14]. □

So, if we accept a memory overflow with probability α then we have a bound $b = l.m/\alpha$.

7 Conclusion and Future Work

We have presented a language for business rules (BRL) and an approach to build a monitor system that is able to check business rules on-the-fly in parallel to a business information system (BIS). The assumption is that we cannot trust the BIS. We have shown how to develop a monitor either as labeled transition system with an infinite state space, or as a colored Petri net with tokens that grow unboundedly in size. In order to be able to evaluate business rules in such a way that we need only a finite memory and that the computations involved will not depend on the size of the event log, we restricted ourselves to a subset of the BRL. This subset covers all the characteristic examples we encountered in practice. The construction method we presented is based on two principles: for the authorization rules and resource balancing rules we have given a fixed colored Petri net where the specific parameters for a particular organization have to be filled in by token values, e.g., for the four eyes principle. For the task-order rules we presented a construction method to extend the colored Petri net in a systematic way. We do not claim that our constructions are unique or the best, but they seem to be rather straightforward. We have shown that the involved computations are often not depending on the length of the event log. For active case rules we have shown probabilistic bounds on the number of cases that need to be verified. If the Petri net cannot execute a transition, then a rule is violated. This violation can be reported or it may generate an interrupt for the BIS. As future work we will try to find a larger subset of business rules that can be translated to colored Petri net patterns that can be glued together to form one colored Petri net in a systematic way. We are involved in a case study in practice using an implementation based on CPN tools (cf. [15]) which shows that the approach is feasible. As future work we also see a more detailed analysis of past stable formulas in BRL and there is a need for a more user friendly form for BRL, by sugaring the syntax or even a graphical language. Last but not least we note that an approach is needed to recover from a violation of the business rules.

References

1. Romney, M.B., Steinbart, P.J.: Accounting Information Systems. 11 edn. Pearson International Editions (2009)
2. Geerts, G.L., McCarthy, W.E.: An ontological analysis of the economic primitives of the extended-REA enterprise information architecture. International Journal of Accounting Information Systems 3(1), 1–16 (2002)
3. McCarthy, W.E.: The REA accounting model: A generalized framework for accounting systems in a shared data environment. The Accounting Review 57(3), 554–578 (1982)
4. Berg, D.: Turning Sarbanes-Oxley projects into strategic business processes. Sarbanes-Oxley Compliance Journal (2004)
5. IFRS Foundation: The International Accounting Standards Board Web Site (2010), `http://www.ifrs.org/Home.htm`
6. van Hee, K.M., Serebrenik, A., Sidorova, N., van der Aalst, W.M.P.: History-dependent petri nets. In: Kleijn, J., Yakovlev, A. (eds.) ICATPN 2007. LNCS, vol. 4546, pp. 164–183. Springer, Heidelberg (2007)
7. Jensen, K.: Coloured Petri nets: basic concepts, analysis methods and practical use, vol. 2. Springer, London (1995)
8. van Hee, K.M.: Information Systems Engineering, a Formal Approach. Cambridge University Press, New York (1994)
9. van der Aalst, W.M.P., van Hee, K.M.: Workflow Management: Models, Methods and Systems. MIT Press, Cambridge (2002)
10. van der Aalst, W.M.P.: Verification of workflow nets. In: Azéma, P., Balbo, G. (eds.) ICATPN 1997. LNCS, vol. 1248, pp. 407–426. Springer, Heidelberg (1997)
11. Girault, C., Valk, R.: Petri Nets for System Engineering: A Guide to Modeling, Verification, and Applications. Springer, New York (2001)
12. Darondeau, P.: Deriving Unbounded Petri Nets from Formal Languages. In: Sangiorgi, D., de Simone, R. (eds.) CONCUR 1998. LNCS, vol. 1466, pp. 533–548. Springer, Heidelberg (1998)
13. van der Werf, J.M.E.M., van Dongen, B.F., Hurkens, C.A.J., Serebrenik, A.: Process Discovery Using Integer Linear Programming. In: van Hee, K.M., Valk, R. (eds.) PETRI NETS 2008. LNCS, vol. 5062, pp. 368–387. Springer, Heidelberg (2008)
14. Ross, S.: Introduction to Probability Models. Academic Press, London (2007)
15. Jensen, K., Kristensen, L.: Coloured Petri nets: modelling and validation of concurrent systems. Springer, Heidelberg (2009)

A The Formal Syntax and Semantics of BRL

We first recall the syntax of BRL which is defined by the following abstract syntax:

$$E ::= \neg E \mid (E \wedge E) \mid \mathcal{X}.\mathcal{P} \mid (E = E) \mid (E < E) \mid (\mathcal{X} = \mathcal{X}) \mid \\ \mathbb{Q} \mid A \mid T \mid \Sigma(\mathcal{X} : E)\ E \mid (E + E) \mid (E \cdot E).$$

The language is subject to a typing regime, which means that we have type derivation rules that derive for some expressions a result type. If an expression has indeed such a result type then we call it *well-typed*. The expressions that are of type **Boolean** are called *formulas*. The type derivation rules are as follows. In these rules we assume that the variables $e, e_1, e_2, \ldots$ range over expressions in E, and the variable τ ranges over the types in Θ.

$$\frac{e : \textbf{Boolean}}{\neg e : \textbf{Boolean}} \qquad \frac{e_1 : \textbf{Boolean} \qquad e_2 : \textbf{Boolean}}{(e_1 \wedge e_2) : \textbf{Boolean}} \qquad \frac{}{x.p : \theta(p)}$$

$$\frac{e_1 : \tau \qquad e_2 : \tau}{(e_1 = e_2) : \textbf{Boolean}} \qquad \frac{\tau \in \{\textbf{Quantity}, \textbf{Time}\} \qquad e_1 : \tau \qquad e_2 : \tau}{(e_1 < e_2) : \textbf{Boolean}}$$

$$\frac{}{(x_1 = x_2) : \textbf{Boolean}} \qquad \frac{q \in \mathbb{Q}}{q : \textbf{Quantity}} \qquad \frac{a \in A}{a : \textbf{Agent}} \qquad \frac{r \in R}{r : \textbf{Role}}$$

$$\frac{t \in T}{t : \textbf{Task}} \qquad \frac{\begin{array}{c} e_1 : \textbf{Boolean} \\ e_2 : \textbf{Quantity} \end{array}}{\Sigma(x : e_1)\ e_2 : \textbf{Quantity}} \qquad \frac{e_1 : \textbf{Quantity} \qquad e_2 : \textbf{Quantity}}{(e_1 + e_2) : \textbf{Quantity}}$$

$$\frac{e_1 : \textbf{Time} \qquad e_2 : \textbf{Quantity}}{(e_1 + e_2) : \textbf{Time}} \qquad \frac{e_1 : \textbf{Quantity} \qquad e_2 : \textbf{Quantity}}{(e_1 \cdot e_2) : \textbf{Quantity}}$$

Note that we allow that timestamps and quantities are added, and that this results in a new timestamp. In the following of this paper we assume that all expressions in the language are well-typed unless explicitly indicated otherwise.

We proceed with the formal definition of the semantics. A *variable binding* is defined as a partial function $\Gamma : \mathcal{X} \rightharpoonup \mathcal{E}$. For expressions $e \in E$ the semantics are defined by the proposition $\alpha, \Gamma \vdash e \rightsquigarrow v$ which states that the value of e is v for the event log α and the variable binding Γ. For a variable binding Γ and variable $x \in \mathcal{X}$ and event $ev \in \mathcal{E}$ we let $\Gamma[x \mapsto ev]$ denote the variable binding Γ' that is equal to Γ except that $\Gamma'(x) = ev$. The proposition $\alpha, \Gamma \vdash e \rightsquigarrow v$ is defined by the following rules:

$$\frac{\alpha, \Gamma \vdash e \rightsquigarrow b \qquad b \in \{0,1\}}{\alpha, \Gamma \vdash \neg e \rightsquigarrow (1-b)}$$

$$\frac{\alpha, \Gamma \vdash e_1 \rightsquigarrow b_1 \qquad \alpha, \Gamma \vdash e_2 \rightsquigarrow b_2 \qquad \{b_1, b_2\} \subseteq \{0,1\}}{\alpha, \Gamma \vdash (e_1 \wedge e_2) \rightsquigarrow (b_1 \cdot b_2)} \qquad \frac{(p, v) \in \Gamma(x)}{\alpha, \Gamma \vdash x.p \rightsquigarrow v}$$

$$\frac{b \in \{0,1\} \qquad (b=1) \Leftrightarrow \exists_{v \in V}(\alpha, \Gamma \vdash e_1 \rightsquigarrow v \wedge \alpha, \Gamma \vdash e_2 \rightsquigarrow v)}{\alpha, \Gamma \vdash (e_1 = e_2) \rightsquigarrow b}$$

$$\frac{b \in \{0,1\} \qquad (b=1) \Leftrightarrow \exists_{v_1, v_2 \in \mathbb{Q}}(\alpha, \Gamma \vdash e_1 \rightsquigarrow v_1 \wedge \alpha, \Gamma \vdash e_2 \rightsquigarrow v_2 \wedge v_1 < v_2)}{\alpha, \Gamma \vdash (e_1 < e_2) \rightsquigarrow b}$$

$$\frac{b \in \{0,1\} \qquad (b=1) \Leftrightarrow (\Gamma(x_1) = \Gamma(x_2))}{\alpha, \Gamma \vdash (x_1 = x_2) \rightsquigarrow b} \qquad \frac{q \in \mathbb{Q}}{\alpha, \Gamma \vdash q \rightsquigarrow q} \qquad \frac{a \in A}{\alpha, \Gamma \vdash a \rightsquigarrow a}$$

$$\frac{r \in R}{\alpha, \Gamma \vdash r \rightsquigarrow r} \qquad \frac{t \in T}{\alpha, \Gamma \vdash t \rightsquigarrow t}$$

$$\frac{\begin{array}{c} W = \{ev \in \alpha \mid \alpha, \Gamma[x \mapsto ev] \vdash e_1 \rightsquigarrow 1\} \\ f = \{(ev, v) \mid ev \in W \wedge \alpha, \Gamma[x \mapsto ev] \vdash e_2 \rightsquigarrow v)\end{array}}{\alpha, \Gamma \vdash \Sigma(x : e_1)\ e_2 \rightsquigarrow \Sigma_{(ev,v) \in f} v}$$

$$\frac{\begin{array}{c} \alpha, \Gamma \vdash e_1 \rightsquigarrow v_1 \qquad \alpha, \Gamma \vdash e_2 \rightsquigarrow v_2 \\ \{v_1, v_2\} \subseteq \mathbb{Q}\end{array}}{\alpha, \Gamma \vdash (e_1 + e_2) \rightsquigarrow (v_1 + v_2)} \qquad \frac{\begin{array}{c} \alpha, \Gamma \vdash e_1 \rightsquigarrow v_1 \qquad \alpha, \Gamma \vdash e_2 \rightsquigarrow v_2 \\ \{v_1, v_2\} \subseteq \mathbb{Q}\end{array}}{\alpha, \Gamma \vdash (e_1 \cdot e_2) \rightsquigarrow (v_1 \cdot v_2)}$$

It can be observed that for each well-typed expression e such that $e : \tau$ it holds for every event log α and variable binding Γ that there is at most one v such that $\alpha, \Gamma \vdash e \rightsquigarrow v$ and if it exists then $v \in [\![\tau]\!]$. Observe that in the semantics of the summation expression $\Sigma(x : e_1)\ e_2$ the variable x is bound only to the events in α that satisfy e_1, denoted as the set W in the rule. Based on this, the rule defines a partial function $f : W \rightharpoonup V$ that maps each event to the corresponding value of e_2. Then, for each element in W for which f is defined the result of f is summated. Since every event log is finite and the typing will ensure that the result of e_2 is a number if it is defined, the result of the summation is always defined.

Modeling Organizational Units as Modular Components of Systems of Systems

Matthias Wester-Ebbinghaus, Daniel Moldt, and Michael Köhler-Bußmeier

University of Hamburg, Department of Informatics
Vogt-Kölln-Straße 30, D–22527 Hamburg
{wester,moldt,koehler}@informatik.uni-hamburg.de
http://www.informatik.uni-hamburg.de/TGI

Abstract. Modern software systems are frequently characterized as systems of systems. Agent-orientation as a software engineering paradigm exhibits a high degree of qualification for addressing many of the accompanying challenges. However, when it comes to a hierarchical/recursive system decomposition, classical agent orientation reaches its limits. We propose the concept of an *organizational unit* that both embeds actors and is itself embedded as a collective actor in surrounding organizational units. Building upon previous publications that feature an abstract model of organizational units, we supply it with a precise operational semantics in this paper.

Keywords: Multi-Agent Systems, Multi-Organization Systems, Organizational Units, Petri Nets, Nets-Within-Nets.

1 Motivation

While modern software systems are characterized along varying perspectives, metaphors and foci (cf. *ultra large scale systems* [1], *application landscapes* [2] or *software cities* [3] etc.), a widely-held consensus is the fundamental comprehension of modern software systems as large-scale *systems of systems*. According to Maier's [4] conceptual framework for systems of systems, their core distinguishing feature as opposed to other large-scale systems is the operational and managerial independence of the component systems. Component systems are useful in their own right, able to operate independently and maintain a continuing existence independent of the system of systems.

Agent-orientation has emerged as a socially-inspired software engineering paradigm that particularly respects the idea of independent component systems. It advocates flexible, high-level interactions between loosely-coupled, autonomous agents [5]. At the same time, the social foundations of the agent paradigm directly imply possibilities to impose organizational structures to provide global system perspectives [6]. The concepts applied for this cause are congruent to real-world/social concepts: positions, roles, services, authority, delegation, norms, schedules, groups, teams etc.

K. Jensen, S. Donatelli, and M. Koutny (Eds.): ToPNoC IV, LNCS 6550, pp. 174–198, 2010.

However, in the face of large systems of systems, the distinction between only two system levels, namely the overall system of systems and the component systems, is not enough. General system theorists stress that hierarchy is a fundamental feature of complex systems – not so much hierarchy in the sense of power differences but hierarchy as a mechanism of clustering (see the related work section). Thus, in a system of systems setting, a component system can be a system of systems itself.

Unfortunately, such a recursive comprehension of systems of systems poses problems for classical agent-orientation. As analyzed in [7] the *component view* of objects (objects being composed of other objects in a recursive fashion) was lost with the transition from object- to agent-orientation. This observation also holds for approaches where organizational structures are imposed onto a multi-agent system. The organization is seen as a *context* for individual agents. Analogously, groups or teams are seen as sub-contexts within the organization. In social sciences and especially in organization theory it has been recognized for quite some time, that we fail to perceive the importance of *collectivities* (networks of social relations between social actors) in the modern world if we view them only as contexts [8,9]. Instead, collectivities must also be viewed as actors in their own right, as *collective actors*. This is especially true for collectivities in an organizational setting as they offer a higher degree of formalization and goal specificity than other collectivities. Thus, they are more visible and their actions are more comprehensible and accountable. Examples are departments, divisions, enterprises, strategic alliances, virtual organizations, organizational fields or whole industries.

Consequently, the social world offers a rich reservoir of inspirations for *meso level structures* for the transition between the "face-to-face" micro level and the macro level of the overall society. These are available for agent-orientation to exploit with respect to system of systems engineering. So it is not surprising that approaches for extending classical agent-orientation with mechanisms for collective agency have been brought forth. But it is our opinion that these approaches rely too much on an extrapolation of classical agent concepts and technology for the case of collective actors. Unique considerations that arise when a collectivity of actors shall collectively act "as a whole" are neglected. We will elaborate on this criticism in the related work section of the paper.

In our work, we build upon agent-oriented ideas and strongly rely on the actor metaphor. But we focus on the collective actor as a core metaphor of its own rather than as a supplementary construct. As a consequence, conceptualizing a coherent combination of a collectivity's internal functioning with its boundary management in order to act "as a whole" is central to our approach. As we focus on organization theoretical conceptions of collectivities we use the term *organizational unit*. Each organizational unit is both a context for actors and an actor of its own. Provided a universal concept of an organizational unit, it can be applied recursively for component systems at arbitrary levels of a system of systems. Thus, we arrive at a conceptual extension of classical multi-agent thinking and we term systems build upon organizational units as *multi-organization systems.*

The aim of the paper is to provide an *abstract* "thinking model" as well as an *operational* "programming model" of organizational units. We present the abstract model in Section 2. The abstract model focuses on identifying the analytical components of an organizational unit, how they are functionally related and how the relations carry over from one to multiple organizational units. This model can be consulted when talking about a system (of systems) on a high level of abstraction (e.g. early development phases). Section 2 strongly relies on previous publications by us. But it is not just a summary but also a consolidation of previous results with original contributions and figures.

Nevertheless, the main contribution of this paper is the presentation of the operational model in Section 3. We provide a precise model of how the specifications of the abstract model can be operationalized. All aspects concerning system control and openness / boundary management that are featured in the abstract model are transferred into a model with an exact operational semantics. This step provides a technical understanding of the functioning of organizational units and systems composed of them. For this purpose we have chosen the high-level Petri net formalism of reference nets [10] as our modeling technique. The reference net formalism offers powerful and flexible mechanisms for synchronization between different system levels as first-order concepts. Specific benefits of the choice for reference nets will be elaborated alongside the presentation of the operational model. Our reference net model of an organizational unit is elaborated enough to be directly executed. Consequently, it provides a strong guideline of how to actually program organizational units. As an illustration of the operational peculiarities, we present an example scenario in Section 4.

Our concept of an organizational unit is intentionally lean and and relies on fundamental and universal inspirations from general system and organization theory. Together with agent-orientation, they provide the main bodies of related work which will be consulted in Section 5 before we conclude our work in Section 6.

2 Abstract Model

In this section, we present an abstract model of an organizational unit where we study its analytical components. The section is based on results from previous publications by us [11,12]. Here, we give a consolidated synopsis, including original figures and explanations.

An Organizational Unit as a Structure in Threes. At the heart of our approach lies the idea of an organizational unit as a *Janus-faced* entity. We define an organizational unit as being an organizational context for organizational actors and at the same time being itself an organizational actor that has other organizational units as its contexts. This basic understanding is illustrated in Figure 1 in UML notation. By recursively applying this understanding,

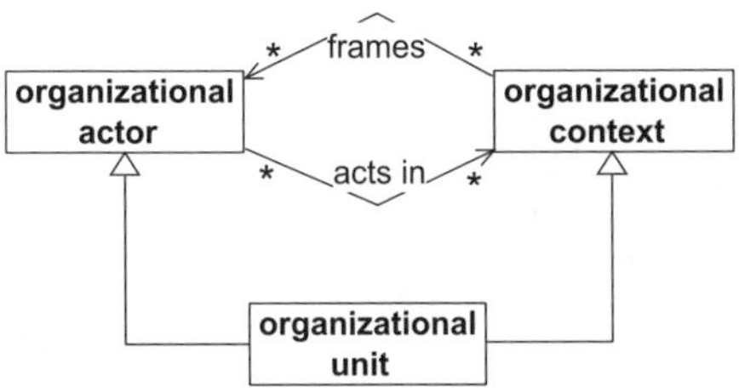

Fig. 1. Basic Definition of an Organizational Unit

we arrive at a (non-disjoint) hierarchy of organizational units, each of which is both an embedding context and itself embedded in other contexts.

It remains to be explained what we mean by organizational units being contexts and actors. As a starting point, we derive three *conceptual directions* that have to be investigated from the viewpoint of every organizational unit: *"looking downwards/inwards"* at embedded organizational units, *"looking at ones own level"* at the organizational principles of the organizational unit in focus and *"looking upwards/outwards"* at embedding organizational units. The first and third direction refer to an organizational unit being a context and an actor respectively while the second direction sits at the intersection between both.

In the following of the section we present how these conceptual directions are respected in our model. As a foundation for the following explanations, we present a first abstract model of an organizational unit as a structure in threes in Figure 2. We define an organizational unit as consisting of three sets of *actors*: operational actors, integration actors, governance actors.

Actors participate in three sets of *activities*: integration activities, governance activities, peripheral activities. Activities are composed of *action* instances of three basic *operations*: addition of actors, modification/usage of actors, removal of actors.

The figure includes all of these elements. It also captures the fact that the three sets of actors may overlap. The outer circle represents the unified set of all actors. An arc with filled arrow tips models a *control channel*, meaning that actors from the associated actor set control the activities from the associated activity set: The actors both enable the activities and constrain them with respect to their content. An ordinary arc models a *participation channel*, meaning that actors of the associated actor set can participate in activities from the associated activity set.

The explanations so far are not meaningful enough as they go hardly beyond denominations of elements. In the following, we describe the peculiarities behind the model from Figure 2. We lay a strong focus on behavioral aspects. More specifically, we explain how the three sets of system activities correspond to the above-mentioned three conceptual directions of an organizational unit and thus to an organizational unit's capacity of being a context and an actor. This entails the coverage of structural aspects in terms of relationships between actor sets and system rules. We omit other aspects like resources for the abstract model.

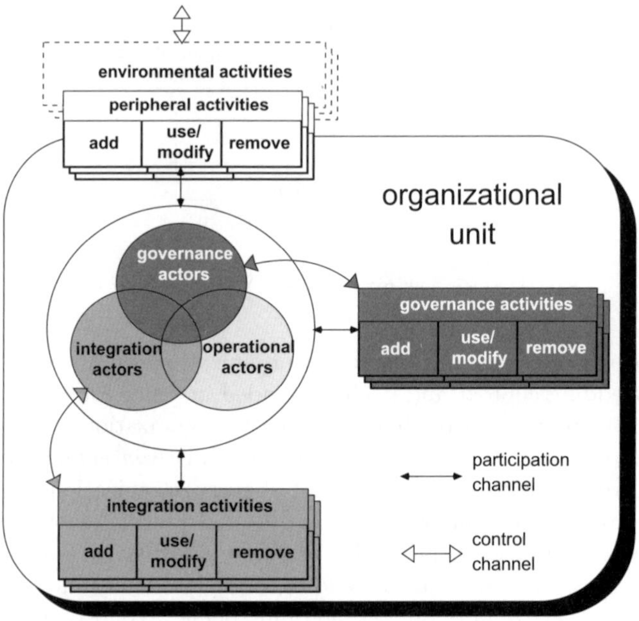

Fig. 2. Organizational Unit as a Structure in Threes

System Control. We distinguish the *analytical aspects* of operation, integration and governance for each organizational unit and classify system actors according to these aspects (see Figure 2). The three aspects are intrinsically interwoven and interdependent. Before presenting a Petri net-based interpretation of the interplay between operation, integration and governance in Section 3, we address their intended conceptual relationships on a more general level in this section. Figure 3 gives an illustration in UML notation.

Governance and integration together embody the system's control. The combination of integration and operation represents the system's (daily) business. The governance actors develop overall system goals and strategies and derive high-level rules that the system's business has to follow. In this paper, we do not systematically distinguish between different kinds of system rules, which may of course be very diverse (c.f. Scott's [9] characterization of regulative, normative and cultural-cognitive features of institutional settings). Instead, we consider system rules generally as an explication of the system's organizing principles that are mandatory for all embedded actors. The integration actors are responsible for applying these rules to the current operational context of the organizational unit and to concretize them accordingly. They develop sub-goals, plans and performance standards according to which they enable, coordinate and regulate the system's operation. Within this context, the operational actors carry out the system's primary tasks/operations and provide (low-level) operational feedback. In addition, the integration actors provide (high-level) strategic feedback to the governance actors. Figure 2 shows that the three sets of system actors may

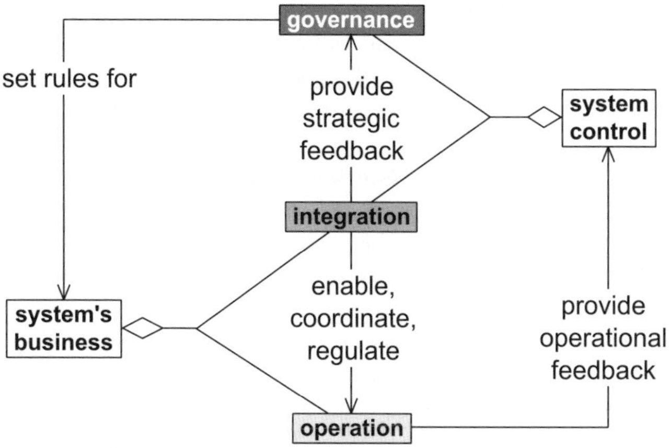

Fig. 3. System Control Concept Diagram

overlap. For instance in an enterprise, a worker (operational actor) might be a chosen representative of the workforce and as such act as a (temporary) member of the enterprise's directorate (and thus being a governance actor).

With these explanations, we obtain a clearer picture of the governance and integration activities from Figure 2. In the course of governance activities, governance actors negotiate system rules, transmit them to the other actors and receive feedback by them of how the rules work out. We interpret governance activities as the conceptual direction of "looking at ones own level" as the organizational unit's overall configuration is under consideration. In the course of integration activities, integration actors coordinate in order to achieve a consistent application of the system rules to the current operational context of the organizational unit. In addition, the integration actors enable rule-compliant activities where operational actors participate to carry out their tasks. We interpret integration activities as the conceptual direction of "looking downwards/inwards" as here the internal functioning of an organizational unit along existing system rules is addressed.

Consequently, integration sits between governance and operation. While governance actors are responsible for *strategic control decisions* (setting system rules), integration actors are responsible for *operational control decisions* (applying/implementing existing system rules) within the strategic frame offered by the governance actors. This separation of concerns targets at attenuating oscillation between high-level control decisions and their effects on the system's operation. The broad conceptualization of control aspects in terms of governance and integration for the general case of an organizational unit is quite generic. It may manifest in a wide distribution of control in specific instances of organizational units. For example, the set of governance actors may actually be a complex and shifting composition of actors that have very different responsibilities and influence concerning governance decisions. Analogously, the implementation of the governance decisions may entail complex relationships between the integration actors, with different responsibilities and hierarchy levels of authority. Consequently, for concrete instances of organizational units, additional actor and activity subsets along with relationships between them may become necessary.

Openness and Boundary Management. An organizational unit is a *Janus-faced* entity. It does not only embed actors but also acts as an actor itself in surrounding organizational units. Consequently, an organizational unit participates in activities of surrounding units. These are the *environmental activities* from Figure 2. Participation takes place via an organizational unit's peripheral activities. They correspond to the third conceptual direction of "looking upwards/outwards". Peripheral activities overlay/interlock with environmental activities. This occurs when an internal actor carries out an action that is at the same time part of a peripheral activity and of an environmental activity. As an environmental activity may again be a peripheral activity for the surrounding unit, such an overlay/interlock may reach across arbitrarily many system levels.

The conception of peripheral activities from Figure 2 is a simplification and we give a more sophisticated illustration in the following. First of all, while environmental activities are controlled by surrounding organizational units, participation in these activities is controlled by internal control actors of the organizational unit in focus. We distinguish between peripheral activities with a governance and an integration character as illustrated in Figure 4.

This leads to an orthogonal observation. When we apply our model recursively, analytical interpretations of activities may differ from system level to system level. We show an example in Figure 5. In this market scenario, we consider the specific activity for forming a strategic alliance between two enterprises. For these two enterprises, participation in this activity has a governance character as the formation of a strategic alliance would result in new and modified business

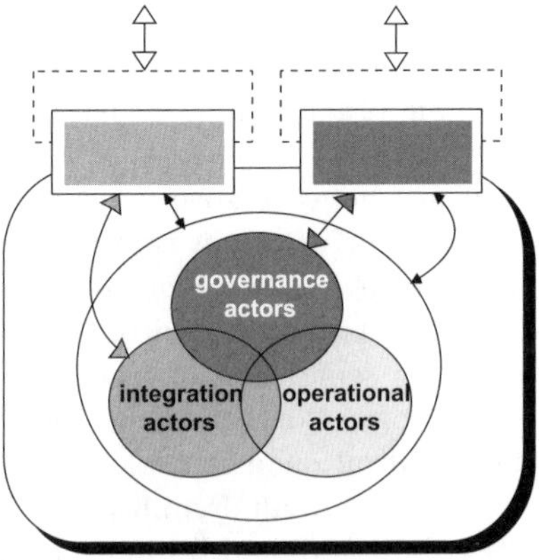

Fig. 4. Control of Peripheral Activities

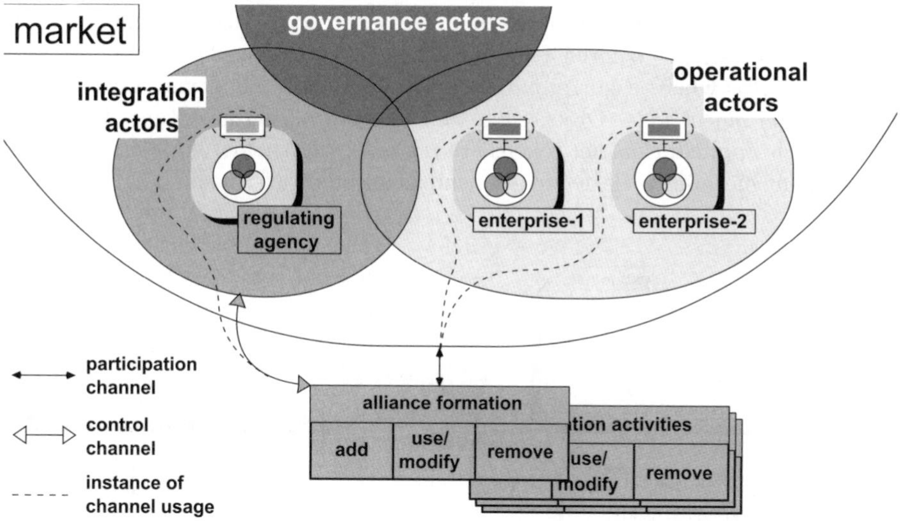

Fig. 5. Example: Different Perspectives on Activities

rules. Consequently, the two enterprises participate via peripheral governance activities. From the perspective of the surrounding market however, the two enterprises just belong to the set of operational actors. Alliance formation between operational actors is part of the market's daily business and has to conform to the market's existing institutional rules. So the activity for alliance formation is an integration activity that has to be enabled and controlled by a regulating agency as an integration actor. For this agency, regulating the alliance formation is part of its common responsibilities and thus the agency participates via a peripheral integration activity.

3 Operational Model

Building on the abstract "thinking model" for organizational units from the previous section, we now turn to a precise "programming model" that provides a technical understanding and an operational semantics for the former abstract concepts. We present the operational model in two steps. As a first step, we concentrate on the realization of recursive system structures based on the fundamental concepts of actors and activities. As a second step, we build on this first operational model and enrich it with the analytical distinctions for operation, integration and governance from the previous section. We rely on the high-level Petri net formalism of *reference nets* [10] as our modeling technique and will point out its advantages for our purpose. Consequently, we begin this section with a short introduction into reference nets. One particular feature of our reference net-based models from this section is that we can directly use them as executable prototypes for deployment in the Renew [13] tool.

Reference Net Modeling. Reference nets offer additional concepts in comparison to "ordinary" colored Petri nets. They implement the *nets-within-nets* concept [14,15] where a surrounding net - the *system net* - can have nets as tokens - the *object nets*. Object nets can be seen as *active tokens*. Reference semantics is applied, thus net tokens are *references* to the actual nets. This way, non-disjoint hierarchies of net relationships can be established.

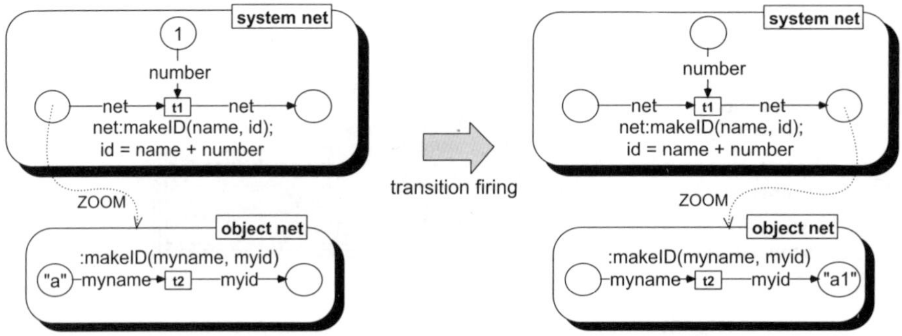

Fig. 6. Reference Nets Example: Firing of Synchronized Transitions

Figure 6 shows an example of a system net and an embedded object net. To facilitate communication between nets, a *synchronous channel* permits a fusion of two transitions for the duration of one firing occurrence. The two transitions can only fire simultaneously. Here, we have the channel :makeID(). A channel is identified by its name and argument signature. Channels are directed, exactly one of the two transitions (the one with a *downlink*, here t1) indicates the net in which the counterpart of the channel (a transition with the corresponding *uplink*, here t2) is located. However, information flow between the fused transitions upon firing is bi-directional and achieved by *unification* over expression inscriptions on both channel sides. The unification mechanism respects the locality of transitions. On both channel sides the choice for variable names is independent from the choice on the other side. Combination is achieved by the requirement that channel arguments at the same position on both sides of the channel have to unify. Consequently, in the example, the variables name and myname on different sides of the channel have to unify and are both bound to the value "a" (analogously for the variables id and myid, being bound to "a1"). If no unifying binding can be found, none of the two transitions can fire.

Figure 6 shows a basic example with just one system net, one object net and one synchronous channel specification. In more complex nets-within-nets models like the ones presented in the following of the section, there typically appear instances of the following situations (often in combination).

- The coupling of the two sides of a synchronous channel is dynamic and is only established for one firing occurrence. From the perspective of a system net, there might be multiple embedded objects nets that offer uplinks matching the system net's downlink. Analogously, from the perspective of an object net, there might be multiple embedding system nets that offer downlinks matching the object net's uplink. If multiple couplings between system and object nets allow for a unifying binding across a synchronous channel, one of the possibilities is chosen non-deterministically for firing.
- The interpretation whether one specific net is regarded as a system net or as an object net depends on the specific embedding situation. In a nets-within-nets hierarchy, the intermediate levels are nets that are both object nets (with respect to embedding nets of the next higher hierarchy level) and system nets (with respect to embedded nets of the next lower hierarchy level). Consequently, the context of each synchronous channel in terms of which nets offer a downlink or an uplink determines the interpretation of system and objects nets.
- While one synchronous channel only takes scope over two transitions, multiple channels can be combined to allow for a fusion of arbitrarily many transitions across arbitrarily many hierarchy levels for one firing occurrence.

Recursive Actor Systems. As a the first step towards an operational model of organizational units we present a preliminary model of *collectivity units* that focuses on an operationalization of actor-activity synchronization in a recursive fashion. Figure 7 shows a collectivity unit modeled as a reference net (details on channel parameters can be found in Figure 9 below). It embeds object nets for actors and activities. Activities comprise multiple actions, each of which is an instance of one of the basic operations mentioned in Section 2: addition of actors, usage/modification of actors, removal of actors.[1] Here, we omit the details of how actors and activities are added or removed.

For actions to occur, actors and activities have to be synchronized and we distinguish between *internal* and *peripheral actions*. In the case of an internal action the collectivity net simultaneously calls an actor via the channel :act() and an activity via the channel :iStep() with the purpose that the actor carries out an action in order to realize an internal activity step. Peripheral actions allow a collectivity to appear as an actor of its own at higher system levels. A peripheral action is also carried out by an internal actor. But from the perspective of a surrounding collectivity, the action is carried out by the collectivity in focus "as a whole". Consequently, the collectivity net does not only call an internal actor via an :act() channel but offers an :act() channel to surrounding collectivities

[1] We do not deepen on activity modeling in this paper. In many cases, modeling activities based on workflow nets [16] and especially inter-organizational [17] or distributed workflow [18] nets is a good option for our purposes. However, we do not prescribe such an approach and instead apply a quite general understanding of activities similar to the UML [19] where an activity models part of a system's behavior by describing how elementary behavioral elements (i.e. *actions*) are combined to more complex behaviors by means of control and data flows.

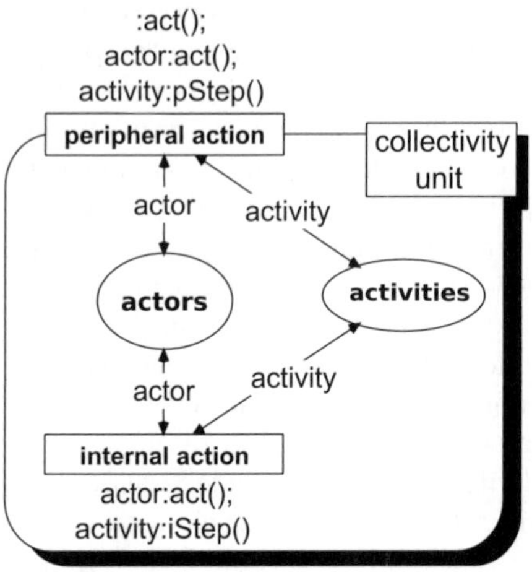

Fig. 7. Preliminary Collectivity Unit Model: Actor/Activity Operationalization

itself. The associated activity is involved via a :pStep() channel. Thus, we arrive at a *technical understanding of collective action*.

Building upon this understanding, Figure 8 illustrates a recursive system of systems structure. It shows a market and an enterprise with their respective activities. It exemplifies the occurrence of a receive-action that takes effect at multiple levels. From the perspective of the market, the receive-action is just an internal action carried out by the enterprise as an embedded actor. For the enterprise however, the same action is a peripheral action, carried out by an actor embedded in the enterprise but at the same time allowing the enterprise to act "as a whole" on the market. Recursive actor nesting according to this mechanism can be arbitrarily deep but of course there has to be a termination at some point. Consequently, the figure also sketches an individual actor – a checker acting in the context of the enterprise. Our modeling approach explicitly targets at collective actors and we do not make further assumptions concerning individual actors here.

We cannot cover all aspects of our operational model in this paper but Figure 9 elaborates on action execution. As there typically exist multiple actors and activities at the same time, we have to make sure that the right actors and activities come together for an action execution. For this reason, actors and activities denote each other mutually (via actorID and activityID/iActivityID). In addition, both provide an action argument that is a complex data structure itself. For peripheral actions, an identifier of the corresponding activity of a surrounding collectivity (pActivityID) has to be included as a further argument. All of these parameters have to unify for an action synchronization. Some variables might not be assigned values beforehand which allows to dynamically bind actors, activities or action parameters into an action occurrence.

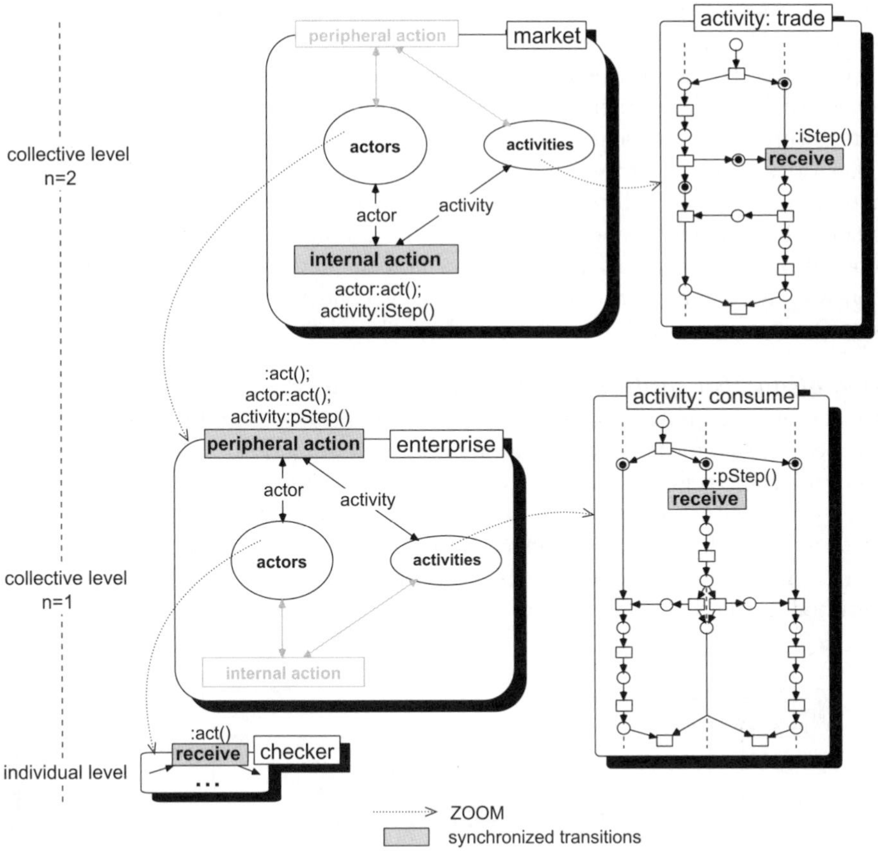

Fig. 8. Action Occurrence in a Recursive System of Systems Structure

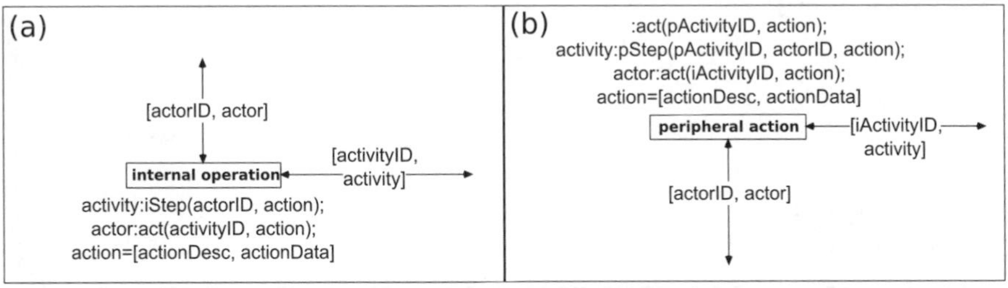

Fig. 9. Details for Action Execution (Zoom into Figures 7 and 8)

Based on the explanations so far, we want to point out the benefits of using reference nets as our modeling technique in this section. We are able to combine well-established approaches of graphical, Petri net-based behavior modeling with the possibility to model structural arrangements in terms of hierarchical system levels. More specifically, our model directly respects the sociological concept of collectivities having an existence of their own but at the same time being *embodied* by their participants. It is important to avoid assigning collective actors anthropomorphic features that they do not possess. The synchronization of transitions allows to straightforwardly model the circumstance that a collective actor's action is actually an action of one of its embedded actors. In software technical implementations of our model that do not rely on direct reference net simulation, approximations of this mechanism may of course be applied. But here we aim at an operational semantics for collective agency that has a most appropriate conceptual fit to the sociological concept.

Operation, Integration, Governance. So far, the operational model does not feature the analytical distinctions made in Section 2 and it does neither offer mechanisms for addition/removal of actors and activities. We will not cover actor addition/removal here. Activity initiation on the other hand is inseparably intertwined with the introduction of the analytical control aspects into our operational model. Controlling activities means controlling the whole functioning of an organizational unit and in this respect, controlling which activities may be initiated in the first place is vital.

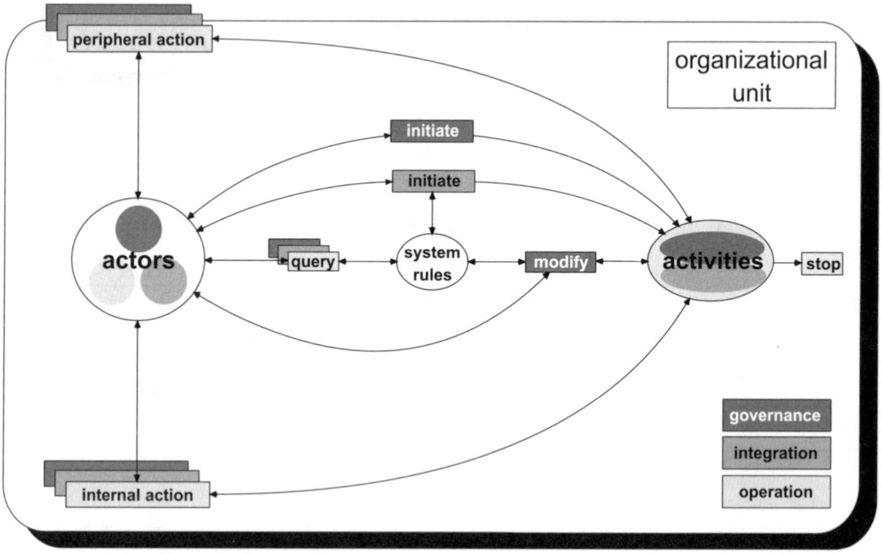

Fig. 10. Operational Model of an Organizational Unit

Figure 10 shows an overview of the operational model of an organizational unit (without inscriptions). It is an elaboration of the former simple operational model of a collectivity unit.The model exhibits the kind of two-level control structure described in Section 2 and embodies a Petri net-based interpretation of the interplay between operation, integration and governance. For illustrative purposes, we have also "colored" the transitions in the figure, indicating which actors are allowed to execute the corresponding actions. An important point is the explication of the concept of system rules. The system rules are embedded as an additional object net. Basically, we require a consistent set of system rules that can be consulted to check whether the initiation of a given system activity is admissible. Only integration and governance actors may invoke system activities. The model respects separation of concerns with respect to *setting* and *applying* system rules as it was propagated in Section 2. This is more evident in the zoom from Figure 11 (where we omit channel parameters).System rules are set and modified by governance actors in the course of governance activities. Any access to system rules other than that is restricted to be read-only. Integration actors may invoke integration activities only if they are in adherence to system rules. Governance actors on the other hand are allowed to invoke governance activities without reference to system rules (but see below). We obtain the desired effect of integration sitting as an intermediary between governance and operation.

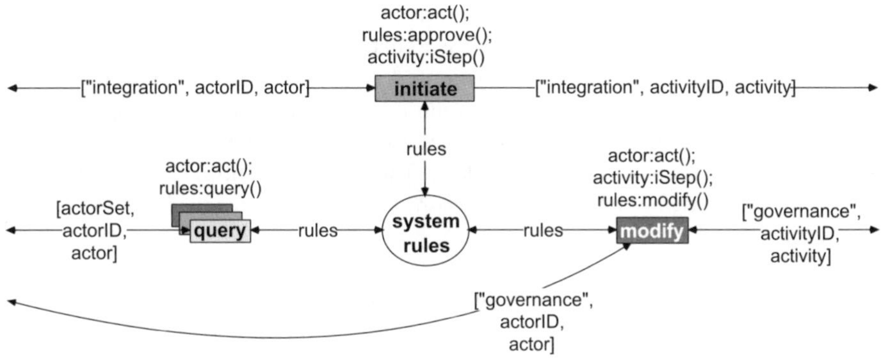

Fig. 11. Channel Interface to the System Rules (Zoom into Figure 10)

We have a closer look at action execution in Figure 12. It illustrates that things have gotten more complicated in comparison to the case of the previous simple operational model. Actors and activities are no longer only associated with an identifier but also with their respective actor and activity sets, where actors may belong to multiple sets.[2] Likewise, actions have received an action type. In the case of an internal action, the action's type has to match the set of the actor that carries out the action.For the case of peripheral actions, there is an

[2] If an actor belongs to multiple actor sets, then this actor is embedded multiply, i.e. there are multiple tokens for this actor and each of these tokens is associated with a different actor set. Of course, the actor net references of all these tokens point to the same actor net respectively.

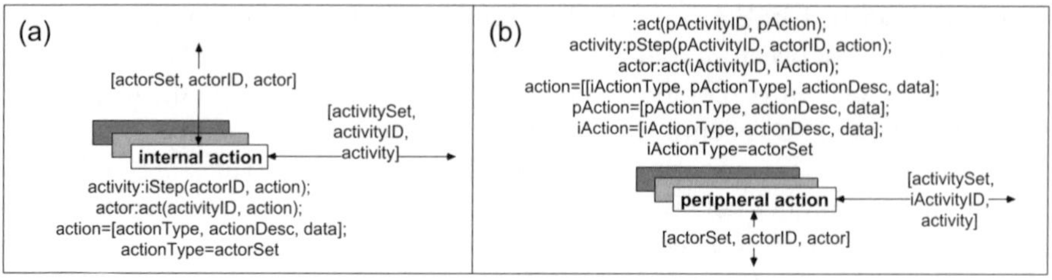

Fig. 12. Details for Action Execution (Zoom into Figure 10)

additional aspect. In Section 2, we described that the analytical interpretations of actions may differ from system level to system level. So the action type of a peripheral action is itself a tuple, consisting of its analytical interpretation from the organizational unit in focus and its analytical interpretation at the level of the surrounding organizational unit.

In Section 2 we have presented an intentionally abstract model of an organizational unit and Figure 2 only includes actors and activities. For the operational model it becomes necessary to be more specific. In Figure 10 we have already explicated system rules as we need them as a first-order concept to provide an operational semantics for the aspects of operation, integration and governance. It is possible to extend the model and explicate further *organizational artifacts* where artifacts can be any kind of function-oriented passive entities like materials, tools or documents (for multi-agent system engineering, an analogous approach has emerged: organizations are conceptualized in terms of active agents and passive artifacts [20]). However, in order to keep the model as simple as possible, one can also model artifacts as "dumb" actors that offer their specific functions in the course of activities.

Governance Rules. Governance of organizational units is a subtle topic. Following Figure 10, governance actors may initiate system activities without any constraints and modify the system rules in the course of these activities. Consequently, governance actors carry a heavy burden of responsibility. As a result, we consider Figure 10 to be inadequate for many cases. Instead, governance very often has to follow rules itself. These are meta-rules that specify who is allowed to modify the "ordinary" system rules in which way. We call the two kinds of rules *governance rules* and *integration rules* respectively. The question arises, where governance rules stem from. The most straightforward solution is that governance rules are set from the system level above as illustrated in Figure 13.

4 Example Scenario

The operational model developed in this paper proposes generic concepts for "programming" organizational units. It can be concretized for various specific approaches in order to combine them in a systems of systems setting. In this section, we elaborate on one specific concretization as an illustrative example.

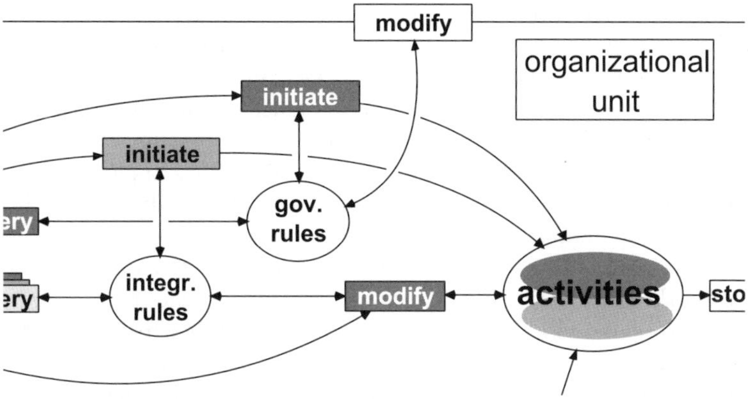

Fig. 13. Integration and Governance Rules

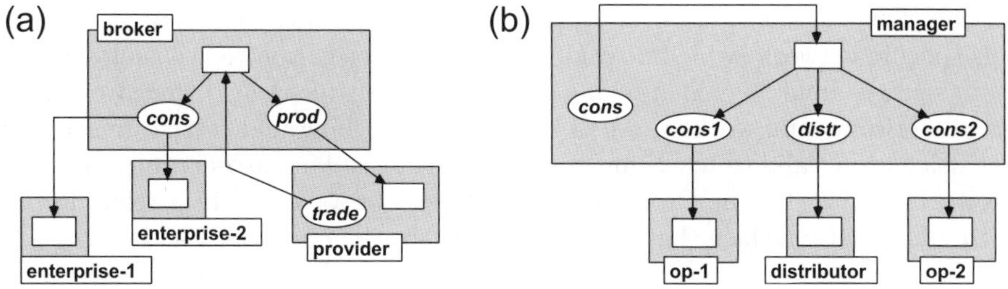

Fig. 14. Delegation Networks: (a) market, (b) consumer enterprise

Figure 14 shows two simple examples of *delegation networks* modeled with Petri nets.[3] A place models a *task* and a transition models the *processing* of a task. For this purpose, each transition has exactly one place in its preset and each place has at least one transition in its postset. Task processing can take on two forms. (1) A transition with an empty postset models the *execution* of a task. (2) A transition with a non-empty postset models the *refinement* of a task into sub-tasks. In the figure, we have partitioned the net into *positions* (the gray boxes) in such a way that an arc from a place to a transition models the *delegation* of a task from one position to another.

[3] We have dealt with delegation networks in some of our previous publications [21,18]. In fact, we have developed the approach SONAR, a mathematical approach to model multi-agent organizations as delegation networks based on Petri nets. SONAR features a comprehensive model for organizational teamwork, from team formation over distributed planning and plan execution to organizational transformations. However, in this paper, we will only use a small fragment of SONAR's modeling capabilities and we will not address any formal properties.

Of course, such delegation networks could also be modeled as simple AND/OR graphs. But by using Petri nets, we can directly relate their operational semantics to delegation processes. Delegation starts with initial tasks – places with an empty preset. When putting a token on such a place, the possible firing sequences until there are no tokens left in the net induce possible *teams*. Consequently, for the example from Figure 14 (a), there is one initial task trade and it leads to two possible teams. Both teams include the provider and broker. Additionally, either enterprise-1 or enterprise-2 is included, depending on who receives the cons task. We assume that each possible team is associated with a *team service* specification that constrains how the final tasks of the team (those that are not further refined, here prod, cons) are to be executed by their respective positions. A specific choice for one execution possibility is a *team plan*.

For deploying delegation networks as organizational units one has to establish an according set of system rules. As the Renew tool allows for an easy integration of Java code, we have chosen to formulate the rules in tuProlog[4]. We obtain built-in reasoning mechanisms and the unification mechanism of Prolog interacts neatly with the unification mechanism of reference nets described in the previous section. For each delegation network, we have predicates (*facts*) that describe this specific network (which positions exist, task delegation relationships, which team services hold for which teams etc.) and predicates (*rules*) that are generic for all networks and work on top of the facts (describing team structures, checking delegation validity, checking team and team service associations etc.). As shown in Figure 15, the Prolog database has to be wrapped in a reference net with a channel interface that is a counterpart to the one from Figure 11.

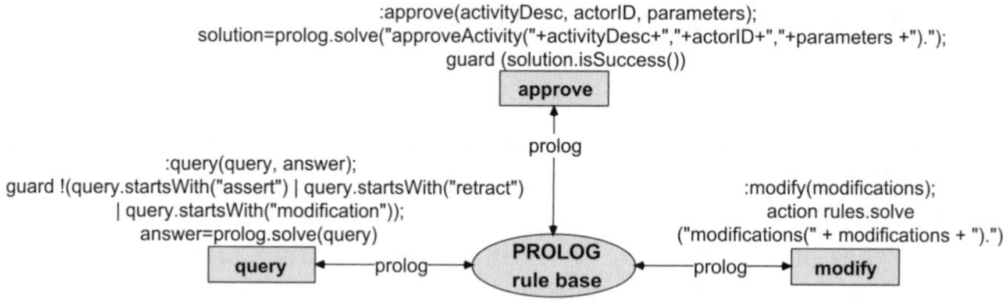

Fig. 15. Channel Interface of the tuProlog System Rules Net (as one possible Counterpart to Figure 11)

We also have to identify the analytical aspects of operation, integration and governance. Identifying these aspects for specific approaches often leaves multiple possibilities. For delegation networks, we adopt the simple view that delegation corresponds to integration and executing final tasks corresponds to operation. Governance corresponds to changing the facts describing the delegation network.

[4] http://www.alice.unibo.it/xwiki/bin/view/Tuprolog/

Here, we will illustrate the interplay between integration and operation and leave out governance aspects. Figure 16 displays the whole process of carrying out the initial task trade in the market network from Figure 14 (a). We have the broker as an integration actor, enterprise-1 and enterprise-2 as operational actors and the provider as both an integration and operational actor. The figure shows which actor is involved in which action at some given point in time. For activity invocation, it is indicated which part of the system rules has to be consulted. At time points t1, t2, t3 delegation activities (top right of the figure, details concerning these activities are omitted) are invoked to eventually build a team. While the system rules state which task delegations are possible, the integration actors have some freedom of choice concerning which delegation mode they prefer (direct assignment, negotiation, bidding, etc.). In this example, the team consisting of provider, broker and enterprise-2 is formed. At time point t4 the provider as the initiator/head of the team invokes a team plan for the execution of the final team tasks prod and cons (activity at the right side of the figure). The system rules state which team services hold for which teams. A team plan results by applying certain constraints to a team service. These constraints are supplied by the head of the team and and the system rule have to approve whether the constraints and thus the team plan itself are valid. At time points

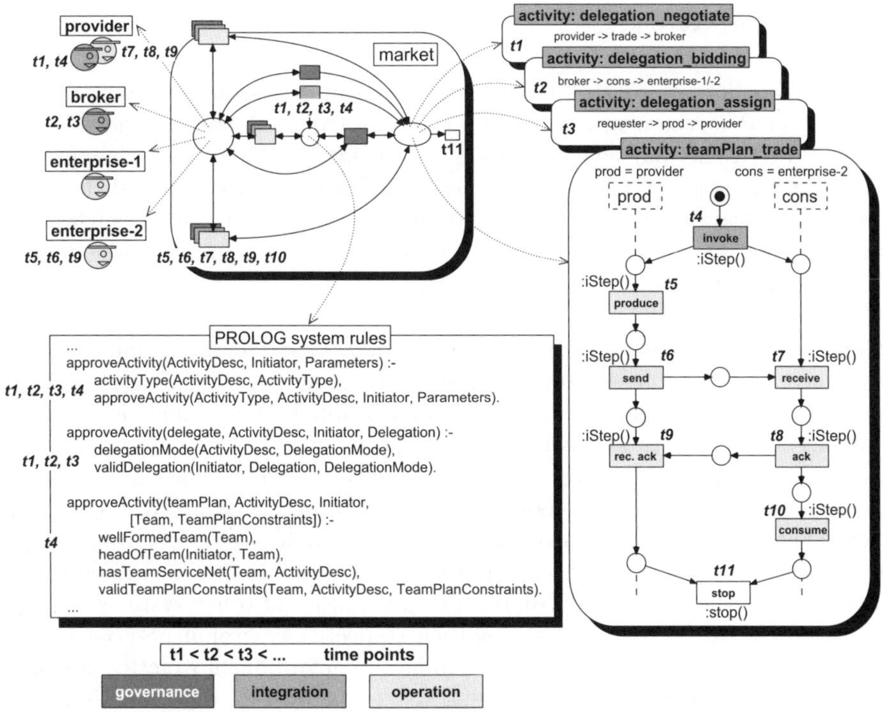

Fig. 16. Example Execution of the Initial Task trade

t5-t10 the provider and enterprise-2 execute the operational actions for the prod and cons parts of the team plan before termination in t11.

We can take advantage of the system of systems character that underlies our approach. We consider the delegation network consumer enterprise from Figure 14 (b) as a sub-network to the market from Figure 14 (a). The task cons models the same task in both cases. However, it is a final task for the market and an initial task for the consumer firm. We deploy the consumer firm also as an organizational unit and embed it as enterprise-2 inside the market. Consequently, the manager of the consumer firm has to take care of "bridging" between team formation activities at both system levels. We do not consider this aspect here and instead concentrate on the execution of team plans. A team plan for the team consisting of manager, distributor, op-1 and op-2 in the consumer firm has to refine the cons part of the corresponding team plan for the team consisting of provider, broker and enterprise-2 on the market. Figure 17 displays such a refinement. The peripheral action arrangement of the activity teamPlan_cons at the consumer firm exactly fits into the cons part of the activity teamPlan_trade at the market. The figure illustrates the transition from individual to collective action. While the consumer firm appears as holistic at the level of the market, the three actions belonging to the cons part of the team plan are actually carried out by multiple actors at the level of the consumer firm.

5 Related Work

As our modeling approach for organizational units rests on quite fundamental concepts and mechanisms, the general range of related work is wide. In this section, we restrict ourselves to address two fields of related research explicitly. The first one is general system and organization theory as it provided a great body of inspirational input. The second one is multi-agent research as it was the starting point of our research and we view our results as a conceptual extension to classical agent-orientation.

General System and Organization Theory. General system and organization theory have a long tradition in studying openness and control of systems. Concerning open systems, we have first of all adopted the common view from [9] (among others) where an open systems (like for instance an enterprise) relies on services and resources of other systems but at the same time constructs and continuously reconstructs its boundaries across which it relates to its environment. The concept of an environment is too important to characterize it simply as "everything else". Instead, our approach is consistent with the systemic perspective that the environment does not only consist of other systems (that in turn view the first system as a part of their respective environments) but is itself a system (c.f. [22,23]). Each open system has an environment exactly *because* of its participation in a greater whole and its characteristics are a function of its fit into this greater context. We obtain a hierarchy of systems embedding other systems and Simon [24] points out that hierarchy in this sense of clustering is a

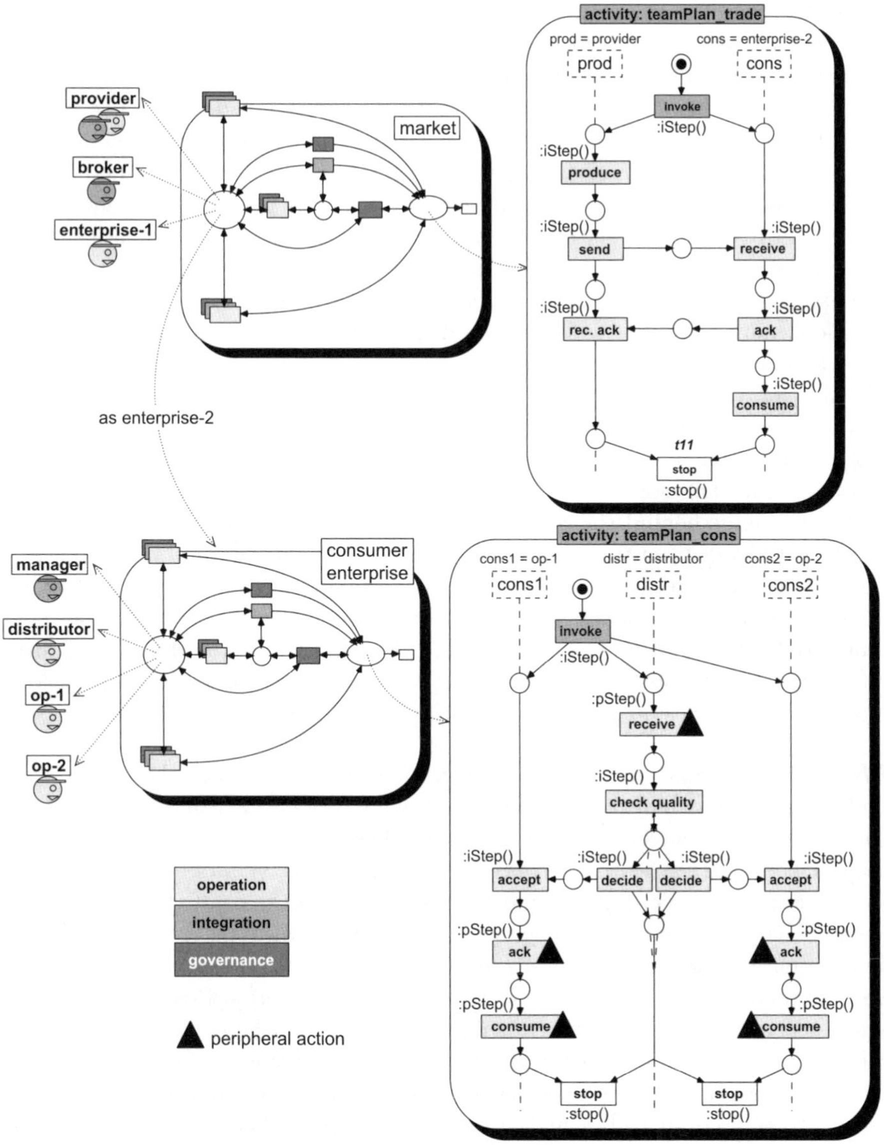

Fig. 17. Team Plan Execution on Different Levels

fundamental feature of *all* complex systems. Each particular system is localized both in terms of its embedded systems and in terms of the systems by whom it itself is embedded. As in our case, this perspective has frequently been applied in a recursive manner, with similar systems at each level (c.f. the concept of a *Holon* [25] or the *Viable System Model* [26]).

In the case of system control, we have drawn on inspiration from cybernetics [27] as a sub-field of general systems theory. It propagates the analytical separation of a controlled part and a controlling part of a system. The variant to carry out a further separation of the controlling part into two is quite popular (c.f. [28,29]). Ashby [30] characterizes this distinction as separating the handling of disturbances "in degree" (applying existing decision rules) from the handling of disturbances "in kind" (determining whether it is necessary to redefine the rules) and it is closely related to what Argyris [31] labels *double-loop learning*. Scott [9] stresses that this principle provides a very powerful and general model of control that is also widely-applied in social organizations. Although organizations may exhibit a considerable degree of structural complexity, both in their technical core and their peripheral components, it is still possible to identify the two underlying aspects of setting and applying system rules (c.f. goal and strategy setting by the *dominant coalition* and the establishment of control/coordination systems to see to it that resources and energies are mobilized to pursue the strategies).

The rationale behind the rooting of our approach in system and organization theory is to learn from the adaptivity, robustness, scalability and reflexiveness of their respective objects of study (especially social systems) and to translate their building principles in effective information technology. We have not only combined and integrated the inspirations concerning openness and system control into our model of organizational units. We have also proposed an operational model that provides a technical understanding of the theoretical concepts.

Multi-Agent System Engineering. We have stressed the relation to multi-agent research in the introduction. We have mentioned that approaches for collective agency have been brought forth. For example, organization-oriented approaches often advocate the concept of groups [32,33,34] as a further decomposition means. While groups are mostly just considered as contexts for individual agent behavior, some approaches go further and regard the grouping concept as a potential basis for a recursive decomposition where collectivities of agents are regarded as actors. For example, *holonic multi-agent systems* [35] or *multi-multi-agent systems* [36] feature a federative approach where one or a few agents represent a collection of agents to the outside. Multiple approaches [37,38,7] propose organizations or teams as specialized agents that can not only play (external) roles themselves but at the same time require their own (internal) roles to be played by others. In [39] an entity that is both an agent and an agent platform is proposed.

We consider these approaches very valuable but in our opinion they focus on rather *technical* considerations of how to align and implement collective agency with classical agent concepts and technology. Our approach can be considered as orthogonal to these efforts. We focus on a *conceptual* model of collective agency. We explicitly address questions related to the content of collective agency. This basically concerns the relation between internal configurations of a collectivity and its boundary management to act as a whole on higher system levels. We specifically refer to collective actors in organizational settings which we term organizational units. We have derived three conceptual directions that have to be addressed for all organizational units and that provide a basis for systematically studying vertical and horizontal relationships between multiple organizational units in a multi-level organizational setting.

In this paper, we have supplemented our previously published abstract model of organizational units with an operational semantics. While the accompanying model provides a technical understanding of collective action, it is still a conceptual model as we aim at a very close fit to the sociological concept of collective action. While we use reference nets to supply operational semantics and our models serve as directly executable prototypes, the underlying mechanisms can also be transferred to other technologies. Doing this, an approximation of the semantics we supplied in this paper is probably necessary. For distributed approaches, the question arises whether to manage system rules as well as actor-activity synchronization centralized or decentralized. In this context, middleware approaches for multi-agent organizations [6] provide a promising starting point as they combine channeling system behavior along explicit system rules with different stages of decentralized middleware management. However, in [12] we have come to the conclusion that actually a nested middleware approach is necessary to account for a system of systems approach.

Consequently, our organizational unit approach sits at the intersection between different directions of multi-agent research: organizational modeling approaches, frameworks for realizing recursive nesting and middleware deployment. To put it differently, we ascribe agent-oriented technology the potential of providing vehicles for the distributed deployment of systems of systems according to our approach. In the opposite direction, we see our model as contributing to agent-oriented efforts that seek to close the gap between classical agent-oriented thinking (individual actors) and the need for hierarchic decomposition mechanisms that respect the actor metaphor as a continuous first-order abstraction.

6 Conclusion

We have presented a modular approach to comprehend systems of systems as being composed of organizational units. Each organizational unit can be regarded under a context perspective (embedding/imprinting the behavior of its participants) and under an actor perspective (acting itself as a holistic entity). We have established a consistent relation between collective agency and internal control structures of an organizational unit. Our model rests on universal concepts and provides a conceptual basis to systematically study and implement different modes of coupling between organizational units, both horizontally and vertically. For example, in [11] we have applied the abstract part of our model to study different levels of a reference architecture for *multi-organization systems*. We have qualitatively distinguished *departments*, *organizations*, *organizational fields* and the *society* as iteratively embedded specific types of organizational units according to the model from Figure 2.

In this paper, we have supplemented our abstract "thinking model" of an organizational unit with an operational "programming model". The underlying purpose is twofold. The main purpose is still to provide a conceptual reference model for the comprehension of and thinking about complex systems as compositions of organizational units. Here, we have supplied a technical understanding of our formerly abstract concepts. This helps to get a clearer picture of how systems of systems based on organizational units function. In addition, such a technical understanding is necessary in order to get a grasp on how to actually build software systems according to our approach. As a result, we have provided a proof-of-concepts by deploying our operational models based on reference nets in the context of the Renew tool. However, while we have taken advantage of reference net semantics, the underlying concepts of operationalization can be transferred to other engineering approaches.

Concerning future work, a model like ours has to be complemented by modeling languages, tools and methodologies that really make it applicable. Now that we have supplied our previously abstract model with an operational semantics, the context and requirements for these developments will be easier to determine. Furthermore, we have so far been concerned with architectural question and operational semantics for our models of organizational units. For this purpose we have taken advantage of the complete expressive power of the reference net formalism. In order to be able to formulate and prove formal properties we will have to look into restrictions of the formalism, at least for chosen aspects of the models.

References

1. Northrop, L.: Ultra-Large-Scale Systems: The Software Challenge of the Future. Software Engineering Institute, Carnegie Mellon (2006)
2. Lankes, J., Matthes, F., Wittenburg, A.: Softwarekartographie: Systematische Darstellung von Anwendungslandschaften. In: Ferstl, O., Sinz, E., Eckert, S., Isselhorst, T. (eds.) Wirtschaftsinformatik 2005: eEconomy, eGovernment, eSociety, Physica-Verlag, Heidelberg (2005)
3. Hess, A., Humm, B., Voss, M., Engels, G.: Structuring software cities - a multidimensional approach. In: Proceedings of the 11th IEEE International Enterprise Distributed Object Computing Conference (EDOC 2007), pp. 122–129 (2007)
4. Maier, M.: Architecturing principles for systems-of-systems. Systems Engineering 1(4), 267–284 (1999)
5. Jennings, N.: On agent-based software engineering. Artificial Intelligence 177(2), 277–296 (2000)
6. Boissier, O., Hübner, J.F., Sichman, J.S.: Organization Oriented Programming: From Closed to Open Organizations. In: O'Hare, G.M.P., Ricci, A., O'Grady, M.J., Dikenelli, O. (eds.) ESAW 2006. LNCS (LNAI), vol. 4457, pp. 86–105. Springer, Heidelberg (2007)
7. Boella, G., van der Torre, L.: Organizations as socially constructed agents in the agent oriented paradigm. In: Gleizes, M.-P., Zhang, S.-W., Zambonelli, F. (eds.) ESAW 2004. LNCS (LNAI), vol. 3451, pp. 1–13. Springer, Heidelberg (2005)
8. Johnson, D.: Contemporary Sociological Theory: An Integrated Multi-Level Approach. Springer, Heidelberg (2008)
9. Scott, W.R.: Organizations: Rational, Natural and Open Systems, 5th edn. Prentice Hall, Englewood Cliffs (2003)

10. Kummer, O.: Referenznetze. Logos Verlag, Berlin (2002)
11. Wester-Ebbinghaus, M., Moldt, D.: Structure in threes: Modelling organization-oriented software architectures built upon multi-agent systems. In: Padgham, L., Parkes, D., Müller, J., Parsons, S. (eds.) 7th International Joint Conference on Autonomous Agents and Multiagent Systems (AAMAS 2008), IFAAMAS (2008), pp. 1307–1311 (2008)
12. Wester-Ebbinghaus, M., Köhler-Bußmeier, M., Moldt, D.: From multi-agent to multi-organization systems: Utilizing middleware approaches. In: Artikis, A., Picard, G., Vercouter, L. (eds.) ESAW 2008. LNCS, vol. 5485, pp. 46–65. Springer, Heidelberg (2009)
13. Kummer, O., Wienberg, F., Duvigneau, M.: Renew – the Reference Net Workshop (2006), `http://www.renew.de/` Release 2.1
14. Valk, R.: Petri nets as token objects: An introduction to elementary object nets. In: Desel, J., Silva, M. (eds.) ICATPN 1998. LNCS, vol. 1420, pp. 1–24. Springer, Heidelberg (1998)
15. Valk, R.: Object petri nets: Using the nets-within-nets paradigm. In: Desel, J., Reisig, W., Rozenberg, G. (eds.) Lectures on Concurrency and Petri Nets. LNCS, vol. 3098, pp. 819–848. Springer, Heidelberg (2004)
16. van der Aalst, W.: Verification of workflow nets. In: Azéma, P., Balbo, G. (eds.) ICATPN 1997. LNCS, vol. 1248, pp. 407–426. Springer, Heidelberg (1997)
17. van der Aalst, W.: Interorganizational workflows. Systems Analysis - Modelling - Simulation 34(3), 335–367 (1999)
18. Köhler-Bußmeier, M., Wester-Ebbinghaus, M., Moldt, D.: A formal model for organisational structures behind process-aware information systems. In: Jensen, K., van der Aalst, W.M.P. (eds.) Transactions on Petri Nets and Other Models of Concurrency II. LNCS, vol. 5460, pp. 98–114. Springer, Heidelberg (2009)
19. Bock, C.: UML 2 activity and action models. Journal of Object Technology 2(5), 43–53 (2003)
20. Hübner, J.F., Boissier, O., Kitio, R., Ricci, A.: Instrumenting multi-agent organisations with organisational artifacts and agents: Giving the organisational power back to the agents. Autonomous Agents and Multi-Agent Systems 20(3), 369–400 (2010)
21. Köhler, M.: A formal model of multi-agent organisations. Fundamenta Informaticae 79(3-4), 415–430 (2007)
22. Parsons, T.: Structure and Process in Modern Societies. Free Press, New York (1960)
23. Luhmann, N.: Soziale Systeme. Suhrkamp (1984)
24. Simon, H.: The architecture of complexity. Proceedings of the American Philosophical Society 106(6), 467–482 (1962)
25. Koestler, A.: The Ghost in the Machine. Henry Regnery Co. (1967)
26. Beer, S.: The Heart of the Enterprise. Wiley, Chichester (1979)
27. Wiener, N.: Cybernetics. Wiley, Chichester (1948)
28. Swinth, R.: Organizational Systems for Management: Designing, Planning and Implementation. In: Grid (1974)
29. Herring, C.: Viable software: The intelligent control paradigm for adaptable and adaptive architectures. Dissertation, University of Queensland, Department of Information Technology and Electrical Engineering (2002)
30. Ashby, W.R.: Design for a Brain. Wiley, Chichester (1960)
31. Argyris, C., Schön, D.: Organizational Learning: A Theory of Action Perspective. Addison-Wesley, Reading (1978)

32. Hübner, J.F., Sichman, J.S.: A model for the structural, functional and deontic specification of organizations in multiagent systems. In: Bittencourt, G., Ramalho, G. (eds.) SBIA 2002. LNCS (LNAI), vol. 2507, pp. 118–128. Springer, Heidelberg (2002)
33. Ferber, J., Gutknecht, O., Michel, F.: From agents to organizations: An organizational view of multi-agent systems. In: Giorgini, P., Müller, J.P., Odell, J.J. (eds.) AOSE 2003. LNCS, vol. 2935, Springer, Heidelberg (2004)
34. Odell, J., Nodine, M., Levy, R.: A metamodel for agents, roles, and groups. In: Odell, J.J., Giorgini, P., Müller, J.P. (eds.) AOSE 2004. LNCS, vol. 3382, pp. 78–92. Springer, Heidelberg (2005)
35. Fischer, K., Schillo, M., Siekmann, J.H.: Holonic multiagent systems: A foundation for the organisation of multiagent systems. In: Mařík, V., McFarlane, D.C., Valckenaers, P. (eds.) HoloMAS 2003. LNCS (LNAI), vol. 2744, pp. 71–80. Springer, Heidelberg (2003)
36. Stockheim, T., Nimis, J., Scholz, T., Stehli, M.: How to build a multi-multi-agent system: The agent.enterprise approach. In: Proceedings of the 6th International Conference on Enterprise Information Systems, ICEIS 2004. Software Agents and Internet Computing, vol. 4, pp. 364–371 (2004)
37. Hahn, C., Madrigal-Mora, C., Fischer, K.: A platform-independent metamodel for multiagent systems. Autonomous Agents and Multi-Agent Systems 18(2), 239–266 (2008)
38. AOS-Group: Jack intelligent agents team manual (2009), http://www.aosgrp.com/documentation/jack/JACK_Teams_Manual_WEB/index.html
39. Rölke, H.: Modellierung von Agenten und Multiagentensystemen. Logos Verlag, Berlin (2004)

A Multi-Agent Organizational Framework for Coevolutionary Optimization

Grégoire Danoy[1], Pascal Bouvry[1], and Olivier Boissier[2]

[1] FSTC/CSC/ILIAS, University of Luxembourg
6 Rue R. Coudenhove Kalergi, L-1359 Luxembourg
gregoire.danoy@uni.lu, pascal.bouvry@uni.lu
[2] SMA/G2I/ENSM.SE, 158 Cours Fauriel
42023 Saint-Etienne Cedex, France
olivier.boissier@emse.fr

Abstract. This paper introduces DAFO, a Distributed Agent Framework for Optimization that helps in designing and applying Coevolutionary Genetic Algorithms (CGAs). CGAs have already proven to be efficient in solving hard optimization problems, however they have not been considered in the existing agent-based metaheuristics frameworks that currently provide limited organization models. As a solution, DAFO includes a complete organization and reorganization model, Multi-Agent System for EVolutionary Optimization (MAS4EVO), that permits to formalize CGAs structure, interactions and adaptation. Examples of existing and original CGAs modeled using MAS4EVO are provided and an experimental proof of their efficiency is given on an emergent topology control problem in mobile hybrid ad hoc networks called the injection network problem.

Keywords: Multi-Agent Systems, Organizational Model, Evolutionary Algorithms.

1 Introduction

Coevolutionary Genetic Algorithms (CGAs) are one of the key evolutions of Genetic Algorithms (GAs) [21] that allow to optimize hard problems with very large search spaces, like many real-world ones. Instead of evolving one homogeneous population of individuals that represent a global solution, the coevolutionary approach involves several populations that represent specific parts of the global solution. Those populations of individuals then evolve through competing or cooperating interaction patterns.

Despite their proven good performance on hard optimization problems, CGAs have not been considered in existing metaheuristics frameworks [2], even in the latest ones based on a multi-agent approach [27]. The multi-agent paradigm [50] has been used as a way to answer to the metaheuristics recent needs for simplicity, flexibility and modularity through its social metaphor, i.e. organization. However the different organizational models proposed in this context do not address all the specification needs for defining CGAs' structure, interactions and

K. Jensen, S. Donatelli, and M. Koutny (Eds.): ToPNoC IV, LNCS 6550, pp. 199–224, 2010.

adaptation. In addition, none of the existing metaheuristics libraries are based one those models.

In this paper we propose DAFO, a Distributed Agent Framework for Optimization, that consists in a multi-agent system dedicated to evolutionary optimization. A key element of this framework resides in its multi-agent organization model, MAS4EVO (Multi-Agent System for EVolutionary Optimization), which is an extension of the $\mathcal{M}$OISE$^+$ model [24]. MAS4EVO addresses the limitations of the existing agent-based frameworks by explicitly defining the CGAs structure and interactions through its organization model and their dynamic adaptation with a reorganization model. This paper also describes the usage of MAS4EVO for modeling existing CGAs and original ones and demonstrates that with limited organizational changes it is possible to define and apply CGAs variants that outperform standard ones on a real-world optimization problem.

The paper is organized as follows. In section 2, we first introduce coevolutionary genetic algorithms. Then in section 3, we analyze the existing metaheuristics frameworks and libraries and identify their limitations. Then we present the foundations and basic components of the DAFO framework in section 4, focusing on its organization model MAS4EVO, and we illustrate its usage for modeling a simple genetic algorithm (SGA). In section 5, two existing CGAs and two original ones (hybrid and dynamic) are modeled with MAS4EVO. A description of the DAFO framework implementation is provided in section 6. Section 7 shows the application and comparison of some of the modeled CGAs on a topology control problem in hybrid ad hoc networks. Finally, section 8 presents our conclusions and future work.

2 Coevolutionary Genetic Algorithms

Genetic Algorithms (GAs) [21] are heuristic methods based on Darwin's principle of evolution [15] (survival of the fittest) among candidate solutions (known as "individuals") with the stochastic processes of selection, recombination and mutation. Unfortunately, "classical" GAs tend to perform poorly or are difficult to apply on some problems especially when they have very large search spaces like many real-world problems such as inventory management [14] or topology control in mobile ad hoc networks [10]. In order to address these kinds of problems, researchers referred again to a nature inspired process to extend evolutionary algorithms: coevolution (i.e. the coexistence of several species [19]).

The main difference between Coevolutionary Genetic Algorithms (CGAs) [32] and GAs comes from the adaptive nature of fitness evaluation in coevolutionary systems: the fitness of an individual is based on its interactions with other individuals from other so-called subpopulations. Thus, instead of evolving a population of similar individuals representing a global solution like in classical GAs, CGAs consider the coevolution of subpopulations of individuals representing specific parts of the global solution and evolving independently with a genetic algorithm. Individuals are evaluated based on their direct interactions with other individuals. These interactions can be either positive or negative depending on the consequences that such interactions produce on the population: (*i*) if positive (case of *cooperative coevolution*), the presence of each species stimulates the growth of the other species, (*ii*) if negative (case of *competitive coevolution*), the presence of each species implies the limitation of the growth of another species.

In the following we describe two CGAs, a cooperative one called Cooperative Coevolutionary GA (CCGA) and a competitive one based on non-cooperative models of game theory called Loosely Coupled GA (LCGA).

2.1 Cooperative Coevolutionary Genetic Algorithm

In [37], Potter and De Jong proposed a general framework for cooperative coevolution that they used for test functions optimization (De Jong's test suite). In this approach, multiple instances of GAs are run in parallel. Each population contains individuals that represent a component of a larger solution. Complete solutions are obtained by assembling representatives from each of the species (populations). The fitness of each individual depends on the quality of the solutions the individual participated in. In some sense, it measures how well the individual cooperates to solve the problem.

In the initial generation *(t=0)* individuals from a given subpopulation are matched with randomly chosen individuals from all other subpopulations. The best individual in each subpopulation is then retrieved based on its fitness value. The process of *cooperative coevolution* starts in the next generation *(t=1)*. For this purpose, in each generation the operations follow a round-robin schedule.

Only a single subpopulation is "active" in one cycle, while the other subpopulations are "frozen". All individuals from the active subpopulation are matched with the best values of the frozen subpopulations. When the evolutionary process is completed, the solution of the problem is the composition of the best individuals from each subpopulation.

Figure 1 presents an example of the application of the CCGA on the Rosenbrock function (part of De Jong's test suite). It illustrates the CCGA general architecture (complete communication graph) and the way each population

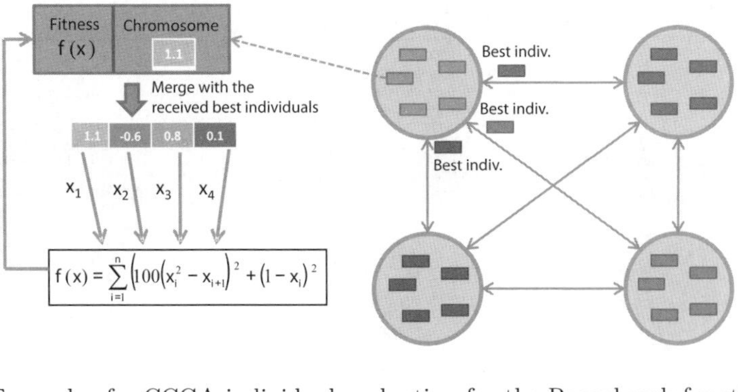

Fig. 1. Example of a CCGA individual evaluation for the Rosenbrock function (n=3)

evaluates its individuals by combining them with the individuals selected from the other species (here with the best individual).

Since their introduction, CCGAs have been widely applied and their properties are still studied, such as the influence of their interactions [34][33] and their parallelization [35]. Cooperative coevolution showed to be efficient on different hard problems like static function optimization [36], rule learning [38] [40], neural network learning [39], and multiagent learning problems [41].

2.2 Loosely Coupled Genetic Algorithm

The Loosely Coupled Genetic Algorithm (LCGA) [45] is a medium-level parallel and distributed coevolutionary algorithm. It explores the paradigm of competitive coevolution algorithms motivated by non-cooperative models of game theory. For an optimization problem described by some function (a global criterion) of N variables, local chromosome structures are defined for each variable and local subpopulations are created for each of them. A problem to be solved is thus firstly analyzed in terms of possible decomposition and relations between subcomponents. They are expressed by a communication graph G_{com}, known as graph of interaction. The function decomposition and the definition of the interaction graph aim at minimizing communications while still ensuring that the fact of reaching local optima for all different players (being a Nash equilibrium point) still leads to a global optimum of the initial function. The interaction graph is therefore hard-coded and this process has to be done manually by taking into account information on the internal structure of the cost function, i.e. of the problem. LCGA was applied to dynamic mapping and scheduling problems [43], a distributed scheduling problem [44] and to test functions [45].

Figure 2 presents the application of the LCGA on the same instance of the Rosenbrock function as in Fig. 1. It illustrates the decomposition used, the

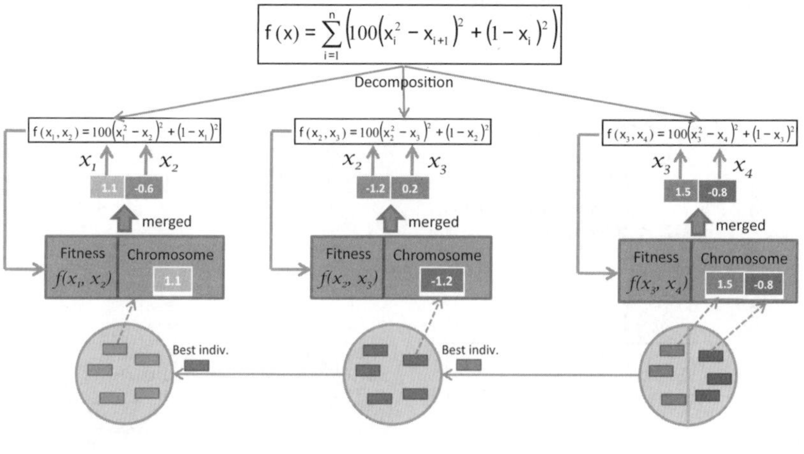

Fig. 2. Example of a LCGA individual evaluation for the Rosenbrock function (n=3)

communication graph it implies (simple list) and the way each evolutionary algorithm evaluates the fitness of its individuals by combining them with the best individual from the neighbor population.

To summarize, the differences between these CGAs lie in the following parameters:

- the topology of communications: complete graph for the CCGA, any topology for LCGA (depends on the problem decomposition)
- the interaction protocols: synchronous exchange from all to one for CCGA, asynchronous exchange for LCGA
- the exchanged information: best or best and random for CCGA, random individuals for LCGA
- their relation to the environment (i.e. to the optimization problem): in CCGA each subpopulation evaluates its solutions on the global problem, in LCGA a subpopulation evaluates its solutions on a subproblem (depending on the problem decomposition).

3 Metaheuristics Frameworks and Libraries

Despite their successful application on many test problems and a few real-world ones, none of the works applying CGAs cited in the previous section provide a framework for designing such metaheuristics or a library for applying them. Therefore, in the following section we propose to analyze existing metaheuristics frameworks and libraries respectively in terms of their capacity to express and implement CGAs.

In I&D Frame, (Intensification and Diversification Frame) [5], metaheuristics are analyzed in terms of intensification and diversification components that correspond to operators, strategies or actions used to conduct the search. This component approach was designed to help designing new hybrid algorithms. ALP (Adaptive Learning Search) [18], which is an extension of AMP [47], is also considering intensification and diversification phases that evolve a memory. This model is adapted to population based metaheuristics. The I&D and ALP frameworks allow describing different metaheuristics using a limited set of generic concepts. However, they do not take into account two key properties of metaheuristics [9], including CGAs: distribution possibility (linked to collective solving) and dynamic adaptation. Indeed, they are based on a black box model, that prevents describing the structure, the interactions and the relations of the system (i.e. the algorithm) to the optimization problem.

Three different agent based frameworks have been proposed to tackle these issues, by benefiting from the autonomous and self-adaptation properties of agents. The following proposes a description and analysis of these frameworks in terms of systems organization, adaptation, distribution and provided methodology to implement the proposed models (see Table 1). The objective is to evaluate their capacity to express the CGAs topology, communications, adaptation at runtime and to apply distributed CGAs.

Table 1. MAS Metaheuristics Frameworks

	Organization	Adaptation	Distribution	Methodology
MAGMA	Functional	No	Functional	No
MAS-DGA	Structural	Rule based	Cooperative Agents	No
AMF	Structural	Self-adaptation	Cooperative Roles	Yes

MAGMA (MultiAGgent Architecture for Metaheuristics), introduced in Roli's PhD thesis [42] and later in [28], consists in a multi-level architecture where each level contains one or several specialized agents implementing an algorithm. This architecture provides a high modularity but its organizational model is limited to a functional description (one or more agents = one task) and therefore to a functional distribution. Finally it neither takes into account dynamic adaptation possibilities nor provides a methodology for instantiating the developed models.

In MAS-DGA (Multi-Agent System for Distributed Genetic Algorithms) [30], each basic GA is encapsulated into an agent that must keeps knowledge of the search, learning, or optimization problem it operates on. Agents are coordinated by a set of rules stipulating the topological and communication (migration) aspects. These rules can be fixed a priori or set during run-time. MAS-DGA therefore includes a simple organizational and reorganizational model based on a structural specification. Distribution is achieved through distributed genetic agents. However, no detail concerning this model, the corresponding methodology or its implementation are given in the single paper mentioning MAS-DGA.

Finally, AMF (Agent Metaheuristic Framework) presented in [16] proposes a framework based on an organizational model which describes a metaheuristic in terms of roles. These roles correspond to the main components or tasks in a metaheuristic: intensification, diversification, memory and adaptation or self-adaptation. AMF is based on a specific organizational model, however it is limited to its structural specification (i.e. RIO - Roles Interactions Organization [26]). AMF is the only framework providing a complete methodology for developing metaheuristics, from analysis to model and implementation.

The aim of such frameworks is to ease the modeling and analysis of metaheuristics. To implement and apply metaheuristics, many libraries, independent from the previous models, have been proposed and analyzed in several surveys from which we can cite [2] and [7]. The prominent libraries being ParadisEO (PARAllel and DIStributed Evolving Objects) [8], MALLBA (MAlaga + La Laguna + BArcelona) [1] and iOpt [17]. Such libraries permit extensive distributed executions of metaheuristics, but none of them implements "standard" CGAs like the CCGA or the LCGA introduced in section 2. Another main issue mentioned in [27] is the gap between the proposed general frameworks and the existing libraries. Indeed, the multi-agent paradigm is a commonly used concept in metaheuristics as proven by the various frameworks proposed in the literature. The advantages of using multi-agent and organizational models can be justified by the robustness of MAS [28] and the metaheuristics need for flexibility and modularity [48] answered by MAS social metaphor (i.e. organizations).However there exists a real lack of tools, as only the AMF framework allows to instantiate

Table 2. Analogy between CGAs and organizational MAS

Coevolutionary GAs	Organizational MAS
Subpopulation running GAs	Autonomous Agents
Communication topology (interaction graph)	Organization model
Interaction graph adaptation	Reorganization model

its models, but based on an organizational model limited to a structural specification (definition of roles and interactions between roles).

Based on the conclusions drawn in section 2 and on the advantages of the agent paradigm for modeling distributed population based metaheuristics, a parallel can easily be drawn between the CGAs properties and an organizational MAS as presented in Table 2.

Subpopulations composing a CGA can be modeled as autonomous agents collectively acting to achieve their goal (i.e. optimize a given problem) in a distributed and decentralized way. The topology and content of the agents interactions driven by the cooperative or competitive nature of the CGA can be modeled using organizations. Finally the dynamic adaptation of CGAs can be modeled by extending the organization model with reorganization capabilities. This answers limitations identified in [9].

However, none of the available agent frameworks dedicated to metaheuristics provide the required complete organizational and reorganizational description as they only allow partial structural or functional specifications and no explicit modeling of the organization adaptations. For this reason, a novel framework dedicated to coevolutionary optimization, DAFO (Distributed Agent Framework for Optimization) that includes the MAS4EVO (Multi-Agent System for EVolutionary Optimization) organizational and reorganizational model have been developed. The latter is described in the next section.

4 Multi-Agent Organization Model for Optimisation

A general view of DAFO's underlying model is provided in Fig. 3. It is composed of three types of agents interacting together and able to perceive and react to the environment in which they are situated. The environment represents the optimization problem which is provided and specified by the user. Depending on the problem, the environment can be either static or dynamic. The considered types of agents are: (*i*) *problem solving agents (PSA)* in charge of optimizing a fitness function using a metaheuristic (i.e. executing the algorithms considered in GA or in CGAs), (*ii*) *fabric agents (FA)* which instantiate and configure the running application and (*iii*) *observation agents (OA)* which observe the problem solving agents and provide output interfaces to the end user(s).

The interactions between the agents use the FIPA ACL [31] restricted to the *inform* and *agree* performatives. They also use FIPA-SL propositions[1] to express the content of the messages. This content is composed of either organizational

[1] FIPA-SL specifications: http://www.fipa.org/specs/fipa00008/SC00008I.pdf

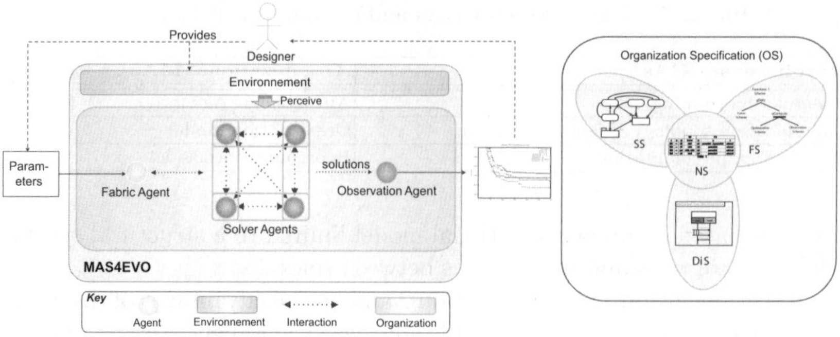

Fig. 3. DAFO Overview with its organization model

information or computational information (i.e. individual(s)). Interaction protocols structure and express the sequence of messages according to the strategy of solutions exchange (best, random, etc) between the different GAs embedded in the agents.

Finally, the coevolutionary strategies are represented by defining a multi-agent organization, using the MAS4EVO organization model, used to impose global patterns of cooperation on the behaviors of the agents. Thanks to the explicit representation of the organization, agents are able to change and reorganize the global functioning of the system. We focus here on MAS4EVO since it is the core of the DAFO Framework. It is based on $\mathcal{M}$OISE^{+} [24] and dedicated to evolutionary optimization by the set of roles, groups and goals that are used. The abstract definition of cooperation patterns of the MAS builds what we call the organization Specification (OS). When a set of agents adopts an OS, they form an organization Entity (OE). The OS is defined using four different specifications: structural, functional, dialogic and normative.

The following sections provide a detailed description of those four specifications. The example of the modeling of a simple GA (SGA) using MAS4EVO as presented in Fig. 4 will be used to illustrate the different concepts those specifications are based on (an exhaustive description of these specifications can be found in [11]).

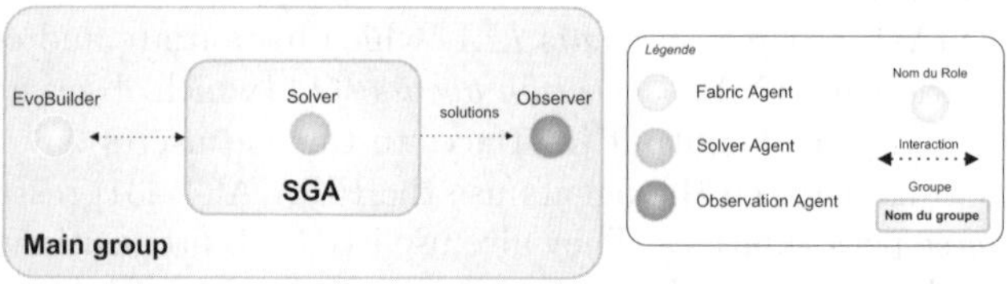

Fig. 4. Schematic view of a SGA modeled using MAS4EVO

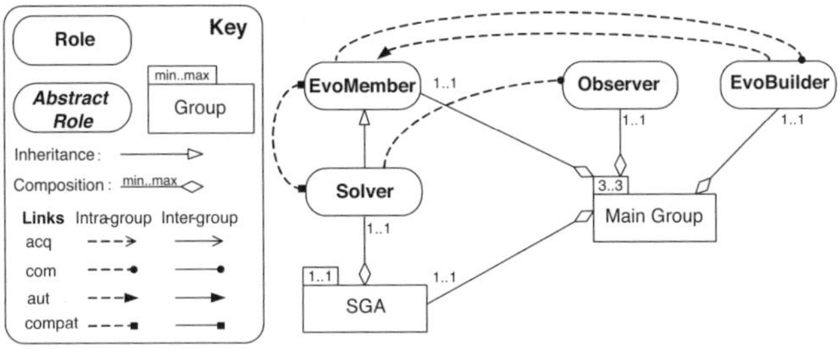

Fig. 5. Graphical Representation of the Structural Specification of the SGA Example

4.1 Structural Specification

The Structural Specification (SS) expresses the structure of an organization in terms of *roles*, *links* between roles and *groups*. A *role* is a label which allows attaching a set of constraints described in the other specifications of $\mathcal{M}$OISE$^+$. An agent is expected to respect these constraints as soon as it accepts to play that role. A *group* is defined by a composition of non-abstract roles (composition link), a set of intra-group links, a set of inter-group links, roles and groups cardinalities and agent cardinality (i.e. the number of agents which can play a role in the group). *Links* are the relations which have a direct influence on the agents' interactions. They can be of three types: (*acq*) for constraining the agent acquaintances graph, (*com*) for the interaction graph between the agents and (*aut*) for the authority and control structure bearing on the agents. A set of constraints is defined and used when the OS is enacted when the agents adopt roles in the created groups. These constraints express inter-roles compatibilities, links scope (intra-group and inter-group) and maximum/minimum number of adopted roles and created groups that could exist in the OE.

In Fig. 5 is shown the example of the SS of a simple GA. The root group is the *Main Group* group. It is composed of a single group *SGA* (cardinality "1..1"). The *Main Group* group is composed of three agents (cardinality "3..3"): one playing the *EvoBuilder* role, another one the *Observer* role and another one the *EvoMember* role. Each of these roles can only be adopted once (cardinality "1..1"). The *SGA* group is composed of one agent (cardinality "1..1") playing the role *Solver*. The *Solver* role inherits its constraints from the *EvoMember* role. The *EvoBuilder* role possesses an authority link on the *EvoMember* role since it will control the lifecycle of the *EvoMember* (e.g. instantiation). The *EvoMember* possesses a communication link with the *EvoBuilder* role. This link will be used to provide information concerning the *EvoMember* lifecycle (e.g. ready to compute). The *Solver* role also has a communication link but with the *Observer* role to send results of its computation process (e.g. the best individual per generation). Finally the *EvoMember* role and the *Solver* role have a compatibility link. This means that the same agent can play both roles in the same instance of the *Main Group* (we do not mention the *SGA* group since it is a subgroup of *Main Group*).

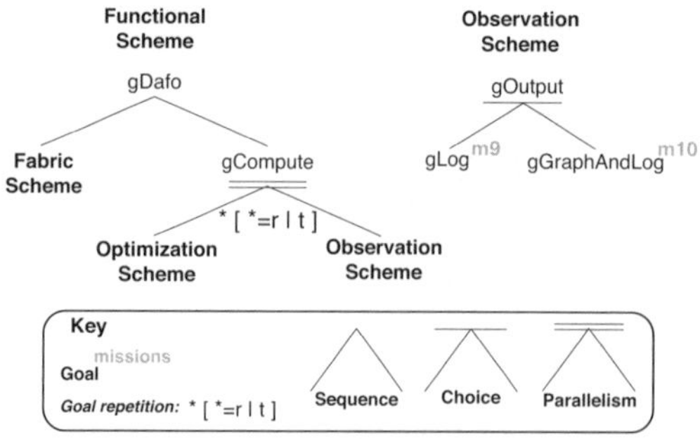

Fig. 6. Graphical Representation of the Functional Specification of the SGA Example

4.2 Functional Specification

The Functional Specification (FS) describes a set of social schemes corresponding to the collective plans to be executed by the OE. These goals are grouped into missions which are attached to the roles in the normative specification. Missions are assigned to the agents as soon as they adopt the corresponding roles. Different types of goals and social schemes have been introduced. They can be functional, as in $\mathcal{M}$OISE$^+$, but also interactional, organizational or regulatory. In addition to the initial version of $\mathcal{M}$OISE$^+$, the possibility to associate a repetition constraint on a goal has been added, i.e. a guard condition that will stop the iterated achievement of the goal according to some repetitions number or time constraint. Interactional goals use one generic interaction protocol specified in the dialogic specification. It must mention the source and destination roles as well as the information exchanged if necessary. The organizational goals imply an action on the organization entity (e.g. instantiation of new agents). Therefore they provide reorganization capabilities. Regulatory goals imply a monitoring of the organization so as to start a plan once a predefined criterion is reached. They can be used for instance to trigger a reorganization process. Finally, artificial goals are goals that can not be reached. They are only used for specification purposes.

In Fig. 6 two out of the four social schemes of the FS of the SGA are presented. The functional scheme (left side) is considered as the main scheme of the FS. Its root goal, *gDafo*, is to run the DAFO framework. It is satisfied when the *Fabric Scheme* and the artificial goal *gCompute* are satisfied in sequence. The goal *gCompute* is itself achieved once its repetition condition is satisfied. An iteration of the *gCompute* goal will be achieved when goals *Optimization Scheme* and the *Observation Scheme* are achieved in parallel.

Concerning the *Observation Scheme* (right side of Fig. 6), its artificial root goal *gOutput* is satisfied if one of the two functional goals *gLog* or *gGraphAndLog* are achieved, i.e. an output of the results is obtained by the GA. The *gLog* goal saves the received best individual of one generation and the calculated average in each generation in log files. The *gGraphAndLog* additionally draws the corresponding graphs.

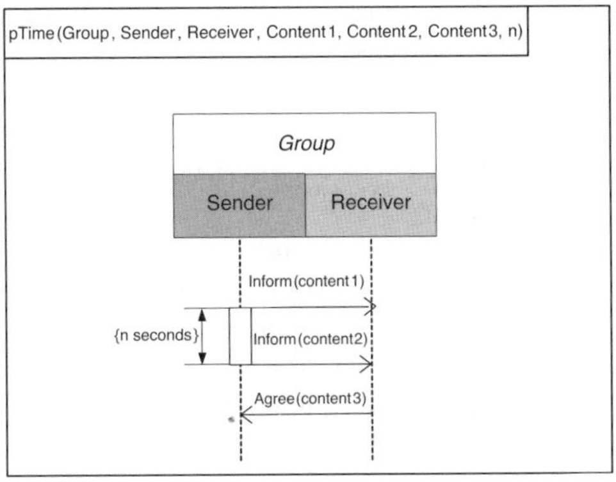

Fig. 7. Graphical Representation of the Dialogic Specification of the SGA Example

4.3 Dialogic Specification

The Dialogic Specification (DiS) is an extension to the initial $\mathcal{M}$OISE$^+$ model. It is used to specify parameterizable generic interaction protocols in an independent manner of the roles and groups specified in the structural specification (SS). These interaction protocols are a variant of both AUML sequence diagrams [3] and AGR organizational sequence diagrams [20]. In Fig. 7 is presented the *pTime* protocol defined using the DiS. This protocol requires seven parameters, a *group name*, a *sender role*, a *receiver role*, three different *message contents* and a time constraint. The n value represents a timing constraint, i.e. the number of seconds between the first *Inform* message that contains the parameter *content1* sent from the sender to the receiver and the second one that contains the parameter *content2*. Finally, the receiver has to send back an *Agree* message to the sender with the parameter *content3*.

The graphical representation of the DiS has two dimensions: (i) the vertical dimension represents the time ordering and (ii) the horizontal dimension represents generic groups and roles that will be specified as parameters. Messages in sequence diagrams are ordered according to a time axis. This time axis is usually not rendered on diagrams but it goes according to the vertical dimension from top to bottom.

4.4 Normative Specification

During the execution of the organization, the agents will have: (i) to play roles within groups as specified in the structural specification (SS), (ii) to commit to missions and to achieve the corresponding goals defined in the functional specification (FS) and, (iii) finally to communicate following the interaction protocols depicted in the dialogic specification (DiS). In order to link these three specifications, we define the Normative Specification (NS) adapted from the one introduced in $\mathcal{M}$OISE^{Inst} [6]. This specification is composed of a set of *normative expressions* involving a deontic operator (permission, obligation or interdiction) with terms from the SS, FS and DiS.

A norm n is defined as:

$$n : \varphi \rightarrow op(bearer, m, p, s)$$

where φ is the norm validity condition, *op* is the deontic operator defining an obligation, a permission or an interdiction, *bearer* refers to an entity of the SS (role or group) on which the deontic operator is applied, m refers to a mission defined in the FS, p is an optional set of parameters used for the instantiation of the mission m, s is the functional scheme of the FS to which the mission m belongs.

For instance, the following norm:

$$N04 : true \rightarrow obl(EvoMember, m4, -, Fabric)$$

is an obligation for every agent playing the *EvoMember* role to perform the mission $m4$ of the *Fabric* social scheme. According to the definition of mission $m4$, the agent playing the *EvoMember* role is endorsed of the obligation to achieve two organizational goals (creation of the subgroup SGA and adoption of the Solver role in this new group). Given the validity condition of this norm $N04$, the norm is valid.

5 Multi-Agent Organization Modeling of Existing and New CGAs

In the preceding section we have described the different specifications provided by the organization modeling language of DAFO. We have illustrated their use to model a simple GA. We show in this section how it is possible to model different CGAs by using a unique generic agent (i.e. the Problem Solving Agent) and a library of organizational models. This section presents the simple changes needed in the structural specification to switch from the CCGA to the LCGA (cf. Sec. 2). It additionally introduces two LCGA variants developed using DAFO, the hybrid LCGA (hLCGA) that is modeled by changes in the structural specification of the LCGA; and the dynamic LCGA (dLCGA) modeled by changes in the functional specification that provide reorganization capabilities to the LCGA (complete organization models can be found in [11]).

5.1 CCGA MultiAgent Organization Model

CCGA is a cooperative CGA using a complete graph as topology of communication between the different subpopulations. It is therefore necessary to have at least three Problem Solving Agents (PSAs) to represent and compute these subpopulations. Since all PSAs interact with each other, we only use one group to manage them.

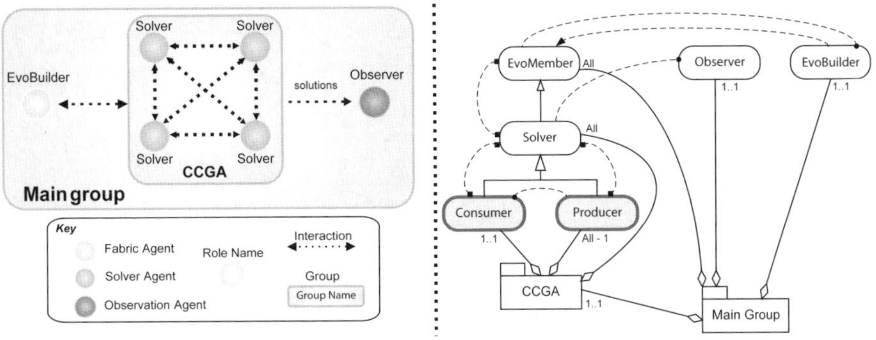

Fig. 8. Example of organization Entity and Graphical representation of the Structural Specification for the CCGA

A specific feature of CCGA is the round-robin process realized in each generation of the algorithm. In this process, one after the other each subpopulation becomes active, i.e. it receives individual(s) from all the other subpopulations and evaluates its own individuals. This is first modeled at the structural level by adding two new roles, *Consumer* and *Producer*, and, second, at the functional level by introducing a regulatory goal. With this goal, each PSA can monitor if it is its turn to become active (i.e. playing role *Consumer*). Organizational goals then allow the PSAs to change role (i.e. switch from *Producer* to *Consumer* and the opposite).

In order to model the complete graph topology of the CCGA in terms of an organizational structure, new roles *Consumer* and *Producer* (compared to the SGA) inheriting from the *Solver* role have been added: (see highlighted roles on the right side of Fig. 8). The *Consumer* role can only be played by a single PSA (cardinality 1..1). It represents the active subpopulation while the *Producer* role is played by all the other PSAs participating to the system (cardinality All-1). Agents playing the *Producer* role are able to send some information (generally individuals) to the agent playing the *Consumer* role. Let us notice that an agent playing the Solver role can also play the *Consumer* or the *Producer* role (compatibility link).

5.2 LCGA Model

As previously mentioned, the LCGA is a competitive CGA that has no restriction concerning the topology of communication between the different subpopulations. Due to the optimization problems tackled in this article, i.e. Inventory Management [14] and Injection Networks [12], we modelled a LCGAs using ring or complete graph topologies. We therefore chose to use topologies based on a ring, in which it is possible to augment the number of neighbours, from 1 to n-1 (n being the number of PSAs) as illustrated in the Fig. 9.

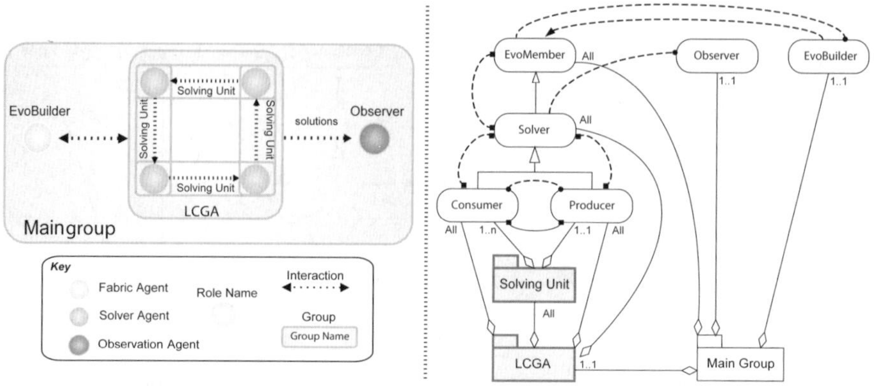

Fig. 9. Example of organization Entity and Graphical representation of the Structural Specification for the LCGA

As for the CCGA, it is necessary to have at least three PSAs to represent the subpopulations. Since in such ring-based topologies one PSA will communicate with one or several neighbours, a new type of group is introduced: *Solving Unit*. This group contains one *Producer* role (cardinality 1..1) and one to several *Consumer* roles (cardinality 1..N). In order to create a ring (see left side of Fig. 9), the same PSA will play the *Consumer* role in one *Solving Unit* group and the *Producer* role in the next *Solving Unit* group. This Solving Unit group is a subgroup of LCGA. These two new groups are highlighted on the right side of Fig. 9. An inter-group compatibility link between the *Producer* and *Consumer* roles has also been added so as to express the possibility for an agent to play both roles in two different *Solving Unit* groups.

Contrary to CCGA, LCGA does not imply synchronous exchanges of individuals between the subpopulations and thus no monitoring of the organization and no modification of the OE (i.e. no swapping from Producer to Consumer roles and vice versa). The individuals exchanged between subpopulations are also different since in LCGA random individuals are sent contrary to the best or best and random of the CCGA. This is converted at the model level with a new parameter in the pInform interaction protocol (i.e. random).

Another difference is the collaborative process introduced in LCGA. Once one subpopulation has calculated the fitness values of its individuals, based on the individuals of its neighbour, these fitness values are sent to the same neighbour population which will use these fitness values to re-evaluate its own individuals (typically the average between the fitness it calculated and the fitness it received). This will be tackled in the functional specification as a new functional goal (gReEvaluate) and new possible parameters in the pInform interaction protocol (i.e. fitnesses).

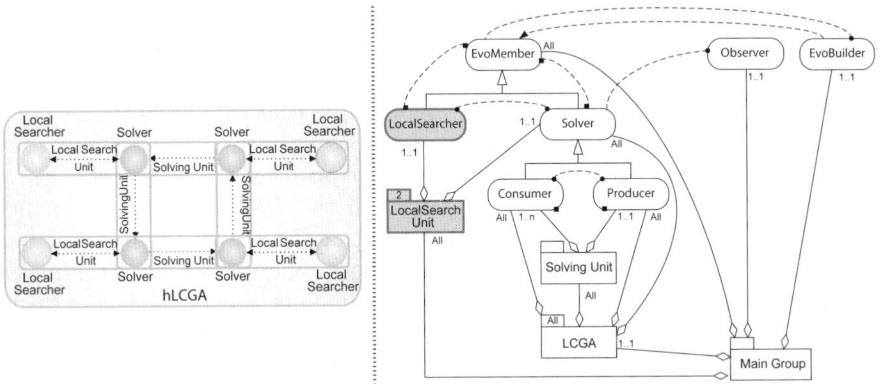

Fig. 10. Example of organization Entity and graphical representation of the Structural Specification for the hLCGA

5.3 hLCGA Model

Hybridization of GAs has been a very active research area. However, hybrid coevolutionary genetic algorithms have been rarely tackled, except in [46] where a CCGA has been hybridized with a hill-climbing algorithm. Due to the few existing researches in this area and benefiting from our multi-agent organization approach, we decided to investigate the hybridization of the LCGA with different local search algorithms.

Although it is possible to make a GA hybrid in different ways, latest published articles [46] have shown that combining GAs with local search algorithms are one of the best approaches for improving the results. The model of this hybrid LCGA is therefore based on the LCGA's presented in the previous section. To hybridize it, each PSA running a SGA and representing one subpopulations of the LCGA will communicate with another new PSA running one local search algorithm (LS). This topology is represented on the left side of Fig. 10.

As for the LCGA, it is necessary to have at least three PSAs to represent the subpopulations. In our hybrid approach, we therefore add three PSAs to run the local search algorithm. In order to allow a communication between these PSAs, a new type of group has been added in the SS, *LocalSearchUnit*. In this group, the PSA running a SGA will play the *Solver* role and the PSA running the LS algorithm will play a new *LocalSearcher* role (see right side of Fig. 10). These new *LocalSearchUnit* groups will have to be created and these new *LocalSearcher* roles will have to be adopted by the additional PSAs. This will be considered in the FS with the addition of the organizational goals CreateSubGroup(LocalSearch, DAFO) and the gAdoptRole(LocalSearcher, SolvingUnit).

Once the OE is instantiated, it is necessary to run the LS algorithm. This is also achieved in the FS by adding the exchange of individual(s) (best individual or population rate defined by the parameter alpha) from the *Solver* role to the *LocalSearcher* with the interactional goal pInform(alpha). Then the LS algorithm is run with the functional goal *gRunLS* and finally the optimized individual(s) are sent back using the same interactional goal *pInform(alpha)*. These new goals will be part of new missions which will be attached to roles in new norms of the NS.

The SS of the hLCGA presented in Figure 10 is thus similar to the LCGA's SS plus the addition of the new group *LocalSearchUnit* which is a subgroup of the *DAFO* group and of the new role *LocalSearcher*. All the instances of the *LocalSearchUnit* subgroup are contained in the *DAFO* group (cardinality "All"). The *LocalSearch Unit* group contains exactly one *Solver* role and one *LocalSearcher* role (cardinality "1..1"). They both inherit from the *EvoMember* role. Those two roles have to be played by two different agents due to the cardinality "2" on the group. The *LocalSearcher* role and the *EvoMember* role have a new compatibility link which means that the same agent can play both roles in the same instance of the *DAFO* group (we do not mention the *LCGA* group since it is a subgroup of the *DAFO* group). Finally, a new intra-group communication link between the *LocalSearcher* and the *Solver* roles and vice versa is added. This will allow the exchange of individual(s) necessary for the LS algorithm.

5.4 dLCGA Model

Few previous researches have considered the adaptive CGAs, also known as dynamic CGAs. The related works focused either on the adaptation of the number of populations [39] or on the adaptation of the parameters [25]. Our contribution consists in building a dynamic LCGA, in which the topology of communication between the populations evolves during runtime. Indeed, contrary to CCGA where the topology is fixed (i.e. fully connected graph), using LCGA makes no restriction on the communication graph, since it fully depends on the decomposition of the optimized problem.

dLCGA is a dynamic version of LCGA. Its interaction structure is modified each n generations of the algorithm. The modification is achieved through a cooperative process starting with the first player that randomly chooses a new position in the graph of interaction and informs all the other players of his local decision. The next player in the graph will then randomly choose a new position among the remaining ones and inform the other players. This process is iteratively executed by all players. Once finished, each player goes to its new position and the algorithm runs again for n generations. Through this random process, each population exchanges information with different populations during runtime, and thus has to evaluate its individuals using different parts of the solution.

Left side of Fig. 11 shows an example of a dLCGA with a ring topology using a simplified view of an organizational entity (OE). After n generations of the algorithm, all *PSAs* leave the roles they play in the *Solving Unit* groups. Consequently, they only play a role in the "base" group *Main Group* and this way they can communicate all together in order to define the groups in which each of them will play a role. Once they all know their new location, they take their roles in the newly defined groups. Since the topology changes consist in moving the PSAs on the ring, this only affects the organizational entity (OE) and not

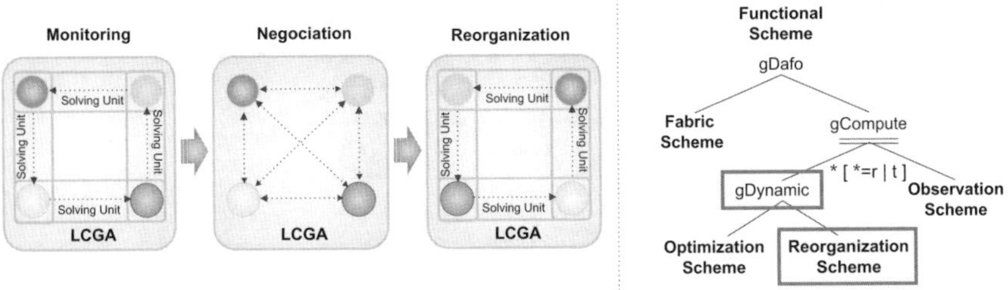

Fig. 11. Example of organization entity evolution and graphical representation of the Functional Specification for the dLCGA

the organizational specification (OS).Therefore, the structural specification of the dLCGA is similar to the LCGA's.

We therefore only describe the changes needed in the FS. The functional scheme is presented on the right side of Fig. 11. A single social scheme has been added to the FS of the LCGA in order to manage the three steps of the reorganization describe hereinbefore (monitoring, negotiation and reorganization). The following details the content of this new *reorganization scheme.* Each PSA will have to monitor its computation in order to verify if the condition is met or not. This is achieved by a new regulatory goal *gMonitoring.* Once this condition is met, each PSA leaves its *Consumer* and *Producer* roles in its *SolvingUnit* groups. This is achieved with two new organizational goals *gLeaveRole(Producer, SolvingUnit)* and *gLeaveRole(Consumer, SolvingUnit).* Then the PSAs will have to negotiate with each other to find their new groups. This negotiation is achieved with a new interactional goal *pNegotiate.* This goal implies the definition of a new interaction protocol in the dialogic specification. Finally the PSAs will adopt their *Consumer* and *Producer* roles in their newly defined *SolvingUnit* groups using the *gAdoptRole(Producer, SolvingUnit)* and *gAdoptRole(Consumer, SolvingUnit)* organizational goals. All these new goals are grouped in the *Reorganization Scheme.*

This section has demonstrated the usage of our approach to model two existing CGAs, the CCGA and the LCGA. Through these first two examples it was shown that with few changes in the organization specifications it is possible to switch from one CGA to the other. We also introduced two competitive coevolutionary genetic algorithms, hLCGA and dLCGA, respectively hybrid and dynamic variants of the LCGA developed using DAFO. Their detailed model using MAS4EVO has been presented, demonstrating the capacity of this new organizational model to describe such new coevolutionary genetic algorithms. Indeed, for the hLCGA it was proved that by adding a new group and a new role in the SS and a few new goals in the FS to the LCGAs (and adapting the NS accordingly) it is possible to create a new hybrid variant. Similarly, by keeping

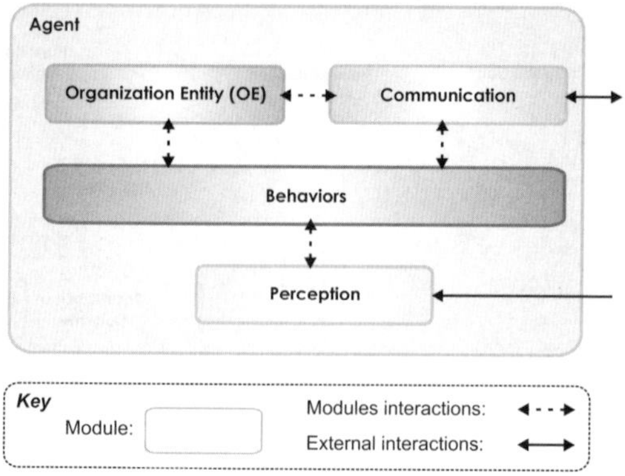

Fig. 12. DAFO's agents modular architecture

the same SS as the LCGA and adding a reorganization scheme in its FS, it is possible to create a new dynamic variant of LCGA.

6 DAFO Framework

In the previous sections we have described the MAS4EVO model and its utilization for modeling different CGAs, the CCGA, the LCGA and two variants of the latter (hybrid and dynamic). The following section provides a short description of the modular implementation of MAS4EVO that we call DAFO, Distributed Agent Framework for Optimization.

The DAFO framework has been built using an existing multiagent API, Madkit [22] which is also based on an organizational model but limited to its structural aspect, AGR (Agent Group Role) [20]. Figure 12 provides a modular view of the DAFO agents architecture (a detailed description of DAFO's implementation using the Unified Modeling Language can be found in [11]). The main module, *Agents*, represents the three different agent types, i.e. PSA, OA and FA. This module embeds an internal engine which manages the lifecycle of the agent and the activation of its different internal modules. The *organization Entity (OE)* module represents the instantiation of the four MAS4EVO organization specifications (SS, FS, DiS and NS). The *Communication* module implements the interaction mechanisms and more particularly the interaction protocols defined in the MAS4EVO's Dialogic Specification. The *Behaviors* module contains the set of behaviors, in a Jade-like way [4], available to the agents. Depending on the missions it has to fulfill, an agent will activate one or several behaviors. A behavior uses some skills to realize the goals corresponding to the mission. The *Perception* allows the agent to perceive its environment, i.e. the other agents of the system and the MAS environment (which is the optimization problem provided by the user).

When developing an optimization framework, computation efficiency is a key feature. In terms of performance, the choice of the Madkit API has been driven by two criteria, the first one being its distribution capabilities that can be used by DAFO, as experimented in [13], the second one is its good performance capabilities compared to other agent platforms [29].

7 CGA for the Injection Network Optimization Problem

A metaheuristic framework is defined in [28] as useful for comparing existing algorithms, designing (new) hybrid algorithms and supporting software engineering. Therefore, after comparing existing CGAs and recently introduced variants (hybrid and dynamic) in terms of organizational specifications (structural and functional) in section 5, the purpose of this section is to present their application using DAFO on a current real-world optimization problem, the injection network optimization problem. More precisely, the objective is to demonstrate that the few changes needed in the Organization Specification to define the hybrid variant of the LCGA (see 5.3) permit, once instantiated, to outperform the "standard" LCGA. The first subsection provides a description of the injection networks optimization problem, and the second one presents the obtained experimental results.

7.1 Problem Description

Mobile multi-hop ad hoc networks most often face the problem of network partitioning. In this application we consider the problem of optimizing *injection networks* which consist in adding long-range links (e.g., using GSM, UMTS or HSDPA technologies) that are also called *bypass links* to interconnect network partitions. An example of such an injection network is presented in Figure13. To tackle this topology control problem, we use small-world properties as indicators for the good set of rules to maximize the *bypass links* efficiency. Small-world networks [49] feature a high clustering coefficient (γ) while still retaining a small characteristic path length (L). On the one hand, a low characteristic path length is of importance for effective routing mechanisms as well as for the overall communication performance of the entire network. On the other hand, a high clustering coefficient features a high connectivity in the neighborhood of each node and thus a high degree of information dissemination each single node can achieve. This finally motivates the objective of evoking small-world properties in such settings. This optimization problem was first introduced in [12]. In order to optimize those parameters (maximizing γ, minimizing L) and to minimize the number of required bypass links in the network, we used three different CGAs modeled in DAFO, i.e. the existing CCGA, LCGA, and the novel hLCGA.

In order to assign a fitness value to the candidate solutions (i.e. sets of possible bypass links) of our algorithms, we use a unique cost function F which combines the two small world measures (L and γ) and the number of created bypass links. The calculation of the characteristic path length L imposes that there exists a path between any given nodes a and b. Consequently, the computation of the fitness function requires that we first test if the network is partitioned. If the

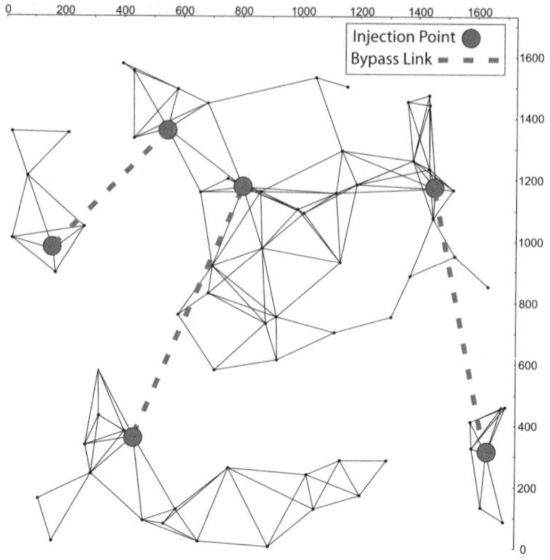

Fig. 13. Example of an injection network

optimized network is still partitioned (the bypass links defined do not achieve to connect all the partitions), the fitness value is assumed to be a weighted term of the number of partitions in the network. On the contrary, if the optimized network is no longer partitioned, the fitness value is assumed to be a linear combination of the clustering coefficient, of the characteristic path length, and of the difference between the number of bypass links defined and the maximum number allowed. The aim of the optimization process is to maximize the clustering coefficient, and to minimize both the characteristic path length and the number of bypass links. By using this fitness function we now face the maximization problem defined in Algorithm 1.

Algorithm 1. Fitness Function

if *Graph connected* **then**
| $F = \alpha * \gamma - \beta * (L - 1) - \delta * (bl - bl_{max})$
else
| $fitness = \xi * P$
end

With weights experimentally defined:
$\alpha = 1$
$\beta = 1 /(N - 2)$
$\delta = 2 / (N * (N-1))$ - WifiConnections
$\xi = 0.1$

where bl is the number of bypass links created in the simulated network by one solution, bl_{max} (defined a priori) is the maximum number of bypass links that can be created in the network, P is the number of remaining partitions in the whole network after the addition of bypass links and N is the number of stations in the global network. Finally, WifiConnections is the number of existing Wi-Fi connections in the network.

7.2 Experiment Results

In this section, we discuss and analyze the results we found during our experiments with the two panmictic GAs (genGA and ssGA) and the three different CGAs (CCGA, LCGA and hLCGA) modeled within DAFO. For hLCGA, the LCGA algorithm was hybridized with the Next Ascent Hill Climbing (NAHC) local search algorithm. In Table 3, we show the parameters used for all the proposed algorithms. Panmictic (i.e. single population) algorithms have a population of 100 individuals, the CCGA, LCGA and hLCGA are run using 5 populations of 20 individuals so as to keep the same total amount of individuals for every algorithm. The termination condition is achieving 50,000 fitness function evaluations, common to all the algorithms, as well as the recombination (the two points crossover –DPX–) and mutation (bit-flip) operators, and their probabilities: $p_c = 1.0$ and $p_m = 1/\text{chrom\_length}$, respectively. The two parents are selected using a binary tournament, except for the two cellular algorithms, for which one of them is considered to be the current individual itself. Finally, all the algorithms follow an elitist strategy (preventing the best individual in one generation to be modified), with the exception of the ssGA.

Table 3. Parameters used for the studied GAs

Number of Subpopulations	5 for CCGA, LCGA, hLCGA
(Sub)Population size	100 (genGA, ssGA)
	20 (CCGA, LCGA, hLCGA)
Termination Condition	50,000 function evaluations
Selection	Binary tournament (BT)
Crossover operator	DPX, p_c=1.0
Mutation operator	bit flip, $p_m = 1/\text{chrom\_length}$
Elitism	1 individual (not for ssGA)

In order to conduct experiment on ad hoc networks, and more precisely to evaluate potential solutions on this topology control problem, we interfaced DAFO with an ad hoc networks simulator, Madhoc [23]. We have defined a square simulation area of 0.2 km^2 and tested three different densities of 150, 210 and 350 devices per square kilometer. Each device is equipped with both Wi-Fi (802.11b) and UMTS technologies. The coverage radius of all mobile devices ranges between 20 and 40 meters in case of Wi-Fi. The studied networks represent a snapshot of mobile networks in the moment in which a single set of users moved away from each other creating the clusters of terminals.

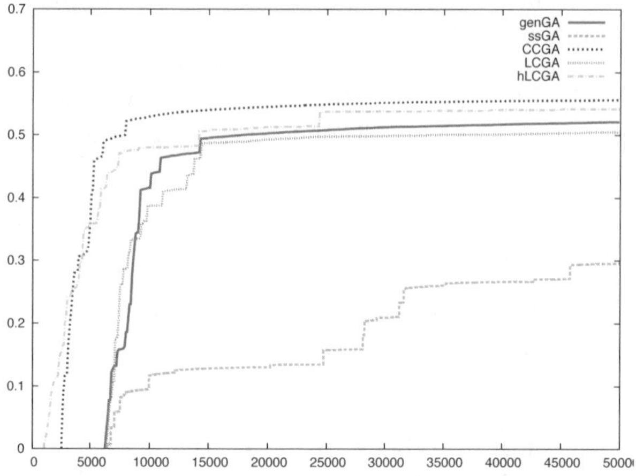

Fig. 14. Evolution of the average best fitness value (30 executions) during the run for the sparse instance

Table 4. Results of all experiments

Network	GA	Best Result	Avg. Result	Hit Rate
	genGA	0.5353	0.5210 ± 0.008	100%
	ssGA	0.5513	0.2956 ± 0.345	100%
Sparse	CCGA	0.5684	**0.5564** $\pm \mathbf{0.005}$	100%
	LCGA	0.5411	0.5050 ± 0.013	100%
	hLCGA	**0.6066**	0.5413 ± 0.045	100%
	genGA	0.6078	0.6028 ± 0.002	100%
	ssGA	0.6081	0.5495 ± 0.197	100%
Interm.	CCGA	**0.6173**	**0.6101** $\pm \mathbf{0.003}$	100%
	LCGA	0.6117	0.6078 ± 0.002	100%
	hLCGA	0.6089	0.6046 ± 0.002	100%
	genGA	0.5926	0.5899 ± 0.0009	100%
	ssGA	0.5903	0.5880 ± 0.0007	100%
Dense	CCGA	0.5937	0.5910±0.001	100%
	LCGA	**0.6139**	**0.6074** $\pm \mathbf{0.004}$	100%
	hLCGA	0.6049	0.5995 ± 0.007	100%

To get confident conclusions, every problem was solved 30 times with each algorithm (independent runs), and a statistical study was made to analyze the results (Shapiro-Wilks and ANOVA or Kruskal-Wallis depending on the data distribution). In Table 4 we show the averaged results, the best ones, and the percentage of runs in which the algorithms found a non-partitioned network (hit rate). The results presented here are statistically significant, i.e. there are meaningful differences among the compared algorithms with 95% probability. The best overall result for every network instance is shown in **bold font**.

It clearly appears in Table 4 that the three CGAs always outperform the panmictic GAs (genGA and ssGA) for all the network instances both in terms of best and average result (except the LCGA on the sparse instance). The new hLCGA reaches the best overall result on the sparse network, while the CCGA provides the best average fitness. On the intermediate instance the CCGA obtains the best results while on the dense instance the LCGA provides the best ones. It can be noticed that the novel hLCGA outperforms the CCGA on the dense instance. Figure 14 demonstrates the superiority of the CGAs in terms of convergence speed on the sparse instance. The improvement brought by the novel hybridization of the LCGA can also be noticed, both for convergence and average best result reached.

8 Conclusion and Future Work

We have proposed in this paper a multi-agent approach dedicated to evolutionary optimization. The resulting DAFO (Distributed Agent Framework for Optimization) provides a novel way of modeling CGAs as a multi-agent organization using the MAS4EVO model that provides a complete specification of the algorithms structure, interactions and adaptation. We have presented how MAS4EVO addresses the exiting frameworks limitations and have shown how it is possible to define multiple CGAs, existing ones (CCGA, LCGA) but also original ones (hybrid LCGA, dynamic LCGA), as different organization specifications. The implementation of DAFO which permits to apply, compare and distribute CGAs on optimization problems with a minimum of coding effort was also introduced.

Finally, we demonstrated that the few changes needed in the Organization Specification to define the hybrid variant of the LCGA (see 5.3) permit, once instantiated, to outperform the "standard" LCGA an emergent business problem related to topology control in mobile hybrid ad hoc networks.

In order to conduct these experiments, we showed that the DAFO framework can be interfaced with other third-party softwares like the Madhoc simulator we used for simulating our injection networks.

In our future work we plan to develop a more adaptive dLCGA by increasing the autonomy of the Problem Solving Agents, allowing them to adapt their parameters and/or their organization according to the problem and/or to their neighbors in the organization, using for instance some learning mechanisms.

References

1. Alba, E., Almeida, F., Blesa, M., Cabeza, J., Cotta, C., Díaz, M., Dorta, I., Gabarró, J., León, C., Luna, J.M., Moreno, L., Pablos, C., Petit, J., Rojas, A., Xhafa, F.: MALLBA: A library of skeletons for combinatorial optimisation. In: Monien, B., Feldmann, R.L. (eds.) Euro-Par 2002. LNCS, vol. 2400, pp. 927–932. Springer, Heidelberg (2002)
2. Alba, E., Tomassini, M.: Parallelism and evolutionary algorithms. IEEE Trans. Evolutionary Computation 6(5), 443–462 (2002)

3. Bauer, B., Muller, J., Odell, J.: Agent UML: A formalism for specifying multiagent interaction (2001)
4. Bellifemine, F.L., Poggi, A., Rimassa, G.: Developing multi-agent systems with JADE. In: Castelfranchi, C., Lespérance, Y. (eds.) ATAL 2000. LNCS (LNAI), vol. 1986, pp. 89–103. Springer, Heidelberg (2001)
5. Blum, C., Roli, A.: Metaheuristics in combinatorial optimization: Overview and conceptual comparison. ACM Comput. Surv. 35(3), 268–308 (2003)
6. Boissier, O., Gâteau, B.: Normative multi-agent organizations: Modeling, support and control, draft version. In: Normative Multi-agent Systems. No. 07122 in Dagstuhl Seminar Proceedings, IBFI, Schloss Dagstuhl, Germany (2007)
7. Cahon, S., Melab, N., Talbi, E.G.: Building with paradisEO reusable parallel and distributed evolutionary algorithms. Parallel Comput. 30(5-6), 677–697 (2004)
8. Cahon, S., Melab, N., Talbi, E.G.: ParadisEO: A framework for the reusable design of parallel and distributed metaheuristics. Journal of Heuristics 10(3), 357–380 (2004)
9. Crainic, T., Toulouse, M.: Parallel Strategies for Meta-heuristics, pp. 475–513. Kluwer Academic Publishers, Dordrecht (2003)
10. Danoy, G., Bouvry, P., Seredynski, F.: Evaluations of Strategies for Co-Evolutionary Genetic Algorithms: dLCGA Case Study. In: Proceedings of the 16th International Conference on Artificial Neural Networks In Engineering (ANNIE 2006), pp. 91–96. ASME publisher, Saint Louis (2006) ISBN 0–7918–0256–6
11. Danoy, G.: A Multi-Agent Approach for Hybrid and Dynamic Coevolutionary Genetic Algorithms: Organizational Model and Real-World Problems Applications. Ph.D. thesis (2008)
12. Danoy, G., Alba, E., Bouvry, P., Brust, M.R.: Optimal design of ad hoc injection networks by using genetic algorithms. In: Lipson, H. (ed.) GECCO, p. 2256. ACM, New York (2007)
13. Danoy, G., Bouvry, P., Alba, E.: Distributed coevolutionary genetic algorithm for optimal design of ad hoc injection networks. Special Session on Parallel and Grid Computing for Optimization (PGCO 2007), Prague (2007)
14. Danoy, G., Bouvry, P., Martins, T.: hlcga: A hybrid competitive coevolutionary genetic algorithm. In: HIS, p. 48. IEEE Computer Society, Los Alamitos (2006)
15. Darwin, C.: The Origin of Species by Means of Natural Selection. Mentor Reprint, 1958, NY (1859)
16. David Meignan, J.C.C., Koukam, A.: An organizational view of metaheuristics. In: AAMAS 2008: Proceedings of First International Workshop on Optimisation in Multi-Agent Systems, pp. 77–85 (2008)
17. Dorne, R., Voudouris, C.: Hsf: the iopt's framework to easily design metaheuristic methods, pp. 237–256 (2004)
18. Dréo, J., Aumasson, J.P., Tfaili, W., Siarry, P.: Adaptive learning search, a new tool to help comprehending metaheuristics. International Journal on Artificial Intelligence Tools 16(3), 483–505 (2007)
19. Ehrlich, P.R., Raven, P.H.: Butterflies and plants: A study in coevolution. Evolution 18(4), 586–608 (1964)
20. Ferber, J., Gutknecht, O., Michel, F.: From agents to organizations: An organizational view of multi-agent systems. In: Giorgini, P., Müller, J.P., Odell, J.J. (eds.) AOSE 2003. LNCS, vol. 2935, pp. 214–230. Springer, Heidelberg (2004)
21. Goldberg, D.E.: Genetic Algorithms in Search, Optimization and Machine Learning. Addison-Wesley Longman Publishing Co., Inc., Boston (1989)

22. Gutknecht, O., Ferber, J.: Madkit: a generic multi-agent platform. In: Proc. of the Fourth International Conference on Autonomous Agents, pp. 78–79. ACM Press, New York (2000)
23. Hogie, L., Bouvry, P., Guinand, F., Danoy, G., Alba, E.: Simulating Realistic Mobility Models for Large Heterogeneous MANETS. In: Demo proceeding of the 9th ACM/IEEE International Symposium on Modeling, Analysis and Simulation of Wireless and Mobile Systems (MSWIM 2006). IEEE, Los Alamitos (October 2006)
24. Hübner, J.F., Sichman, J.S., Boissier, O.: Developing organised multiagent systems using the moise. IJAOSE 1(3/4), 370–395 (2007)
25. Iorio, A.W., Li, X.: Parameter control within a co-operative co-evolutionary genetic algorithm. In: Guervós, J.J.M., Adamidis, P.A., Beyer, H.-G., Fernández-Villacañas, J.-L., Schwefel, H.-P. (eds.) PPSN 2002. LNCS, vol. 2439, pp. 247–256. Springer, Heidelberg (2002)
26. Mathieu, P., Routier, J.-C., Secq, Y.: RIO: Roles, interactions and organizations. In: Mařík, V., Müller, J.P., Pěchouček, M. (eds.) CEEMAS 2003. LNCS (LNAI), vol. 2691, pp. 147–157. Springer, Heidelberg (2003)
27. Meignand, D.: Une Approche Organisationnelle et multi-Agent pour la Modélisation et l'Implantation de Métaheuristiques, Application aux problmes doptimisation de rśeaux de transport. Ph.D. thesis (2008)
28. Milano, M., Roli, A.: Magma: A multiagent architecture for metaheuristics. IEEE Trans. on Systems, Man and Cybernetics – Part B 34(2), 925–941 (2004)
29. Mulet, L., Such, J.M., Alberola, J.M.: Performance evaluation of open-source multiagent platforms. In: AAMAS 2006: Proceedings of the Fifth International Joint Conference on Autonomous Agents and Multiagent Systems, pp. 1107–1109. ACM Press, New York (2006)
30. Noda, E., Coelho, A.L.V., Ricarte, I.L.M., Yamakami, A., Freitas, A.A.: Devising adaptive migration policies for cooperative distributed genetic algorithms. In: Proc. 2002 IEEE Int. Conf. on Systems, Man and Cybernetics. IEEE Press, Los Alamitos (2002)
31. O'Brien, P.D., Nicol, R.C.: FIPA, towards a standard for software agents. BT Technology Journal 16(3), 51–59 (1998)
32. Paredis, J.: Coevolutionary life-time learning. In: Ebeling, W., Rechenberg, I., Voigt, H.-M., Schwefel, H.-P. (eds.) PPSN 1996. LNCS, vol. 1141, pp. 72–80. Springer, Heidelberg (1996)
33. Popovici, E., De Jong, K.: The effects of interaction frequency on the optimization performance of cooperative coevolution. In: GECCO 2006: Proceedings of the 8th Annual Conference on Genetic and Evolutionary Computation, pp. 353–360. ACM, New York (2006)
34. Popovici, E., Jong, K.D.: The dynamics of the best individuals in co-evolution. Natural Computing: An International Journal 5(3), 229–255 (2006)
35. Popovici, E., Jong, K.D.: Sequential versus parallel cooperative coevolutionary algorithms for optimization. In: Proceedings of Congress on Evolutionary Computation (2006)
36. Potter, M.A.: The design and analysis of a computational model of cooperative coevolution. Ph.D. thesis (1997)
37. Potter, M.A., De Jong, K.: A cooperative coevolutionary approach to function optimization. In: Davidor, Y., Männer, R., Schwefel, H.-P. (eds.) PPSN 1994. LNCS, vol. 866, pp. 249–257. Springer, Heidelberg (1994)
38. Potter, M.A., De Jong, K.A.: The coevolution of antibodies for concept learning. In: Eiben, A.E., Bäck, T., Schoenauer, M., Schwefel, H.-P. (eds.) PPSN 1998. LNCS, vol. 1498, pp. 530–539. Springer, Heidelberg (1998)

39. Potter, M.A., Jong, K.A.D.: Cooperative coevolution: An architecture for evolving coadapted subcomponents. Evolutionary Computation 8(1), 1–29 (2000)
40. Potter, M.A., Jong, K.A.D., Grefenstette, J.J.: A coevolutionary approach to learning sequential decision rules. In: Proceedings of the 6th International Conference on Genetic Algorithms, pp. 366–372. Morgan Kaufmann Publishers Inc., San Francisco (1995)
41. Potter, M.A., Meeden, L., Schultz, A.C.: Heterogeneity in the coevolved behaviors of mobile robots: The emergence of specialists. In: IJCAI, pp. 1337–1343 (2001)
42. Roli, A.: Metaheuristics and structure in satisfiability problems. Tech. Rep. DEIS-LIA-03-005, University of Bologna (Italy), phD. Thesis - LIA Series no. 66 (May 2003)
43. Seredynski, F.: Competitive coevolutionary multi-agent systems: the application to mapping and scheduling problems. J. Parallel Distrib. Comput. 47(1), 39–57 (1997)
44. Seredynski, F., Koronacki, J., Janikow, C.Z.: Distributed scheduling with decomposed optimization criterion: Genetic programming approach. In: Proceedings of the 11 IPPS/SPDP 1999 Workshops Held in Conjunction with the 13th International Parallel Processing Symposium and 10th Symposium on Parallel and Distributed Processing, pp. 192–200. Springer, London (1999)
45. Seredynski, F., Zomaya, A.Y., Bouvry, P.: Function optimization with coevolutionary algorithms. In: Proc. of the International Intelligent Information Processing and Web Mining Conference. Springer, Poland (2003)
46. Son, Y.S., Baldick, R.: Hybrid coevolutionary programming for nash equilibrium search in games with local optima. IEEE Trans. Evolutionary Computation 8(4), 305–315 (2004)
47. Taillard, E.D., Gambardella, L.M., Gendreau, M., Potvin, J.Y.: Adaptive memory programming: A unified view of metaheuristics. European Journal of Operational Research 135(1), 1–16 (2001)
48. Talbi, E.G., Bachelet, V.: Cosearch: A parallel co-evolutionary metaheuristic. In: Blum, C., Roli, A., Sampels, M. (eds.) Hybrid Metaheuristics, pp. 127–140 (2004)
49. Watts, D.J.: Small Worlds – The Dynamics of Networks between Order and Randomness. Princeton University Press, Princeton (1999)
50. Wooldridge, M.J., Jennings, N.R.: Agent theories, architectures, and languages: A survey. In: Wooldridge, M.J., Jennings, N.R. (eds.) ECAI 1994 and ATAL 1994. LNCS, vol. 890, pp. 1–22. Springer, Heidelberg (1995)

Author Index

Bakker, Piet J.M. 121
Boissier, Olivier 199
Bouvry, Pascal 199

Danoy, Grégoire 199
Desel, Jörg 1

Evangelista, Sami 21

Hidders, Jan 144
Houben, Geert-Jan 144

Knapik, Michał 42, 98
Köhler-Bußmeier, Michael 174
Kristensen, Lars Michael 21

Mans, Ronny S. 121
Merceron, Agathe 1
Moldt, Daniel 174
Moleman, Arnold J. 121

Niewiadomski, Artur 98

Paredaens, Jan 144
Penczek, Wojciech 42, 72, 98
Półrola, Agata 72, 98

Russell, Nick C. 121

Szreter, Maciej 42, 98

Thiran, Philippe 144

van der Aalst, Wil M.P. 121
van Hee, Kees 144

Wester-Ebbinghaus, Matthias 174

Zbrzezny, Andrzej 72, 98

Printing: Mercedes-Druck, Berlin
Binding: Stein+Lehmann, Berlin